Rethinking Institutional Analysis and Development

A publication of the
International Center for Self-Governance

The mission of the International Center for Self-Governance is to encourage men and women in developing countries to achieve the self-governing and entrepreneurial way of life. In addition to publishing the finest academic studies, such as this edition of Rethinking Institutional Analysis and Development, ICSG also provides practical materials in a variety of readily accessible formats, including manuals, learning tools, and interactive tasks.

For more information on ICSG or its publications, training materials, and videos , please contact:

ICSG
720 Market Street
San Francisco, CA 94102 USA
(415) 981-5353

Rethinking Institutional Analysis and Development

Issues, Alternatives, and Choices

Edited by
Vincent Ostrom, David Feeny,
and Hartmut Picht

Institute for Contemporary Studies
San Francisco, California

© 1993 Institute for Contemporary Studies

This book is a publication of the International Center for Self-Governance, dedicated to promoting the self-governing and entrepreneurial way of life around the world. The Center is a program of the Institute for Contemporary Studies, a nonpartisan, nonprofit public policy research organization. The analyses, conclusions, and opinions expressed in ICS Press publications are those of the authors and not necessarily those of the Institute for Contemporary Studies, or of the Institute's officers, its directors, or others associated with, or funding, its work.

Printed in the United States of America on acid-free paper. All rights reserved. No part of this book may be used or reproduced in any manner without written permission except in the case of brief quotations in critical articles and reviews. First edition published in 1988.

Inquiries, book orders, and catalog requests should be addressed to ICS Press, 720 Market Street, San Francisco, CA 94102. (415) 981-5353. Fax (415) 986-4878. For book orders and catalog requests call toll free in the contiguous United States: **(800) 326-0263**. Distributed to the trade by National Book Network, Lanham, Maryland.

Library of Congress Cataloging-in-Publication Data

Rethinking institutional analysis and development : issues, alternatives, and
  choices / edited by Vincent Ostrom, David Feeny, and Hartmut Picht.
    p. cm.
  Revision of 1989 edition.
  Includes bibliographical references and index.
  ISBN 1-55815-264-4 (acid-free paper)
    1. Economic development—Political aspects. 2. Economic development—Social aspects. 3. Institution building. 4. Developing countries—Economic policy. 1. Ostrom, Vincent, 1919– . II. Feeny, David, 1948– .
III. Picht, Hartmut.
HD88.R48   1993
338.9—dc20   93-16940
                                                                          CIP

Table of Contents

Foreword   *Robert B. Hawkins, Jr.*   xiii
Acknowledgments   xv

Part One
Introduction

CHAPTER 1   **The State of the Art**
Norman Nicholson   3

Policy and Institutions 7
The Character of Goods and Institutions 10
Institutional Innovation: Markets and
    Constitutions 12
Overview of Chapters 17
Summary 34
Notes and Works Cited 37

Part Two
The Challenge of Institutional Analysis: Some Issues and Approaches

CHAPTER 2   **Cryptoimperialism, Predatory States, and Self-Governance**
Vincent Ostrom   43

Recipes for Constituting "New" Nations   45
The Theory of Sovereignty: How the
    Few Exploit the Many   56
Are There Alternatives?   60
Conclusion   66
Works Cited   67

CHAPTER 3 **Tocqueville's *Democracy in America* and the Third World**
Sombat Chantornvong   69

Tocqueville's Analysis and
    the Asian Situation   70
Economic Development in
    the Asian Situation   82
Development and Democracy   89
Notes and Works Cited   96

CHAPTER 4 **Institutional Arrangements and the Commons Dilemma**
Elinor Ostrom   101

The Commons Dilemma   101
Successful Efforts to Cope
    with the Commons   108
What Can Be Learned from
    These Cases?   117
Notes and Works Cited   127

CHAPTER 5 **Reciprocity: A Bottom-Up View of Political Development**
Ronald J. Oakerson   141

Reciprocity   142
Primary Local Units   146
Constitutional Choice   149
Development Processes   151
Conclusion   155
Notes and Works Cited   155

CHAPTER 6 The Demand for and Supply of Institutional Arrangements
David Feeny   159

   The Demand for and Supply of Technological Change   162
   Extending the Metaphor: The Demand for and Supply of Institutional Change   163
   The Demand for and Supply of Institutional Change: Beyond the Metaphor   171
   Conclusions   196
   Notes and Works Cited   198

Part Three

Institutions and Development in Less Developed Countries

CHAPTER 7 Institutional Resources for Development among the Kgalagadi of Botswana
Susan Wynne   213

   Primary Local Units of Collective Action   216
   Hierarchical Principles of Organization   219
   Nonhierarchical Organizational Principles of Kgalagadi *Kgotla*   226
   Conditions for the Productive Operation of Primary Local Units of Collective Action   234
   The Continuing Challenge of Institutional Analysis and Design   235
   Notes and Works Cited   238

CHAPTER 8 The Putu Development Association:
A Missed Opportunity
Amos Sawyer   247

The Role of Participation in
    Development   248
Community Development as
    Self-Governance   250
Background: Putu Society   252
Putu Social Organization   253
Structure of Authority   253
Principles of Association in Putu   255
Contemporary Operational Pattern
    of Authority in Putu   256
A History of the Putu Development
    Association   257
Organizing the Putu Development
    Association   259
Formulating a Program and Mobilizing
    Resources   262
Conflict and Conflict Resolution   265
Lessons from Putu   268
Dilemma of Self-Governance
    Within Hierarchical Orders   269
Notes and Works Cited   272

CHAPTER 9 The Development of Autocracy in Liberia
Amos Sawyer   279

Foundations of African Political Order   281
Creating the Liberian Political Order   285
Forming the New Society   292
Conjectures and Conclusion   300
Notes and Works Cited   303

CHAPTER 10 The Coevolution of Property Rights and
Political Order: An Illustration from
Nineteenth-Century Hawaii
James Roumasset and Sumner J. La Croix   315

The Coevolution of Property Rights
and Political Order 317
An Application to Nineteenth-Century
Hawaii 322
Concluding Remarks 330
Notes and Works Cited 332

Part Four

Market Institutions and Contingent Considerations

CHAPTER 11 **How Markets Alleviate Scarcity**
Louis De Alessi   339

Characteristics of a Market System   341
How Markets Are Used to Solve the
    Economic Problem   353
Limitations of the Market and of Some
    of Its Alternatives   360
Conclusions 369
Works Cited 372

CHAPTER 12 **The Ethical Foundations of the Market**
John F. A. Taylor   377

Works Cited 388

CHAPTER 13 **Opportunity, Diversity, and Complexity**
Vincent Ostrom   389

Complexities and the Conceptualization
    of Patterns of Order in Human
        Societies   389
Entrepreneurship in the Public Sector   394
The Pursuit of Development
    Opportunities   396
Conclusion 404
Works Cited 405

CHAPTER 14 Currency Competition: A Constitutional Perspective
Hartmut Picht   407

From Monetary Functions to Monetary Services   410
Jointness of Use and Feasibility of Exclusion   411
Joint Supply and Synthetic Joint Use of Monetary Services   414
Economies-of-Scale External and Internal to Producers   416
Pricing Pattern in the Case of Cash Media of Exchange   419
Production Externalities with Respect to Unit-of-Account Stabilization Services   422
Constitutional Implications for Currency Competition   424
Currency Competition in the Light of Alternative Options   427
Notes and Works Cited   430

Part Five

The Continuing Challenge

CHAPTER 15 Institutional Analysis and Development: Rethinking the Terms of Choice
Vincent Ostrom, David Feeny, and Hartmut Picht   439

Contingencies, Conceptions, and Social Realities   439
Choice Among Institutions   446
Institutions as Contractual Arrangements   452

Toward Convergence in a Theory of
Institutional Choice and a
Theory of Inquiry   458
Notes and Works Cited   463

About the Authors   467
Index   471

Foreword

In reissuing this book, the International Center for Self-Governance recognizes that it is even more important now than when it was first published, in 1988. It deserves to be read as widely as possible in the countries where ICSG is working to promote the self-governing and entrepreneurial way of life.

In the farming villages and the barrios of the Dominican Republic, among the small business owners of Guatemala, in the ethnic subgroups of Nepal, and in countless other settings, citizens have begun to band together to invest in themselves and their communities. This flowering of self-governance that we have begun to see in developing countries must not be allowed to perish. The key to sustaining the life of these self-organizing activities is the creation of a strong enabling environment.

Institutional analysis permits us to understand how to design—or redesign—the institutional arrangements that will allow self-governing and entrepreneurial efforts to be initiated and borne out. It is becoming increasingly clear that supporting productive human development will require that we pay more attention to the art of crafting institutions—at both the micro-level and the macro-level—so that individuals and organizations can build sound self-governing and entrepreneurial structures.

The enduring distinction of this volume is its challenge to traditional economic thinking. That thinking had always sought to explain economic growth in terms of resources, technologies, and human preferences. These factors, however, cannot account fully for economic growth. The editors of *Rethinking Institutional Analysis and Development*, Vincent Ostrom, David Feeny, and Hartmut Picht, argue that a fourth component—institutions—is the missing link. They and the thirteen contributors demonstrate that the influence of institutions is considerable.

Institutions embody the basic rules that govern all public and private actions—from individual property rights to the ways in which communities deal with public goods. They affect distribution of income, efficiency of resource allocation, and the development of human resources. These rules, in their power to enable self-governing impulses to be enacted and find support in the society, constitute a vital public resource. True public life, in contrast to what is either narrowly private or dominated by government authority, needs vigorous institutions. They are an essential element of what it means to be public.

In bringing together a series of important papers addressing both the theoretical and practical dimensions of institutional choice, Ostrom, Feeny, and Picht present a firm basis for recognizing the crucial role of institutions in economic development.

Robert B. Hawkins, Jr., Ph.D.
President
Institute for Contemporary Studies

Acknowledgments

The development and preparation of this volume was made possible by a grant from the United States Agency for International Development, DAN-5433-GSS4052. The agency's concern was with the relationship of institutions to development. Since institutions are ways of ordering choice, the focus of our early discussion was on the terms on which alternatives are available. That is also a definition of price. We thus pursued a dialogue about what implications institutions might have for "getting the prices right," a dialogue that involved discussion of economic development in the Third World. A conference on "Getting the Prices Right" was held by the Workshop in Political Theory and Policy Analysis at Indiana University, Bloomington, from September 17 to 20, 1985. The papers given at this conference were revised and some new papers added in order to make up this book. I wish to express my appreciation to all of those who participated in the conference and who have prepared the papers presented here. Above all, I wish to express my personal appreciation for the considerable efforts that my coeditors, David Feeny and Hartmut Picht, have devoted to the preparation to this volume.

Members of the professional staff at USAID, including Ed

These acknowledgments pertain to the original version of this book, which was published in 1988 and has become a widely used resource. Because of repeated demand from people who wish to have current access to the volume, ICSG is reissuing the paperback edition. Publication of this edition was funded by the United States Agency for International Development.

Connerley, Ken Kornher, Norman Nicholson, Chris Russell, Bob Shoemaker, and Ruth Zagorin, have been helpful colleagues in pursuing ideas about institutional analysis and development. Jamie Thomson, Sheldon Gellar, Goran Hyden, James Wunsch, Dele Olowu, Mohammed Labib, Ladipo Adamolekun, and Brian Loveman have also made important contributions to these discussions.

Finally, I owe a special debt of gratitude to colleagues in the Workshop in Political Theory and Policy Analysis. Patty Zielinski assumed the major responsibility for putting the manuscripts together. Kristin Crose, Linda Smith, and Susan Wynne kept correspondence and communication among authors and editors going. Their devotion to the enterprise made the work a pleasure.

Vincent Ostrom
Co-Director
Workshop in Political Theory
and Policy Analysis

Part I

Introduction

1   *Norman Nicholson*

The State of the Art

Introduction

Over the past twenty years, we have acquired a growing appreciation of how prices and markets shape economic development. Prices guide the allocation of resources in a society: the goods and services produced, how they are produced, and how they are distributed. If the price system works effectively, the allocation of resources will approximate the aggregate preferences of the community. Similarly, an effective price system will signal growing inefficiency in the economy and reward innovation and reallocation of resources to reduce those inefficiencies.

Only fairly recently, however, have we begun to understand in any systematic way how these economic forces interact with the institutional and political arrangements at work in any society. This book

---

The views expressed are those of the author and do not represent the views of the Agency for International Development.

is concerned with how those institutional and political arrangements affect economic development.

Institutional structure is important because of its role in expanding human choice, which is a fundamental goal of economic development. To be sure, there are other sources that serve to expand human choice. Economic growth per se constitutes a significant expansion of human choice through the expansion of the resource base and the accumulation of capital. Improvements in human capital (education, technology, and health), which "empower" individuals, also expand choice. But institutional structure is a third component.

Institutions affect human choice by influencing the availability of information and resources, by shaping incentives, and by establishing the basic rules of social transactions. Institutional innovation contributes to development by providing more efficient ways of organizing economic activity, ways that often lead to fundamental restructuring of an economy.

Students of development have long been concerned with institutional arrangements and how they influence the rights of individuals and communities to exercise choice. A significant focus of this literature has been the detrimental impact of development on the choices of the small rural communities that were the bedrock of the "traditional" order. Much of the early sociological and anthropological literature focused on how the emergence of worldwide markets and the national state tended to destroy the efficacy of the local community. The local communities seemed powerless in the face of these enormous national and international forces. Furthermore, it was argued, the normative foundations of those national institutions, and their power, were at odds with those of the traditional society. As those institutions grew in strength, they undermined the values of reciprocity and ascriptive status on which these communities were organized, it was argued. Thus, the local communities began to lose even their ability to manage their own local affairs. It seemed to matter little whether the community prospered or became poorer in the modernizing process; the results were the same.

This perception gave rise to two different schools of thought in the development literature. One placed emphasis on restoring to the local community a degree of control over its own fate. This has been variously described as "community development," "decentralization," or "local participation." The second approach was to advance the new nation-state as the appropriate vehicle for restoring social control over the economy and the direction of change. Drawing on local adaptations of European socialism, this approach emphasized state capitalism, extensive regulation of the economy, and comprehensive planning. Neither of these solutions has been entirely successful, however. Both the national- and local-level institutions are characterized by inefficiency and exploitation.

In short, the existing institutional context has neither the broad-based participation of the population of the Third World in the processes of choice, nor an institutional environment in which resources are allocated in socially efficient ways that facilitate development. The purpose of this book, then is to examine the requirements for increasing participation and efficiency in social choices, after a thorough reexamination of the institutional foundations of developing countries.

Another role of institutional analysis in economic development lies in addressing the problem of "getting the prices right," which is important for a number of reasons. Even in the most effective of market systems, there is potential for "market failure." Market failure may result from the character of the goods in question (i.e., public goods), externalities, inadequate information or asymmetries of information, or high transaction costs.

Getting the prices right is also important because, as they grow in size and power, governments can cause distortions in the price structure through the impact of their authority and budgets. This is not to say that the effects of public policy are inevitably negative, but that, insofar as those policies are determined by nonmarket forces, they have great potential for becoming increasingly distorting in the absence of careful monitoring and control of policy measures.

While all economic institutions—capital markets, contract systems, property rights, etc.—try to order economic transactions by imposing rules, they can contribute to deviations from pure market efficiency. Almost any institution engenders the germ of price distortion because of the inertia inherent in any established order. For example, institutionalized property rights may need significant alteration before new technologies can have a broad impact on productivity. Biotechnology and information systems are recent instances.

The role of institutional analysis in getting the prices right is especially important because fundamental price distortions are introduced by the constitutional order that forms the basic structure of the political economy. This occurs as the constitutional order determines the "representativeness" and "accountability" of those who exercise public authority, and also establishes the basic law governing the resolution of conflict among diverse groups, institutions, and individuals. Perhaps most importantly for the study of development, the constitutional order shapes the rate and direction of institutional change within the polity.

This book explores the impact of institutions and political arrangements on development. It illustrates how some institutional arrangements exacerbate market distortions and inefficiencies while others facilitate structural change and development. The insights offered by these essays serve to elucidate strategies that will improve the efficiency of institutional choices.

The past decade has produced substantial evidence of how institutional weaknesses in developing economies have slowed development. Even if allowances are made for the detrimental impact on developing countries of global and external events (for example, declining primary commodity prices, increasing protectionism, fluctuations in oil prices, and the vagaries of weather), it is clear that many of these countries are enduring the consequences of inappropriate institutional and policy choices that were made in the past.

It has also become clear how political power and political institutions shape the economy. The economic choices made in most of these countries reflect, in most cases, neither the free play of market forces nor popular political choice, but rather the conscious designs of political elites. In the case of Korea, Taiwan, and Singapore, authoritarian regimes have contributed to rapid growth and a substantial reduction of poverty. Elsewhere, elites have encouraged inefficiencies in both the public and private sectors, which permit only the sparse benefits of exceedingly modest growth to eventually "trickle down" to the masses. However, there are almost no examples of the combination of liberal democracy and free-market economy that characterized British and American development.

In considering these issues, it has not been uncommon for development practitioners to make a distinction between, on the one hand, policy reforms and structural adjustment programs and, on the other hand, institutional development. Whereas policy reform and structural adjustment programs are perceived as short-term issues, it is argued that institutional development makes a more basic and long-term contribution to development. "Getting the prices right," in other words, is often perceived as a short-term problem that can be treated independently of institutional development. Institutional development efforts are commonly viewed as involving training, incremental improvements in management systems, and construction of facilities, but pay little attention to "getting the prices right."

These are conceptual errors that need to be corrected. First, institutional development and design are part of the process of "getting the prices right," because the interaction of supply and demand is mediated through institutions. Second, bad policies will, over time, fundamentally corrupt and distort institutional performance. Third, policy reform and structural adjustment effects, by starting the process of "getting prices right," are essential to the process of institutional change in economic development. These interactions can be illustrated in three different areas: policy choices, the character of goods provided by the public sector, and the constitutional order.

Policy and Institutions

In any economy bad policy encourages inefficiency. Bad policy may be a simple matter of setting prices inappropriately. At a second level, however, basic choices among policy types, pursued long enough, may cause those distortions to be embedded in institutional arrangements that become self-perpetuating. I do not refer here to the common list of policy distortions that can be found in any International

Monetary Fund stabilization program—overvalued exchange rates, controlled interest rates, etc. Rather, I refer to Theodore Lowi's typology in which he distinguishes among distributive, redistributive, regulatory, and constitutive policies (Lowi, 1972). To summarize it, the four types (distributive, regulatory, redistributive and constitutive) are distinguished by: (1) the extent to which coercion is imminent and (2) the degree of directness of their impact on the individual (in contrast with the environment of individual choice). Thus, the choice of policy type determines the conditions of individual choice in the face of the exercise of public authority. In consequence, institutional arrangements become specialized to the style of individual interaction with government authority that is associated with particular policy types.

"Distributive" policies have been a particularly common source of price distortion in developing countries. Distributive policies make benefits available generally to the population. They apply directly to individuals, but are not coercive. The relationship between the benefits received by individuals and the costs incurred by the government in providing these benefits are typically indirect and vague. Social services, subsidies, and public goods (e.g., infrastructure) are examples of such distributive policies. They are politically popular because there are no apparent losers, only winners. These policies are the mainstay of patronage politics, and their popularity with constituents provides a continual pressure to expand the benefits—an expansion limited only by budget constraints.

Large cumbersome bureaucracies have grown up to manage these distributive programs. The key incentive in such bureaucracies is ostensibly the expansion of services. Quality control, cost-effectiveness, and opportunity costs receive little attention. Performance is often weak, and attempts to improve management frequently founder on the combined opposition of both the bureaucracy and their clientele, both of which benefit from the existing arrangements.

Thus, two development problems are engendered by distributive policies. First, costs grow excessively until budget deficits and debts force an adjustment. Second, because of the lack of effective controls, the considerable resources committed to the distributive programs are typically used inefficiently and, therefore, the overall development effort is weakened. For example, general food subsidies, while popular, are not a very efficient way either to keep food prices low or to benefit the poorest. Further, they divert resources from other developmental efforts, such as agricultural development, that would offer long-term solutions.

This is not to argue that there is no role for distributive policies in development. What is suggested, however, is that these political regimes appear to have few effective means for "pricing" these distributive policies. The immediate "price" for the policies appears when food riots break out in the wake of a reduction in subsidies. The real costs, however, become clear only when a structural adjustment program forces a reconsideration of the role of government in the economy and a systematic shift in government priorities. It is noteworthy that these events are usually sparked by external forces. It is also noteworthy that analysts usually measure the "cost" to the poor in terms of the higher food prices associated with the reforms, rather than of the slow growth in jobs associated with the prevailing price distortions.

Distributive policies, and associated price distortions, are pervasive throughout developing economies. Subsidies on a wide range of goods (including electricity, credit, irrigation water, transportation infrastructure, fertilizer, and capital goods) frequently provide benefits to groups of recipients at little cost to themselves. The damage done by these subsidies goes beyond the opportunity cost of the resources tied up in them. The price distortions can fundamentally corrupt key development institutions.

Although the benefits of distributive policies are freely available to the target population, the resources are scarce to society and thus may become exceptionally valuable to the recipients. It is not surprising, therefore, that individuals attempt to appropriate these benefits to themselves. Typically this is done by controlling the intermediary institutions that distribute the benefits.

The results are various. First, the powerful find it relatively more profitable to seek the "rents" engendered by the differences between the real value of the good and the subsidized price than to seek increasing efficiency, find new markets, discover new products, etc. In proportion to the magnitude of these rent-seeking activities, the economy loses the contribution of these entrepreneurial services to development. Second, the economy is distorted as businessmen, or farmers, divert resources into those areas where the largest rents are to be had. Third, for the bulk of the target group, there is commonly an increase in transaction costs as bribery and factional politics become endemic. This produces an increasing level of cynicism concerning developmental institutions and destroys the trust and sense of reciprocity essential to institutional development.

As we search for improved efficiencies in development, we must understand better how the policy framework influences the performance of key economic institutions. Among the greatest futilities in development efforts are the unsuccessful attempts to bring about improvements in institutional efficiency through training and improved management techniques that run counter to the incentives engendered by the policy framework.

The Character of Goods and Institutions

In addition to the price distortions in the private sector introduced by bad policy, distortions are introduced by pricing problems within the public sector. The problem of pricing "public goods" has been well established in the literature and need not be repeated here.[1] Inefficiencies in producing goods or services in the public sector occur not because they have the character of "public goods," but for a number of other reasons: perceived "market failures," a desire to plan and manage the economy, the search for public revenues, or a conviction that certain goods or services are vested with a considerable public interest. The same is true of many public services.

Whatever the reason for preferring public production of goods, the proliferation of inefficient public-sector enterprises has served to weaken development efforts. It is not uncommon that such enterprises are over-capitalized, ignore comparative advantage, and operate without concern for either production costs or markets. These conditions stem from attempting to manage a firm independently of market forces. Typically, they run large operating deficits that must then be met from general revenues.

The detrimental effects of inefficient public-sector enterprises on development commonly go beyond the budget drain. These enterprises are frequently protected from both domestic and international competition and are the major beneficiaries of overvalued exchange rates that reduce the cost of their imported capital requirements. They drain capital from more productive sectors and are protected by regulatory policies that spread distortions throughout the economy. When the system of public production is sufficiently large and encompasses key industries, the distortions may become substantial.

The remedy for such distortions lies initially in the recognition that it is very difficult to maintain an adequate system of prices for the factors of production, or to assess demand for the product, when that production is managed independently of market forces. Where the product is clearly a "private good," such as matches, the simple solution is divestiture. The solution is more complex when the products are "mixed goods" (V. Ostrom and E. Ostrom, 1977).

A few examples illustrate the character of "mixed goods." For example, some of the benefits of an educated work force accrue to the community at large, while others accrue to the individual directly. Alternatively, it is possible to weaken the non-exclusionary character of many public goods by the simple devise of denying individuals membership in the beneficiary community. For instance, U.S. cattlemen once attempted to exclude sheepherders from common range lands, and nations today extend their territorial waters to protect fishing and mining rights in "international waters." It is also important to make a distinction among the various stages in the supply and consumption of a good in considering its "public" character. For example, because of economies-of-scale in public utilities, we have treated them as natural monopolies. In electric power, however, we find that the economies lie in the distribution grid, not necessarily in either production or consumption. Thus competitive power generation, sold to the "common" grid, may permit the introduction of some market efficiencies into a "natural monopoly."

This category of goods is very difficult to price correctly. The market will tend to underproduce these goods, and the public sector will tend to overproduce them, as was demonstrated in the case of distributive policies. Whether the government solves this problem by ownership or regulation—both typical solutions—inefficiencies are sure to occur. However, many of these mixed goods are particularly critical for development—irrigation systems, education, and market facilities, for example. It is because of the critical nature of these goods that the question of institutional choice and design—including experimentation and innovation aimed at getting the prices right and allocating resources more efficiently—becomes an integral part of the development process.

We have already alluded to some of the possibilities. Public ownership and public regulation have historically been institutional alternatives. For example, public regulations that require property owners to have their garbage removed regularly permit homeowners to do it themselves, or to contract with competing suppliers of the service. Subsidies are a familiar technique of creating social benefits that exceed either individual benefits or the commercial value of a good or service; population control through the subsidization of condoms in a pronatalist culture would be one example. Scale has been considered an important variable in getting prices right. For example, it has often been argued that decentralization and smaller scale will provide better opportunities for getting the prices right if goods and services must be provided in the public sector.

As our understanding of the problems of public goods and mixed goods becomes clearer and the evidence of institutional experiments is increasingly documented, a variety of institutional options may be found for dealing with the problems of the public sector and for providing substantially improved efficiencies and pricing. In this respect, one cannot help but be struck by the variety of institutional solutions to these common social problems within the traditional cultures compared to the paucity and uniformity of the options currently available in the modern-sectors of these same societies.

Institutional Innovation: Markets and Constitutions

The simplest growth models portray economic development as a function of the accumulation of capital. As increments of capital are added, the productive capacity of an economy also increases, growing in size and complexity. More recent discussions of growth have attempted to include technological change in the model. With a given technology, additional increments of production are added at an increasing cost as the factors of production become scarce, resulting in slower growth. Without technological innovation, it is argued, stagnation will appear in one sector after another until growth stops.

With an adequate investment in technological development, on the other hand, new ways of producing products can be found that economize on the scarce factors of production. Laborsaving devices economize on labor; skyscrapers or high-yielding varieties of grain economize on scarce land; new methods of producing steel, with lower energy costs, may reduce the cost of capital goods. If factor markets are working properly, relative factor prices will signal both the need for technological change and indicate the appropriate direction (Ruttan, 1978: ch. 12). However, in the absence of technological change, the potential rents available to those who control the scarce factors of production become quite large. Protection of those rents may constitute a substantial motive for resisting change. The potential rewards for technological innovation may be even larger, but the risks are typically great and institutional arrangements (the "mixed-good" character of the innovation) may significantly reduce the rewards appropriable by the innovators.

Technological innovation is not entirely a market phenomenon. As the economy and production techniques grow in complexity and sophistication, technology depends increasingly on the stock of basic science from which it draws. Basic science, and indeed much of the technology it engenders, have the characteristics of a public good: lead times are long, investment in human capital substantial, commercial profitability very risky, and the benefits of success hard to appropriate. The process of technical innovation, therefore, depends on a complex set of institutional arrangements. Not only those institutions that produce the innovations are involved (for example, the agricultural research system), but also those that define ownership and new forms of contract, or allocate the risk of negative externalities (such as environmental pollution, unemployment and safety risks.) In fact, technological innovation depends to a considerable extent on institutional investments and innovation, which are not exclusively, or even primarily, market events.

Even without incorporating technological change into a development model, we can see that an increase in the size and complexity of the economy alone will necessitate significant institutional change. Rising transaction costs, associated with a complex economy, may require changes in laws governing contract, incorporation, antitrust, etc. (Williamson, 1985). Capital markets develop specialized institutions for mobilizing capital and even such a basic institution as money may undergo considerable transformation. Again, while changes in the structure of the economy may well signal the need for such changes and motivate them, they do not depend primarily on market processes.

At significant points in the growth and development of an economy, further progress will require major changes in its structure. At the most basic level these changes are associated with increasing scale, with major changes in factor ratios (as from labor-deepening to capital-deepening production), in sectoral shifts (as from agriculture, to industry and, eventually, to service as the leading sectors), and in shifts in the role of trade in the economy. But structural change need not lead to growth or development. To achieve growth and development, and to move structural change in productive ways, major shifts in the way in which economic institutions allocate resources, incentives, and information are required. Without these changes, economic activity will turn in increasingly inefficient and unproductive directions. The benefits will return to rent-seekers rather than to entrepreneurs. It was this phenomenon that Clifford Geertz described in *Agricultural Involution* (1968), and Karl Polanyi in *The Great Transformation* (1957). Both books chronicled the pernicious effects of societal failure to provide institutional innovations in the face of significant structural change in the economy induced by population growth.

Thus, the structural transformation of economies to higher levels of efficiency and productivity, accommodating to changing environments, is not an automatic consequence of market forces. Rather, it is very much a consequence of the legal and policy framework that governs institutional change and experimentation. New forms of association must receive legal sanction in due course if they are to flourish and to provide a general model of interaction. Institutional rules must eventually be enforceable by public authority and, therefore, must be compatible with the higher legal order. In short, institutional change is very much a "political economy" event that depends on the interaction of political and economic forces.

Vernon Ruttan has observed that the "supply" of institutional change depends on two factors: the knowledge base, and the cost of innovation (in relation to benefits). With regard to knowledge, most development practitioners are aware of the frustrations involved in development activities in the absence of a clear understanding either of the state of the economy or of the processes at work. The more social science knowledge we have, Ruttan argues, the better we will design and implement institutional change. Practitioners are also well aware of the value of an opportunity to experiment, and of the danger of premature closure in institutional innovation. The cost of institutional innovation may also be great. In certain political environments the cost can literally be death. But even without such severe sanctions, the costs of innovation may be prohibitive because of the costs involved in legislative changes, court cases, and overcoming the political power of vested interests.

It is important to consider the factors identified by Ruttan that influence the supply of institutional innovation. One of these factors, the constitutional order (Ruttan, 1978), is explored in depth in this book.

The constitutional order influences institutional innovation in four ways. First, it may be conducive to free inquiry and social experimentation, or it may be fundamentally repressive. To the extent that it is the latter, the knowledge base on which institutional change rests will be reduced and change will be distorted or retarded. Second, the constitutional order directly influences the cost of entry into the political system and the ease with which the legal foundations of new institutions can be established. Third, as we have seen in previous sections, the constitutional order affects the pattern of use of public authority and, therefore, the types of distortions introduced by public policy into the economy. To the extent that those distortions are great, the market signals that, in Ruttan's terms, induce institutional change will be misdirected. Finally, a stable and vital constitutional order introduces into the political economy a sense of civil order—an agreement on basic values and processes for conflict resolution—that considerably reduces the cost or risk of innovation.

The essays presented in this volume make a powerful case for the profound impact of the constitutional order on the course of economic development. Nevertheless, of the three institutionally based sources of price distortions within an economy that we have discussed, the constitutional level is probably the least subject to change in the interests of development. The constitutional order is also the area of institutional analysis where the prescriptions for improved performance are least clear. It is not evident, for example, that liberal constitutional orders will outperform authoritarian ones. One would be hard pressed to argue that the recent economic success of the states belonging to ASEAN (Association of Southeast Asian Nations) is associated with liberal political systems (see chapter 3 of this book). On the other hand, it is not implausible to argue that regimes characterized by arbitrary tyranny and political instability have performed far below their economic potential. It is important, therefore, to pursue the line of inquiry initiated in this book to address two questions. First, how does the constitutional order shape the evolution and efficiency of a market economy? Second, how does the constitution influence the pace and direction of technological and institutional change? Without powerful theoretical analysis and clear evidence, Third World nations will be even less likely to heed advice favoring constitutional reform than the advice they receive regarding economic reform. The advantage that the current inquiry has over previous attempts to deal with these questions is the recognition that the impact of the constitutional order on the economy is mediated through a set of market institutions of considerable diversity. It appears likely that a multilevel approach, in which constitutional norms interact with institutional rules which in turn interact with individual choices, is an approach with considerable potential.

The State of the Art

Overview of Chapters

In part two, "The Challenge of Institutional Analysis: Some Issues and Approaches," the authors focus on the identification and consequences of conditions that encourage the free association of individuals in pursuit of their common interests. An important distinction is made between market institutions, in which individuals and groups meet to enter into the exchange of goods and services, and political institutions, in which individuals associate to pursue common benefits.

The authors share a normative position, common in classical Greek philosophy, that the individual is only truly "free" or fully "developed" when he is "self-governed." The authors do not address the social-psychological literature, which raises questions about the existence of a generic human thirst for freedom.[2] Rather, like the Greek philosophers, they take the position that human beings have a capacity for freedom that can either be nurtured (leading to self-fulfillment) or constrained (leading to slavery). The focus of attention, therefore, becomes social conditions and their impact on this desired self-fulfillment. This normative position leads them to seek circumstances in the developing world that truly promote self-governance. Instead, however, they find hierarchy with few checks, regimes that severely limit or discourage free association and experiments in self-governance, and powerful tendencies at work that concentrate power and authority.

One essay in the group, by Sombat Chantornvong (chapter 3), draws on Alexis de Tocqueville's argument that the prevalence of free association, which he found in North America, rested on the equality of conditions and the abundant resource base there. However, as with earlier attempts to correlate democracy and development, the empirical case here is difficult to validate.[3] Thus, the ASEAN states, which have witnessed rapid growth and a significant reduction in poverty associated with that growth, have not been noteworthy for the growth of democracy. Chantornvong is forced to conclude, with Tocqueville, that the cause lies as much with the "spirit of the people" as with empirical conditions.

The general line of argument in the collection lies in a different direction, however. It is not wealth, equality, or other empirical conditions, per se, that create the conditions of self-governance. Political development is not derivative from economic conditions, as has been argued fairly systematically in the social science literature for the past twenty years, but derives from the nature of the constitutional rules that govern collective action. The bedrock of self-governance, it is argued, is the capacity to experiment with various forms of association in order to solve common problems and pursue common goals. Individuals must be free to associate and to set the terms of that association. They must have the rights to appropriate the benefits of that association. They must be able, in extremis, to enforce the rules of that association. The constitution and the state can assist them in this by lending the authority of the state to encourage innovation and association. Or, at the other extreme, the state can monopolize authority, initiative, and resources.

But a population learns self-governance by practicing it, motivated by common problems and on terms found mutually agreeable. Under this approach local groups are the source of innovation, of lower-level rules, and of an existential appreciation of democracy. The sources of a "spirit of democracy" are essentially local and at the community level. Two observations are important here. First, this approach does not argue that "small is beautiful." As societies grows in scale and complexity, the scale of problems grows, transaction costs increase, and externalities multiply. In consequence, secondary or tertiary levels of association must evolve to deal with the society's needs. Second, this approach does not suggest that anarchy is the solution. Public, even national, authority is essential to establish and maintain the constitutional rules and deal with the largest-scale problems. But by implication, and consistent with the "mass society" literature of the 1950s and 1960s, if the community base is lost, the mass scale becomes inherently unstable (see Kornhauser, 1959).

This is essentially an American "pluralist" model of political development. It does not deny the importance of the development of the central nation-state; clearly, the emerging nations confront problems of national proportions. But it does suggest that if the institutions of the nation-state are developed at the expense of diverse and relatively autonomous local institutional change, the culture of democracy cannot be expected to emerge. One does not have to believe that all societies are "ready" for large-scale democracy—certainly the Greek philosophers did not believe that. Nor does one have to believe that the "modern" forms of association are inherently different from "traditional" forms, as did Ferdinand Tonnies ([1887] 1957) with his distinction between *Gemeinschaft* (community) and *Gesellschaft* (society), and the other classic writers on the sociology of development in Europe. In fact, the authors of this book seem to agree that one is well advised to build on forms of association known and understood by the local culture.

The authors have revived a set of questions that were eagerly pursued twenty years ago by Martin Lipset, Gabriel Almond, Reinhard Bendix, Ralf Dahrendorf, and others, concerning the relationship of political participation, group association, and democratic values to the development of modern society. But a number of issues still remain to be settled. B. R. Ambedkar was surely not the first to point out, in the arguments over untouchability in India, that the local community was not a font of liberal and humanitarian ideals, let alone of equity. Theodore Lowi has argued forcefully that the evils of abrogating public authority to "private" groups can be as great as the evils of excessive concentration of public power (Lowi, 1979). Finally, although there is ample micro-level evidence, some presented in this volume, that local communities have a remarkable capacity to solve "development" problems, the evidence is less convincing at the macro level.

David Feeny's contribution, "The Demand for and Supply of Institutional Arrangements" (chapter 6) develops a framework for making a bridge between the several contributions in this volume that focus on "constitutional" issues and the more general development literature. He builds this framework by bringing clarity and order to two critical components of the political economy of institutional change. The first component builds on the growing literature on "rent seeking," showing how power can alter economic rewards and incentives. Thanks to this component, it becomes possible to search for institutional rules that shape these incentives in ways that also increase overall economic efficiency and growth. The second component suggests the importance of providing a constitutional order that encourages institutional innovation and differentiation and is, therefore, consistent with rapid economic development.

In chapter 2, Vincent Ostrom argues that the logical requirement for some form of public authority does not automatically lead one to conclude that a "Leviathan," or supreme sovereign, is essential to civil society. Rather, it is important to recognize that the development of the nation-state and its administrative apparatus in the developing world, to which international donors have contributed, is fraught with opportunities for rent-seeking, exploitation, and tyranny. Four key sets of institutions (rules) can serve to restrain those tendencies: freedom of association; the right to property and free economic exchange; due process of law; and the capacity of communities to invest in "public goods" in a way that establishes some relationship between supply and demand. It is the key function of governance, he argues, to make the rules that govern these four processes. The rules should specify process, not content. They should be open and visible, not cryptic. Above all, political development must be viewed as a process that expands power—that is, expands society's capacity to identify and mobilize resources to solve problems—rather than concentrating it.

Nothing in this argument will alter the tendency of men to seek and exploit power. But insofar as the establishment of constitutional regimes is frequently an act of collective will that embodies the aspirations and assumptions of the founders, it can correct a fatal and critical misconception engendered by the nation-building literature. All civil society rests on stability, predictability, and order. However it is essential to recognize that these requisites can be achieved as effectively—perhaps more effectively—by the stable and orderly evolution of the rules as by the concentration of power.

Chapter 3, by Sombat Chantornvong, has already been mentioned. He chronicles the single-minded strengthening of the state bureaucracy in developing countries, drawing heavily on Tocqueville to argue that democracy rests on three foundations: equality of conditions, laws, and the "spirit of the people." But the most critical contribution, according to the author's study of Tocqueville, comes from the experience of self-governance itself. The power of the author's argument rests in his demonstration that it is indeed possible to make a constitutional compact in which prosperity (based on sound macro policies) and social services (provided by the government) are exchanged for the concentration of power in the hands of the elite. Furthermore, it is possible to succeed. If democracy is to be defended, it must be defended in its own right—not as a cause of general economic development. Similarly, although one may find socioeconomic conditions that encourage free association, as have authors from Tocqueville to Dahrendorf, the most important cause is a constitutional and legal order that permits and encourages it.

In chapter 4, Elinor Ostrom picks a particular developmental problem, management of the "commons," to explore the issue of the role of changing associational forms in economic development. Contrary to much of the game-theory literature and to Garrett Hardin's well-known arguments on the subject, Ostrom argues that the stark choice between privatization and dictatorship is not a necessary outcome of the dilemma of the commons. Rather, a review of the case studies reveals that people learn from their mistakes over time, even showing great ingenuity in crafting new institutional forms for resolving dilemmas. Secondly, the solutions are diverse, involving different combinations of technological advance, management procedures, adjudicative institutions, property rights, etc. In other words, even in the "worst case" of common property with enormous externalities, local ingenuity prevails over central dictates across a wide diversity of cultures.

Even more to the point, Ostrom argues that development projects and development administration, like game theory, deal with the static case of how to play most effectively within the rules. What is required, she concludes, is a "constitutional" level of analysis that permits us to modify the rules in order to foster better learning, institutional innovation, and problem solving at the local level.

In chapter 5, Ronald Oakerson develops the case for the small, primary social unit as the source of experience in self-governance. It is in these settings that individuals learn about the interaction of self-interest and reciprocity that is the basis of political development. Because citizens first confront the problems associated with social change in the small, primary social unit, it is here that we find a great capacity for innovation and entrepreneurship in dealing with those problems. While Oakerson does not develop this point in order to make a case for the utility of free association to economic development (as does the literature on decentralization, participation, and development), such an argument is clearly engendered here (see Uphoff, et al., 1979; Esman and Uphoff, 1984). The constitutional order rests on rules of association and on the rules that govern changes in them. The management of development generally operates within the existing institutional rules, and this is the familiar arena for most development projects. But the most dynamic aspect of development is when the rules are exploited to formulate new institutional forms, or when the rules themselves evolve.

In chapter 6, David Feeny develops the framework for institutional change that was briefly discussed above. Building on the work of Douglass North, Vernon Ruttan, and others, Feeny argues that entrepreneurs, motivated by changing factor prices, develop new institutional arrangements that provide increased organizational efficiency and reallocate costs and benefits. However, institutional change is shaped by the society's power structure, which may inhibit innovation in order to protect elite interests. Feeny's recognition that political power influences the direction of economic change is hardly new. However, his attempt to bring power and economic development together within a single framework through the vehicle of institutional analysis represents a major advance in development theory.

Feeny points out that institutional change has the potential to alter both the distribution of income and the efficiency of resource use within the economy. There is ample evidence in the development literature of institutional changes that accomplish the former but not the latter and, in consequence, have little developmental impact. Yet income and its effects are a motivating force for innovation. The practical problem in development is to provide an environment in which incentives to innovate are channeled in socially useful ways that improve economic efficiency.

Feeny argues that the demand for institutional change is generated by the growing inefficiencies in the economy (indicated by price shifts), changing technology, the character of the market (including size), and the "constitutional" order (which shapes the way in which individuals and groups can assert and defend their respective interests). The "supply" of institutional change, in turn, also rests on the "constitutional" order insofar as it tolerates or constrains innovation in the rules governing association and changes in the distribution of costs and benefits. Feeny recognizes that the supply of institutional change depends on the "cost" of institutional design and the knowledge base that informs the search for alternatives. In short, market forces, shaped by an institutional policy environment represented by the "constitutional" order, drive institutional innovation.

Part three, "Institutions and Development in Less-Developed Countries," contains four essays exploring institutional changes that foster economic development at the local level. It is important to clarify the relationship between participation and development, because it has remained murky in the literature. It seems evident, for example, that technological change or a sound structural adjustment program can produce significant economic development without increasing democratization. Nevertheless, there is a broad variety of literature that argues that development projects frequently fail without provision for "real" local participation.

The first point stressed by this literature is that local (or "traditional") communities, have not survived for generations without evolving mechanisms for solving the social and economic problems that commonly confront them. Not surprisingly, therefore, these communities evince remarkable energy, ingenuity, and effectiveness in dealing with the collective challenges of development, when given an opportunity to do so. This adaptive capacity has been attributed to several sources.

One source of adaptation commonly referred to is the indigenous culture. In generations of adapting to the local environment, perhaps through trial and error, communities have evolved effective techniques of dealing with common problems. Knowledge of these techniques is social "capital," which is available to assist development if the opportunity arises.

There is, however, a second level of explanation that forms a recurring pattern in the "decentralization" literature, namely, that community organizations—being inherently simpler, less hierarchical, and "closer" to the problem—are more dynamic than centralized, large-scale hierarchies. This represents a direct rejection of the Weberian assumption that bureaucracy should be the epitome of efficient and rational organization in human society.

A third argument has been made from time to time that cuts across those above. One might argue with Ralf Dahrendorf that there are certain ecological and cultural requisites for "group formation" (1959: chs. 5, 7). Where these are missing—in ethnically diverse and poorly integrated economies, for example—the most effective organizations are likely to be small ones located at the community level.

At the operational level the distinctions among these arguments are probably not important, as they tend to converge on fairly common prescriptions for project design. However, for those interested in the analysis of institutional change, the distinctions are significant. An early and exceptionally well documented argument about the vitality and utility of "traditional" institutions for development is to be found in the work of the Rudolphs (L. Rudolph and S. Rudolph, 1967). But the institutions of "traditional" Hindu society to which they referred were not community-level organizations but the principles of caste that constituted the very structure of Hindu society. They found in caste the cultural capacity for large-scale organization that could rival class as the foundation for political and economic action. It is also advisable to recall the argument of Clifford Geertz (1968) that not all adaptations of "traditional" community institutions prove to be viable development tools. Some, indeed, are pathological. Nevertheless, the overall point is well taken: human communities are indeed generally highly adaptive in the right environment.

There has been a tendency to view institutional innovation and change at the local level as "adaptive." Cultures have evolved their institutional capital as they have responded to environmental challenges in order to survive. There is little in most of the "participation" literature to suggest that human institutions may evolve in order to pursue human definitions of the "good, the advantageous, and the just." But if participation is not a process of choice, then it is simply good management, to be evaluated on efficiency grounds. This book, then, is important since it puts local participation in the constitutional context of expanding human choice, to which project design and implementation are secondary.

The arguments presented here make a strong case for building on "traditional" organizational forms. This is good advice for the project officer, who has limited control over his environment. It is also good advice at the constitutional level of institutional change. For example, in the Bhagavad Gita, Mohandas Gandhi found a vital part of traditional Hindu culture: a formula for selfless non-violence that fired a nationalist movement. His predecessors had found in the same text an equally powerful formula for communal violence. In both cases, the culture had provided a recognizable metaphor for action and change. Much of the anthropological literature has tended to view institutional change as an exceedingly slow process and culture as the source of continuity rather than a source of innovation. But this is not necessarily the case. Institutional and cultural change may be rapid, for example, if conditions change rapidly and dramatically, if incentives for innovation are strong, and if opportunities for learning new organizational and cognitive forms are afforded. It is important to view culture as a basis for expanding choice, not limiting it.

As these essays search local communities for evidence of community initiative, it is not surprising that they find institutional arrangements that exploit both hierarchy and reciprocity. Nor is it unusual for larger-scale institutions to be built on these community-level building blocks. For example, many national-level political organizations are simply an aggregate of local factional traditions (Nicholson, 1972). What is uncommon in simpler rural communities, Karl Polanyi argues, is the presence of market institutions governing such basic economic interactions as contract and property (Polanyi, 1957). In fact, the disruptive impact of market forces on traditional communities has fascinated Western observers of economic change since the nineteenth century. It is clear that national elites throughout the Third World have attempted to reduce the impact of market forces on local institutions, frequently with disastrous economic consequences.

We find, then, contrasting explanations for the erosion of local institutions. Karl Polanyi, much of the anthropological tradition, and many nationalist leaders in the Third World have found the "collapse" of local institutions engendered in the spread of the market economy. This book, in contrast, finds much of the explanation in a hierarchical constitutional tradition exploited by "predatory elites." In fact, the two explanations are not mutually exclusive. Both the market and a centralized political order permit "predatory elites" to create private opportunities for profit that are beyond the control of local communities and existing institutions. Nor are "traditional" institutions immune from corruption. In fact, as Susan Wynne (chapter 7) suggests, many of these local institutions were merely older versions of similarly predatory strategies. Thus the character and contribution of local institutions depends to a great extent on the character of the broader regime within which they exist. The role of local institutions will depend on such factors as the strength of market forces, the vertical distribution of authority, the character of intermediate institutions, and the broad constitutional norms that govern the formation of associations.

The final essay in part three, by James Roumasset and Sumner J. LaCroix, makes an important contribution to institutional analysis by arguing forcefully that the performance of institutions cannot be deduced a priori from their structure or, one might add, from their consistency with the historical traditions and culture of the society. Rather, institutions—old and new—must be evaluated in the context of the "political economy" environment in which they appear and by whether, within that environment, they serve to increase or decrease efficiency and promote growth.

In chapter 7, Susan Wynne reviews the "stock of cognitive resources" upon which African nations can draw to fashion development institutions. Exploring the traditions of the Kgalagadi of Botswana, she finds a fairly recent evolution of more "consensual" relationships within certain groups, replacing the hierarchy of the past. She attributes this institutional innovation to the migration of some communities into the arid desert of western Kweneng, where coping with the harsh environment engendered a more flexible set of social arrangements. Another contributing factor was the appearance of employment opportunities in South Africa for the young men, giving them greater independence. There are undoubtedly tensions in these local communities. Wynne stresses autonomy, and the concomitant freedom of experimentation that it affords the community, as major contributors to successful community problem solving.

In chapter 8, Amos Sawyer illustrates the close relationship existing between participation and development within local communities in Liberia, with participation serving both as a goal and as a means of development. Citing the experience of the Putu Development Association, he demonstrates the importance of local self-organization in achieving development objectives. The Putu Development Association rested on the adaptation of recognized indigenous organizational principles that had been used in the past to manage communal land and settle disputes. Successful as a local initiative, the association nevertheless foundered because of government opposition. Both the "constitutional" environment and the lack of effective intermediate institutions for the settlement of external disputes proved the undoing of the organization. The author concludes: "The survival of local units of collective action depends upon their being nested in a larger system of federated authority relationships." The chapter also touches on the importance of political exchange, such as community support for national elites in exchange for local autonomy, in establishing local autonomy.

Amos Sawyer examines the Liberian experience with autocracy in chapter 9. He finds a movement toward autocracy in Liberia that is characteristic of postcolonial Africa. The origins of this tendency lie in the pre-colonial traditions, the centralized character of colonial authority, the decolonialization process itself, and the integrative strategies of the nationalist regimes. Curiously, although these experiences differ greatly among African regimes, the political consequences appear to be similar.

Before the establishment of Liberia, the indigenous population was organized into diverse ethnic communities, in an environment into which the slave trade had introduced a high level of conflict and instability. With the repatriation of American slaves and the establishment of the new constitution, a strongly centralized political order was superimposed. Within this constitutional order, power steadily gravitated toward the presidency, a development that culminated in the personal rule of President Tubman (1944–1971). What has resulted is a predatory regime in which personal power is unrestrained by law.

The story of Liberia raises challenging questions about the sources of such autocratic tendencies in Africa. Does it simply reconfirm an argument that ethnic diversity does not necessarily replicate the preconditions of the American pluralist political tradition? Did the repatriated slaves simply replicate an exploitative colonial political order? Did halting economic growth inhibit the economic and political integration of the country, leaving the national leadership unchecked by countervailing political forces? In any case, the emergence of national political power in Liberia, as is frequently the case elsewhere, has been fundamentally destructive of local autonomy and initiative.

Returning to Roumasset and La Croix, we see them, in chapter 10, explore current conceptual problems concerning institutional change in the context of nineteenth-century Hawaii. At the most general level, the authors challenge current thinking in economics, which argues that institutional change—in this case the intervention of public authority to establish political rights in property—is a direct consequence of changing market conditions. Rather, they assert that political change must be viewed as an autonomous process, although it may well respond to the same forces that are acting on the market.

They make a second, equally important argument that the efficiency of alternative institutional arrangements cannot be deduced a priori from their structure. Rather, the performance of any such arrangements is an empirical question that will depend on a variety of factors, including both their structure and their interaction with their political and market environments. Specifically, they argue that private property cannot automatically be assumed to be more efficient than common property; it depends upon the particular environment. Further, because political and economic change are related but autonomous, it cannot be taken for granted that rent-seeking behavior is always contrary to increased efficiency and growth. It may well be the case that, in the right circumstances, the efforts of the powerful to alter institutional arrangements to permit themselves to capture more rents may move institutions in more efficient directions.

This essay should be read in conjunction with David Feeny's (chapter 6), which it complements. In effect, what Roumasset and La Croix assert is that political and institutional changes are not an automatic consequence of changes in factor prices. Political and institutional changes, as Feeny argues, have costs and risks associated with the shifts in power, income shares, and institutional rights engendered by the changes. One must understand why political entrepreneurs would take those risks and pay the costs. There is, of course, a tradition in political science that posits that political entrepreneurs are driven by the desire for "power" in the same way that economic entrepreneurs are driven by the desire for wealth (see Lasswell, 1960: ch. 13; Frohlich, Oppenheimer, and Young, 1971: 57). In certain circumstances, this may be sufficient to explain the emergence of a centralized state, increased tax demands, and other autonomous changes in the political economy, as Roumasset and La Croix suggest. However, it is equally plausible that the economic gains from rent-seeking will be sufficient to induce economic entrepreneurs to become political entrepreneurs.

Part 4, "Market Institutions and Contingent Considerations," contains three papers that explore the institutional requisites of a market economy. At the most basic level, the market system is considered to rest on society's fundamental values, namely, the ones that define property rights, the right to associate and organize for economic gain, and the limits placed on individual choice. The market is perceived as an institutional arrangement that maximizes the individual's ability to order his consumption preferences and to pursue them freely. Consequently, market institutions rest on a fundamental conviction regarding the individual's capacity for instrumental rationality. In addition, with the exception of problems that center on a variety of "market failures," the market will provide the most efficient means of allocating consumption and the factors of production in order to assure that the society's resources are used to maximize the aggregate satisfaction.

In economics, much of the discussion of "public choice" has

centered on public interventions that compensate for instances of "market failure." Market failure may rest in information asymmetries, or gaps, that inhibit rational choice on the individual's part. Failure may also rest on the character of the goods in question; "public goods," for example, are difficult to price and supply through market mechanisms. Goods that are characterized by large "externalities" also present difficulties.

But the discussion in this book goes beyond this traditional focus of "public choice." In doing so, it invites an exploration of the institutional foundations of the market economy itself. What are the factors that permit and encourage institutional change within the market economy? How do various definitions of institutional rules (or rights) influence the performance and outcomes of market institutions?

In a brief essay he prepared for the Agency for International Development, Theodore Lowi listed the "institutional requisites" of a market economy (Lowi, 1985). Among them were: (1) law and order, (2) a stable currency, (3) property law and property rights, (4) contract law, (5) laws governing exchange, (6) regulations for the conveyance of public domain to private hands, (7) provision of public goods, (8) provision and regulation of human capital (labor), and (9) pooling of risk. Several of these are discussed in greater depth in this book. There is a growing recognition in the development literature of the contribution of improved market institutions to the efficient use of development resources. The variety and complexity of the institutional underpinnings of an effective market economy are less frequently recognized, however. But as John Taylor's essay in part four indicates, an understanding is needed of how the foundations of the political community interact with the foundations of a market economy.

Furthermore, neither the economy nor market institutions are stagnant. Markets are not simply established for all time. As the economy grows in complexity and sophistication, the evolution of market institutions must follow. In their ground-breaking work on "institutional innovation," Hans Binswanger and Vernon Ruttan (1978) suggest that economic forces themselves "induce" institutional change through the increasing costs associated with increasingly inefficient and outdated institutional arrangements. In such circumstances, the potential gains to both individuals and society from such innovation become very large. Ruttan's concern is predominantly with the process of technological change, but also touches on such fundamental economic institutions as property and contract. Hartmut Picht's essay in this book (chapter 14), which searches for alternatives to public monopolies in the supply of currency, bears directly on this question.

In chapter 11, "How Markets Alleviate Scarcity," Louis De Alessi pursues three themes. First, he explores the implications of Adam Smith's observations that individuals respond in predictable ways to opportunities for gain, and that the process of economic exchange is fundamental to society. Starting with certain basic principles of economic exchange, De Alessi then explores how, for example, different systems of property rights may alter the character of those exchanges.

Among many possible systems of exchange, the market system is deemed efficient because it permits individuals maximum freedom to pursue individualized preferences. In fact, De Alessi comments, in a market system the welfare of individuals is closely related to the consequences of their own decisions. The market then allocates resources and production according to those principles. The function of government is to define rights (such as rights to property) and protect them. The market system also performs a second order of functions in that, beyond the regulation of production and consumption, it also determines the future of the economy by directing investment—that is, by allocating capital and risk. De Alessi also discusses "market failure" and the role of government in alleviating it. The problem of "getting prices right" in an economy is not a regulatory problem but an institutional one, namely, establishing the set of rules and rights that governs the process of individual choice.

In chapter 12, "The Ethical Foundations of the Market," John Taylor explores further the market as a social institution. Whereas De Alessi argued that market institutions depend on a publicly determined set of rules and rights, Taylor suggests that these rights must have their basis in the bonds and values of the political community.

The key to a system of exchange lies not in the ability of the government to enforce institutionalized rights but in the community's recognition and acceptance of those rights. Ultimately, he suggests, economic exchange is not an exchange of goods but of rights over those goods. The key community values that support market exchange are reciprocity and voluntarism in the exchange.

In chapter 13, "Opportunity, Diversity, and Complexity," Vincent Ostrom discusses the interrelationship between markets and public authority. He discusses economic institutions—or any other kind of institution—as a form of "public good" that facilitates exchange. In consequence, the constitutional order, which regulates the application of public authority and creates the normative context for the establishment of economic institutions, determines in large measure the character of the market economy. Although Ostrom criticizes Polanyi's concept of an autonomous market as a logical impossibility, there is much in common between Ostrom's and Polanyi's views. Polanyi describes an environment in which rapid demographic and economic change has destroyed the foundations of "community." The scale and complexity of the emerging nation-state and the emerging national economy effectively remove these processes from community control, Polanyi argues. The processes and the consequences that Polanyi describes in Europe resemble the conditions Ostrom describes in the modern developing world. Furthermore, Polanyi argues, market forces themselves are poorly understood by the same elites that benefit from them—hence the appearance of the Poor Laws in England. Europe was forced, Polanyi implies, to correct this situation by reintegrating its populace into the political community—presumably, as Reinhard Bendix (1964) suggests, by the concept of "citizenship" and, as Karl Deutsch (1953) has argued, through the force of nationalism. Britain and America effected this change through liberal political and economic institutions; continental Europe effected it through other constitutional traditions (for which see, for example, Shonfield, 1965).

Ostrom, drawing on the work of P. T. Bauer, suggests that the institutions of political control in the Third World have permitted political elites to exploit market forces for their benefit. In addition, these political economies have not been able to find effective institutional alternatives to the market nor to counteract the effects of bad policy environments on their growth rates. Ostrom makes a powerful case that regimes designed to maximize political control and rent-seeking by the few are unlikely to afford opportunities for institutional experimentation by individuals striving to resolve their own economic problems and to capture personal opportunities for increased efficiencies and growth. In short, the constitutional order may greatly inhibit the "institutional innovation" that Ruttan seeks.

In chapter 14, "Currency Competition: A Constitutional Perspective," Hartmut Picht explores institutional solutions to a common problem of economic policy: unstable currency. The origins of Picht's inquiry lie in the critical role that a stable currency plays in social exchange generally, and in a market economy in particular. Picht explores suggestions that have been made in recent years to "privatize" currency, that is, to eliminate the governmental monopoly on currency systems, and to introduce a competitive system of privately supplied currencies as a way to reduce the scope for bad government policy. In a careful institutional analysis, Picht argues that the institutional requirements for a successful competitive market in currencies are unlikely to appear in the current international setting.

Picht also suggests (as Milton Friedman has) that a "constitutional" provision for automatic adjustment of the money supply, based on the impact of productivity advances on prices, will produce analogous effects at lower institutional cost. He suggests that it may be possible to establish effective property rights in specialized "units of account" that would permit privatization and differentiation of this key function of currency.

Picht's discussion of institutional options for managing currency systems is interesting as a way of addressing currency problems. Conceptually, however, it has a broader significance. First, his analysis suggests the necessity, as economies grow in size and complexity, for greater differentiation, specialization, and sophistication in key economic institutions. Second, it demonstrates how rigorous institutional analysis can suggest changes in rules and rights, perhaps at the constitutional level, that can encourage this process of differentiation. This suggests an important relationship between economic change and institutional change. Economic forces and economic analysis may reveal growing inefficiencies in an economy and, in consequence, there are opportunities for economic gains from institutional "innovation." The analytic tools for exploring and understanding such institutional innovation, however, demand the capacity to deal effectively with the interaction of rules (even at the constitutional level) and the performance of markets.

Part five, "The Continuing Challenge," by the editors, provides an excellent presentation of the arguments presented in the whole book. I shall conclude by highlighting the specific contributions the book makes to improving the practice of development.

Summary

The key problems facing the developing world today are sustainability and efficiency. Sustainability refers to the inability of developing countries to maintain the investments that have been made. This can be seen in virtually every sector. The Green Revolution (development of high-yield hybrid cereals and other improvements) represented a remarkable breakthrough in Asian agriculture. But there is now serious concern about the ability of Asian research systems to stay ahead of pests and diseases and to sustain the growth rates that have occurred over the past two decades. Rural road systems, irrigation canals, and other infrastructure deteriorate for lack of maintenance. Malaria, thought to be near eradication in South Asia, is resurgent again in the Himalayan foothills. The sustainability problem cannot be blamed on a preoccupation with artifacts rather than human capital, institutions, and systems. Training and management systems have been a continual focus of development efforts. U.S. development efforts, for example, have stressed long-term commitments to institution-building in universities, local governments, and the key development ministries.

Efficiency is the other major concern. In Asia, for example, economies have continued to grow, except when interrupted by human disasters. However, the return on resources invested is unfortunately low in comparison with the needs. Children start school, but do not stay long enough to emerge literate. Bad policy directs capital into inefficient uses. Water is carried through irrigation systems at enormous cost and then much is lost through leakage, or wasted through improper cultivation techniques—often resulting in growing salination.

This is not to suggest that there is neither growth nor good news. For example, world-class science has emerged in Asia. Also, most Asian economies have weathered the vagaries of shifting oil prices and maintained steady, if modest, growth rates without falling into debt traps. Nevertheless, it is reasonable to conclude that neither the public nor the private sector in much of the developing world has developed institutional arrangements that allocate resources efficiently. Furthermore, the growing national wealth and the expanding choices are both concentrated in relatively few hands.

What do the approaches presented in this volume have to offer in the context of these problems? I will outline the principal findings.

1. Much development effort is misdirected because of misdiagnosis. For example, many of the efforts directed toward institutional development focus on training and internal management systems. Yet this is likely to be ineffective if rent-seeking drives incentives in detrimental directions. We need to understand and undertake management improvements in the context of changing incentives.

2. While there are remarkable exceptions, the environment for institutional experimentation and innovation is poor throughout the developing world. Attempts by the communities to provide their own public goods frequently falter from the opposition of national elites or the lack of a legal environment that permits initiative. It is vital to understand that sovereignty is not a zero-sum game, and that variety in the organization of public authority is both possible and productive.

3. Although the public sector in developing countries is not large by the standards of developed ones, it is clear that the government sector has grown very rapidly in a context of considerable concentration of political power. Consequently, the institutions

of representation and control are frequently unable to keep pace with the capacity of political and military elites to affect economic choices at both the macro and micro levels. Furthermore, the influence of the elites is not illegal in any sense of the term. Without any expectation of major constitutional changes, it may nevertheless be possible to suggest incremental changes that will shift power in the direction of greater, rather than less, growth and economic efficiency.

4. In the face of momentous changes in the Asian economies over the past twenty years, markets have been very slow to react for a variety of reasons. For example, there has been a shift from subsistence to predominantly commercial agriculture within this period. Yet the marketing structures for key inputs and for intermediate-term capital have frequently not responded. In the face of rising budget deficits and foreign exchange shortages, several countries in Asia are engaged actively in the privatization of public sector enterprises and in trade liberalization. Yet there is real concern that the indigenous capital market will be unable to keep up with this structural change in the economy. It is reasonable to argue that, in many of these countries, public authority has not been directed toward improving market institutions and market efficiency. Even more recently, the development goal has been stated—incorrectly I would argue—as one of expanding the private sector, rather than of developing market institutions. We need to understand clearly the character of the public functions and policies that encourage expansion and innovation in a market economy.

This book represents a self-conscious attempt to look at the process of development as the interaction of public and private choice. It attempts to demonstrate how the process of public choice can expand or diminish private choice. It contends, furthermore, that in all circumstances the political process will structure private choices through its influence on key economic institutions. The methodologies presented in this volume can illuminate these interactions. Through this improved knowledge, we can aspire to improved policy and improved institutional innovation.

Notes

1. The classic exposition is found in Samuelson (1954); see also Musgrave (1973): ch. 3.
2. The classic argument is found in Fromm (1941). It engendered a series of studies that attempted to find the roots of totalitarian movements in the psychological stress associated with the breakdown of traditional European society, and the uncertainty and challenge to the individual of the modern industrial society.
3. The strongest argument is found in Lipset (1960). In the development literature, Almond and Verba made the case in *The Civic Culture* (1963). An empirical study focused on participatory values in India was inconclusive: compare Jacob (1971).

Works Cited

Almond, Gabriel A., and Sidney Verba (1963) *The Civic Culture*. Princeton: Princeton University Press.

Bendix, Reinhard (1964) *Nation Building and Citizenship*. New York: Wiley.

Binswanger, Hans P., and Vernon W. Ruttan (1978) *Induced Innovation*. Baltimore: Johns Hopkins University Press.

Dahrendorf, Ralf (1959) *Class and Class Conflict in Industrial Society*. Stanford: Stanford University Press.

Deutsch, Karl W. (1953) *Nationalism and Social Communication*. New York: Wiley.

Esman, Milton J., and Norman T. Uphoff (1984) *Local Organizations*. Ithaca, N.Y.: Cornell University Press.

Frohlich, Norman, Joe A. Oppenheimer, and Oran R. Young (1971) *Political Leadership and Collective Goods*. Princeton: Princeton University Press.

Fromm, Erich (1941) *Escape from Freedom*. New York: Farrar & Rinehart.

Geertz, Clifford (1968) *Agricultural Involution*. Berkeley: University of California Press.

Jacob, Philip E., ed. (1971) *Values and the Active Community*. New York: Free Press.

Kornhauser, William (1959) *The Politics of Mass Society*. Glencoe, Ill.: Free Press.

Lasswell, Harold D. (1960) *Psychopathology and Politics*. New York: Viking Press.

Lipset, Seymour M. (1960) *Political Man*. Garden City, N.Y.: Doubleday.

Lowi, Theodore (1972) "Population Policies and the American Political System." In A. E. Kier Nash, ed., *Governance and Population: The Governmental Implications of Population Change*. Commission on Research Reports, vol. 4, Population Growth and the American Future. Washington, D.C.: U.S. Government Printing Office, 283–300.

—————— (1979) *The End of Liberalism*. New York: Norton.

—————— (1985) "The Public Character of Private Markets." Paper prepared for the U.S. Agency for International Development, Bureau for Science and Technology, Office of Rural and Administrative Development, July.

Musgrave, Richard A. (1973) *Public Finance in Theory and Practice*. New York: McGraw-Hill.

Nicholson, Norman K. (1972) "The Factional Model and the Study of Politics." *Comparative Political Studies* (Oct.), 291–313.

Ostrom, Vincent, and Elinor Ostrom (1977) "Public Goods and Public Choices." In E. S. Savas, ed., *Alternatives for Delivering Public Services: Toward Improved Performance*. Boulder, Colo.: Westview Press, 7–49.

Polanyi, Karl (1957) *The Great Transformation*. Boston: Beacon Press.

Rudolph, Lloyd I., and Susanne H. Rudolph (1967) *The Modernity of Tradition*. Chicago: University of Chicago Press.

Ruttan, Vernon W. (1978) "Induced Institutional Change." In Hans P. Binswanger and Vernon W. Ruttan, eds., *Induced Innovation*. Baltimore: Johns Hopkins University Press, 327–357.

Samuelson, Paul A. (1954) "The Pure Theory of Public Expenditure." *Review of Economics and Statistics*, vol. 36 (Nov.), 387–389.

Shonfield, Andrew (1965) *Modern Capitalism*. New York: Oxford University Press.

Tonnies, Ferdinand (1957) *Community and Society.* Charles P. Loomis tr. and ed. East Lansing, Mich.: Michigan State University Press. First published in 1887 as *Gemeinschaft und Gesellschaft.*

Uphoff, Norman T., et al. (1979) *Feasibility and Application of Rural Development Participation: A State-of-the Art Paper.* Monograph Series no. 3. Rural Development Committee, Cornell University: Center for International Studies.

Williamson, Oliver E. (1985) *The Economic Institutions of Capitalism.* New York: Free Press.

Part II

The Challenge of Institutional Analysis: Some Issues and Approaches

2

Vincent Ostrom

Cryptoimperialism, Predatory States, and Self-Governance

Introduction

People everywhere have recognized that the end of World War II presented a major challenge. That war was seen as the end of imperialism and the opening of a new era in civilization, an era that would be marked by the liberation of colonial peoples and the creation of a free world. But the end of imperialism, as associated with the disappearance of self-proclaimed empires, has not been accompanied by the liberation of the world's peoples. The conditions of many of the peoples in the Third World have not been marked by progressive patterns of development but by seriously degenerative tendencies. The world has not been made safe for democracy.

A preliminary draft of this paper was presented on March 21, 1985, as a lecture at McMaster University, Hamilton, Ontario. I owe a substantial debt to Mohammed Labib for calling my attention to the "recipe" contained in what I refer to as the Copeland formula, and to Miles Copeland's *The Game of Nations: The Amorality of Power Politics* (New York: Simon and Schuster, 1969).

Human aspirations have diverged radically from the patterns of development that have actually occurred. Why has this been the case?

In an effort to explain what has happened, I shall argue that coping with "crises" by calling for imperative actions has yielded new forms of cryptoimperialism. The basic formulae for two different types of cryptoimperialism were worked out some years ago. One is advanced in *The Game of Nations* by Miles Copeland, who identifies himself as having been associated with "cryptodiplomacy" (Copeland, 1969: 12). Cryptodiplomacy is hidden diplomacy. I have viewed Copeland's reference to cryptodiplomacy as an invitation to extend the use of the prefix crypto- to imperialism. Cryptoimperialism is the more general structure of relationships that has come to prevail. Cryptoimperialism is a theory for creating cryptoempires, hidden empires in which the control apparatus is concealed by a veil of secrecy behind rhetoric about "freedom" and "liberation." The other formula was worked out by V. I. Lenin. The success of Lenin's revolutionary efforts marked the end of Imperial Russia and created the Union of Soviet Socialist Republics and its association with other socialist states governed in accordance with Marxist-Leninist principles. Lenin's approach to revolutionary struggles for liberation yields a form of cryptoimperialism analogous to Copeland's.

The crises associated with cryptoimperialism are also reflected in the ideology used to organize the new nations of the Third World. In the second part of this essay, I use the theory of sovereignty to demonstrate how sovereign states are likely to become predatory states. Wherever liberation efforts draw upon concepts of state-building and state-to-state relationships as the keys to development in the Third World, we can expect extraordinary opportunities to exist for a few to exploit the many. We can begin to understand some of the sources of human tragedy—crises—in the contemporary world.

In continuing this analysis, I suggest that alternatives may be made available by drawing upon principles of self-governance. Understanding those alternatives depends upon a much fuller elaboration of the terms upon which alternatives are available in the constitution of human societies. Such an approach requires as much attention to the role of infrastructures in the fashioning of human societies as to that of the superstructures reflected in institutions of national governments.

The task we confront in seeking to understand the terms on which alternatives are available is one of challenging proportions, beyond the competence of individual human efforts. Instead, that challenge is potentially tractable to inquiry by many people of diverse capabilities. Other papers in this volume begin to explore some of the terms on which alternatives may be available. This approach opens the possibility of choice among alternative institutional possibilities, rather than presuming that human beings can only respond to crises with no-choice imperatives.

Recipes for Constituting "New" Nations

To a significant degree, human beings shape their own social realities. These realities are grounded in conceptions that refer to ordering principles and imply a computational logic. We can thus turn to the explanations that are offered about how to proceed in constituting ordered relationships in human societies as a way of supplying us with the theoretical conjectures that are constitutive of human social relationships. This is why the Copeland formula and the Lenin formula provide us with computational logics for understanding what has happened in the constitution of the new nations that have come into being following the collapse of the major imperial systems after World War II.

The Copeland Formula. Miles Copeland's *The Game of Nations* (1969) is an account of American efforts to establish a stable regime in an unstable situation in Egypt following British efforts to reduce their imperial commitments in the Middle East. Instability is incompatible with both freedom and development; progress in building a free world requires stability. Prior efforts to cope with comparable instabilities in Syria were the immediate background to the Egyptian developments. In Syria, these efforts began with a coup d'état undertaken by Husni el Zaim, the chief of staff of the Syrian army. According to Copeland's account, Zaim was aided by a "political action team" of American cryptodiplomats who "suggested to him the idea of a coup d'état, advised him how to go about it, and guided him through the intricate preparations in laying the groundwork for it" (Copeland, 1969: 50). Other coups followed. "The problem, then," as Copeland indicates, "was not of bringing about a change of government" by a military coup, "but of making the change stick" (p. 54).

Working out arrangements for making a change of government "stick" required a much greater elaboration of the necessary structural conditions for doing so. These were worked out in the coup d'état organized by Gamal Abdelnasser who is known to the world today simply as Nasser. According to Copeland's account, a team of cryptodiplomats was intimately involved in preparing the coup and in continuing discussions about how to build a stable structure of relationships that would be secure against further coups and counter-revolutionary efforts.

James Eichelberger, a State Department political scientist, was, according to Copeland's account, assigned directly to the American ambassador "to work out various situation estimates and recommendations for action" (p. 86). Among the papers said to have been prepared by Eichelberger was one called "Power Problems of a Revolutionary Government," which is published as an appendix to Copeland's book. This paper, Copeland says, "was translated into Arabic, commented upon by various members of Nasser's staff, translated back into English for further editing by Eichelberger, and so on back and forth between English and Arabic until a final version was produced" (p. 87). "The final version was passed off to the outside world," in Copeland's account, "as the work of Zakaria Mohieddin, Nasser's most thoughtful and (in Western eyes) reasonable deputy, and accepted at face value by intelligence analysts of the State Department, the CIA, and, presumably, similar agencies of other governments" (p. 87). Copeland also indicates that Eichelberger later "went to great lengths to disown any connection with it" (p. 87).

Since the analysis contained in "Power Problems of a Revolutionary Government" is the foundation for Copeland's analysis in *The Game of Nations* and is published there, I shall refer to it as the Copeland formula even though that statement may have been variously contributed to by Eichelberger, Mohieddin, and others. The statement is of fundamental importance in specifying the basic conditions for achieving stability in a revolutionary government undertaken by a military coup. We can also view the statement as being of constitutional importance by the extent to which this formulation serves as a model for aspiring leaders in the new nations of the Third World.

A constitution can be conceived as specifying the terms and conditions of government. This is what the Copeland formula addresses; it is a recipe for organizing a stable revolutionary government undertaken by the leaders of a military coup. These terms and conditions provide us with an understanding of the way that systems of government have been organized among the "new nations" of the Third World. In fact, some of these nations are, like Egypt, as old as recorded history; others were little more than administrative units in European empires. What they shared in common was colonial dependency in one form or another; and their newness is reflected in claims to independent standing in the family of nations.

The Copeland formula lays down two principles about the maintenance of governmental power. First, power is based on "*repressive* action or on *constructive* action" (p. 284). Second, "*everything that a government does has an effect on its power base*" (p. 285). That power base, in its most essential structure, rests upon instruments for repressive action. All actions, then, need to be assessed for the way that they contribute to control over instrumentalities for repressive action in a society.

Revolutionary governments, the Copeland formula emphasizes, are not bound by considerations of legality. Revolution is by its nature illegal. The task of a revolutionary government is to do whatever is necessary to actualize a maximum of power that is subject to its control. This it does by placing itself in a position to exercise a monopoly over both repressive and constructive measures of collective action. A "policy of drift and compromise," according to the statement, is "dangerous in the extreme" because it forsakes power for popularity (p. 287).

In consolidating its power base, a revolutionary government, according to the Copeland formula, relies upon repressive powers exercised through: (1) legislation, (2) police, (3) an organized intelligence service, (4) propaganda facilities, and (5) military force. Having seized power illegally, a revolutionary government is subject to no legal constraint in exercising a monopoly over all legal political activity. This is done by prohibiting all "organized political activity not favored by the government" (p. 291). All opposition is made illegal. Legislation, in the form of revolutionary decrees, becomes the foundation of state security and formulates the duties and obligations of citizens. Magistrates, according to the Copeland formula, are presumed to be under the control of the revolutionary government.

Since "police are the bulwark of the security system," control over police is a matter of high priority. "This means, essentially, that the police should be 'politicized' and should become, to whatever extent is necessary, a partisan paramilitary arm of the revolutionary government" (p. 292). A carefully concealed intelligence or secret service is the "nerve center of the whole security system of a revolutionary state." This service, disguised within the structure of government or even located outside of government, must have access to the work of all other security and intelligence services and be capable of penetrating and dealing with "any suspected antirevolutionary activity" (p. 293).

Propaganda activity must, according to the Copeland formula, be mobilized to support the use of repressive power and justify its continued use. Steps need to be taken by assigning press officers to all news media to offer guidance about publication. "The authority of these officers can be reinforced when necessary by evoking the security legislation . . . or by threatening the overstrict or 'nuisance' enforcement of various laws or taxes" (p. 293).

The military force deserves special attention to assure "a loyal and efficient army" and to "build a countersubversive intelligence system in the army." Everything should be done to keep a "happy army" (p. 293).

The repressive apparatus has priority in laying the foundations for the constructive measures that are to be initiated on behalf of the revolutionary movement. Of critical importance is the creation of a "mass organization" as an "extragovernmental association in which the leaders of the revolution, together with other governmental officials and employees, join with a large mass of private citizens for the declared purpose of supporting and furthering the accomplishments of the revolution" (p. 295). This mass organization is to serve as a "propaganda front for the government and to build a political party for the future" (p. 296).

The mass organization is to serve as a "clearinghouse" for anyone wishing to influence the government or dealing with governmental officials. The mass organization is a way of obtaining "satisfaction" (p. 297) for citizens having difficulties with the government. In return for its services, "the mass organization can expect the adherence of many people who otherwise might remain indifferent, and financial contributions or other types of active support should be much easier to solicit" (p. 297). Copeland elsewhere identifies such a mass organization as providing citizens with "the freedom to vote without the freedom to argue about what is being voted upon— except, that is, within the confines of the one party set up by the state" (p. 127). In these circumstances, "the party is an instrument of the state whereby the state influences the people to think the way the leader of the state wants them to think" (p. 127).

In the Copeland formula, the "working cadre" of the mass organization "can be found in the civil service, for all government employees can and should be required to join on an active basis as the condition of continued governmental employment" (p. 296). Copeland elsewhere emphasizes a principle of "big government." He asserts that the purpose of government "is not so much to serve the public as to keep a large segment of the public off the streets— a segment that could be extremely dangerous if left unemployed" (p. 128). People absorbed into government employment are kept occupied and under surveillance. At the same time they act, in part, as brokers to secure satisfaction for those whose interests are being impeded by other officials; and in part, to influence people to think the way that the leader of the state wants them to think.

As the structure of government is stabilized, the Copeland formula anticipates the preparation of a new constitution. Two features are considered of "utmost importance, however, if the revolutionary power base is to be perpetuated with maximum effect" (p. 297). First, the written constitution should contain only general provisions without legal force. All such provisions should depend upon further legislation. Second, the constitution should depend upon a "strong executive, popularly elected by plurality" (p. 298). The statement anticipates that the revolutionary party as the only lawful political party "will be in a position for some time to come to 'write the constitution' in accordance with its own requirements" (p. 298) and control the selection of the executive. "It is impossible," the statement insists, "to overemphasize the importance of these two propositions—that the formal constitution (the 'written constitution') should consist of broad general provisions, and that it should provide for a strong executive" (p. 298). It warns against "legalistic documents...produced by constitutional commissions" composed "largely of professors and jurists" and "drawn up with great regard for complicated concepts of government that appear in textbooks and with the niceties of theoretical justice" (p. 299).

The Copeland formula, viewed as constitutional design, suggests an unlimited center of power that has at its disposal extensive instrumentalities for repressive action. Such a system of government is not bound by lawful limits. Revolutions and coups d'état are by their nature illegal. Those who lead revolutions and coups are free to be outlaws and pursue a wide range of temptation strategies in oppressing and exploiting others. They are capable of exercising dominance over a society where people are told what to think and what to do. The laws in such a society are subject to arbitrary enforcement. They become instruments of harassment for a press that displays independence; and instruments of corruption in the hands of party cadres who are prepared to extend favors in exchange for active support. The scenario for constructive action implies a commitment to wipe out traditional institutions that stand in the way of progress as conceived by the leaders of a revolutionary government; to mobilize an uncritical devotion to the revolutionary cause; and to secure obedience in undertaking those measures proclaimed by the revolutionary leadership as essential to the revolution. A strong executive and a one-party system form the core of the longer-term constitutional structure.

When we take the design formulated in Copeland's account, we have an explanation that enables us to understand the events that have transpired and are transpiring in the Third World. There, coups d'état and revolutions are the standard methods for changing governments. The standard form of government is the "strong executive," that is, some variant of dictatorship. A politicized police, a secret service, a happy army, an inflated bureaucracy, a mass movement organized as a one-party system, and a propaganda service to tell people what to think are the key instrumentalities of control. Citizens are expected to obey and not to oppose measures of the government. Traditional institutions that have helped to sustain a way of life are subject to assault; and new ways that are amenable to mass appeals and maximization of the regime's control over society are put in their place. Revolutionary rhetoric about socialism is used to nationalize economic enterprises and control economic activity. Costs of government escalate, while productivity declines. The tragedies of the Third World ensue. New forms of cryptoimperialism, managed by cryptodiplomats and dictatorial governments, replace the older forms of imperialism run by colonial officers.

The Lenin Formula. Lenin, as an active professional revolutionary, was explicit about the task of organizing a socialist revolutionary movement. Without a theory of revolution, Lenin argued, there can be no successful revolution. Lenin was preoccupied first with organizing a successful revolutionary movement. Then, once the movement was successful, he hoped to transform society. A brief newspaper article, "Where to Begin?" (May, 1901) and a more extended account in *What Is To Be Done?* (written 1901–1902) provide the basis for understanding how Lenin viewed the task of constituting a revolutionary movement; and *State and Revolution* ([1917] 1932) indicates how political authority should be organized after a successful revolution to achieve the transformation of society.

The organization of government in Imperial Russia relied upon principles of autocracy that gave the czar ultimate authority to control the apparatus of government. Autocracy also implied "self-rule" on the part of the czar. No limits to that autocracy were acknowledged. The czar, as the personification of autocracy, ruled over society.

In "Where to Begin?" Lenin poses the basic revolutionary task as establishing a strongly organized party for the purposes of winning not only a "few concessions, but the very *fortress* of the autocracy" (Lenin, [1901] n.d.: 16, my emphasis). The stress is upon establishing a fighting organization where "our military forces mainly consist of volunteers and rebels" (p. 18). The effort is a long-term one of fashioning "an organization that will be ready at any moment to support every protest and every outbreak, and to utilize those for the purposes of increasing and strengthening the military forces fit for the decisive battle" (p. 18). The organizers of a revolution must be prepared for the "decisive battle" and "capable of leading that battle" in light of the "spontaneous outbursts" or "unforeseen political complications which constantly threaten it [the tsarist autocracy] from all sides" (pp. 22–23).

The core of this effort is to be achieved through the organization of an all-Russian newspaper. A clandestine newspaper will provide an instrument of publicity, the rudiments of a command apparatus in its distributional network, and an intelligence apparatus in its newsgathering arrangements. The appeal of the revolutionary movement must be to create as large a base of support among the population as possible.

> We must take upon ourselves the task of organizing a universal political struggle under the leadership of our Party in such a manner as to obtain all of the support possible of all opposition strata for the struggle and for *our Party*. (Lenin, [1902] n.d.: 103, Lenin's emphasis)

Lenin explicitly rejects models of organization based upon trade unions, student circles, and broad democracy. All of these patterns of organization would expose the leadership to being captured by the police and the destruction of its fighting potential at the very time when the decisive battles are to be engaged. Leaders of trade unions are known to the world: they bargain with the opposition. Student circles march "to war like peasants from the plough, snatching up a club" (p. 116). Party organization based upon "broad democracy" is "nothing more than a *useless and harmful* toy" (p. 154, Lenin's emphasis). Instead, Lenin argues, "the only serious organizational principle the active workers of our movement can accept is strict secrecy, strict selection of membership and the training of professional revolutionaries" (p. 155). Furthermore, "secrecy is such a necessary condition that all the other conditions must be subordinated to it" (p. 150).

The function of Lenin's revolutionary party is to exercise leadership of a revolutionary movement. The unity of a revolutionary movement depends upon the unity of its leadership. A "dozen professional revolutionaries" centralizing "the secret part of the work" will increase many times over the active participation of the broad masses in the revolutionary struggle. The revolutionary party, thus, is the vanguard of the revolutionary movement performing the secret leadership functions that organize and direct the revolutionary movement as a whole. The basic principles that apply to the party as the vanguard of the revolutionary movement are: (1) strict secrecy, (2) strict selection of membership, (3) strict discipline, and (4) careful training of a small core of professional revolutionaries who exercise leadership of the revolutionary movement. It is such a fighting organization that will lead a revolutionary movement capable of winning "the very fortress of the autocracy."

Lenin's theory of revolution relies upon a command apparatus that is practically a mirror image of the autocracy he sought to destroy. A unified leadership exercises command over a revolutionary movement in much the same way that an autocratic imperial government exercises a unity of power in its command over society. Leadership is exercised by a few professional revolutionaries who in turn select their own membership, in contrast to an imperial tradition based upon patrimonial principles of inheritance. But, in both cases, it is the leadership that exercises command over others in accordance with principles of strict secrecy, strict discipline, strict rules of selection, and professional training to exercise command and control functions.

Once the revolutionary struggle has won the fortress of the autocracy, how is the transformation of society to be achieved so that human beings may be liberated from the circumstances where the few exploit the many? Lenin, in *State and Revolution*, draws upon Karl Marx to make his diagnostic assessment of the basic task to be achieved: the transformation of society that will liberate people from exploitation by the creation of a new socialist society.

Marx's analysis is grounded in the presupposition that private ownership of the modes of production in a capitalist society is the essential element in human exploitation. Those who own the modes of production are capitalists; and they share a class interest in the use of their property to exploit those who are workers. Competitive dynamics yield an increasingly narrow and more powerful class of owners as weaker ones are eliminated and the exploitation of workers intensifies. The state becomes an organ of the capitalist class to maintain its dominance over society through the coercive instrumentalities of the military, the police, and the bureaucracy. Workers become the object of oppression as irreconcilable class antagonisms intensify, yielding a revolutionary potential.

Lenin's theory of revolution is designed to take advantage of this revolutionary potential by seizing the very fortress of the state apparatus. Seizing state power and crushing and destroying the state apparatus are not sufficient, however, to yield a new society free of human exploitation and without class antagonism. New patterns of property relationships need to be established once the oppressed—the proletariat—have seized state power through a dictatorship of the proletariat. The oppressed can use state power to eliminate the oppressors and undertake the reconstruction of society.

The reconstruction of society is achieved by using state power to expropriate private property. The means of production will then be owned by the working class thanks to its control of state power through a dictatorship of the proletariat. The working class as owner of the means of production will then reap the fruits of its own labor, exploitation will be eliminated, and a classless society will exist. The state will no longer have a reason for existence and will wither away. A communist society will come into being and that society will be both classless and stateless. Lenin conceives of the communist party as being the vanguard party exercising leadership on behalf of the dictatorship of the proletariat in achieving a revolutionary transformation where human exploitation will cease to exist.

This same account as offered by Marx and Lenin can be read in a different way. A small core of revolutionaries can be viewed as exercising leadership of a revolutionary movement by control over the secret leadership functions of command and control. Once the fortress of the prevailing leadership of the state is seized, the revolutionary leadership assumes control over the state apparatus, expropriates private property, and establishes command and control over all socialized property. Opposing forces are eliminated and the revolutionary leadership, as the ruling apparatus, exercises command over state power. The revolutionary leadership achieves autocratic control over the state apparatus. A new autocracy replaces the old autocracy and preserves the autocratic principles of governance: strict secrecy, strict discipline, strict selection of membership in the ruling autocracy, and careful training of those who become professional rulers. The more things change, the more they remain the same.

The New Ruling Classes. We have here two contending sets of conjectures. The Marxist-Leninist argument sees a revolutionary struggle culminating in the use of state power to liberate human beings from exploitation and achieve a classless and a stateless society. The Copeland formula sees the use of state power on behalf of a revolutionary movement as achieving the stability necessary for a free world to develop. Both have actually led to a continued effort to consolidate the power of central governments.

Milovan Djilas, a leading figure in the Yugoslav communist movement, describes the results of the Soviet effort.

> Everything happened differently in the USSR and the other Communist countries from what the leaders—even such prominent ones as Lenin, Stalin, Trotsky, and Bukharin—anticipated. They expected that the state would rapidly wither away, that democracy would be strengthened. *The reverse happened.* (Djilas, 1957: 37, my emphasis)

The state was strengthened and a new ruling class came to dominance, "its power more complete than the power of any other class before in history" (p. 38). In seeking the liberation of people from human exploitation, the communist party has itself created another form of cryptoimperialism.

Much the same observation might be made about the end of imperialism and the blossoming of a free world that was expected to emerge following World War II. Everyone expected that imperialism would rapidly wither away and that democracy would be strengthened. *The reverse has happened.* Cryptoempires are engaging in power struggles that strengthen the repressive capabilities of predatory states and state functionaries to prey upon their own subjects, whose autonomous cultural infrastructures are threatened with destruction without their opportunities for self-governance being increased. American cryptoimperialism may have achieved some measure of short-term stability at the cost of both freedom and long-term stability.

Both the Copeland formula and the Lenin formula rely upon a unity of command to achieve stable forms of control over society. Each relies upon the military, police, and an intelligence apparatus (including the secret police) to deny fundamental human rights and control society. Leadership is exercised by a disciplined elite operating in secrecy. A party apparatus, to mobilize people to support the regime, and censorship, to control public information, are collateral forms of control available to those who exercise leadership prerogatives. Men aspire to be free, as Rousseau long ago explained the human condition, but they are everywhere in chains.

Why do such conditions prevail? This is the subject of the next section.

The Theory of Sovereignty: How the Few Exploit the Many

Basic institutions in human societies are organized to create structures of incentives and deterrents that lead people to behave in predictable and thus ordered ways. There is a type of logic or rationality imbedded in the structure of human institutions. Our effort, then, will be to clarify the logic of state organization and establish why it is that a theory of the state has to provide opportunities for the few to exploit the many. A theory of sovereignty, defined as the authority to govern society, is well elaborated in Thomas Hobbes's *Leviathan* ([1651] 1960) and provides us with a computational logic for the organization of sovereign states.

The problem pertaining to authority to govern arises because human beings order their relationships with one another in societies by references to rules. Rules are linguistic devices that rely upon norms or standards to order choice by distinguishing what is forbidden from what is permitted and required. By interposing limits upon all possible actions, human beings are able to achieve predictability in their relationships with one another and still leave sufficient openness to allow for latitudes of choice. By using a common set of rules of the road, for example, automobile drivers are able to respond to one another in predictable and orderly ways and still have sufficient freedom of choice to proceed by distinguishable and unique routes to unique destinations. Drivers in socialist societies are as dependent upon enforceable rules of the road as drivers in capitalist societies.

The pattern of order in any society depends then upon a body of common rules that enable a multitude of individuals to act with a shared community of understanding. It is a common set of rules that transforms a multitude into an ordered community of relationships. Rules, however, are not self-formulating, self-enforcing, or self-modifying. Instead, they are human creations that depend upon human agents to formulate, enforce, and alter them if there are to be orderly relationships in human societies. It is this complex task of formulating, enforcing, and modifying rules that is the basic function of government. Thus, the authority to govern pertains to what can be referred to as the rule-ruler-ruled relationship.

Without authority to enforce rules, human beings will always be tempted to ignore them and pursue opportunities that are beyond the bounds of lawful relationships. If they do, the resulting conflicts are likely to escalate into violence and destruction. Rule-ordered relationships depend upon some who exercise prerogatives of enforcement in order to make rules binding in human relationships.

A theory of sovereignty—the authority to govern—begins then with a presupposition that law is necessary for ordered social relationships in any society. Further, law is required to have a coherence that can be characterized as a "unity of law." For a unity of law to exist, the further presupposition is made that a "unity of power" is necessary to the peace and concord of society. One single center of authority must exercise the ultimate prerogatives of government. It is this ultimate center of authority that is "sovereign" and has the last say in the governance of a society. A theory of sovereignty presumes a unity of power—a unity of command—where those who exercise sovereignty rule over society (Hobbes, [1651] 1960).

This conception, that the unity of law depends upon a unity of power, has been fundamental to organizing the structure of government in most societies throughout recorded history. The character of any such relationship involves deep puzzles and extraordinary tensions for human societies. In order to make rules binding in human relationships and to limit temptations to pursue opportunities that arise from the violation of law, those who exercise the prerogatives of rulership must have access to instruments of coercion to achieve the advantage of rule-ordered relationships. Several implications follow.

One implication is that those who exercise rulership prerogatives in a society achieve positions that are radically unequal to those who are the subject of rules. Rules imply rulers and ruled (subjects). The most radical source of inequalities in human societies is the rule-ruler-ruled relationship. Furthermore, those who exercise the prerogatives of rulership have access to instruments of coercion and force to impose punishment upon those who follow temptation strategies that arise from ignoring or violating law. Rulers have access to instruments of evil (i.e., instruments of punishment) to achieve the advantages that accrue from orderly relationships in human societies.

The rule-ruler-ruled relationship, then, is a Faustian bargain in which human beings have recourse to instruments of evil to do good. These conditions apply alike to the revolutionary who seeks to use state power in order to transform society and eliminate human exploitation; to cryptodiplomats who seek to establish stable regimes in a world plagued by coups d'état and revolutionary struggles; and to social reformers who rely upon central governmental authority to undertake measures to advance social welfare. Life in human societies is plagued by radical inequalities in the rule-ruler-ruled relationship and by the circumstance that these inequalities are distinguished by assigning authority to some who can lawfully use instruments of force or coercion to impose deprivation upon others. The presumption that the peace and prosperity of any people depends upon a unity of law, and that the unity of law depends upon a unity of power, further implies that any such center of authority should exercise a *monopoly* over the legitimate use of force in a society. This is the attribute that is used to define the state: in most modern works in the social sciences, the state is the entity that has a monopoly of the legitimate use of force in the governance of society. All instruments of coercive power not controlled by the central authority of the state are presumed to be without legitimacy; they are presumed to be illegal.

Building upon these presuppositions, a theory of sovereignty carries the further implication that those who are sovereign and monopolize the legitimate use of force in a society exercise an authority that is both *unlimited* and *indivisible*. Those who have the ultimate authority to govern, and have a monopoly of the legitimate use of force in a society, exercise an authority to determine all other authority relationships. Sovereigns, then, are the source of law and cannot themselves be held accountable to a rule of law. All others are *subjects* in the presence of a *sovereign*; and sovereigns, not being limited to any enforceable rule of law, stand outside the law, that is, are outlaws in relation to those who are subjects.

Those who are sovereign have access to extraordinary opportunities to use the instrumentalities of governance to dominate the allocation of values in society and exploit others. Sovereigns, and those who act on their behalf, are free to become predators and prey upon others, who are reduced to a position of being relatively defenseless subjects (Levi, 1981; Rotberg, 1971: see esp. ch. 10). State-building, where the preoccupation is with establishing strong central governments that exercise a monopoly over the legal instrumentalities of coercion in a society, creates unique opportunities for a few to exploit the many. In such circumstances, the exercise of state power can be used to reduce all other potential sources of power to submission. Predatory states created either in the image of American or Soviet cryptoimperialism can be expected to yield impoverishment in the Third World.

Organizing aid to the Third World on a state-to-state basis does not alter the fundamental structures of relationships. Each state, within a world of sovereign states, is presumed to exercise control over its own internal affairs. Military and economic aid, under such circumstances, can be used to enhance the repressive and predatory characteristics of the regime in power. Efforts to modify such tendencies place the contending world powers in the position of relying upon whatever instruments of command are available to the respective heads of state. In the American case, this means that the instrumentalities of cryptodiplomacy are available in the diplomatic, military, and intelligence services. In the Soviet case, these instrumentalities of cryptodiplomacy are reinforced by the command apparatus that is available in the leadership structure of Lenin's revolutionary party. Lenin's vanguard party yields such an advantage in the imperial struggle for domination that the Soviet form of cryptoimperialism can be expected to prevail so long as human freedom and liberation are conceived only with reference to states and state-to-state relationships.

Are There Alternatives?

When we conceive of price as the terms on which alternatives are available, we need not confine our reference to monetary prices. Any effort to "get the prices right" requires a course of inquiry to go beyond market calculations. The possibility of both cryptoimperialism and predatory states implies that market deficiencies cannot always be resolved by turning from markets to states. State officials, or those who control state power, can be as predatory as the most self-serving and avaricious capitalists.

We cannot, however, assume that all heads of state are birds of prey even when some of them view corruption as the lubricant that keeps the machinery of state in motion and consider the modus vivendi of politics as learning how to "steal cleverly" (Hyden, 1980: 196). Some heads of state are also motivated by a strong passion to do good rather than prey upon others. But puzzles arise even in these circumstances.

Those who exercise the ultimate authority to govern and simultaneously command the legitimate use of force in a society may, in their passion to do good, seek to eliminate all obstacles that stand in their way. These are the circumstances that yield the most extreme forms of oppression in human societies. Great dangers arise whenever human beings with strong convictions about the rightness of their cause are authorized to use instruments of evil to do good. The results can reach genocidal proportions.

Other circumstances can also prevail where those who exercise the ultimate prerogatives of government are aware of their own limitations as fallible creatures, and seek to use those prerogatives to advance human welfare. Grave difficulties exist even then. I shall draw upon two examples: the emancipation of serfs in Imperial Russia and the emancipation of slaves in the United States.

Czar Alexander II, after extended inquiry and persistent effort, issued his Edict of Emancipation on February 19, 1861. At that time serfs comprised approximately 80 percent of the population in Imperial Russia. What did an imperial edict accomplish given the immensity of this task? Important changes in the nexus of legal relationships occurred; but as Edward Crankshaw shows in *The Shadow of the Winter Palace*, such a decree could only be a small but important step in the liberation of serfs. Infrastructures in Russian society that might have enabled serfs to achieve freedom and self-governance were tragically lacking. Radical new expectations were formed. In the absence of appropriate institutional arrangements for achieving self-governance, an exceedingly precarious situation was created. Revolutionary disturbances erupted in 1905. The regime itself collapsed in the revolutionary struggle of 1917. Eventually, the regime gave way to one led by Lenin's vanguard party. Whether the collectivization of Soviet agriculture has yielded the liberation of the peasantry or created a new form of serfdom remains an issue some 125 years after the Edict of Emancipation.

Much the same assertion can be made with regard to President Abraham Lincoln's Emancipation Proclamation, issued on September 22, 1862. Putting words on paper was not sufficient to make free men of former slaves. Access to education and the understanding and skills that accrue from education had to be achieved. Among these essential skills were the ones associated with making the legal and political system work to the advantage of the "freed" amid a status quo dominated by their erstwhile oppressors. Blacks could vote with their feet to find a more congenial status quo. But achieving freedom is a long and enduring struggle. Though what Alexander II and Lincoln did were important events in the chronicle of human liberation, the terms on which freedom becomes possible require much more than can be accomplished by heads of state.

A free world, then, depends upon a much more complex configuration of institutional arrangements in human societies. If we human beings are to be free enough to be first and foremost our own governors, we must be prepared to recognize basic human rights and correlative obligations that extend those same rights and obligations to others. Rights to freedom of speech, worship, and assembly; rights to gain access to information and knowledge, to enter into voluntary exchange arrangements, to hold property, and to enter into associated arrangements with others; rights to specify terms and conditions of governance through processes of constitutional choice and to due process of law; all are of fundamental importance if human societies are to be constituted so that freedom may prevail, and people can participate in the governance of society and fashion their own course of development.

The structure of opportunity in a free society allows individuals wide latitude of choice to pursue opportunities consistent with their own aspirations. Freedom of opportunity depends upon the capacity of individuals to relate to others through exchange arrangements and through teamwork. The correlative of exchange arrangements is a lawful right to what is exchanged, that is, to property. The correlative of teamwork is a right to share in the fruits of joint efforts. Freedom cannot exist without constitutionally guaranteed rules of association and property rights.

Problems associated with common-property resources—goods subject to collective use or consumption—and with conflict and conflict resolution require recourse to involuntary patterns of association. But even these can be formulated under terms and conditions that meet the requirements of fairness, and that hold those who exercise extraordinary prerogatives of government accountable to a public trust specifiable under the limits of constitutional law. All such arrangements require that governance occur in an open public realm (*res publica*), where everyone exercises some basic prerogatives of governance and no one exercises unlimited prerogatives of governance.

It follows that a free society depends upon an elaborate structure of institutional arrangements that conform to two basic rules. One is the ancient moral precept, "Do unto others as you would have others do unto you." This precept can be developed into a method of normative inquiry, where human beings take the perspective of others, discount partialities associated with self-love, and strive for impartiality (Kaufmann, Majone, and Ostrom, 1986: ch. 11). The other rule is W. R. Ashby's law of requisite variety: To realize specified effects, there must exist as much variety in the strategies available as there is variety in the conditions that obtain (Ashby, 1956: 206-213). In short, simple institutional arrangements will not suffice for a complex world.

Adam Smith, in *The Theory of Moral Sentiments*, warns against those who imagine that they can arrange "the different members of a great society with as much ease as the hand that arranges the different pieces on a chess-board" ([1759] n.d.: 380-381). Human societies are, instead, composed of "pieces" that are capable of thinking and acting on their own, for "in the great chess-board of human society, every piece has a principle of motion of its own altogether different than the legislature might choose to impose on it" (p. 381). Only when principles of legislation can be used to fashion institutional arrangements that are consonant with the principles of motion that activate individual human beings can "the game of human society . . . go on easily and harmoniously" and yield results that are "likely to be happy and successful" (p. 381).

Getting the prices right, then, requires more than markets and states. It depends upon appropriate configurations of rule-ordered relationships. Infrastructures are necessary that enable people to have recourse to self-organizing and self-governing institutions appropriate to the pursuit of diverse opportunities. These include the capacity to: (1) organize teamwork and teams of teams in complex patterns of organization appropriate to the task to be accomplished; (2) have access to free-exchange relationships with correlative systems of property rights; (3) undertake communal patterns of organization to arrange roads, schools, waterworks, and other essential communal services and facilities; and (4) have access to governing institutions that operate in accordance with due processes of law.

Many such structures can be fashioned by following Amilcar Cabral's (1973) advice to "return to the source" and to build upon the experiences that are part of the cultural tradition of people in their present circumstances. Every people that has survived to this point in time has acquired some capabilities for teamwork, exchange relationships, and communal organization. These capabilities need to be built upon and extended to meet the opportunities for life in the contemporary world.

It would be naive to assume that people, if left to themselves, will do good. It is possible for human societies to develop where no one trusts anyone else—societies where each is prepared to "do others in or to be done in." If such conditions are to be avoided, the interdependencies of life need to be organized on the basis of reciprocity by "doing unto others as you would have others do unto you." This is the foundation for the common relationships experienced as *res publica*—an open public realm—that is constitutive of democratic, self-governing societies. The task of the analyst concerned with achieving productive potentials in human societies is to "return to the source" as Cabral suggests, understand the conditions that prevail, and develop a self-conscious awareness that alternatives exist and that choices are possible.

The command-and-control structures for fashioning cryptoimperial systems with their predatory states, whether of the American or the Soviet variety, cannot suffice to fashion free societies any more than emancipation proclamations or edicts of emancipation can create free peoples. Instead, the great chessboard of human society must allow for the pieces to move themselves in accordance with rules that facilitate mutually respectful and productive relationships, and afford methods for processing and resolving conflicts so as to maintain a fair game open to the pursuit of diverse opportunities.

Freedom can be achieved when the pieces on that chessboard are capable of acting, setting rules, and holding each other to account in accordance with that most basic constitutive rule, "Act in relation to others as you would have others act in relation to you." This is the law of laws that gives unity to self-governing societies. The other condition is to meet the law of requisite variety that is necessary to all forms of artisanship if they are to yield the artifacts that help to sustain human life in meaningful ways. These requirements can be met when people acquire capabilities for self-governance under whatever circumstances.

Copeland's formula for fashioning a cryptoimperialism appropriate to a "Free World" is the antithesis of the principles used in the constitution of American democracy and other systems of democratic governance in the modern world. These principles were reasonably well articulated in studies by Montesquieu, Locke, Rousseau, Hume, Smith, Hamilton, Madison, and Tocqueville, among many others who have contributed to a theory of governance in accordance with rules of constitutional law (V. Ostrom, 1987). But these principles cannot prevail in systems of state-to-state relationships grounded in theories of sovereignty. This is why the fashioning of a truly free world depends upon building the fundamental infrastructures that enable different peoples to become self-governing. Otherwise, efforts in the name of the "Free World" or "Peoples Liberation" based upon either the Copeland formula or the Lenin formula will be destructive of human freedom.

The big task in setting the terms on which alternatives are available (i.e., getting the prices right) is to specify principles of human association, as James Madison has suggested, that build upon "the capacity of mankind for self-government" (Hamilton, Jay, and Madison, [1788] n.d., no. 39: 243). This is why Tocqueville asserts: "A new science of politics is needed for a new world" ([1835] 1945, vol.1:7). That new science of politics is a science of association that enables peoples to design, create, and maintain systems of governance where they can be self-governing. Such self-governing societies can be conceived as being both classless and stateless societies, for not all systems of governance need be viewed as states that exercise a monopoly of the legitimate use of force in a society. What is nominally viewed as a "state" in the family of "nation-states" need not be ruled by a sovereign. The constitution of a free world cannot be fashioned by theories of sovereignty and cryptoimperialism. Alternatively, federative principles of organization can be used to constitute self-governing societies (V. Ostrom, 1987).

Conclusion

It would be irresponsibly cynical to presume that all states are monstrous birds of prey devouring their own subjects. On the other hand, it may also be irresponsibly naive to presume that all states are benevolent creations that can always be relied upon to correct the ills of society and to get the prices right, so to speak. It is essential to address the reality that exists in human societies, and to recognize that the computational logic inherent in the theory of sovereignty, and the associated structures of both American-type and Soviet-type cryptoimperialism, create extraordinary opportunities for a few to exploit the many.

When we begin to recognize the distinct likelihood of predatory states, it may then become possible to mobilize our analytical capabilities to explain the terms on which alternatives become available in human societies. These are the prerequisites for choice; and choice is the prerequisite for a free world. Choice pertaining to the terms and conditions of government is possible; but revolutionary struggles and coups d'état are not effective ways to clarify the terms on which those alternatives are available. Problems of development in the contemporary world can only be clarified in light of: (1) the choice of alternative institutional arrangements and what this implies for the constitutional choices people might make; (2) the collective choices that might be taken, given the terms and conditions that apply to the organization and conduct of governments; and (3) the great multitudes of operational choices that become available when people can relate to one another through diverse institutional arrangements, organized according to rules that are constitutive of fair games.

Works Cited

Ashby, W. Ross (1956) *An Introduction to Cybernetics*. New York: Wiley.
Cabral, Amilcar (1973) *Return to the Source: Selected Speeches*. New York and London: Monthly Review Press.
Copeland, Miles (1969) *The Game of Nations: The Amorality of Power Politics*. New York: Simon and Schuster.
Crankshaw, Edward (1986) *The Shadow of the Winter Palace*. London: Papermac.
Djilas, Milovan (1957) *The New Class*. New York: Praeger.
Hamilton, Alexander, John Jay, and James Madison (n.d.) *The Federalist*. Edward Mead Earle, ed. New York: Modern Library. First published in 1788.
Hobbes, Thomas (1960) *Leviathan or the Matter, Forme and Power of a Commonwealth Ecclesiasticall and Civill*. Michael Oakeshott, ed. Oxford: Blackwell. First published in 1651.
Hume, David (1948) *Hume's Moral and Political Philosophy*. Henry D. Aiken, ed. New York: Hafner.
Hyden, Goran (1980) *Beyond Ujamaa in Tanzania: Underdevelopment and an Uncaptured Peasantry*. Berkeley and Los Angeles: University of California Press.
Kaufmann, Franz-Xaver, Giandomenico Majone, and Vincent Ostrom, eds. (1986) *Guidance, Control, and Evaluation in the Public Sector*. Berlin and New York: de Gruyter.
Lenin, V. I. (n.d.) "Where to Begin?" In *Selected Works*, vol. 2. New York: International Publishers, 15–23. First published in 1901.
_____ (n.d.) *What Is To Be Done?* In *Selected Works*, vol. 2. New York: International Publishers, 25–192. First published in 1902.
_____ (1932) *State and Revolution*. New York: International Publishers. First published in 1690.
Levi, Margaret (1981) "The Predatory Theory of Rule." *Politics and Society*, vol. 4, 431–465.
Locke, John (1952) *The Second Treatise of Government*. Thomas P.

Peardon, ed. Indianapolis: Bobbs-Merrill. First published in 1690.

Montesquieu, Charles Louis de Secondat (1966) *The Spirit of the Laws*. New York: Hafner. First published in 1748 as *De l'esprit des loix*.

Ostrom, Vincent (1987) *The Political Theory of a Compound Republic: Designing the American Experiment*. Rev. ed. Lincoln: University of Nebraska Press.

Rotberg, Robert A. (1971) *Haiti: The Politics of Squalor*. Boston: Houghton Mifflin.

Rousseau, Jean-Jacques (1978) *On the Social Contract*. Roger D. Masters, ed. New York: St. Martin's Press. First published in 1762 as *Du contrat social*.

Smith, Adam (n.d.) *The Theory of Moral Sentiments*. Indianapolis: Liberty Press. First published in 1759.

Tocqueville, Alexis de (1945) *Democracy in America*. Two vols. Phillips Bradley, ed. New York: Knopf. First published in 1835.

Wicksteed, Philip H. (1933) *The Common Sense of Political Economy*. Lionel Robins, ed. London: Routledge and Kegan Paul.

3

Sombat Chantornvong

Tocqueville's *Democracy in America* and the Third World

Introduction

While the average American nowadays would probably not be much interested in reading Alexis de Tocqueville's *Democracy in America*, it may still be safe to assume that American readers would be more likely than any others to be curious about what Tocqueville had to say about their society. But why should anyone from the Third World bother to read a lengthy book written in the last century by a French nobleman about the United States? Is *Democracy in America* in any way relevant to the problems facing non-Western nations today? Can an African or Asian reading the book learn something from it that might help him better understand the situation of his own and neighboring societies, most of which are classified as "underdeveloped" or "developed" or "less developed"? What parts of Tocqueville's

---

The author would like to express his sincere gratitude to Saneh Chammarik, William Klausner, and, especially, Montri Chenvidyakarn for their valuable comments.

analysis and which of his prescriptions are still not only valid but applicable to other societies? To try to answer such a question requires that an African or Asian read *Democracy in America* with an entirely different set of questions in mind than he would if he read the book for a description of early nineteenth century American society. This paper grows out of such an attempt. Just as Tocqueville's references to the Old World are mostly limited to his French homeland, the Third World perspective and experiences related in this paper will be limited to my homeland, Thailand, and some of her Southeast Asian neighbors.

Tocqueville's Analysis and the Asian Situation

"No novelty in the United States," Tocqueville begins, "struck me more vividly during my stay there than the equality of conditions" ([1835] 1969: 9).[1] He adds that "the more I studied American society, the more clearly I saw equality of conditions as the creative element from which each particular fact derived" (p. 9). "Equality of conditions," as used by Tocqueville, seems to mean the state of society in which the concept of equality has been actualized, at least for white males; all men have equal opportunities, for example, to receive education and to take part in the general leveling of wealth, and they are uniformly assured of political rights. The United States is a place where the principle of popular sovereignty happily coincides with equality of conditions. Thus, it was easy for democracy to take root and develop. According to Tocqueville,

> Anglo-Americans brought equality of conditions with them to the New World. There were neither commoners nor nobles there, and professional prejudices were always as unknown as prejudices of birth. So with this democratic social state it was not hard for democracy to establish its sway. (Tocqueville, [1835] 1969: 305)

But if Tocqueville had journeyed to Asia, he would most likely have said that the one single principle that struck him as the most pervasive and the most influential in Asian societies, past and present, was that of inequality. Prior to the middle of the nineteenth century, the social and political inequality that existed and served as a moving principle of Asian agrarian societies was basically the inequality associated with birth. People were simply born to different social classes, each with its own duties and functions (see, for example, Wales, 1965).

With the coming of Western imperialism and colonialism, new dimensions were added to this inequality. To begin with, Western imperialism significantly distorted the internal cohesiveness of self-sufficient village economies, forcing economic activities to shift from subsistence agriculture to plantation production of raw materials and foodstuffs for world markets (Watnick, 1952: 28). The colonized Asians now acquired a taste for new consumer goods. This was the beginning of their dependence on external forces beyond their control. The inroads of capitalism by way of colonization also led to the formation of new social classes—the small entrepreneurial middle class and the new educated bureaucratic elite.

In the West the expansion of the economic base of the entrepreneurial class had led to the liberalization of the absolutist, mercantilist monarchies. Tocqueville himself observes that "trade makes men independent of one another and gives them a high idea of their personal importance; it leads them to want to manage their own affairs and teaches them how to succeed therein. Hence it makes them inclined to liberty" ([1835] 1969: 637). The emergence of the entrepreneurial "middle class" in colonial Asia did not, however, produce a similar effect. Part of the reason was that the newly formed and very small middle class of businessmen consisted mostly of alien Asian immigrant populations—notably Indians and Chinese—not the natives of the land (Bastin and Benda, 1968: 72–74).

Colonial administration had also created a new educated elite that proved to be more significant for the immediate future of Asia. This small group of men was most receptive to the key ideas of Western democracy—freedom and equality (Vella, 1955: 362). It was the exposure of Western-educated elites to the idea of Western democracy that sparked revolutionary nationalism in Asia. These native elites advocated democratic forms of government, espoused the course of nationalism, and led the uneducated masses in the struggle against colonialism. The single mass party, also a new creation, was organized by nationalist leaders as the chief instrument with which to achieve the goal of independence. The issue of independence dominated all other issues. Internal differences and divisions were subsequently played down. On the surface, it appeared as though the end of colonization and newly won independence must bring an Asian-style utopia.

While, as Tocqueville observes, "the Revolution in the United States was caused by a mature and thoughtful taste for freedom, not by some vague, undefined instinct for independence" ([1835] 1969: 72), the so-called national revolutions of Asia, which involved violence and the disruption of existing structures of authority, were aristocratic in nature. The masses did not originate the revolutions. It was always the elitist few who called for national revolution. In most cases, ordinary individuals who participated in the nationalist movement played the role of loyal followers. Instead of challenging all traditions, all moral rules, established rights, and social values, and substituting new ones based on democratic standards, most nationalist movements seemed to focus primarily on taking over the state apparatus. In many cases, the indigenous elites, many of whom had previously served as colonial intermediaries, simply took over the political and bureaucratic machinery left behind by their colonial masters (Marcos, 1971: 69).

Thus, national revolutions in Asia tended to strengthen the power of the state but did not go very far in transforming the spirit of the society. At first most former colonies adopted the political forms of the imperial powers. The case of the Philippines, the only country in Asia whose constitution was patterned after that of the United States, serves as a good example. Unlike the Anglo-Americans, who had been brought up in an atmosphere of political and civil liberty and had therefore taken naturally to politics, the masses of Asia had neither the desire nor the skills necessary for modern-day political participation.

The small number of new elites who were entrusted with the responsibility of governing an independent country felt that they should be allowed a great deal of flexibility for the maneuvers required by paternalistic authoritarian rule. It was difficult for the nationalist leaders, whose different social background, educational achievements, and administrative and political experience distinguished them from the rest of the people, to accept the latter as their equals (Foltz, 1963: 119). Although it is true that many were genuinely concerned about the miserable state of the masses, theirs was certainly not the kind of concern that one had for one's equals. In short, despite their dedicated role in the uprooting of foreign and exploitative rule, the Western-educated elites often turned out to be a new kind of aristocracy in their own countries.

The end of Western imperialism, therefore, did not necessarily mean the beginning of freedom or the birth of democracy. Instead, it brought more inequality as the desire of the Western-educated leaders to transform their country into something like the powerful West called for specialized administrative and technical skills. The result was the emergence of a modern bureaucracy. According to Tocqueville, the predominance of social equality, the adequate education of the average citizen, the prosperity of trade and industry, and the abundance of land in the United States, made the people more inclined to seek the channels of private enterprise rather than official bureaucratic positions as the means to improve their lot.

> In the United States, when a citizen has some education and some resources he tries to enrich himself either by trade and industry or by buying a field covered in forest and turning into a pioneer. All he asks from the state is not to get in his way while he is working and to see that he can enjoy the fruit of his labor. (Tocqueville, [1835] 1969: 632-633)

By contrast, in the newly independent countries administrative positions have become the main objectives of ambitious men. Unlike Tocqueville's United States, in which official appointments were few, ill-paid, and insecure (pp. 632-633), Asia has made the public bureaucracy the main source of employment for the educated class. In Thailand, for example, the bureaucracy, until lately, has been the primary outlet for its most ambitious and educated citizens (Siffin, 1966: 131). As a privileged group, having, in a sense, their own class interests to promote, the bureaucrats in Asian countries have enlarged their power, influence, and interest to the point that no other forces capable of limiting or controlling them exist. In Thailand, the domination of bureaucratic organization in the armed forces, the police, and the civil administration is so conspicuous that the kingdom is sometimes called a bureaucratic polity (see, for example, Riggs, 1966). The American, according to Tocqueville, shied away from seeking official appointment, and also avoided political positions because of the "daily breeding [of] new and impatient desires" occasioned by the equality of conditions.

> In the United States it is men of moderate pretensions who engage in the twists and turns of politics. Men of parts and vaulting ambition generally avoid power to pursue wealth; the frequent result is that men undertake to direct the fortunes of the state only when they doubt their capacity to manage their private affairs. (Tocqueville, [1835] 1969: 205)

The opposite is true in Asia. In the new Asian states, politics, like bureaucracy, is the monopoly of the ambitious few. After all, political independence turned these new elites into an element of the new ruling class, charged with the main responsibility of nation-building and modernization. In addition, political independence often meant that the immediate task of its leadership was to win the loyalty of quarreling factions that threatened to break up the new nation as soon as the common enemy was out of sight.

Unlike the citizens of Tocqueville's America, who spoke the same language, believed in the same religion, shared common beliefs, and lived under the same material conditions and the same laws (p. 56), the citizens of many new Asian states, such as Burma and Malaysia, still face problems of divisive cultural pluralism (Bastin and Benda, 1968: 102–106). In sharp contrast to Tocqueville's observation that even religion in the United States is republican ([1835] 1969: 397), church and state in several Asian countries are either at odds with each other or are too closely linked. In either case—whether a state religion is officially established or serious antagonism exists between the secular state and the church—prejudice, resentment, and conflicts are bound to exist. Faced with unyielding opposition movements and irredentism, both real and imagined, most leaders argue for the greater centralization of political authority. They argue that the new nations of Asia need the kind of regime that is strong enough to run the affairs of state effectively and efficiently (Muang, 1969: 300).

Even in a relatively more homogenous society like Thailand, the new elites still face serious problems rooted in the feudal and colonial past. Unlike in the United States where, as Tocqueville argues, equality was the accepted principle of social relations ([1835] 1969: 9), in Asia the idea of class hierarchy, which includes respect for age, status, rank, education, and wealth, and deference to authority, is still very much alive. In fact, it might be said that, for the most part, the inhabitants of the former colonies regard themselves more as "subjects" of traditional regimes, than as "citizens" of new democratic nations.

Without an adequate social basis—without equality of conditions—the political institutions and the rituals of democracy that were imposed from above have served merely to legitimize the power of the ruling class—traditional landowners, hereditary rulers, members of religious hierarchies, and military and civilian bureaucrats. Even a free and popular election, though seen as an indispensable aspect of democratic rule, in practice has often meant manipulation of the political process with attendant corruption. Most political parties, which have proliferated, have bases that are more personal than ideological. They function mainly to control the masses and to perpetuate personal rule. Typically, wealth is the assured way of gaining power through the electoral process.

Unlike the citizens of Tocqueville's America, where every village was a sort of republic accustomed to self-rule ([1835] 1969: 386), the villagers of Asia are no more than festival spectators in electoral rituals. At best they tend to view election time as the time to make some small private gain in the vote-selling business. The electorate exercises no real choice. Free elections thus do not lead to substantial social or political change but serve merely to legitimize the rule of old oligarchs or new elites. After all, the supply of qualified candidates is limited and their characters and attitudes seem to have changed very little. Despite the right to vote, the masses of Asia remain unfree.

Without a democratic social condition, the private institutions that Tocqueville believed were factors in the maintenance of independence can exist only in form. Newspapers, which, according to Tocqueville, are essential for the development and maintenance of any concerted action of democratic citizens (pp. 517–520), are the tools or are under the control of a special class or group. Likewise, civil associations, which Tocqueville regards as very important in the formation of an independent spirit (pp. 520–524), often come under the state's control or regulation. In Thailand, for example, the government agencies concerned must examine and authorize the statutes of any kind of association, including academic associations, before it can be formed. Even today no association is allowed to take part in political activities (Chenvidyakarn, 1979).

As if the inequality of conditions and other unfavorable factors mentioned above were not enough, the conditions of Asian nations are far less conducive to the growth of democracy in other significant ways. Unlike the United States, which was located in relative geographical isolation and therefore had no neighbors or enemies to fear, most new nations are often hard-pressed by both internal divisions and external threats. The military elites, which were the first to receive Western training in the technological fields and which led the masses in the nationalist struggle for independence, are therefore in a very good position to assume political leadership (Novack and Lakacham, 1964: 244). How unfortunate this situation can be with regards to the development of democracy may be judged from the following remarks by Tocqueville.

> The Americans have no neighbors and consequently no great wars, financial crises, invasions, or conquests to fear; they need neither heavy taxes nor a numerous army nor great generals; they have also hardly anything to fear from something else which is a greater scourge for democratic republics than all these others put together, namely, military glory. (Tocqueville, [1835] 1969: 278)

Furthermore, under military rule, the suppression of opposition groups or leaders and the application of other strong-arm tactics are not uncommon. General respect for the rule of law and peaceful resolution of conflicts, which are important American habits or customs favorable to the maintenance of freedom according to Tocqueville, are conspicuously absent.

By Tocqueville's standard, most postindependence Asian states would be classified as aristocracies or oligarchies. Yet the new aristocrats, or rather, the new oligarchs of Asia must not be too readily identified with the kind of aristocracy Tocqueville has generally described. While aristocracy is a social system based on the inequality of men, according to Tocqueville, it is not simply rule by the rich and powerful. Traditional aristocracy was also, in Tocqueville's view, a system that evoked a man's highest spiritual qualities, since an aristocrat was someone who was attached to causes beyond himself (Zetterbaum, 1967: 22). Even the relationship between a master and his servants in aristocracies was not simply that of an employer and employees.

> In aristocracies the master comes to think of his servants as an inferior and secondary part of himself, and he often takes an interest in their fate by the extended scope of his selfishness. The servants, for their part, see themselves in almost the same way, and they sometimes identify themselves so much with the master personally that they become an appendage to him in their own eyes as well as in his. (Tocqueville, [1835] 1969: 575)

More broadly, the relationship between the rich and the poor in a traditional aristocracy was also one that was psychologically free from oppression or struggle.

> In nations where an aristocracy dominates society, the people finally get used to their poverty just as the rich do to their opulence. The latter are not preoccupied with physical comfort, enjoying it without trouble; the former do not think about it at all because they despair of getting it and because they do not know enough about it to want it. (Tocqueville, [1835] 1969: 531)

The new oligarchs of Asia, on the contrary, have never felt free of all wants nor have they been content with their lot. Seeking not just power or glory but also wealth, they have not looked beyond their own class interests (see Wilson, 1964: 60; Riggs, 1966: 251).

An aristocracy, observes Tocqueville, also contributes indirectly to the defense against any tyranny over the people by defending its own privilege or "aristocratic liberty."

> [O]nly an aristocracy can preserve the people from the oppression of royal tyranny and from the miseries of revolution, [so] that the privileges which seem established in the sole interest of those who possess them do also form the best guarantee for the tranquility and prosperity even of those who do not have them. (Tocqueville, [1840] 1959: 73).

Again, it is evident that the new oligarchs of Asia could not perform this function because their interests do not coincide with those of the masses. In this sense, the masses of the new Asian states are worse off than those living under an European aristocracy of the "ancien régime." Unlike the average American who, thanks to the equality of conditions, is never satisfied with his present fortune and is "constantly trying a thousand ways to improve it" (Tocqueville, [1835] 1969: 637), the average Asian looks to the government for guidance and accepts his fate as inevitable, taking refuge in the hope for a higher status in the next world. According to Tocqueville, "when inequality is the general rule in society, the greatest inequalities attract no attention" (p. 538). In an Asian society where conditions were generally unequal and where the hierarchy of command appeared to be firmly established, it naturally would not matter to the majority of the people if the new military or bureaucratic elites should acquire more "liberties" or "privileges" than others. Indeed, it would not matter if the so-called democracy were given up altogether. In such a society Tocqueville's fear of the vice of democracy unchecked—the tyranny of the majority acting through an uncontrolled political assembly—is not applicable. After all, for a tyranny by the majority to develop, the people must first be free. The society in which they live must also be truly democratic so they can exercise their political rights to the full.

While political democracy may be readily given up in some countries on the ground that it is a peculiar product of Western civilization and historical experience, the much desired modernization and industrialization are never easily forsaken. As a matter of fact, it has often been argued that the failure of democracy to function effectively in these countries is largely due to the inability of the leaders to provide a solid base from which processes of modernization and industrialization might take off. Modernization and industrialization, thought to be essential to these nations' existence, have, however, led to greater centralization and increased inequality of conditions. In order to industrialize, for instance, a nation, as Tocqueville has observed, requires infrastructures such as roads, canals, and ports that in Asia only the central government provides and that in the United States are provided by local and state instrumentalities of government. The power of the central government grows because only it is authorized to expand in order to produce these infrastructures. The growth of industry also brings with it a new and complicated system of human relations that requires uniform regulation and control. The end result, according to Tocqueville, is further administrative centralization (pp. 684-687). Modernization and industrialization have exacerbated a situation in which the problems of urbanization, overpopulation, the high cost of technological transfers and development, the emergence of technocracy, and the expansion of bureaucracy already seem ungovernable.

In addition, the rise of large-scale industry, observes Tocqueville, may result in the emergence, on the one hand, of a "new industrial aristocracy," and on the other, of an increasingly debased and impoverished class of workers.

> When a workman is constantly and exclusively engaged in making one object, he ends by performing this work with singular dexterity. But at the same time, he loses the general faculty of applying his mind to the way he is working. Every day he becomes more adroit and less industrious, and one may say that in his case the man is degraded as the workman improves....

While the workman confines his intelligence more and more to studying one single detail,

> the master daily embraces a vast field in his vision, and his mind expands as fast as the other's contracts. Soon the latter will need no more than bodily strength without intelligence, while to succeed the former needs science and almost genius. The former becomes more

and more like the administrator of a huge empire, and the latter more like a brute. (Tocqueville, [1835] 1969: 555-556)

To Tocqueville, "[this] state of dependence and poverty affecting part of the industrial population in our day is an *exceptional fact* running counter to conditions around it" (p. 584, emphasis supplied). He is not overly concerned with the possibility that unrestrained pursuit of material well-being will become characteristic of any particular group of people, for "such particularistics would soon be lost in the general picture" (p. 543). But in Asia, where inequality of conditions prevails, the pursuit of wealth by an industrial-loving artistocracy has had a different effect. The emerging industrial aristocrats find it to their advantage to join hands not merely among themselves but also with the rulers to exploit the masses. Even the members of a small middle class, in those cases in which one has developed as a result of the modernization process, may also go along with a bureaucratic-capitalist partnership so long as they can maintain their interests. To understand the position taken by the new upper classes of an Asian society, one probably needs only to remind oneself of Tocqueville's remark that people are moved not so much by "the quiet possession of something precious" as by "the imperfectly satisfied desire to have it and the continual fear of losing it again" (p. 530). Meanwhile, the poor masses, thrown helplessly under the yoke of a mercantilist capitalist economy, eventually come to depend on state authorities for the improvement of their lot.

Again, the Asian context of industrialization highlights the equality of conditions and other fortunate circumstances that later made the United States a great commercial republic. Yet, at first glance, it would seem that it was America's almost unlimited natural resources and general prosperity alone that made it all possible. Because, according to Tocqueville, "the territory of the Union . . . provides inexhaustible supplies for industry and for labor," political ambition is replaced by love of money, "and prosperity quenches the fires of faction" (p. 306). In fact, it sounds as if Tocqueville is praising the passion of Americans for profit making in the development of their virgin continent.

> In Europe we habitually regard a restless spirit, immoderate desire for wealth, and an extreme love of independence as great social dangers. But precisely those things assure a long and peaceful future for the American republics. Without such restless passions the population would be concentrated around a few places and would soon experience, as we do, needs which are hard to satisfy. What a happy land the New World is, where man's vices are almost as useful to society as his virtues! (Tocqueville, [1835] 1969: 131)

The crux of the matter is, as one scholar points out, that the desire for well-being inevitably accompanies equality of conditions, quite independently of climatic or geographic factors (Zetterbaum, 1967: 128-129). In other words, it is the equality of conditions that gives birth to the love of wealth—the spirit of commerce that, in turn, not only makes the country great but also promotes social stability. Or, as the same scholar puts it, "Tocqueville believed that the spirit of commerce would produce a social state in which most men owned some property, thus ending the contrast between the few rich and the many poor that he considered the main source of social instability" (p. 131).

In Asia, on the other hand, the limited resources available and the inequality of conditions seem, instead, to bring out the negative side of human self-interest (Marcos, 1971: 56).[2] The problems of hunger, poverty, diseases, violence, and wretchedness have become more visible. The results of modernization and industrialization efforts appear to threaten the political elites themselves. Economic inequality not only weakens social cohesion but also breeds injustice and inevitably breaks the political bonds that bind the society. Now more than ever, it is possible to imagine that the masses, feeling that poverty is indeed a social product, not something predestined, may ask for radical political, social, and economic changes. Here, Tocqueville's remark concerning the relationship between the rich and the poor states of the Union is quite appropriate: "It is difficult to conceive of a lasting relation between two peoples, one of whom is poor and weak, the other rich and strong, even if it is proved that the strength and wealth of the one are in no way the cause of the weakness and poverty of the other" ([1835] 1969: 381).

Economic Development in the Asian Situation

Today, the response of most new nations to the basic problem of economic inequality is planned development. But, if economic prosperity is a necessary condition for political stability, can it be argued in reverse? Does the quest for economic development, defined as economic growth plus more equal income distribution, necessarily imply the exclusion of democratic processes (Gerling, 1981: 54–55)? For Asian countries that have not yet adopted the central planning system of industrialization, it seems that persisting internal and external threats leave them no choice. The only way they can progress is to establish effective administrative machinery for economic development. In claiming that the government now has the moral obligation to improve the conditions of the poor, the regime's leaders often declare that they are working against economic oppression. They call upon the people to sacrifice political freedom in order that the state may break up the concentration of economic powers and promote economic growth for all.

Interestingly enough, it is with regard to the relationship between economic development and freedom that Tocqueville's ideas are proving to be highly relevant to Asia. As mentioned earlier, Tocqueville's observations of a social and historical nature have shed light on the reason why a democratic tree could grow in America but could not survive and grow in Asia. Yet, at the same time, one cannot simply dismiss Tocqueville's fear of the coming of a new kind of despotism—the one characterized by its drive towards depoliticizations and the emergence of an administrative state ([1835] 1969: 540).

Actually in Asia today such a danger sometimes creeps in almost unnoticed. Consider the cases of the Philippines and Singapore. In the Philippines, former President Marcos had vowed to eliminate economic inequality, charging that "the wealth of the few, like the power of the few, is a violence on the poor." He then demanded a "democratic revolution"—the building of a New Society in which property would be regulated for collective human ends (Marcos, 1971: 119). It was the job of a democratic government to serve as a faithful instrument of the people's revolutionary aspiration, he argued. From now on it would be the poor who would shape the future of the Philippines (Marcos, 1976: 56).

President Marcos was, however, far from being a Marxist. His so-called democratic revolution, he maintained, was actually aimed at preventing a communist revolution that would be destructive of human freedom. While he did not try to please just one particular class, he nevertheless tried to make his New Society everything to everybody. Thus, in explaining that his democratization of wealth simply meant the sharing of private wealth with the society, and not a total abolition of private ownership, he promised the rich security against the communist threat. He offered peace and order to the middle class, and pledged to the poor that his definition of "equality" meant giving each citizen "three square meals, a roof over his head, efficient public transport, schooling for his children and medical care for his family" (p. 116). But in order to produce such a society, in which economic activities both private and public would join together in promoting the interest of each individual and the welfare of the whole, the authority of the government had to be exerted whenever these ends were not being served (p. 124).

In the New Society, the state alone is presumed to be neutral and thus free from any political ideology (Magno, 1983: 10). Only political authority can establish the priorities and provide the mechanism of equalization. What is further needed is the modification of the political culture of the Filipinos from being populist, personalistic, and individualistic to being one of citizens who are equally conscious of the collective or social interest (Marcos, 1976: 59). Implicit in this idea is not just Marcos's attempt to raise the status of the state now characterized as a paternal authority above the reach of any particular class interest, but apparently his belief in the necessary links between social conditions and the citizen's habits of mind. The new social conditions, Marcos seems to say, can be freshly created. Understandably, he was evasive when talking about the legitimacy of the authority he assumed in order to bring about these changes.

Not many people have taken Marcos's words seriously. They are often dismissed as mere political rhetoric—a crude attempt to justify his rule by martial law. He has been judged by what has actually been going on in the Philippines, not by what he proposed to do. The picture of a society deeply troubled by worsening economic crisis, widespread corruption in high places, political assassinations, daily protests and demonstrations, internal divisions, and local insurgency, however, can draw us away from a more fundamental question: What would have happened if he had succeeded in delivering the goods? Had Marcos been able to make good his promises of a better society, would his rule have been more acceptable? After all, the socioeconomic programs he implemented, which were aimed at reducing mass poverty and at mobilizing mass support for a crumbling regime, helped generate the demands that were being made on it. What would it have meant if the regime had been able to handle all these demands? For a student of Tocqueville, answers to these questions should come before our concern over the final fate of the regime. In other words, one should take seriously the warning of Tocqueville that the threat to liberty may lie no less in citizens refusing the responsibilities of freedom than in their being refused an opportunity to exercise the responsibilities of freedom ([1835] 1969: 540).

A New Society of the type Marcos sought has been realized in Singapore, often considered the most "successful" new nation of Southeast Asia, if not the whole of Asia. Since Singapore separated from the Federation of Malaysia and became a fully independent state in 1965, it has become a showcase of economic progress and political stability (*Asia Week*, September 7, 1984, p. 34). In 1984, 2.5 million Singaporeans enjoyed the highest per capita GNP (U.S. $5,900) in Asia except for Japan, and had only 3.3 percent unemployment. In view of this economic prosperity, the majority of Singaporeans may well be content.

The People's Action Party (PAP), which has ruled the island republic since its birth, accepted from the very start the goal of advancing the welfare of the people. A subsidized public housing program, aimed at alleviating the acute housing shortage among low-income groups, was the first among several other welfare services provided by the social democratic government. In retrospect, it can be seen that the housing development program has not only served as a means to get the economy going but has also brought solid political support for the Lee Kuan Yew regime. By encouraging the poorer sections of the society to accumulate property by purchasing government apartments on an easy installment plan, the PAP government has succeeded in giving them a vested interest in the status quo (George, 1974: 205). In order to ensure the success of its industrialization policy and the expansion of welfare services, the government of Singapore through its efficient bureaucrats and state enterprises has become actively involved in other commercial, industrial, and financial projects. Today, by all counts, the government of Singapore is the most important entrepreneur in the island economy, and Singapore has become one of the most successful and prosperous "capitalist" countries in the world (*Asia Week*, September 7, 1984, p. 34).

The difficulties of achieving economic development and improved public welfare, however, have been used by the regime as pretexts for disciplining the Singaporean people and demanding their total obedience. The regime can point to the fact that Singapore is one of the most racially heterogeneous societies in the world. It suggests that in order to ensure the dynamism of its economy, the regime must also organize all aspects of the social life of the people, including family planning.[3] Yet implicit in this drive for popular discipline is a conscious desire on the part of the government to make its citizens into New Men. Those who admire the system often regard this socialization in a new political culture through strict schooling and community control as a process of nation-building. They are quick to point to the desirable manners, respect for the law, communal harmony, work ethic among labor, popular support for the armed forces, and the spirit of patriotism as being among the moral virtues and social precepts successfully inculcated by the government over the years (p. 34).

If one were to take a critical look at this whole process of socialization, what has been created in Singapore is nothing but a culture designed to discourage conflict, disruptive confrontation, and free bargaining, and to encourage instead stability and low-risk, orderly petition (Chee, 1975: 43). The education system, for example, has been completely "officialized." Not only does the regime emphasize the importance of technical and vocational training over humanities and liberal arts but, apparently as a means of controlling the minds of the youth, it also goes so far as to appoint cabinet ministers to the staff of the university (George, 1974: 134).[4] In the meantime, the government also employs various tactics to ensure that only young Singaporeans with the right kind of attitude and background are enrolled in college. It has succeeded in instilling in the students, many of whom were born and have lived most of their lives under PAP's rule, their rulers' conviction that "liberal democracy" is dispensable in a society that "must put survival above everything else" (George, 1974: 132).

Newspapers may have grown in terms of circulation, but they are under strict government control. Claiming that the main task of a newspaper consists in disseminating facts and information, and citing the need to prevent waste of resources and duplication of services, the regime has recently forced the merger of small newspapers under the control of a single corporation. The rationale given by the minister involved is quite characteristic of the regime itself. "Competition alone does not make a quality newspaper. Quality people working in a company that is financially sound make a quality paper" (*Asia Week*, September 7, 1984, p. 40). Radio and television are also tightly controlled by the government.

Since economic growth and the improvement of the people's living conditions seem to endorse the PAP's program, the ruling elites have become increasingly authoritarian in their exercise of political power. The regime tolerates no political dissent. It has carried out a systematic policy of rigorous internal repression of all opposition groups. The last strike recorded in Singapore was in 1977. Given the small size of the island (226 square miles), it is not difficult to understand why PAP's drive for the monopolization of power has succeeded so well. In 1967, PAP successfully turned Singapore into a single-party regime when it won all the parliamentary seats in the general election. Since 1968, it has swept all the general elections, each time with a larger number of votes. Rapid economic and social development in Singapore, the regime now argues, necessitates the shift of emphasis from politics to economics. According to PAP leaders, they can succeed in promoting the welfare of the people only when they can give up their excessive concern with "politics" by turning Singapore into a one-party system (Chee, 1975: 53). The regime's achievements in the fields of public housing, transportation, health, education, and community organization have already convinced most of the satisfied populace that there are simply no means of ensuring economic survival other than those offered by PAP. A popular election now turns out to be an exercise in popular mobilization that serves only to maintain the system and to reinforce the power of the ruling party. It seems, as one perceptive observer puts it, that "politics" has disappeared from Singapore. There is just no politics any more; there is only "an administrative state" (p. 48). Apparently, the regime has succeeded too well in producing materially satisfied citizens, who are willing to forego all of what the government denies them and obey the government absolutely.

The disappearance of politics and the emergence of the "administration of things," predicts Tocqueville, will result in the tremendous growth of government activities ([1835] 1969: 515). This has been the case in Singapore as the regime has assumed a direct role in the expansion of the economy. It has enlarged and extended the role of bureaucracy to cover many new areas of responsibilities. Civil servants are now appointed to preside over public enterprises and private companies. While the regime seeks to retain its socialist-style grass-roots organizations, it increasingly draws its parliamentary candidates from a highly educated technocratic class and from the teaching staff of its university. Senior officers of public enterprises resign from their posts to run for political offices.

Centralization is another main feature of the regime. Long ago, the regime merged the city council with the central government, apparently in a move to ensure national unity. The degree of centralization has now reached the point where a license is needed for everything in Singapore. No business—whether banking, operating a newspaper or a taxi, or hawking—can be done without one. Most licenses have to be renewed each year (*Asia Week*, September 7, 1984, p. 37).

The following words of Tocqueville could have summarized that very situation.

> The central power not only fills the whole sphere of former authorities, extends, and goes beyond it, but also acts with greater speed, power, and independence than it had ever done. All the initiative taken away from private people is constantly going to enrich that of the government. As a result, public administration not only depends on one sole power but also is more and more controlled from one spot and concentrated in ever fewer hands. The government centralizes its activity at the same time that it increases its prerogatives; hence, a twofold growth of power. (Tocqueville, [1835] 1969: 683)

Yet it is only natural for other Asian leaders to aspire to see their countries become another Singapore. Compared to others, Singapore must appear to be an ideal society. But a student of Tocqueville might ask: What is the point of being one of the best-fed, best-administered, best-educated nations, if the major outlet for grievances and frustration available to ordinary citizens is the letters column in the newspaper or the political rumour mill (Chee, 1975: 56–58)? Is this not in fact symptomatic of a suppressed society where no real political participation and no free press exists? Worse still, does this "capitalist totalitarianism" not remind us of Tocqueville's unnamed new despotism in which the government manages nearly every important aspect of life for its people who, welcoming all of this, think of nothing or cannot think at all (George, 1974: 109)?[5] What good is it to have people whose only concern in life seems to be material interests—people who know "the price of everything and the value of nothing" (p. 202)? Or, as Tocqueville puts it:

> What good is it to me, after all, if there is an authority always busy to see to the tranquil enjoyment of my pleasures and going ahead to brush all dangers away from my path without giving me even the trouble to think about it, if that authority, which protects me from the smallest thorns on my journey, is also the absolute master of my liberty and of my life? (Tocqueville, [1835] 1969: 93)

With this awareness, one may suggest that countries like Singapore and the Philippines, though seemingly worlds apart, in reality belong to the same category. The only difference is that one happens to be economically successful while the other is a disaster. In between these extremes, many other nations exist that can claim both successes and failures. From a comparative perspective, the situation in the Philippines under Marcos, bad as it was, was not bad in *all* respects. At least politics in the sense of conflicts and choices of ends, which presupposes the will to liberty on the part of the populace, existed and still exists there.

The failure of Marcos's economic development plan should be viewed as a blessing in disguise because it may have made it easier for the people to shun his authoritarian rule. More and more Philippine businessmen and professionals of the middle class, who, according to Tocqueville, would be a "natural enemy of any violent commotion" (p. 636), joined hands with other political dissidents in their protest against his regime. All of this resistance would not have been possible if the Philippines (once a showcase for a working democracy in Southeast Asia) had had no experience with democratic rule. Despite its past abuses, the tradition of political democracy in the Philippines provided the opposition groups with precedents and recognized means with which to overcome one-man rule. Moreover, as Tocqueville argues, just as in defending its own "liberty" or "privilege," the aristocracy will end up defending the general liberty (pp. 72, 88), so the emergence of the new opposition groups apart from the traditional ones in the Philippines should be regarded as something conducive to the resuscitation of liberal democracy.

Development and Democracy

The relevance of *Democracy in America* to Asia having been argued, it now remains to determine whether a would-be "democratic leader" can draw any guidance from Tocqueville. At first glance, it may appear that such a possibility does not exist. In reading *Democracy in America*, an Asian may find that Tocqueville has indeed brought our attention to a fundamental problem facing any would-be democratic nation today. Foremost in the mind of an average Asian reader of Tocqueville is probably the problem of the existing inequality of conditions in his own society. He most likely would argue that it is basically the pre-existence of democracy, actualized in the form of the equality of conditions, that makes popular rule in the

United States a success. It is this peculiar social state that prevents the dogma of popular sovereignty from being just "an isolated doctrine, bearing no relation to the people's habits and prevailing ideas" (Tocqueville, [1835] 1969: 397). Tocqueville himself remarks that "the social state of America is a very strange phenomenon. Men there are near equality in wealth and mental endowments, or, in other words, more nearly equally powerful, than in any other country of the world or in any other age of recorded history" (p. 56).

To an Asian reader, Tocqueville could not have stressed the significance of this "strange phenomenon" of equality of conditions too much. Consider, for example, the case of the United States, in which the prevailing equality of conditions leads to the emergence of the democratic mores of individualism. First, such individualism has two sides: the exaltation of individual reason (something not necessarily bad); and second, the concentration on self-interested and largely materialistic ends (Lively, 1962: 85). In the new aristocracy of Asia, the introduction of the democratic process resulted in the emergence of individualism of the second kind only. This self-centered, self-interested concentration on personal ends was at the very beginning limited to the upper classes and the newly emerging middle classes only, because they were the ones who took full advantage of the new political structure. Then, thanks to modernization efforts, the poor masses began to demand that the government must provide them with a better standard of living. But neither the "individualism" of the middle and upper classes in Asia nor the rising expectations of the masses seem to have led to aggressive, individualistic self-assertion.

In most cases, Asian individualism and the Asian mode of modernization has caused most classes to shy away from social obligations, leaving public affairs to the government which has, as a result, extended state power. In a country where the taste for physical pleasures has been more rapidly absorbed by the people than either education or the experience of free institutions, a few men can easily seize control of the machinery of government and maintain themselves in power as long as they can satisfy the people's material needs. In short, the introduction of formal democratic institutions and processes into a society in which inequality of conditions is the rule may turn that society into something very close to "capitalist totalitarianism," as the case of Singapore suggests.

A question may, then, be raised: Is it possible to modify the existing social state or to construct out of the old one a society that is favorable to the emergence of democracy? Before any answer can be given, let us first find out what that state is. As used by Tocqueville,

> the social state is commonly the result of circumstances, sometimes of laws, but most often of a combination of the two. But once it has come into being, it may itself be considered as the prime cause of most of the laws, customs, and ideas which control the nation's behavior; it modifies even those things which it does not cause. Therefore one must first study their social state if one wants to understand a people's laws and mores. The striking feature in the social condition of the Anglo-Americans is that it is essentially democratic. (Tocqueville, [1835] 1969: 50)

The combination of "circumstances" and "laws" constitutes a "social state," which, in turn, characterizes the whole regime. Circumstances and laws also make up two of the three major categories of factors that contribute to the maintenance of democratic rule in the United States, the other being social mores or "habits of minds." Tocqueville concluded that the reasons for the success of democracy in the United States fell into three categories. "The first is the peculiar and accidental situation in which Providence has placed the Americans. Their laws are the second. Their habits and mores are the third" (p. 277).

Of these, the most vital one is the third factor—the spirit of the people, the feelings, the beliefs, the ideas, the habits of the hearts and minds of men (p. 308). A people may differ with regards to an assortment of things. Some may be rich and some may be poor but, as Jack Lively says in his study of Tocqueville, they can live together if they share the same mores.

> Differences between social and economic functions would naturally persist, differences between rich and poor might persist, what would go would be the division of society into groups with distinctive mores. And this would result from the egalitarian insistence on the basic comparability of all individuals and their subjection (recourse) to common rules. (Lively, 1962: 244)

To Tocqueville, the ultimate social and political reality is the totality of ideas and sentiments that form the habits of men's hearts and minds. To truly understand what any society means one must understand these generally held ideas, sentiments, and standards, not just the formal institutions (Lively, 1962: 236). Tocqueville stresses the importance of mores in the following words.

> Europeans exaggerate the influence of geography on the lasting powers of democratic institutions. Too much importance is attached to laws and too little to mores. Unquestionably those are the three great influences which regulate and direct American democracy, but if they are to be classed in order, I should say that the contribution of physical causes is less than that of the laws and that of laws less than mores.
>
> I am convinced that the luckiest of geographical circumstances and the best of laws cannot maintain a constitution in despite of mores, whereas the latter can turn even the most unfavorable circumstances and the worst laws to advantage. (Tocqueville, [1835] 1969: 308)

To an Asian reader of Tocqueville, the factors conducive to the actualization of democracy and the ones that maintain it therefore seem to overlap. Thanks to the social conditions, that is, the circumstances and laws combined, the idea of popular sovereignty can be actualized. The development of "democratic mores" then contributes to the maintenance of democratic rule. Yet it is clear that the social conditions and mores, significant though they may be, are not beyond the reach of human influence. Both of them, as Tocqueville says, can be altered by laws. "A law can modify that social condition which seems most fixed and assured, and everything changes with it" (p. 297). In other words, just as every law and political institution to be effective and lasting must be based on or reflect social mores, so it is possible that, once put into action, laws and political institutions may themselves be able to modify social mores in light of sentiments and the way people think. There are of course cases in which factors affecting social mores themselves, as well as the inclinations those factors encourage, may be rather difficult to alter; such are the habits formed by climate, past history, economic abundance or scarcity, sentiments, and ways of thinking

(Lively, 1962: 237). But there are also cases that show the creation of certain laws or political institutions may have resulted in the emergence of some other passions not intended in the first place. At any rate, to find democratic devices that will fit in with one's particular social condition and to construct "democratic mores" through legislation is not impossible. Indeed, Tocqueville seems to provide plenty of encouragement for such an attempt.

> American laws and mores are not the only ones that would suit the democratic peoples, but the Americans have shown that we need not despair of regulating democracy by means of laws and mores. . . . If other peoples, borrowing this general and creative idea from the Americans, but without wishing to imitate the particular way in which they have applied it, would try to adapt it to the social state which Providence has imposed on the men of our time and should seek by this means to escape the despotism of anarchy threatening them, what reasons have we to believe that they are bound to fail in their endeavor? (Tocqueville, [1835] 1969: 311)

It is not the intention of this paper, nor is it possible within its limits, to specify how one would go about "adapting" democratic ways to fit in with his particular society, or influence the development of "democratic mores" through legislation. The rudiment of a method can be indicated when we recognize that each "operational plan," in Tocqueville's opinion, must be based on the principle of self-interest. An American, Tocqueville observes, "obeys the society, not because he is inferior to those who direct it nor because he is incapable of ruling himself—but because union with his fellows seems useful to him and he knows that the union is impossible without a regulating authority" (p. 66). Or, as he later sums it up: "The individual is the best and only judge of his own interest and that society has no right to direct his behavior unless it feels harmed by him or unless it needs his concurrence" (p. 66).

Translated into a strategy for future development, this method simply means that the problem of balanced development is basically the problem of self-development, of freedom and self-interest, and that as such it should be treated as a problem in democratic self-governance. To think otherwise is to run the risk of imposing an order that is destructive of the social mores—the social glue that holds the society together. In fact, Tocqueville would have argued, under a nondemocratic regime no socioeconomic program sponsored by the government can be truly good, since it has the tendency to limit or separate the ties that bind a citizen's individual freedom to his sense of social responsibility. How can we expect any kind of constructive "development" to grow out of a relationship in which the government, taking a paternalistic position, treats the people not as its constituency to whom it is accountable, but rather as something to be patronized and thus controlled? The idea of freedom—beginning with the freedom to choose—must be regarded as an essential part of any development effort (David, 1984). Democratic mores must be cultivated and this can only be done through meaningful citizen participation. In fact, development itself must be viewed not merely as a goal but as a process in which people can constructively associate with one another. Ways must be devised to make citizens equal partners in development. Says Tocqueville: "[T]he most powerful way, and perhaps the only remaining way, in which to interest men in their country's fate is to make them partake in its government" ([1835] 1969: 236).[6]

Of course, there is a danger that the people may lack political maturity. Tocqueville himself is aware of this possibility and often warns that nothing is harder than freedom's apprenticeship.

> It cannot be repeated too often: nothing is more fertile in marvels than the art of being free, but nothing is harder than freedom's apprenticeship . . . . It is hard to make the people take the share in government; it is even harder to provide them with the experience and to inspire them with the feelings they need to govern well. (Tocqueville, [1835] 1969: 240, 315)

But then the only way the people can learn to know the law is by taking part in the framing of the legislation, just as the only remedy for the weakness of association in any society is through experience in associating. Tocqueville is never tired of making this observation; an American, he says, learns the law by legislating and government by governing. "The great work of society is daily performed before his eyes, and so to say, under his hands" (p. 304).

The task of an Asian leader, then, is to see to it that the ideas of democracy and freedom guide all socioeconomic programs. The goals of development must be to achieve the kind of society in which these ideas are cherished. Application, of course, may vary according to different circumstances, but the principle must remain the same. Granted the existence of a myriad of problems facing Asian nations today, we can definitely say that such a development task, to be a success, would have to be carried out by the greatest and most intelligent statesmen. Yet, in a somewhat similar situation, Tocqueville offers as food for thought the proposition that self-interest must be combined with political freedom.

> But sometimes there comes a time in the life of nations when old customs are changed, mores destroyed, beliefs shaken, and the prestige of memories has vanished, but when nonetheless enlightenment has remained incomplete and political rights are ill-assured or restricted. . . . What can be done in such a condition? . . . [I]t is essential to march forward and hasten to make the people see that individual interest is linked to that of the country, for disinterested patriotism has fled beyond recall. Certainly I am far from claiming that in order to reach this result the exercise of political right must immediately be granted to every man; but I do say that the most powerful, and perhaps the only remaining ways, in which to interest men in their country's fate is to make them take a share in its government. (Tocqueville, [1835] 1969: 236)

For Tocqueville, in order to be fully "developed," a country as well as an individual must first be free. To question whether development without democracy is desirable is misleading (see Huntington, 1984: 193–218). Without democracy—that is, without freedom—we cannot have development in the true sense. Development can be accomplished as people learn how to govern themselves and societies become self-governing. To trade democracy for economic development under despotic rule would be a poor bargain, for in the words of Tocqueville,

> if it is true that there will soon be nothing intermediate between the sway of democracy and the yoke of a single man, should we not rather steer toward the former than voluntarily submit to the latter? And if we must finally reach a state of complete equality, is it not better to

let ourselves be leveled down by freedom rather than by the despot? (Tocqueville, [1835] 1969: 315)

Notes

1. All subsequent references to *Democracy in America* are from this edition. However, in part 3, in order to avoid possible conceptual confusion, George Lawrence's term "social state" should be understood to mean what Henry Reeve translated as "social condition." See Alexis de Tocqueville, *Democracy in America*, the Henry Reeve text rev. Francis Bowen, corr. and ed. Phillips Bradley (New York: Vintage Books, 1945).

2. Ferdinand Marcos, as President of the Philippines, had this to say regarding his country: "There seems to be individual but no national progress. Everyone had his own strategy for personal survival but there was no strategy for national survival."

3. Prime Minister Lee Kuan Yew, sensing the adverse effects of low fertility among the more educated Singaporean women, has urged female professionals, who tend to stay single, to marry and raise a family.

4. The following are some excerpts from the "Code of Conduct" for Vigilante Corps members that may be considered as guidelines for Singapore's ideal citizen. "Human beings have basic needs. Human beings have basic obligations. Basic Human Needs. Food, water and clothes. Housing. Medical care. Education. Security. The State provides our basic needs. The Republic of Singapore is our society. We elected our government and the Government is responsible for the organization of our society. It is through the efforts made by the Government, on our behalf, that we are able to obtain our basic needs."

5. The following telephone conversation took place between a visiting Asian editor and his friend, a minister in the PAP government.

MINISTER: Well, now how do you find Singapore?
EDITOR: (*casually*) Great.
MINISTER: What do you mean?

EDITOR: Just great.

MINISTER: I don't think I like the tone of your voice.

EDITOR: I have just come from Djarkarta and Manila. Nothing worked there. Here my telephone works, my flush flushes, everything is clean and antiseptic. Singapore is simply great.

MINISTER: All right, old chap, what's bothering you?

EDITOR: Look, what does it all mean? What about people? Don't they have minds? I see no evidence of people here having minds of their own, feelings of their own.

MINISTER: They are happy. See those modern high-rise buildings? We gave them decent places to live in.

EDITOR: What have you done to their minds?

MINISTER: Well, we are thinking about it. Having given them a clean city, modern amenities, and a strong economy, we are now thinking of what culture we should give them.

EDITOR: (*after a pause*) Is the culture factory also going to be in the Jurong industrial estate?

(*End of conversation*)

6. Here I have substituted Reeve's phrase "to make them partake" for Lawrence's "to make them take a share."

Works Cited

Asia Week, September 7, 1984.

Bastin, John, and Harry J. Benda (1968) *A History of Modern Southeast Asia: Colonialism, Nationalism, and Decolonization*. Englewood Cliffs, N.J.: Prentice-Hall.

Chee, Chan Heng (1975) "Politics in an Administrative State: Where Has the Politics Gone?" In Seah Chee Meow, ed., *Trends in Singapore: Proceedings and Background Papers*. Singapore: Singapore University Press.

Chenvidyakarn, Montri (1979) "Political Control and Economic Influence: A Study of Trade Associations in Thailand." Ph.D. diss., University of Chicago.

David, Randolf S. (1984) "Dictatorship and Development: The End of an Illusion." Lecture for Global Community Lecture Series, sponsored by Sophia University, the United Nations, and International University of Japan, Tokyo, March 30–31.

Foltz, William J. (1963) "Building the Newest Nations: Short-Run Strategies and Long-Run Problems." In Karl W. Deutsch and William Folly, eds., *Nation Building*. London: Atherton Press, 117–131.

George, T.J.S. (1974) *Lee Kuan Yew's Singapore*. Worcester and London: Trinity Press.

Gerling, John L.S. (1981) *The Bureaucratic Polity in Modernizing Societies: Similarities, Differences, and Prospects in the ASEAN Region*. Singapore: Institute of Southeast Asian Studies.

Huntington, Samuel P. (1984) "Will More Countries Become Democratic?" *Political Science Quarterly*, vol. 99, no. 2, 193–218.

Lively, Jack (1962) *The Social and Political Thought of Tocqueville*. Oxford: Clarendon Press.

Magno, Alexander R. (1983) "Developmentalism and the 'New Society': The Repressive Ideology of Underdevelopment." The Philippines in the Third World Papers Series, no. 35: Third World Studies Center.

Marcos, Ferdinand E. (1971) *Today's Revolution: Democracy*. Quezon City: Third World Studies Center, University of Philippines.

_____ (1976) *Notes on the New Society of the Philippines*. Manila: Marcos Foundation.

Muang, U. Muang (1969) *Burma and General Newin*. New York: Asia Publishing House.

Novack, David E., and Robert Lakacham (1964) *Development and Society: The Dynamics of Economic Change*. New York: St. Martin's Press.

Riggs, Fred W. (1966) *Thailand: The Modernization of a Bureaucratic Polity*. Honolulu: East-West Center Press.

Siffin, William J. (1966) *The Thai Bureaucracy: Institutional Change and Development*. Honolulu: East-West Center Press.

Tocqueville, Alexis de (1959) *The European Revolution and Correspondence with Gobineau*. John Lukacs, ed. and trans. Garden City, N.Y.: Anchor Books. First published in 1840.

_____ (1969) *Democracy in America*. J. P. Mayer,

ed., George Lawrence, trans. Garden City, N.Y.: Doubleday. First published in 1835.

Vella, Walter F. (1955) *The Impact of the West on Government in Thailand*. Berkeley and Los Angeles: University of California Press.

Wales, H. G. Quaritch (1965) *Ancient Siamese Government and Administration*. New York: Paragon.

Watnick, Morris (1952) "The Appeal of Communism to Underdeveloped Peoples." *Economic Development and Cultural Change*, vol. 1, no. 1 (March), pp. 22–36.

Wilson, David A. (1964) "Thailand." In George M. Kahin, ed. *Government and Politics of Southeast Asia*, Ithaca, N.Y.: Cornell University Press, 2–72.

Zetterbaum, Marvin (1967) *Tocqueville and the Problem of Democracy*. Stanford, Calif.: Stanford University Press.

4

Elinor Ostrom

Institutional Arrangements and the Commons Dilemma

The Commons Dilemma

Since Garrett Hardin's captivating article in *Science* (December 1968), the expression, "the tragedy of the commons," has come to symbolize the degradation of the environment that is to be expected whenever many individuals use a scarce resource in common. Kenneth Godwin and W. Bruce Shepard (1979: 265) refer to Hardin's article as "the dominant framework within which social scientists portray environmental and resource issues." To illustrate the logical structure of his theory, Hardin asks the reader to envision a pasture "open to all." He then examines the structure of this situation from the perspective of a rational herdsman. Each herdsman receives a

---

An earlier version of this paper was presented as the Distinguished Faculty Research Lecture, Indiana University, April 3, 1986. I am grateful for the support made available through National Science Foundation Grant SES 83-09829, and for the helpful comments of Christi Barbour, Fikret Berkes, William Blomquist, David Feeny, Vincent Ostrom, Rick Wilson, and James Wunsch.

direct benefit from his own animals and suffers delayed costs from the deterioration of the commons when he and others overgraze. The herdsman is motivated to add more and more animals because he receives the direct benefit of his own animals and bears only a share of the costs resulting from overgrazing. Hardin concludes:

> Therein is the tragedy. Each man is locked into a system that compels him to increase his herd without limit—in a world that is limited. Ruin is the destination toward which all men rush, each pursuing his own best interest in a society that believes in the freedom of the commons. (Hardin, 1968: 1244)

Hardin was not the first to notice the tragedy of the commons. Aristotle had long ago observed that "what is common to the greatest number has the least care bestowed upon it. Everyone thinks chiefly of his own, hardly at all of the common interest" (*Politics* 2.3, Jowett's translation). Over 150 years ago, William Forster Lloyd ([1833] 1977) sketched a theory that predicted improvident use for property owned in common. More than a decade before Hardin's article, H. Scott Gordon, in "The Economic Theory of a Common-Property Resource: The Fishery" (1954), clearly expounded what has become a classic on its own.

If the only "commons" of importance were a few grazing areas or fisheries, the "tragedy of the commons" would be of little general interest. This is not the case. Hardin himself used the grazing commons as a metaphor for the general problem of overpopulation. The tragedy of the commons has been used to describe such diverse problems as the Sahelian famine of the 1970s (Picardi and Seifert, 1977), the problem of acid rain (R. Wilson, 1985), the organization of the Mormon Church (Bullock and Baden, 1977), the inability of the U.S. Congress to limit its own capacities to overspend (Shepsle and Weingast, 1984), urban crime (Neher, 1978), public sector-private sector relationships in modern economies (Scharpf, 1985), the problems of international cooperation (Snidal, 1985), and communal conflict in Cyprus (Lumsden, 1973).[1]

Analytically, Hardin's theory has been formalized as an N-Person, Commons Dilemma Game (Dawes, 1973, 1975). When the stark features of the formal representation are examined, the decision facing the herdsman in an open-access commons has the same underlying structure as the decision facing each prisoner in the Prisoner's Dilemma (PD) game.[2] For each of the players in this dilemma, the "don't cooperate" strategy strictly dominates the "cooperate" strategy. The equilibrium resulting from each player selecting his "best" individual strategy is, however, not the best joint outcome. Each player seeking to obtain the best result (the temptation payoff) and to avoid the worst result (the sucker's payoff) ends up with a third-rate outcome.

The normal form to represent the structure of a PD game is

	PLAYER 2	
PLAYER 1	Cooperate	Don't cooperate
Cooperate	Second-best result for both	Worst result for 1, best result for 2
Don't cooperate	Best result for 1, worst result for 2	Third-best result for both

The Prisoner's Dilemma game has fascinated many scholars. The paradox that individually rational strategies lead to collectively irrational outcomes seems to challenge a fundamental faith that rational human beings can achieve rational results. In the introduction to his *Paradoxes of Rationality and Cooperation*, Richmond Campbell explains the "deep attraction" of the dilemma.

> Quite simply, these paradoxes cast in doubt our understanding of rationality and, in the case of the Prisoner's Dilemma, suggest that it is impossible for rational creatures to cooperate. Thus, they bear directly on fundamental issues in ethics and political philosophy and threaten the foundations of the social sciences. It is the scope of these consequences that explains why these paradoxes have drawn so much attention and why they command a central place in philosophical discussion. (Campbell, 1985: 3)

The deep attraction of the dilemma is also illustrated by the number of articles written about it. At latest count—over a decade ago—more than two thousand papers had been devoted to the Prisoner's Dilemma game (Grofman and Pool, 1975).

When the game is viewed as a situation that will be repeated for a predetermined number of rounds known to all participants, most theorists predict that players will select their dominant strategy in each round so that there is a deficient equilibrium in each and every game in the series of games. Several predictions are made for an iterated Commons Dilemma game when the number of iterations is unknown to the players. Some theorists still argue that a rational player should play the "don't cooperate" strategy in every round (see, for example, Sobel, 1985). Others argue that rational players facing one another for an unknown number of plays could use contingent strategies to "teach" one another the benefits of selecting cooperative strategies (see, for example, Braybrooke, 1985; R. Hardin, 1982), or Bayesian estimates of subjective probabilities to resolve the dilemma (see J. Wilson, 1986; Aumann, 1987). Still other models assume that resolute players can use strong threats of permanent retaliation, instead of cooperative moves and forgiveness, to develop models of repetitious games that predict the selection of cooperative strategies by all (see Levhari and Mirman, 1980; Lewis and Cowens, 1983; Cave, 1984; Bendor and Mookherjee, 1985). Taking an evolutionary approach, Robert Axelrod (1981, 1984) has analyzed strategies that may be collectively stable under varying conditions of long-term play, and Ulrich Witt (1986) has examined how frequency-dependent learning may help avoid a deficient equilibrium. In a review of the literature on multiagent exploitation of fishery resources, Veijo Kaitala (1986) describes the wide diversity of predicted equilibria in recent game-theory models of commons situations.

With few exceptions (R. Hardin, 1982; Braybrooke, 1985; Orbell and Wilson, 1978), analyses of the Commons Dilemma have focused on the structure of the game as given.[3] From within the game, participants are trapped in an eternal struggle of tragic proportions. Even when analysts have examined situations that would extend for infinite periods of time, the presumption is usually made that the participants themselves have no control over the structure of the situation in which they find themselves.[4] The prisoners in the story upon which the PD game is based were indeed trapped. The physical constraints of separate cells in a prison and a resolute prosecuting attorney imposed an immutable structure upon them. Is this immutability a temporary conceptual and methodological constraint or a deeper substantive necessity? I shall argue that the structure is conceptually and methodologically necessary for analysis, but not an empirical necessity. The inability of participants to change the structure may be a feature of empirical reality in some situations; however, it is not characteristic of all situations.

All analysis is based on assumptions that keep some conditions constant and allow others to vary. Without considering some variables as exogenous to the situation under analysis, it is not possible to analyze that situation. Taking the structure of a Commons or Prisoner's Dilemma as given allows the analyst to derive the likely results that would occur if individuals were to find themselves in a situation that meets the conditions of the model. In the ongoing, complex, multilevel world of action, what is exogenous at one level of analysis may be endogenous at another.[5] Fixation on the rigidity of analytical constraints has had unfortunate consequences when prescriptions are based on this view. The grim predictions generated by many analysts about the Commons Dilemma has led to policy recommendations of an equally grim character. William Ophuls (1973: 228) has, for example, argued that "because of the tragedy of the commons, environmental problems cannot be solved through cooperation . . . and the rationale for government with major coercive powers is overwhelming." Ophuls concludes that "even if we avoid the tragedy of the commons, it will only be by recourse to the tragic necessity of Leviathan" (p. 229).

Garrett Hardin himself argued a decade after his earlier article that we are enveloped in a "cloud of ignorance" about "the true nature of the fundamental political systems and the effect of each on the preservation of the environment" (1978: 310). The "cloud of ignorance" did not, however, prevent him from presuming that the only alternatives to the Commons Dilemma are what he calls "a private enterprise system" on the one hand or "socialism" on the other (p. 314). With the assurance of someone convinced that "the alternative of the commons is too horrifying to contemplate" (1968: 1247), Hardin indicates that change must be instituted and with "whatever force may be required to make the change stick" (1978: 314). In other words, "if ruin is to be avoided in a crowded world, people must be responsive to a coercive force outside their individual psyches, a 'Leviathan,' to use Hobbes's term" (p. 314).

The presumption that Leviathan is necessary to avoid tragedies of the commons leads to recommendations of central government control of most natural resource systems. Robert L. Heilbroner (1974) has opined that "iron governments," perhaps military governments, are necessary to achieve control over ecological problems. In a less draconian view, David W. Ehrenfeld (1972: 322) suggests that if "private interests cannot be expected to protect the public domain then external regulation by public agencies, governments, or international authorities is needed" (see also Carruthers and Stoner, 1981). Peter Stillman (1975: 13) points out that those who see "a strong central government or a strong ruler" as a solution, implicitly assume that "the ruler will be a wise and ecologically aware altruist" even though these same theorists presume that the users of common-pool resources will be myopic, self-interested, and ecologically unaware hedonists.[6]

In contrast, other analysts call, in equally strong terms, for the imposition of private property rights whenever resources are owned communally (Demsetz, 1967; Welch, 1983). "Both the economic analysis of common property resources and Hardin's treatment of the tragedy of the commons" leads Robert J. Smith (1981: 467) to suggest that "*the only way to avoid the tragedy of the commons* in natural resources and wildlife *is* to end the common-property system *by creating a system of private property rights*" (my emphasis).

I have no quarrel with the argument that dividing a commons and assigning individual property rights enhances efficiency in many situations (see, for example, Feeny, 1982). Similarly, I have no quarrel with the argument that administering some resources through central-government authority may avoid the tragedy of overuse in other situations. I do take issue with the presumption that either central-government administration or private-property rights is "the only way to avoid the tragedy of the commons." Limiting institutional prescriptions to either "the market" or "the state" would mean that the social-scientific "medicine cabinet" contained only two remedies.

Tools exist to analyze far more complicated situations than the simple game that is used repeatedly to "illustrate" the Commons Situation. Those prescribing simple solutions have allowed themselves to be "hung up" on simple, one-level, paradoxical situations.[7] Immense scholarly energy has been devoted to trying to prove that individual rationality in a perverse situation will somehow avoid an irrational outcome. Why should we expect perfectly rational individuals placed in highly irrational structures, with no opportunity to change the structure, to achieve collective rationality? There is no more irrational way to structure any enduring situation than that represented by the PD game: no communication among the participants, no previous ties among them, no anticipation of future interactions, and no capacity to promise, threaten, or cajole.

Would reasonable humans, trying to order their own long-term relationships in a productive manner, structure a situation in such a perverse way? Reasonable humans may, of course, structure situations in this manner when they wish to *prevent* the participants in a situation from cooperating with one another. Some cooperation among participants may lead to harms externalized on others, as in criminal conspiracies or economic cartels. Cooperation is not an unambiguous good in all situations (see Ullmann-Margalit, 1977). Is the only "choice" available to rational human beings a "choice" within the constraints of an externally imposed structure? Once we accept this limited view of choice, we are doomed to accept the imposition of structure by external authorities as the only way out of perverse situations such as the Commons Dilemma. I do not accept such a limited view of choice; I now turn from this critique to a more positive approach to the study of Commons Dilemmas.

In the next section I will briefly describe four commons situations that have not resulted in tragedy. If we are to understand how individuals can escape from tragedy, we need to study "success stories" carefully. These stories are particularly interesting because none of them relies on central control or market mechanisms as its primary mode of management. Empirical cases provide the grist for further theoretical development. Once I have presented these four cases, then, I will turn to several substantive and methodological lessons to be learned from analysis of them.

Successful Efforts to Cope with the Commons

West Basin, California. Given the arid conditions of Southern California, the development and use of water resources has been crucial to the growth of that area during the twentieth century. Luckily, metropolitan Los Angeles happens to overlie a complex set of interrelated groundwater basins. In addition to the construction of several major aqueducts to bring water from the Owens Valley, from the Colorado River, and finally from Northern California, water producers in Southern California have been dependent upon underground basins for storage as well as for the flow of fresh water. Building surface structures or towers to store water for peak periods is extremely costly. Since groundwater basins can provide some of this peaking capacity at low cost, the value of the Los Angeles groundwater basins for their storage potential (in contrast to their yield of a water flow) has become their most important function in a complex, conjunctive use system. The loss of one of the groundwater basins underlying metropolitan Los Angeles would be a major economic disaster.

The incentives facing producers of water from an underground basin depend, in part, on the type of property rights system in force at a particular point in time. When groundwater resources were first developed in Southern California, legal relationships were governed by a quasi-riparian doctrine: one could not purchase groundwater rights without purchasing land. Once land had been purchased, however, overlying landowners had the rights to put as much water to beneficial use as they could withdraw. As long as the demand for groundwater did not exceed the average, long-term supply, no problems resulted from open access to all landowners.

As population and industry increased during the 1930s and 1940s, however, demand for water also increased. An annual overdraft (more water being withdrawn than was being replaced) occurred each year. Several of the basins were located immediately adjacent to the Pacific Ocean. Overdraft in these basins meant not only less water in storage but increased the risk of destroying the basin itself through salt-water intrusion. As water levels fell, each producer was tempted to increase production in order to establish a proportionately larger claim to future pumping rights. The remaining water flowed to the lowest water levels in the basin—allowing sea water to flow in. The short-run incentive was to pump as much as possible before disaster hit.

However, other possibilities existed. If all, or even most, of the pumpers would cut back on production, they could jointly benefit from the prevention of salt-water intrusion. A substantial common good could be achieved if most producers halted their accelerated use. Hundreds of water producers pumped from each basin. No mechanism existed for them to come to agreement concerning joint strategies. No governmental authority had boundaries coinciding with any of the groundwater basins. Portions of eleven cities lay over West Basin, the most exposed one in the series. The County of Los Angeles contained many of the basins within it, but was larger than any one of them.

The problem facing water producers in West Basin by the end of World War II can be clearly represented as a Commons Dilemma. Given the large number of participants and the absence of any ways to communicate and develop enforceable joint production strategies, one would predict from the theory of the commons that the basin would be destroyed by salt-water intrusion within a few years.

But this is a success story. Today, West Basin is in better condition than it was forty years ago. Local water producers found a way to reduce their production from the basin and to create several special districts that now enable them to manage the basin in a productive manner. This "success" was not imposed on West Basin by the State of California or the U.S. government. The initiatives to cope with their water problems came from the producers themselves and from local governmental officials.

How did this success come about? First, the users established a voluntary private association—the West Basin Water Association—to provide a forum for face-to-face discussion about their common problems. The producers used this forum to obtain the best available evidence about the current conditions of the basin and to discuss alternative joint production strategies. The association was supported by voluntary dues paid by producers based on the volume of water produced. A decision was made within the association to use equity court procedures in helping to solve the problems they faced. Through legal discovery and reference procedures, the producers were able to obtain reliable information on past and current supply and demand conditions.

In the shadow of the court, producers were able to negotiate a contingent contract. This contractual device enabled a producer to agree to limit production if, and only if, 80 percent of the other producers also agreed to limit their production. A contingent contract effectively eliminates being played for a sucker while others pursue temptation strategies. The choice for each producer in deciding whether to sign a contingent contract is between: (1) cooperating in a situation where most others are also cooperating or (2) not cooperating in a situation where most others are also not cooperating. The contingent contract operated as an interim court decree for several years before it became the final court decree and was imposed on nonsigners as well as those who had signed the original agreement. In addition, the court decision assigned each producer defined rights to the flow of water for the basin that could be purchased independently of land. Once rights were so defined, a market for groundwater could and did develop. A water master was appointed to continue to monitor production and ensure that producers remained within agreed limits.

While utilizing court procedures, West Basin producers also initiated proceedings to create several special districts. The first one enabled producers to supplement the underground supply with a surface supply; the second one enabled them to tax themselves on the amount of water they produced, and to use that tax revenue to engage in replenishment efforts along the coast as well as inland. Replenishment efforts involved several more local public districts that agreed to cooperate in a series of contractual arrangements (see E. Ostrom, 1965, for details; and Blomquist and E. Ostrom, 1985, for a recent analysis).

The participants themselves, in the West Basin Commons Dilemma, were the major actors in designing a series of institutional arrangements to meet their particular needs. Cost-sharing arrangements were developed for each step in the resolution process. The use of proportionate cost sharing began with a voluntary association. Dues were assessed based on the amount of groundwater extracted (thereby creating an incentive to understate use), while votes on association matters were based on the same measure (an offsetting incentive to overstate use). In the court case, costs of investigation and litigation were proportioned to the benefit obtained in the judgment—that is, the prescribed rights to water. The cost of monitoring compliance was again proportioned to rights, with a portion being borne by the State of California. The state has an interest in accurate information about groundwater conditions and in providing facilities to help avoid the tragedy of the commons.

Alanya, Turkey. Our second case stands in marked contrast to the highly modernized political economy of the Los Angeles metropolitan area. The inshore fishery of Alanya in Turkey is a relatively small operation. Fikret Berkes (1986), a human ecologist at Brock University in Ontario, Canada, has provided an excellent description of the fishery and its institutional arrangements. Many of the 100 local fishermen operate in two- or three-man boats using various types of nets. Half of the fishermen belong to a local producers' cooperative and half do not. The economic viability of the fishery in Alanya was threatened in the early 1970s by two factors. First, unrestrained use of the fishery created conflict among the users. Second, competition among fishermen for the better fishing spots greatly increased production costs and uncertainty regarding the harvest potential for any particular team of fishermen.

Early in the 1970s, members of the local cooperative began to discuss and implement a rather ingenious system for allotting fishing sites to the local fishermen.

- Each September, a list of eligible fishermen is prepared, consisting of all licensed fishermen in Alanya, regardless of co-op membership.
- Within the area normally used by Alanya fishermen, all usable fishing locations are named and listed. These spots are spaced so that the net set in one does not block the fish that should be available at the adjacent spot.
- These named fishing locations are in effect from September to May.
- In September, the eligible fishermen draw lots and are assigned to named fishing locations.
- From September to January, each day, each fisherman moves to the new location to the east. After January, the fishermen move west. This gives each fisherman an equal opportunity at the stocks which migrate east to west between September and January, and reverse their migration from January to May through the area. (Berkes, 1986: 73–74)

Each year the list of fishing sites is endorsed by each fisherman and deposited with the mayor and local gendarme. The few infractions that incur are "dealt with by the fishing community at large, in the coffee house. Violators may come under social pressure and, on occasion, threats of violence" (p. 74). If needed, the local gendarme is prepared to help in the enforcement of the agreement. Enforcement has, however, not been a major problem because the system is supported by most of the fishermen themselves. The system helps to allocate the best fishing sites to all fishermen on an equitable basis and has severely reduced conflict as well as production costs.

Toerbel, Switzerland. The third case is that of Toerbel, a village of about six hundred people located in the Vispertal of the Upper Valais region of Switzerland. Netting (1972: 133) identifies the most

Institutional Arrangements and the Commons Dilemma 113

significant features of the environment as: "(1) the steepness of its slope and the wide range of microclimates demarcated by altitude, (2) the prevailing paucity of precipitation, and (3) the exposure to sunlight." For centuries, Swiss peasants have planted their privately owned plots with bread grains, garden vegetables and fruit trees, and hay for winter fodder. Cheeses produced by a small group of herdsmen, who tended village cattle pastured on the communally owned alpine meadows during the summer months, have been an important part of the local economy.

Written legal documents dating back to 1224 provide information regarding the types of land tenure and transfers that have occurred in the village and the rules used by the villagers to regulate the five types of communally owned property: the alpine grazing meadows, the forests, the "waste lands" (stony areas without much vegetation), the irrigation systems, and the paths and roads connecting privately and communally owned properties. On February 1, 1483, Toerbel residents signed articles formally establishing an association to achieve a better level of regulation over the use of the alp, the forests, and the waste lands.

> The law specifically forbade a foreigner (*Fremde*) who bought or otherwise occupied land in Toerbel from acquiring any right in the communal alp, common lands, or grazing places, or permission to fell timber. Ownership of a piece of land did *not* automatically confer any communal right (*genossenschaftliches Recht*). The inhabitants currently possessing land and water rights reserved the power to decide whether an outsider should be admitted to community membership. (Netting, 1976: 139)

The boundaries of the communally owned lands were well established long ago as indicated in a 1507 inventory document.

Not only was access to well-defined **common** property strictly limited to citizens, who were specifically **extended** communal rights, but regulations written in 1517 specified that "no citizen could send more cows to the alp than he could feed during the winter" (p. 139). This regulation, which Netting reports is still enforced, imposed severe fines for any attempt by villagers to appropriate a larger share of grazing rights. The rules regulating the use of irrigation water involved an intricate rotation system based on sun and shadow movements on the surrounding mountains. Timber for construction and wood for heating were marked by village officials and assigned by lot to groups of households who then were authorized to enter the forests and harvest the marked trees.

Regulations also stated the obligations of those with use rights to provide labor inputs related to the cleaning of springs, the maintenance of an extensive irrigation system, the construction and maintenance of roads and paths, rebuilding avalanche-damaged fences, and redistributing manure on common pasture lands. A codification of these regulations signed in 1531 included twenty-four separate articles regulating such diverse activities as "immigration to or emigration from the community, hunting on the alp, stock damage to private plots, the spread of cattle disease, dispute settlement, participation in village government, alp pasturate rights, and compulsory communal building" (pp. 139–140).

In addition to a detailed system of communal rights, private rights to land are also well developed in Toerbel and other Swiss villages. Most of the meadows, gardens, grainfields, and vineyards in Toerbel were owned by separate individuals, but complex condominium-like agreements were also worked out for the fractional shares that siblings and relatives might have in barns, granaries, or multistoried housing units.

Hirano, Nagaike, and Yamanoka Villages in Japan. The last case study involves several villages located in a mountainous region of Japan. For centuries in that country, extensive common lands have existed and been regulated primarily by local villagers. In an important study of traditional common lands in Japan, Margaret A. McKean (1986) estimates that about twelve million hectares of forests and uncultivated mountain meadows were held and managed in common by thousands of rural villages during the Tokugawa period (1600–1867), and that about three million hectares are so managed today.

Three Japanese villages—Hirano, Nagaike, and Yamanoka—are similar in many respects to Toerbel. The villages are also established on steep mountains where many microclimates can be distinguished. Peasants cultivate their own private lands raising rice, garden vegetables, and draft animals. The common lands in Japan produce a wide variety of forest products of value to local peasants including timber, thatch for roofing and weaving, animal fodder of various kinds, and plant and forest residue for fertilizer, firewood, and charcoal.

Each village in earlier times was governed by an assembly. The assembly was usually composed of the heads of each of the households that had political standing in the village. The basis for political status varied substantially by village. In some villages the standing of households was based on cultivation rights in land, in some on taxpaying obligations, and in some on ownership rights in land. In some villages almost all households had political standing and rights to the use of the commons. In others, these rights were more narrowly held (McKean, 1986: 551).

Each village assembly established a relatively complex set of rules regulating both use and enhancement of the commons owned by the village. Boundary rules clearly demarcated which lands were held in common and which in private ownership. Entry rules unambiguously specified who was authorized to use the communally owned land. Ownership of the uncultivated lands near a village devolved from the imperial court to the villages through several intermediate stages involving land stewards and locally based warriors. National cadastral surveys were conducted late in the sixteenth century at a time of land reform that assigned "most of the rights to arable land that we today consider to be 'ownership' to peasants who lived on and cultivated that land" (p. 537). In the earlier systems the owners of large estates had employed agents in each village and authorized these agents to regulate access to the uncultivated lands. As villages asserted their own rights to these lands, they shared a clear image of which lands were private and which were held in common, and of how the lands held in common needed management in order to serve the long-term interests of the peasants dependent upon them. In traditional Japanese villages, the household was the smallest unit of account. Each village contained a carefully recorded, defined number of households. Households could not divide into multiple households without permission from the village. Rights of access to the communally held lands were accorded on a pro rata basis to each household. Consequently, households with many members had no advantage, and considerable disadvantages, in their access to the commons. Population growth was extremely low (0.025 percent for the period 1721–1846) and ownership patterns within villages were stable (p. 552).

In addition to delimiting the ownership status of all lands, village assemblies also established detailed partitioning rules (Oakerson, 1986), which specified in various ways how much of each valued product a household could harvest from the commons.

> Different villages arrived at different arrangements for guaranteeing an adequate supply of the products from the commons. For items that were needed regularly and that the commons yielded in abundance, a village might allow co-owners free and open entry as long as they abided by certain rules to make sure that a self-sustaining population of mature plants or animals was left behind. To enter the commons, one might need to go to village authorities to obtain an entry permit, carved on a little wooden ticket and marked 'entrance permit for one person.' The rules would probably restrict the villager's choice of cutting tools or the size of the sack or container used to collect plants. Everyone would be expected to abide by the village headman's instructions about leaving so much height on a cut plant so that it could regenerate, or taking only a certain portion of a cluster of similar plants to make sure the parent plant could propagate itself, or collecting a certain species only after flowering and fruiting, and so on.
>
> Villagers usually set aside closed reserves . . . for items that had to be left undisturbed until maturity and harvested all at once at just the right time, or that the commons supplied in only adequate, not abundant, amounts. The village headman would be responsible for determining when the time had come to harvest thatch or winter fodder or other products, and would schedule the event. (McKean, 1986: 555)

The tailoring of village rules to the specific needs of each village and the ecological condition of a particular commons also required input from the villages to enhance and maintain the yield of the commons.

There were written rules about the obligation of each household to contribute a share to the collective work to maintain the commons—to conduct the annual burning..., to report to harvest on mountain-opening days, or to do a specific cutting of timber or thatch. Accounts were kept about who contributed what to make sure that no household evaded its responsibilities unnoticed [and] if there was no acceptable excuse, punishment was in order. (McKean, 1986: 559)

McKean's study is also strong testimony that it is possible for local communities to devise effective rules for managing their own common-property resources. The establishment of the rules, the monitoring of behavior, the monitoring of the conditions in the commons, and the assignment of punishment were all conducted primarily in the village. McKean concludes that the long-term success of these locally designed rules systems indicates "that it is not necessary for regulation of the commons to be imposed coercively or from the outside" (p. 571).

What Can Be Learned from These Cases?

Let me turn first to the substantive lessons that can be learned from these four success stories. I will follow this with a discussion of the methodological lessons.

The Substantive Significance. The most important substantive lesson to be learned from these four cases is that it is *possible* for individuals facing a Commons Dilemma in natural settings to design their own institutional arrangements that change the very structure of the situation in which they find themselves. A self-conscious process of institutional change occurred in West Basin and in Alanya. The participants designed new structures for themselves that have enabled them to use common-pool resources in a productive manner. In West Basin, a rich supporting institutional structure enabled participants to enter into contingent contracts, to agree to create special districts with specific powers to tax, and to engage in a creative form of public entrepreneurship to manage the commons. In Alanya, relatively poor fishermen, living in marginal circumstances, were able to extricate themselves from a deteriorating Commons Situation by inventing an ingenious set of rules for rotating fishing sites, enabling everyone to have a fair opportunity to obtain the catch.

These are not unique cases. In Southern California, participants in other groundwater basins have developed similar institutional arrangements to those of West Basin (Weschler, 1968; Rolph, 1982; Blomquist, 1987). While the designs are similar, each is tailored to meet particular circumstances. Besides Alanya, Berkes describes two other inshore fisheries owned communally where local fishermen have developed effective institutions for regulating use. The rules used in these other fisheries are different from those used in Alanya. Swiss peasants living in other alpine villages besides Toerbel have evolved their own systems for allocating the use of common grazing land (Wiegandt, 1977). Many other success stories are recorded in the literature (Siy, 1982; Wade, 1986; Cruz, 1986; Berkes, 1985a, 1985b; Uphoff, 1985; McCay, 1980; Berkes and Pocock, 1981; Acheson, 1975; Cordell and McKean, 1986).

Success is, of course, not the only outcome. In Northern California, Arizona, and New Mexico, many groundwater basins are currently threatened with excessive depletion (Knapp and Vaux, 1982). Several inshore fisheries on the Turkish coast, not far from Alanya, face resource depletion and severe user-group conflicts (Berkes, 1986). Establishing a *possibility* is not the same as establishing *necessity*.

West Basin and Alanya illustrate how individuals can engage in self-conscious design to change patterns of behavior within a relatively short period of time. These cases illustrate what I think Giddens (1979: 56–57) means by the reflexive monitoring of action. Giddens considered this reflexive monitoring to be related not only to the actions taken in a situation but also to the "monitoring of the *setting of interaction*" (his emphasis). The Swiss and Japanese villages illustrate how institutions that evolved in the distant past can be well adapted to particular environmental and cultural circumstances. That the inhabitants of these extremely fragile mountain environments have been able to use them intensively for centuries, while harvesting a rich variety of forest and forage products, is strong testimony to the possibility of long-term, stable outcomes that are not the tragedies posited in theory.

Another lesson to be obtained from these cases is the futility of presuming that there is "one best way." There cannot be "one best way" for relating to an infinite variety of different problematical situations. None of the four institutional arrangements that enabled participants to overcome a Commons Dilemma is either a strict market or a central-government arrangement. While the West Basin "solution" involves firm property rights to the flow of water, the basin itself is not privately owned. A "market" for water rights emerged subsequent to the court decree allocating rights to water. But that is not all that emerged. Water producers created several local, public jurisdictions with regulatory and taxing authority to supplement their own efforts to use equity court procedures to assign firm rights to the flow of water and thus control the total withdrawals from the basin. A complex series of private and public agencies jointly manage this sensitively balanced system. Nor is the polycentric, locally governed system, involving both private and public enterprises, a central-government solution.

In none of the other systems do the rights to use even approach fully marketable rights. In Alanya, one must be a registered fisherman living in Alanya to qualify for the annual lottery. One fisherman cannot sell his annual schedule of fishing spots to another. Rights to the Toerbel commons are individually inherited, but an outsider cannot buy rights to use the commons as an outsider can buy water rights in West Basin. Rights to use of the Japanese village commons are assigned to family units and remain with family units from one generation to the next.

None of the four systems resembles a central-government solution, either. The participants themselves decided which rules are to apply for allocating use. The administrative structure in all four cases is minimal. The users of the commons are also the governors of the commons.

The primary substantive lesson from these cases is that it is possible for humans to break out of the logic that yields a tragedy of the commons and to restructure the situation itself. Thus it is important for policy analysts to recognize the difference between making assumptions during an analysis and presuming these assumptions are immutable. There cannot be "one best way" of organizing the management of natural resource systems. We have much more to learn from careful analysis of existing institutional arrangements.

The Methodological Significance. These cases not only teach us substantive lessons; they also raise methodological issues about how to study institutions and institutional change. In my earlier discussion, I referred to most current analyses of Commons Dilemmas as single-level analyses. The analysis is completely contained within the structure of a given situation. The problem in understanding institutions is that one must use multiple levels of analysis. Several ways exist to identify levels. One method is to separate levels of operational choice, collective choice, and constitutional choice (see Kiser and E. Ostrom, 1982). The typical way of modeling a Commons Dilemma is at the level of operational choice. Analyzing how individuals might change the rules of a situation involving operational choice is at a level of collective choice. Analysis of the rules for making rules is at a level of constitutional choice (Buchanan and Tullock, 1962). When we move from an analysis at one level to a prescription for changing the rules used by people to structure that level, we need self-consciously to use multiple levels of analysis (see V. Ostrom, 1985: ch. 13).

This is a central theme in Douglas Hofstadter's *Godel, Escher, Bach* (1979). Hofstadter distinguishes between systems in which the levels are well separated in time, in space, and in the language used to describe them, and systems in which they are not well separated.

In multilevel systems that are well separated in time and space, no more than one level of analysis must be kept in mind at any one time. Our minds can effectively jump from one level to another depending upon the context of discourse and thought. In many physical systems, for example, various levels of analysis are effectively separated by large gaps in space and/or time.[8] The vast differences in time and space between many levels of physical systems have enabled physical scientists to develop a technical language and theoretical apparatus to explain phenomena at each level relatively independently of other levels.

There are, however, physical systems where the macroscopic behavior of the system emerges from the "independent behaviors of a multitude of microscopic entities" (Courtois, 1985: 592). Ilya Prigogine (1978) has called some of these systems "dissipative structures." They occur in both the physical and biological worlds. Problems of analysis for physical and biological phenomena that are more tightly linked across levels turn out to be far more difficult than analysis where levels can be kept separate. Social and political phenomena are similar in structure to such tightly linked systems and present similar difficulties of analysis.

Hofstadter discusses such difficulties when he argues that what is most confusing "is when a single system admits of two or more descriptions on different levels which nevertheless resemble each other in some way" (1979: 287). He warns that when levels tend to resemble one another closely, "we find it hard to avoid mixing levels when we think about the system, and can easily get totally lost" (p. 287). Hofstadter illustrates the confusion that can result when similar language is used to describe multilevel systems with the problems faced in designing, managing, and fixing errors in computer systems, with their complex layering of programming languages. Those of us who have taught a friend to use a microcomputer are all too familiar with the initial confusion of a novice when faced with the multiple language systems he or she must learn to use. Since all communication with the computer occurs on the same flat screen, the novice interprets the symbols as all coming from the same level. Sorting out what an operating language does from what other, higher-level, languages do is a major task for anyone who works with a computer.

In a similar manner, many social scientists would view the various actions undertaken by participants in West Basin or in Alanya as occurring at one level—what we might refer to as "local level" phenomena. Social scientists tend to distinguish phenomena in terms of space, whether local, regional, national, or international, and time—the Dark Ages, the Middle Ages, the Enlightenment, and the Modern Era, for instance.[9] Another device for grouping similar and dissimilar events is the distinction between government and nongovernment. With this distinction, activities undertaken in West Basin would be classified as part of local government, while the activities undertaken in Alanya would be classified as occurring in the private sector. In the approach presented here, however, the water producers in West Basin and the fishermen in Alanya are both conceptualized as involved in a *similar* but *multilevel* series of activities. They solve a similar problem (the Commons Dilemma) at an operational level by restructuring, at a different level (the collective choice level), the rules affecting their use of the commons.[10] They function at a constitutional level in doing so.

Game theory has developed a rich and useful set of tools to enable scholars to predict outcomes once the structure of a situation is represented as a game. We need to develop a complementary "rules theory" with its own set of tools to enable us to predict the structure of the game that will be produced by particular configurations of rules when used in combination with the physical laws of the environment (see Elkin, 1985, for a similar argument). A theory of rules, combined with game theory, would then provide the basis for rule modifications that may improve rather than diminish human welfare. We have a rich literature in political philosophy to draw upon in developing a theory of rules.[11] Further, considerable work in formal logic, particularly deontic logic, and in artificial intelligence, communications theory, sociolinguistics, developmental cognitive psychology, and linguistics itself is relevant to the study of rules.

One of the problems facing scholars who have been interested in the rules used by people to order their relationships with one another has been the extraordinary variety of particular rules. Until a technical language is developed to express in a more generic form the particular rules found in practice, one rule configuration cannot be compared to another. Rules in use are described either in everyday language or in the legal language of a particular legal system. The variety of rules, if one relies entirely on the specific wording of rules found in practice, is beyond our capacity to analyze.

Institutional Arrangements and the Commons Dilemma

In our current research, my colleagues and I at the Workshop in Political Theory and Policy Analysis are developing a method to represent rules in a generic fashion. We are attempting to identify what is common to a set of specific rules and to capture that commonality in as simple a statement of rules as we can. A complete generic rule configuration affecting the structure of a game would contain rules clarifying the following:

- What positions participants may, must, or must not hold (*position* rules);
- What characteristics participants may, must, or must not have to enter positions (*boundary* rules);
- The authorized actions participants may, must, or must not take independently (*authority* rules);
- The formula that participants may, must, or must not use for decision making when multiple persons must decide (*aggregation* rules);
- The information that participants may, must, or must not reveal to others (*information* rules);
- The states of the world that participants may, must, or must not affect (*scope* rules);
- The rewards or penalties that may, must, or must not be assigned to actions or outcomes (*payoff* rules).[12]

This is not the appropriate place for a detailed examination of the methods we are developing. Let me illustrate them, however, by concentrating on eight generic rules that were changed in West Basin, four of which were also changed in Alanya. While in both cases other rules are also involved, these eight rules were the focus of attention in West Basin. A generic formulation of each rule is presented in Table 4.1.

Four rules were changed in the Alanya case: (1) local civil authorities became official monitors for the fishing agreement, (2) fishermen were limited in the number of days they were allowed to

Table 4.1
Rules That Were Changed in the Alanya or West Basin Cases

	"BEFORE"		"AFTER"	
RULES CHANGED	Alanya	West Basin	Alanya	West Basin
Position rules				
P1. Position of monitor exists	N	N	Y	Y
Entry rules				
E1. Must live (or own land) in local area to be a user	Y	Y	Y	N
E2. May purchase entry rights	N	N	N	Y
Authority rules				
A1. Quantity of use restricted	N	N	Y	Y
A2. Location of use restricted	N	N	Y	Y
Payoff rules				
R1. Sanctions could be imposed on use patterns	N	N	Y	Y
R2. Payments assessed on quantity of use	N	N	N	Y
R3. Payments assessed on assets	N	N	N	Y

fish, (3) fishermen were limited in the location where they could fish, and (4) sanctions could be imposed on those who did not adhere to the restrictions placed on use patterns. In West Basin, all eight of the rules listed in Table 4.1 were changed over a twenty-year period.

By stating the rules in a general rather than a specific form, we can now observe that these eight rules were similar in both Alanya and West Basin "before" they were changed because participants in both locations faced a Commons Dilemma. The similarity in the underlying rule structure is otherwise hidden in the complexity of a modified quasi-riparian water rights doctrine and an open-access fishery regime. In our current research, we are beginning to examine the rule configurations underlying a series of cases similar to those described above in order to ascertain how similar generic rules are related to Commons Dilemmas. From our early results, we know that the generic rule configurations underlying such dilemmas are subject to greater variance than those that apply to Alanya and West Basin. But it will still be possible to associate some types of rule configurations with some types of situations in a systematic manner.

While the "before" rules are identical in their generic structure, the "after" rules are not. Entry rights may be purchased in West Basin and not in Alanya. It is necessary to live in the local area in Alanya and not in West Basin. Further, payments for use as well as payments on assets are assessed in West Basin and not in Alanya. The system to regulate use patterns in Alanya is a far simpler system than the one developed to regulate use in West Basin. Furthermore, in West Basin, users have organized themselves for the purpose of enhancing and regulating the supply of water to the basin as well as regulating the use patterns made of the basin.

The Alanya rule configuration is quite similar to the ones that evolved in Toerbel and in Harano (to take one of the Japanese villages as an example). The generic rules we compared can also be applied to the success cases: the traditional systems that evolved in

	Generic rule number							
	P1	E1	E2	A1	A2	R1	R2	R3
Toerbel, Switzerland	Y	Y	N	Y	Y	Y	N	N
Harano, Japan	Y	Y	N	Y	Y	Y	N	N
Alanya, Turkey ("after")	Y	Y	N	Y	Y	Y	N	N
West Basin, California ("after")	Y	N	Y	Y	Y	Y	Y	Y

Toerbel and in Harano and the "after" situations of Alanya and West Basin.

The similarity in the pattern for these eight rules for Toerbel and Harano is striking. This portion of the rule configuration is identical for two systems that evolved in widely separated, fragile mountain regions in Switzerland and Japan.[13] Without transforming the particularities of the actual rules used in each of these settings into a general form, this underlying similarity in structure is difficult to observe. Although our work on generic rule formulation is just beginning, we can begin to see what it means to sort out multiple levels of analysis and develop technical languages appropriate to each of the levels. Analysis of rule configurations requires an examination of how particular patterns in rules-in-use affect the structure of the situations humans confront. Analysis of these situations, in turn, requires an examination of how incentives so produced lead to particular types of behavior and aggregate outcomes. To develop a cumulative and effective form of policy analysis, we need to pursue *both* types of analysis as rigorously as we can. Without the analysis of rules, the analysis of given situations leads to a focus on the immutable structure of the situation. Without the analysis of situations, the analysis of rules does not tell us how people will behave once rules have been changed (see Majone, 1986: 70).

By learning to understand how rules can be used to restructure such nasty social traps as Commons Dilemmas, we may come to appreciate that alternatives are available for resolving other social dilemmas. Human beings not only face choices about how to act in given situations; they also have the capacity to think about, formulate, and select different ways of structuring choice situations. Choices occur in different contexts and at different levels. When people learn not only how to use a commons but how to govern a commons, they are laying the foundation for developing and maintaining self-governing, democratic societies.

Notes

1. Recent historical work has challenged the validity of the presumption that there was a tragedy of the commons in the use of English open-field grazing lands, but the metaphor of the commons is still quite useful in other settings (Dahlman, 1980).

2. Attributed to Merrill M. Flood and Melvin Dresher and formalized by Albert W. Tucker (Campbell, 1985: 3), the game is described as follows.

> Two suspects are taken into custody and separated. The district attorney is certain that they are guilty of a specific crime, but he does not have adequate evidence to convict them at a trial. He points out to each prisoner that each has two alternatives: to confess to the crime the police are sure they have done, or not to confess. If they both do not confess, then the district attorney states he will book them on some very minor trumped-up charge such as petty larceny and illegal possession of a weapon, and they will both receive minor punishment; if they both confess they will be prosecuted, but he will recommend less than the most severe sentence; but if one confesses and the other does not, then the confessor will receive lenient treatment for turning state's evidence whereas the latter will get "the book" slapped at him. In terms of years in a penitentiary, the strategic problem might reduce to:

Prisoner 2

	Not Confess	Confess
Prisoner 1		
Not confess	1 year each	10 years for 1, 3 months for 2
Confess	3 months for 1, 10 years for 2	8 years each

(Luce and Raiffa, 1957: 95).

Richard Kimber (1981) challenges the appropriateness of using the PD game to represent Commons Dilemmas.

3. Scholars engaged in experimental work have examined a variety of factors that may affect the proportion of cooperative vs. noncooperative strategies (see, in particular, R. Wilson, 1985; van de Kragt, Orbell, and Dawes, 1983; Dawes, McTavish, and Shaklee, 1977).

4. In an important article that presumes that there may be different institutional solutions to such situations, Orbell and Wilson (1978) examine the effect of using a single dictator, majority rule, or unrestrained choice to determine who cooperates and who defects under different environmental conditions.

5. Anthony Giddens (1979: 5) has stressed this basic recursiveness of social life by pointing out that "structure is both medium and outcome of the reproduction of practices."

6. In a fascinating study of the unintended and perverse consequences of national governmental regulation of coastal fishery resources, Anthony Davis (1984) points out that officials of the Canadian Federal Department of Fisheries are firmly convinced that a "tragedy of the commons" will occur in all fisheries without a uniform imposition of central regulations. These national regulations ignore and, in some cases, are contrary to local regulations for managing small-boat fisheries that have been in practice for several generations. The national policies are generating substantial threats to the long-term viability of small-boat fisheries that had been ecologically viable for a long time.

7. Substantial work has been undertaken in modern game-theory literature on much more complex situations than the standard PD or Commons game in modern game theoretical literature (see, for example, Selten, 1975, 1978; Shubik, 1982; Guth, 1985).

8. In a kinetic model of a chemical reaction, the differential equations used to represent the chemical reaction rely on an assumption that the process under analysis can be isolated from its environment. P. J. Courtois has described these multilevel, chemical systems in the following way.

> On the one hand, the environment is supposed to remain unaffected and is held constant; it is represented by a few parameters with fixed

values. On the other hand, underlying processes, at finer scales in time or space, are hidden. Their dynamics are completely ignored. They are supposed to be in a state of equilibrium.... The success and the accuracy of these isolated analyses are, of course, to a great extent due to the large values of the differences in the time and size scales of the structures involved. (Courtois, 1985: 591)

9. A glance at the curriculum for many social science departments reveals some variant of the above spatial or temporal divisions. While these temporal and spatial classifications are useful for many purposes, they are not the only useful ways of examining the layers of interlinked systems of human action.

10. Biology and linguistics both advanced rapidly once the multileveled nature of these disciplines was recognized and a different language developed for each level. Both genotypes and phenotypes are basic structures used in the analysis of living systems. Analysis of a genotype explores the genetic constitution of an organism; analysis of a phenotype looks at the physical manifestations of the individual members of a species. The methods of analysis and scientific language used to describe and explain phenomena at each of these levels differ markedly even though, to understand evolution, one needs to understand both types of structure and how they are related. Modern linguistics has also been well served by a conscious separation of the level of sentence structure from the deeper transformational grammatical structure. This has represented a slow development over time of the work of Humboldt (1836), de Saussure ([1916] 1960), Wittgenstein (1953), and Searle (1969). One of Chomsky's great contributions has been to show that the technical language appropriate for describing and theorizing about a deep transformational grammar is not the same language or level that is used to analyze surface structure (see Chomsky, 1965, 1975, 1978). The analysis of institutional arrangements in the social world needs a similar methodological severing of conceptually close systems and the development of different technical languages for each level of analysis. This does not mean that the levels are severed in everyday life, but that they are perceived as separable by social scientists for analytic purposes. The linkages among levels are so intimately intertwined that it is extraordinarily difficult to separate them for analysis.

11. See Buchanan and Tullock (1962), Hayami and Ruttan (1985), North (1981), V. Ostrom (1980, 1982, 1987), and Shepsle (1979a, 1979b).

12. See E. Ostrom (1986a, 1986b, 1987) and Kiser and E. Ostrom (1982) for discussion of the relationship of particular types of rules to the elements of an action situation. See Feeny (1986) for a discussion of related methodological issues that arise in studying Commons Dilemmas.

13. Most of the other rules used in these two cases are also quite similar. They differ primarily in regard to how rights are transferred across generations and the freedom individuals have to leave their villages (see E. Ostrom, 1987, for a more thorough description).

Works Cited

Acheson, James M. (1975) "The Lobster Fiefs: Economic and Ecological Effects of Territoriality in the Maine Lobster Industry." *Human Ecology*, vol. 3, no. 3, 183–207.

Alchian, Armen, and Harold Demsetz (1973) "The Property Rights Paradigm." *Journal of Economic History*, vol. 33, no. 1 (March), 16–27.

Aumann, Robert J. (1987) "Correlated Equilibrium as an Expression of Bayesian Rationality." *Econometrica*, vol. 55, no. 2 (Jan.), 1–18.

Axelrod, Robert (1981) "The Emergence of Cooperation among Egoists." *American Political Science Review*, vol. 75, no. 2 (June), 306–318.

_____ (1984) *The Evolution of Cooperation*. New York: Basic Books.

Bendor, Johnathan, and Dilip Mookherjee (1985) "Institutional Structure and the Logic of Ongoing Collective Action." Working paper, School of Business, Stanford University, Calif.

Berkes, Fikret (1985a) "The Common-Property Resource Problem and the Creation of Limited Property Rights." *Human Ecology*, vol. 13, no. 2 (June), 187–208.

_____ (1985b) "Fisherman and 'The Tragedy of the Commons'." *Environmental Conservation*, vol. 12, no. 3

(autumn), 199–206.

_____ (1986) "Marine Inshore Fishery Management in Turkey: Some Examples, Problems and Prospects." In National Research Council, *Proceedings of the Conference on Common-Property Resource Management.* Washington, D.C.: National Academy Press, 63–83.

Berkes, Fikret, and Dorothy Pocock (1981) "Self-Regulation of Commercial Fisheries of the Outer Log Point Bay, Lake Erie." *Journal of Great Lakes Research*, vol. 1, no. 2, 111–116.

Blomquist, William (1987) "Getting Out of the Trap: Changing an Endangered Commons." Ph.D. diss., Indiana University, Bloomington, Ind.

Blomquist, William, and Elinor Ostrom (1985) "Institutional Capacity and the Resolution of a Commons Dilemma." *Policy Studies Review*, vol. 5, no. 2 (Nov.), 383–393.

Braybrooke, David (1985) "The Insoluble Problem of the Social Contract." In Richmond Campbell and Lanning Sowden, eds., *Paradoxes of Rationality and Cooperation.* Vancouver, B.C.: University of British Columbia Press, 277–305.

Buchanan, James, and Gordon Tullock (1962) *The Calculus of Consent: Logical Foundations of Constitutional Democracy.* Ann Arbor: University of Michigan Press.

Bullock, Kari, and John Baden (1977) "Communes and the Logic of the Commons." In Garrett Hardin and John Baden, eds., *Managing the Commons.* San Francisco: Freeman, 182–199.

Campbell, Richmond (1985) "Background for the Uninitiated." In Richmond Campbell and Lanning Sowden, eds., *Paradoxes of Rationality and Cooperation.* Vancouver, B.C.: University of British Columbia Press, 3–41.

Carruthers, Ian, and Roy Stoner (1981) "Economic Aspects and Policy Issues in Groundwater Development." World Bank Staff Working Paper no. 496. Washington, D.C.: The World Bank.

Cave, Jonathan A.K. (1984) *The Cold Fish War: Long-Term Competition in a Dynamic Game.* Santa Monica, Calif.: RAND Corporation.

Chomsky, Noam (1965) *Aspects of the Theory of Syntax.* Cambridge, Mass.: MIT Press.

———————— (1975) *Reflections on Language.* New York: Random House.

———————— (1978) *Rules and Representation.* New York: Columbia University Press.

Cordell, John, and Margaret A. McKean (1986) "Sea Tenure in Bahia, Brazil." In National Research Council, *Proceedings of the Conference on Common-Property Resource Management.* Washington, D.C.: National Academy Press, 85–113.

Courtois, P. J. (1985) "On Time and Space Decomposition of Complex Structures." *Communications of the ACM,* vol. 28, no. 6 (June), 590–603.

Cruz, Wilfrido D. (1986) "Overfishing and Conflict in a Traditional Fishery: San Miguel Bay, Philippines." In National Research Council, *Proceedings of the Conference on Common-Property Resource Management.* Washington, D.C.: National Academy Press, 115–135.

Dahlman, Carl (1980) *The Open Field System and Beyond.* Cambridge: Cambridge University Press.

Davis, Anthony (1984) "Property Rights and Access Management in the Small Boat Fishery: A Case Study from Southwest Nova Scotia." In Cynthia Lamson and Arthur J. Hanson, eds., *Atlantic Fisheries and Coastal Communities: Fisheries Decision-Making Case Studies.* Halifax, N.S.: Dalhousie Ocean Studies Programme, 133–164.

Dawes, Robyn M. (1973) "The Commons Dilemma Game: An N-Person Mixed-Motive Game with a Dominating Strategy for Defection." *ORI Research Bulletin,* vol. 13, no. 2 (Sept.), 1–12.

———————— (1975) "Formal Models of Dilemmas in Social Decision Making." In Martin F. Kaplan and Steven Schwartz, eds., *Human Judgment and Decision Processes: Formal and Mathematical Approaches.* New York: Academic Press.

Dawes, Robyn M., Jeanne McTavish, and Harriet Shaklee (1977) "Behavior, Communication, and Assumptions about Other People's Behavior in a Commons Dilemma Situation." *Journal of Personality and Social Psychology,* vol. 35, no. 1 (Jan.), 1–11.

DeAlessi, Louis (1980) "The Economics of Property Rights: A Review of the Evidence." *Research in Law and Economics,* vol. 2,

1–47.

Demsetz, Harold (1967) "Toward a Theory of Property Rights." *American Economics Review*, vol. 62, no. 2 (May), 347–359.

Ehrenfeld, David W. (1972) *Conserving Life on Earth*. New York: Oxford University Press.

Elkin, Stephen L. (1985) "Economic and Political Rationality." *Polity*, vol. 18, no. 2 (winter), 253–271.

Feeny, David (1982) *The Political Economy of Productivity: Thai Agricultural Development 1880–1975*. Vancouver, B.C.: University of British Columbia Press.

─────────── (1986) "Where Do We Go From Here?: Observations on the Implications for the Research Agenda." Paper prepared for a meeting of the Panel on Common Property Resource Management of the Board on Science and Technology for International Development (BOSTID), National Academy of Sciences/National Research Council, Washington, D.C.

Giddens, Anthony (1979) *Central Problems in Social Theory: Action, Structure and Contradiction in Social Analysis*. Berkeley: University of California Press.

Godwin, Kenneth, and W. Bruce Shepard (1979) "Forcing Squares, Triangles and Ellipses into a Circular Paradigm: The Use of the Commons Dilemma in Examining the Allocation of Common Resources." *Western Political Quarterly*, vol. 32, no. 3 (Sept.), 265–277.

Gordon, H. Scott (1954) "The Economic Theory of a Common-Property Resource: The Fishery." *Journal of Political Economy*, vol. 62, no. 2 (April), 124–142.

Grofman, Bernard, and Jonathan Pool (1975) "Bayesian Models for Iterated Prisoner's Dilemma Games." *General Systems*, vol. 20, 185–194.

Guth, Werner (1985) "An Extensive Game Approach to Modelling the Nuclear Deterrence Debate." *Zeitschrift fur die gesamte Staatswissenschaft*, vol. 141, 525–538.

Hardin, Garrett (1968) "The Tragedy of the Commons." *Science*, vol. 162 (Dec.), 1243–1248.

─────────── (1978) "Political Requirements for Preserving Our Common Heritage." In Howard P. Brokaw, ed., *Wildlife and America*. Washington, D.C.: Council on Environmental Quality, 310–317.

Hardin, Russell (1982) *Collective Action*. Baltimore: Johns Hopkins University Press.

Hayami, Yujiro, and Vernon Ruttan (1985) *Agricultural Development: An International Perspective*. Baltimore: Johns Hopkins University Press.

Heilbroner, Robert L. (1974) *An Inquiry into the Human Prospect*. New York: Norton.

Hofstadter, Douglas R. (1979) *Godel, Escher, Bach: An Eternal Golden Braid*. New York: Basic Books.

Humboldt, Wilhelm von (1836) *Uber die Verschiedenheit des Menschlichen Sprachbaues*. Berlin: Druckerei der Koniglichen Akademie der Wissenschaften.

Kaitala, Veijo (1986) "Game-Theory Models of Fisheries Management—A Survey." In T. Basar, ed., *Dynamic Games and Applications in Economics*. Berlin: Springer-Verlag, 252–266.

Kimber, Richard (1981) "Collective Action and the Fallacy of the Liberal Fallacy." *World Politics*, vol. 33, no. 2 (Jan.), 178–196.

Kiser, Larry, and Elinor Ostrom (1982) "The Three Worlds of Action: A Metatheoretical Synthesis of Institutional Approaches." In Elinor Ostrom, ed., *Strategies of Political Inquiry*. Beverly Hills: Sage, 179–222.

Knapp, Keith, and H. J. Vaux (1982) "Barriers to Effective Groundwater Management: The California Case." *Groundwater*, vol. 20, no. 1 (Jan./Feb.), 61–66.

Kragt, Alphons J.C. van de, John M. Orbell, and Robyn M. Dawes (1983) "The Minimal Contributing Set as a Solution to Public Goods Problems." *American Political Science Review*, vol. 77, no. 1, 112–122.

Levhari, D., and L. Mirman (1980) "The Great Fish War: An Example Using a Dynamic Cournot-Nash Solution." *Bell Journal of Economics*, 322–334.

Lewis, Tracy R., and James Cowens (1983) "Cooperation in the Commons: An Application of Repetitious Rivalry." Dept. of Economics, University of British Columbia, Vancouver, B.C. Mimeo.

Lloyd, William F. (1977) "On the Checks to Population." In Garrett Hardin and John Baden, eds., *Managing the Commons*. San Francisco: Freeman. First published in 1833.

Luce, R. Duncan, and Howard Raiffa (1957) *Games and Decisions: Introduction and Critical Survey*. New York: Wiley.

Lumsden, Malvern (1973) "The Cyprus Conflict as a Prisoner's Dilemma." *Journal of Conflict Resolution*, vol. 17, no. 1 (March), 7–32.

Majone, Giandomenico (1986) "Policy Science." In F. X. Kaufmann, G. Majone, and V. Ostrom, eds., *Guidance, Control, and Evaluation in the Public Sector*. Berlin and New York: de Gruyter, 61–70.

McCay, Bonnie J. (1980) "A Fishermen's Cooperative: Indigenous Resource Management in a Complex Society." *Anthropological Quarterly*, vol. 53, no. 1 (Jan.), 29–38.

McKean, Margaret A. (1986) "Management of Traditional Common Lands (Iriaichi) in Japan." In National Research Council, *Proceedings of the Conference on Common-Property Resource Management*. Washington, D.C.: National Academy Press, 533–589.

Neher, P. A. (1978) "The Pure Theory of the Muggery." *American Economics Review*, vol. 68, no. 3 (June), 437–445.

Netting, Robert McC. (1972) "Of Men and Meadows: Strategies of Alpine Land Use." *Anthropological Quarterly*, vol. 45, no. 3, 132–144.

―――― (1976) "What Alpine Peasants Have in Common: Observations on Communal Tenure in a Swiss Village." *Human Ecology*, vol. 4, no. 2 (June), 135–146.

North, Douglass C. (1981) *Structure and Change in Economic History*. New York: Norton.

Oakerson, Ronald J. (1986) "A Model for the Analysis of Common-Property Problems." In National Research Council, *Proceedings of the Conference on Common-Property Resource Management*. Washington, D.C.: National Academy Press, 13–30.

Ophuls, William (1973) "Leviathan or Oblivion." In Herman E. Daley, ed., *Toward a Steady State Economy*. San Francisco: Freeman.

Orbell, John M., and L. A. Wilson (1978) "Institutional Solutions to the *N*-Prisoners' Dilemma." *American Political Science Review*, vol. 72, no. 2 (June), 411–421.

Ostrom, Elinor (1965) "Public Entrepreneurship: A Case Study in Groundwater Management." Ph.D. diss., University of California at Los Angeles.

————— (1986a) "An Agenda for the Study of Institutions." *Public Choice*, vol. 48, 3–25.

————— (1986b) "A Method of Institutional Analysis." In F. X. Kaufmann, G. Majone, and V. Ostrom, eds., *Guidance, Control, and Evaluation in the Public Sector*. Berlin and New York: de Gruyter, 459–475.

————— (1986c) "Multiorganizational Arrangements and Coordination: An Application of Institutional Analysis." In F. X. Kaufmann, G. Majone, and V. Ostrom, eds., *Guidance, Control, and Evaluation in the Public Sector*. Berlin and New York: de Gruyter, 495–510.

————— (1987) "Institutional Arrangements for Resolving the Commons Dilemma: Some Contending Approaches." In Bonnie J. McCay and James Acheson, eds., *The Question of the Commons*. Tucson: University of Arizona Press, 250–265

Ostrom, Vincent (1980) "Artisanship and Artifact." *Public Administration Review*, vol. 40, no. 4 (July/Aug.), 309–317.

————— (1982) "A Forgotten Tradition: The Constitutional Level of Analysis." In Judith A. Gillespie and Dina A. Zinnes, eds., *Missing Elements in Political Inquiry: Logic and Levels of Analysis*. Beverly Hills: Sage, 237–252.

————— (1985) "The Constitution of Order in Human Societies: Conceptualizing the Nature and Magnitude of the Task in Institutional Analysis and Development." Paper presented at the International Political Science Association meetings, Paris, July, 15–20.

————— (1987) *The Political Theory of a Compound Republic: Designing the American Experiment*. Rev. ed. Lincoln: University of Nebraska Press.

Picardi, A. C., and W. W. Seifert (1977) "A Tragedy of the Commons in the Sahel." *Ekistics*, vol. 43 (May), 297–304.

Plott, Charles R. (1979) "The Application of Laboratory Experimental Methods to Public Choice." In Clifford S. Russell, ed., *Collective Decision Making: Applications from Public Choice Theory*. Baltimore: Johns Hopkins University Press, 137–160.

Prigogine, Ilya (1978) "Time, Structure, and Fluctuations." *Science*, vol. 201, no. 4358 (Sept.), 777–785.

Rolph, Elizabeth (1982) "Government Allocation of Property Rights: Why and How." Technical report. Santa Monica, Calif.: RAND Corporation.

Saussure, Ferdinand de (1960) *Course in General Linguistics*. London: Peter Owen. First published posthumously in 1916 as *Cours de linguistique generale*.

Scharpf, Fritz W. (1985) "Ideological Conflict on the Public-Private Frontier: Some Exploratory Notes." Working paper. Berlin: Wissenschaftszentrum.

Searle, John (1969) *Speech Acts: An Essay in the Philosophy of Language*. London: Cambridge University Press.

Selten, Reinhard (1975) "Reexamination of the Perfectness Concept for Equilibrium Points in Extensive Games." *International Journal of Game Theory*, vol. 4, 25–55.

─────────── (1978) "The Chain-Store Paradox." *Theory and Decision*, vol. 9, no. 2 (April), 127–159.

Shepsle, Kenneth A. (1979a) "Institutional Arrangements and Equilibrium in Multidimensional Voting Models." *American Journal of Political Science*, vol. 23, no. 1 (Feb.), 27–59.

─────────── (1979b) "The Role of Institutional Structure in the Creation of Policy Equilibrium." In Douglas W. Rae and Theodore J. Eismeier, eds., *Public Policy and Public Choice*. Sage Yearbooks in Politics and Public Policy, vol. 6. Beverly Hills: Sage, 249–283.

Shepsle, Kenneth A., and Barry Weingast (1984) "Legislative Politics and Budget Outcomes." In G. Mills and J. Palmer, eds., *Federal Budget Policy in the 1980s*. Washington, D.C.: Urban Institute, 343–367.

Shubik, Martin (1982) *Game Theory in the Social Sciences: Concepts and Solutions*. 2 vols. Cambridge, Mass.: MIT Press.

Siy, Robert Y., Jr. (1982) *Community Resources Management:*

Lessons from the Zanjera. Quezon City: University of the Philippines Press.

Smith, Robert J. (1981) "Resolving the Tragedy of the Commons by Creating Private Property Rights in Wildlife." *CATO Journal*, vol. 1, no. 2 (autumn), 439–468.

Snidal, Duncan (1985) "Coordination Versus Prisoners' Dilemma: Implications for International Cooperation and Regimes." *American Political Science Review*, vol. 79, no. 4 (Dec.), 923–942.

Sobel, Jordan Howard (1985) "Utility Maximizers in Iterated Prisoner's Dilemmas." In Richmond Campbell and Lanning Sowden, eds., *Paradoxes of Rationality and Cooperation*. Vancouver, B.C.: University of British Columbia Press, 306–319.

Stillman, Peter G. (1975) "The Tragedy of the Commons: A Reanalysis." *Alternatives*, vol. 4, no. 2, 12–15.

Ullmann-Margalit, Edna (1977) *The Emergence of Norms*. New York: Oxford University Press.

Uphoff, Norman (1985) "People's Participation in Water Management: Gal Oya, Sri Lanka." In Jean Claude Garcia-Zamor, ed., *Public Participation in Development Planning and Management: Cases from Africa and Asia*. Boulder, Colo.: Westview Press, 131–178.

Wade, Robert (1986) "Common-Property Resource Management in South Indian Villages." In National Research Council, *Proceedings of the Conference on Common-Property Resource Management*. Washington, D.C.: National Academy Press, 231–257.

Welch, W. P. (1983) "The Political Feasibility of Full Ownership Property Rights: The Cases of Pollution and Fisheries." *Policy Sciences*, vol. 16, no. 2 (Nov.), 165–180.

Weschler, Louis F. (1968) *Water Resources Management: The Orange County Experience*. California Government Series no. 14., Institute of Governmental Affairs, University of California at Davis.

Wiegandt, E. B. (1977) "Communalism and Conflict in the Swiss Alps." Ph.D. diss., University of Michigan, Ann Arbor.

Wilson, John (1986) "Subjective Probability and the Prisoner's Dilemma." *Management Sciences*, vol. 32, no. 1 (Jan.), 45–55.

Wilson, Rick K. (1985) "Constraints on Social Dilemmas: An

Institutional Approach." *Annals of Operations Research*, vol. 2, 183–200.

Witt, Ulrich (1986) "Evolution and Stability of Cooperation without Enforceable Contracts." *Kyklos*, vol. 39, 245–265.

Wittgenstein, Ludwig (1953) *Philosophical Investigations*. Oxford: Blackwell and Mott. Published posthumously.

5

Ronald J. Oakerson

Reciprocity: A Bottom-Up View of Political Development

Introduction

Development is usually viewed from one of two angles, assumed to be complementary. One is economic development, associated with the growth of markets, firms, and industries. The other is political development, associated with the rise of democratic states—sovereign governments, each with an appropriate administrative apparatus (a bureaucracy), political apparatus (competitive political parties and a representative parliament), and legal apparatus (a unified system of courts). Both economic and political development tend to be viewed as "national" in character—as different aspects of an integrated process of "nation-building." Building a new nation is frequently thought to entail the destruction of diverse organizational capabilities associated with an older order. Instead of adding incrementally

---

I am very grateful to David Feeny, John Kincaid, Elinor Ostrom, Vincent Ostrom, Hartmut Picht, and Susan Wynne for their insightful comments on earlier drafts.

to an existing organizational infrastructure, the task of nation-building is presumed to involve the creation of a new and dominant mode of organization, the nation-state, that largely displaces traditional patterns of association labeled, often pejoratively, as manifestations of "colonialism" and "tribalism."

The purpose of this paper is to offer a new conception of political development different from that implied by "nation-building," drawing upon the following ideas: (1) reciprocity, (2) primary local units of collective action, and (3) constitutional choice. A discussion of development processes in these terms then follows.

Reciprocity

At the core of economic thought, including development economics, lies the concept of exchange. This concept denotes the economic nexus, the basic relationship between individuals in a market model. An exchange is based upon an explicit quid pro quo between two parties. It is a productive relationship in the Pareto-superior sense that both parties are left better off while no one is left worse off. An exchange is also a relatively complete transaction, that is, its value does not depend on future exchanges (though some of the transactions we ordinarily treat as exchange do not quite meet this criterion). As economic development occurs, the range of opportunities for exchange increases. When we look upon economic development as a process over time, rather than as the state of a system at a point in time, what we observe is an expanding set of choices for constituting exchange relationships.

Is there a similar process that can be said to characterize political development? Political activity does not consist of exchanges in the market sense of the term. This point was recognized clearly by John Dewey (1927), who defined a "public" as a group of people affected by a transaction but not party to it. A political process consists of activity that secures the representation of those interests not fully accounted for in market transactions. Since Dewey, economists have, beginning in the 1950s, elaborated numerous models of such relationships—externalities, common-pool resources, and public goods. These problems cannot effectively be addressed by the creation of markets organized to facilitate exchanges among affected persons.

The question, however, is whether there is some analogous relationship that, like exchange in the case of economic development, characterizes political development. (I am assuming development of a democratic character, but I leave aside for the moment the problem of defining democracy.) The standard economic analysis simply presumes a "government" capable of addressing "nonmarket" issues.[1] What those "nonmarket" or governmental relationships might consist of is usually left unspecified. The implicit model of political development as nation-building presumes that national elections, national legislation, and national administration are the central processes that characterize political development. Unanswered in this conception, however, is the character of the political nexus—the sort of relationship among persons out of which a productive political community is constructed. Is the nexus of political development one that is productive in the sense that exchange is productive?

I suggest that *productive political relationships* follow a pattern of "reciprocity," and that reciprocal behavior is the activity that characterizes a productive politics. Political development, parallel to economic development, consists of the expansion of opportunities for productive reciprocity.

Reciprocity is similar to exchange (Boulding, 1972; Oakerson, 1985). Both exchange and reciprocity are mutually productive transfers. Both increase social welfare. Reciprocity is different from exchange, however, in its lack of discreteness. Not a series of discrete exchanges, reciprocity is more like one on-going "exchange" over time, a continuing relationship between or among persons based upon mutual expectations of behavior. In a reciprocal relationship, each individual contributes to the welfare of others with an expectation that others will do likewise, but without a fully contingent quid pro quo. One can withdraw from *future* participation, but cannot withhold participation contingent upon the participation of others. Unlike exchange, where each party's action is fully contingent upon the action of others, reciprocal relationships are exposed to the possibility of "free rider" behavior, the strategy of enjoying the contributions of others while contributing nothing oneself. "Shirking" is a form of "easy riding," where one does less than expected in a reciprocal relationship.

The considerations relevant to the establishment and maintenance of reciprocal relationships also differ significantly from those relevant to simple exchange. While it is useful, for some purposes of economic analysis, to abstract from the "real" world and create a simplified mental construct of exchange relationships that are devoid of moral and personal considerations, to treat reciprocity in the same manner is to miss its most important dimensions. The establishment and maintenance of reciprocity depends critically upon the properties of trust, fairness, and mutual respect. The language and precepts of moral reasoning are fundamental to reciprocity (see chapter 12 of this book). While it is possible for exchange to occur on quite a narrow base of agreement, reciprocity requires broader agreement on the basic norms of social interaction.

The exchange "model," which I have described, must, of course, be distinguished from the range and variety of "exchanges" that are known to occur.[2] This exchange model is in some cases more a caricature than an accurate representation. Yet it embodies a set of assumptions that underlies most of the analytics in microeconomics. Some economists (Williamson, 1979; R. McKean, 1975) have recognized that certain "exchanges"—labor contracts, for example—involve the establishment of long-term relationships not easily understood in terms of ordinary exchange. The contract becomes more like a "constitution" that articulates in general terms the basic rules of a continuing association. Outcomes then depend more upon the degree of reciprocity that develops in a continuing relationship than upon the explicit terms of an "exchange" that occurs at the time a contract is signed.

Reciprocity occurs as both pair-wise (two-person) and N-person relationships. Pair-wise reciprocity tends to be treated in sociological circles as "social exchange"; N-person reciprocity is generally denoted as "collective action"[3] (Olson, 1965). Both involve the ability of people to make extended commitments to one another over time.

Much more than an ordinary exchange relationship is involved, even when some of the language and procedure of exchange is used. Coercive arrangements can be used in the maintenance of reciprocal relationships, as in the maintenance of exchange relationships by means of contract law; but coercion is distinctly secondary in both exchange and reciprocity insofar as individuals contribute to the well-being of one another. The problem of collective action, as developed by Mancur Olson (1965), for example, is greatly clarified when we realize that it is the establishment and maintenance of reciprocity, not simply the introduction of coercion, that is at issue.

It is widely recognized that political development turns upon the creation of new capabilities for collective action in order to provide public goods and to manage common-pool resources. The conclusion frequently drawn, however, is that instrumentalities of coercion need to be strengthened as a substitute for ordinary social relationships based upon willing consent. Potential recourse to coercion may be a necessary condition of reciprocity in large groups; it may be a convenient tool of reciprocity even in smaller groups; but it is never a sufficient condition of reciprocity in any group. *How to make coercive instrumentalities serve the interests of reciprocity is the central problem of politics and political development.* This is a much more delicate and complex task than the mere creation and use of coercive capabilities.

Taming the use of coercion is not the only difficulty involved in the establishment and maintenance of reciprocity as a base for development. Indeed, the inability to draw freely upon coercion underscores the critical need for trust and mutual adherence to norms of fairness in order to sustain reciprocity. Trust and fairness depend in part upon the mental constructs that individuals use to understand their relation to one another. It follows that development is constrained by the conceptions of social order that prevail in a society.[4] If individuals share an image of society that is extremely hierarchical, or egalitarian but cutthroat, reciprocity will be slow to emerge. In such a society, much of the task of development is intellectual or philosophical. It entails the creation and dissemination of *ideas* capable of transforming the basic conception of social relationships that, for the society in question, establishes the parameters of permissible social change.

Primary Local Units

National development efforts easily become preoccupied with human relationships on a grand scale. Massive projects are frequently an important ingredient in development. Overlooked, neglected, or taken for granted in this perspective are the social infrastructures of development, consisting of a network of relationships among people that requires, in the aggregate, large investments of time and effort to build. In order for large-scale development efforts to serve the interests of discrete communities in a society, these efforts must be tied to infrastructures that are rooted in human associations based upon reciprocity.

Near the base of the social infrastructure in any society can be found collective units—one step removed from family relationships—that tend to nurture reciprocity. Tocqueville referred to the "village or township" as "the only association which is so perfectly natural that, wherever a number of men are collected, it seems to constitute itself" (Tocqueville, [1835] 1945: 62). Such small-scale associations can be viewed as the *primary local units* of collective action in a society. Whether formally or informally constituted, they are ubiquitous. Tocqueville went on to point out, however, that "although the existence of the township is coeval with that of man, its freedom is an infrequent and fragile thing" (p. 62). His subsequent account of the early American township can also be read as a theoretical argument that the freedom and autonomy of primary local units, such as the township, are positively related to citizen reciprocity and local productivity (Oakerson, 1986).

Primary local units, although they may acquire coercive capabilities, emerge from the voluntary face-to-face interactions of people who join together to provide themselves with collective goods. They tend, therefore, to be limited to those who directly benefit from those collective efforts. These local efforts can become the basis for a wider range of collective activities that extend beyond the immediate community; or, contrariwise, larger collectivities can impose restrictions upon primary local units that inhibit their productivity. In general, the productivity of primary local units depends upon a number of factors both internal and external to their organization.

A wide variety of primary local units exist in both highly developed and less developed countries. Some part of what is called "local government" might be construed as a set of primary local units, but not all. In addition to residential communities, or neighborhoods, primary local units can be discovered in fisheries, pastures, and woodlots, among other common-property resources (see National Academy of Sciences, 1986). New primary local units are emerging in relation to public housing units and work places. In the realm of religion, the parish or local congregation is the primary local unit of church organization. The common interests that bring communities together vary. (See chapter 7 of this book for a detailed discussion of a primary local unit based on kinship in Botswana.) Vincent Ostrom (1987a) has emphasized the broader political significance of the great variety of primary local units in maintaining a *res publica*, or public realm of interaction and communication outside the official realm of government, even in the face of repressive regimes.

Despite the ubiquity of primary local units, the degree to which general units of government give formal recognition to and make explicit use of these community-based associations varies widely. *Internally*, primary local units tend to be self-governing, being governed directly by those persons who derive immediate benefits from the collective activities. *Externally*, some primary local units have de facto autonomy, but no political guarantee of that autonomy. Others, including (historically) Tocqueville's townships, have legal autonomy, and are subject only to general rules of law, not to administrative control by general units of government.

The immediate advantage of a greater reliance on primary local units is a higher level of local productivity. Citizens, instead of "spinning their wheels" in seeking action from central bureaucracies or distant governments, practice self-help. They apply their resources to productive activity, as opposed to "rent-seeking" (seeking to gain at the expense of others), which is usually considered to be unproductive economic behavior. Most literature on rent-seeking assumes this behavior to be virtually synonymous with political activity. If political development is grounded in primary local units, then politics can become a means of increasing the "common wealth" of a society, and so contribute to the total set of goods available.

The willingness of citizens to contribute to productive social activity depends upon institutional arrangements that link individual self-interest with reciprocity. To pursue one's self-interest and to practice reciprocity with others are rational, consistent behaviors. Yet individuals can also interpret their self-interest in ways that are inconsistent with reciprocity, ways that lead to various manifestations of free-rider behavior. Tocqueville's reference to "self-interest rightly understood" ([1835] 1945 vol. 2: 131) is to self-interest practiced within the limits of reciprocity. Primary local units support the pursuit of "self-interest rightly understood" by providing a social context that encourages self-interested individuals to behave with reciprocity. The returns enjoyed in common from the joint efforts of individuals are visible and apparent to each member of a community. Individuals have an interest in enlisting the contributions of others; but it is difficult to ask others to contribute without reciprocating. Out of self-interest, therefore, individuals tend to observe the norm of reciprocity, leading each person to contribute with others to a stream of joint undertakings that, on balance, benefit everyone.

The long-term advantage of relying upon primary units is of still greater significance, that is, the learning that occurs among local citizens who engage in patterns of reciprocity, and the extension of that reciprocity to more specialized relationships involving larger communities of interest. Reciprocity learned among local citizens can be transferred to relationships among local communities and, by a variety of principal-agent relationships, to the governance of larger communities of interest including "the nation." Learning, and the extension of learning to new circumstances, is a developmental process. On reflection, it is difficult to imagine a process of political development without parallel processes of learning. The processes of development must therefore be consistent with the conditions for learning and its diffusion as new opportunities are created and new problems arise.

The opportunity for individuals to learn how to function in a mutually productive manner depends upon a plentiful number of situations in which social knowledge can be generated, conjectures tried out, and errors corrected. A multiplicity of primary units may therefore be a necessary condition of the social learning that is relevant to political development. It was in this sense that Tocqueville characterized local institutions as the primary schools of democracy.

Learning and reciprocity are closely tied to the capacity of primary local units for self-governance. In a face-to-face community, officers can be held accountable as much by social processes of pair-wise reciprocity as by formal procedures of election. Reliance on professionals need not be a dependency relationship, and a large number of opportunities can be made available to ordinary citizens to participate in local affairs. Yet the productivity of primary local units also depends upon the scope of action allowed to them by more inclusive political communities. Primary local units can be regulated or preempted by overriding political (or, in the case of the church, ecclesiastical) authority to such an extent that the costs of productive local action become prohibitive to the individuals involved.

Primary local units of collective action bring the processes of human reciprocity to bear upon the problems and opportunities created by jointness and interdependence—publicness—among human beings. Primary local units are to political reciprocity as a marketplace is to economic exchange: a means of association framed by *a set of rules designed to facilitate mutually productive behavior in relation to a particular set of common problems and opportunities.*

Constitutional Choice

Constitutional choice is the choice of rules used to design political institutions. As such, a constitution consists of *a set of rules designed to facilitate reciprocal behavior in relation to particular sets of common problems and opportunities.* In the context of nation-building, constitutional choice may be viewed as providing a point of departure but little more. One of the keynotes of "modern" political science is that constitutions are rhetorical devices used to justify rather than design arrangements of government. In the nation-building model of political development, this is probably the case. But in the alternative model of political development being urged here, constitutional choice is more than a point of departure—more than a rhetorical device of those who rule. It is, rather, a legal capability, enjoyed by an indefinite number of communities within a society, to constitute and reconstitute mutually productive associations (see Ostrom, 1987b).

For constitutional choice to work—and to serve as an instrument of political development—a variety of communities must be able to create a variety of different types of association. Among these communities will be found "the nation." In any political system there must be at least one, but not necessarily only one, general unit of government. It is not necessary that a general unit of government directly create or constitute all other governmental units. The creation of primary local units, especially, can be reserved to citizens, acting through processes of constitutional choice established for this purpose. The constitution of general units of government is simply one essential element in a broader constitutional order.

The *rules of association* in a society are of a fundamental constitutional order. These include rules of voluntary association and varying degrees of involuntary association according to specified procedures. Rules of association lay the foundation for continuing processes of constitutional choice in a society. In the American context, the basic rules of association would include the First Amendment of the U.S. Constitution; state constitutional and statutory provisions relating to the creation of corporate charters (both private and public); and general (state) enabling legislation allowing for the creation of various units of governance in relation to specified types of problems.[5] In the creation of public units, rules of association relax the rule of willing consent that is the standard for private units. The choice of an appropriate set of collective decision rules for the creation of public units will tend to vary from one type of unit to another, in response to the different types of problems for which those units are designed. A society therefore requires *at least two* levels of *constitutional* choice, one to specify (and modify) rules of association, and another to use those rules for constituting new associations in relation to discrete problems and opportunities. While this can be conceptualized as a bi-level phenomenon, a large and complex democratic society may create a complex constitutional order that consists of many opportunities for constitutional choice.

Constitutional choices contrast to program choices or operational choices. A national development orientation tends to focus on the latter, viewed as a series of management or implementation problems. The potential for development comes to be viewed as an administrative challenge, to be met by marshaling resources through bureaucratic processes. Lost in this conception is a view of development as an expansion of the capabilities of individuals in various communities to respond to their collective problems through a variety of associations. Multiplying the opportunities for collective action is a development process that depends more critically upon constitutional choice than upon public management.

Development Processes

With these three intellectual tools—reciprocity, primary local units, and constitutional choice—we can construct an alternative conception of political development. That conception begins with the recognition, little more than a truism, that any process of development is *incremental* (Ostrom, 1987a, refers to "emergent" properties). The truism alerts us to a critical consideration: efforts directed toward encouraging development ought to pay careful attention to the existing base. In general, a useful maxim in development work would be "Don't destroy the base!"[6] Or, more precisely, "Decide what part of the existing structure of society constitutes a useful base, and seek to preserve and build upon it." In any society, the potential development base consists of existing patterns of exchange and reciprocity.

We know that local communities, if simply let alone by a central government, can frequently develop elaborate patterns of reciprocity in relation to specific problems and opportunities—for example, in the governance of various common-pool resources.[7] These patterns of reciprocity are characterized as "informal" by those who consider only state instrumentalities to be "formal." The evidence is, nevertheless, that such patterns reflect *enduring forms* of organization. New institutional arrangements can be built on this durable base. To do otherwise is to waste scarce institutional capital.

Institutional development of this sort can take a number of forms. One is for existing *primary* units to develop *secondary* units designed to enhance primary-unit productivity, perhaps by taking into account somewhat larger communities of interest or by capturing greater economies-of-scale. Secondary units need not exhibit the same self-governing characteristics as primary units if closely tied to primary units in an interorganizational milieu.[8] (Many secondary units can be purely private associations, organized on the model of trade associations or consortia.) Another possibility is for individuals facing new problems and opportunities to establish new primary local units. A new housing development, new conditions of scarcity in a common-pool resource, the establishment of a school, problems of street crime and disorder—any of these circumstances can provide an occasion for the organization of new primary local units. New primary and secondary units both grow out of, and extend further, the existing patterns of reciprocity among persons and their agents.

For this sort of development to occur, the rules of association in a society must be sufficiently open to allow for new associations to emerge and, in the case of public associations, must make available certain powers of government. Instead of a monopoly on the powers of government, a system based upon a reiteration of constitutional choice allows for a dispersion of powers, not simply among existing institutions and offices, but within an expanding set of public units. Inchoate communities must be able to overcome holdout problems in order to establish new patterns of reciprocity. A strict reliance on a rule of unanimity may induce individuals to abandon reciprocity instead of cultivate it. Rules of association may therefore relax the rule of unanimity in circumstances that are carefully circumscribed by law. This will allow various communities to exercise constitutional prerogatives.

The importance of reciprocity in patterns of political development is to ensure that development is mutually beneficial among the individuals and communities concerned. In the absence of reciprocity, politics becomes a zero-sum game in which some individuals use the instrumentalities of government to make themselves better off at the expense of others. The long-run consequence of such a process is apt to be negative-sum, resulting in an escalation of poverty, violence, and revolution. Political development without reciprocity makes as much sense as economic development without exchange.

The major objection to reciprocity as a process of political development is the view that it is confined to very small associations, organized on the basis of face-to-face relationships, and that it cannot, therefore, be used to constitute a large society. As argued above, reciprocity is indeed nurtured in primary local units, and the proliferation of such units is instrumental in the process of development. But primary local units are not sufficient. Primary units can develop secondary units to address larger-scale concerns. General units of government are required to maintain a general framework of social order. To what extent can patterns of reciprocity predominate in relation to general units of government in a large and complex society? The usual answer given is, Very little if at all.

The central issue is coercion. How can coercion be consistent with reciprocity? A coerced exchange is a nonexchange. How can reciprocity be any different? This is a basic puzzle in political theory.[9] One solution that has been developed in Western thought is to structure the institutions of coercion on the same pattern as reciprocity. The use of coercion itself must be reciprocal: one who coerces others today is subject to potential coercion tomorrow. It is this configuration of relationships that we refer to as a "rule of law." Only to the extent that those who exercise the prerogatives of government in a society are themselves subject to a rule of law, on the petition of citizens, can the processes of reciprocity extend to patterns of political development.

Many less-developed nations exhibit severe asymmetries in the distribution of political authority. The impoverishment of these societies is as much political as it is economic. The absence of a rule of law confines reciprocity to face-to-face communities where individuals engage in repeated interactions and there is an underlying symmetry of their social condition. The extension of reciprocity to a broader set of relationships is sharply curtailed. Rules of association are then designed to inhibit rather than to facilitate the establishment of autonomous units, and patterns of dominance and subordination prevail over patterns of reciprocity.

Even highly asymmetric political relationships nevertheless exhibit some degree—however small—of reciprocity. Rulership always comes at a price, and those on top will be keenly aware of the political price they must pay to stay where they are. To begin to modify a general constitution in which serious asymmetry exists, what needs to be done is to raise the price of rulership. To do this, one must find ways of introducing new elements of symmetry in order to leverage greater reciprocity from rulers. Success will depend upon a capacity to sustain such relatively autonomous organizations as private businesses, labor unions, churches, and local governments, which are able to constrain the decisions of rulers. The broad political significance of these organizations can come to overshadow their ostensible purposes. Only the development of countervailing structures of authority and power can introduce greater reciprocity into the general constitution of a society in which serious political asymmetries exist.

In many less-developed societies there can be little progress in the extension of reciprocity without prolonged political struggle. But, as V. I. Lenin has taught us, every such political movement must have a theory. If the theory that informs the struggle is one in which the purpose of the movement is to seize control of the center of power in order to exercise the prerogatives of rulership, such a movement cannot afford to extend patterns of reciprocity. To succeed in extending reciprocity, the purpose of the struggle must be to alter the conditions of rulership, not simply to displace those who rule. The gradual extension of reciprocity in a society must be accompanied by patterns of social learning in which individuals learn to take account of one another and to act in relation to one another only within limits. Learning those limits, and gradually institutionalizing those limits, is the essential condition of productive political relationships.

Conclusion

Development is built on human aspirations. It has many dimensions: economic, social, political, and intellectual. To enable a people to realize—or to reach toward—its aspirations requires many different institutions. Efforts to provide tools of development must not lose sight of the essential development processes: exchange and reciprocity. Both are also highly dependent upon a process of learning. *Institutions* of development must be designed to foster essential *processes* of development. Primary units of association and structures of constitutional choice are perhaps foremost among these institutions. Moreover, exchange and reciprocity are not independent phenomena. The establishment and maintenance of the institutions of exchange—markets, firms, laws, courts—are highly dependent upon productive politics, that is, upon reciprocity. If political development is to serve the fulfillment of human aspirations, it can not be divorced from reciprocity, any more than economic development can be divorced from exchange. Development must both spring from reciprocity and serve it.

Notes

1. An alternative tradition in economic theory, usually labeled as "public choice," has explicitly addressed the difficulties inherent in constituting governments able to correct market deficiencies. The seminal work is that of James M. Buchanan and Gordon Tullock (1962).

2. By the same token, a reciprocity model compels a distinction between the simplified characteristics of the model and the rich array of reciprocal relationships that occur in any society.

3. Both "social exchange" and "collective action" are in a sense misnomers. Social exchange is not exchange in the market sense; it cannot be explained on the basis of immediate return. (There is a large literature that draws upon social-exchange theory; see Blau [1974]: 204–211], for a discussion of the concept of social exchange in much the same terms as reciprocity.) Collective action, by the same token, is not the action of a collectivity, but rather the reciprocal actions of individuals in relation to one another. Collectivities can

make choices; but only individuals can act. To the extent that individuals "act" collectively, they do so by virtue of mutual understanding and coordination.

4. I am indebted to Susan Wynne for suggesting this point to me.

5. One would also include Article IV, Section 3, of the U.S. Constitution pertaining to the admission of new states to the union (not an unimportant provision in the course of American political and economic development); and Article VI, which includes treaties as a part of the supreme law of the land and, thus, includes the possibility of constituting multinational communities of which the United States is a constituent member.

6. This maxim was recognized by Amilcar Cabral (1973) in his advice to "return to the source" (see especially "National Liberation and Culture," 39–56).

7. See especially the essays by Berkes, Wade, and McKean in National Academy of Sciences 1986.

8. In Tocqueville's account of early America, the county is a secondary unit used to provide goods and services local in nature but beyond the capability of individual townships.

9. Thomas Hobbes (in *Leviathan*) and J. J. Rousseau (in *On the Social Contract*) each developed interesting responses. In order for reciprocity to prevail in ordinary human relationships, Hobbes thought it necessary to allow the absolute dominance of a sovereign ruler who functioned as the source of law. In Hobbes's conception, social relationships are based upon reciprocity, but political relationships are based upon dominance. The productivity of social relationships depends upon a rule of law that is exogenously imposed. Rousseau developed the antithesis of Hobbes's solution: reciprocity occurs naturally or spontaneously in ordinary human relationships, but must be extended artificially to include rulers. A rule of law is then endogenous to society, rather than imposed by a Hobbesian sovereign. Hobbes's explanation is consistent with the nation-building tradition of development (though much more attentive to the requirement of reciprocity in society), while Rousseau's account provides a basis for the alternative conceptualization advanced in this paper.

Works Cited

Berkes, Fikret (1986) "Marine Inshore Fishery Management in Turkey." In National Research Council, *Proceedings of the Conference on Common-Property Resource Management*. Washington, D.C.: National Academy Press, 63–83.

Blau, Peter M. (1974) *On the Nature of Organization*. New York: Wiley.

Boulding, Kenneth E. (1972) "The Household as Achilles' Heel." *Journal of Consumer Affairs*, vol. 6, 111–119.

Buchanan, James M., and Gordon Tullock (1962) *The Calculus of Consent: Logical Foundations of Constitutional Democracy*. Ann Arbor: University of Michigan Press.

Cabral, Amilcar (1973) *Return to the Source: Selected Speeches of Amilcar Cabral*. New York and London: Monthly Review Press.

Dewey, John (1927) *The Public and Its Problems*. New York: Holt.

Hobbes, Thomas (1960) *Leviathan or the Matter, Forme and Power of a Commonwealth Ecclesiasticall and Civill*. Michael Oakeshott, ed. Oxford: Blackwell. First published in 1651.

McKean, Margaret A. (1986) "Management of Traditional Common Lands (Iriaichi) in Japan." In National Research Council, *Proceedings of the Conference on Common-Property Resource Management*. Washington, D.C.: National Academy Press, 533–589.

McKean, Roland N. (1975) "Economics of Trust, Altruism, and Corporate Responsibility." In Edmund S. Phelps, ed., *Altruism, Morality, and Economic Theory*. New York: Russell Sage, 29–44.

National Research Council (1986) *Proceedings of the Conference on Common-Property Resource Management*. Washington, D.C.: National Academy Press.

Oakerson, Ronald J. (1985) "Reciprocity, Its General Relevance to Politics." Working paper, Workshop in Political Theory and Policy Analysis, Indiana University, Bloomington, Ind.

——— (1986) "The Meaning and Purpose of Local Government: A Classical Perspective." Working paper, Advisory Commission on Intergovernmental Relations, Washington, D.C.

Olson, Mancur (1965) *The Logic of Collective Action*. Cambridge,

Mass.: Harvard University Press.

Ostrom, Vincent (1987a) "Constitutional Foundations for a Theory of System Comparisons: An Inquiry into Problems of Incommensurabilities, Emergent Properties, and Development." Paper presented at the Radein Research Seminar, Redagon, Italy, February 14–25.

——————— (1987b) *The Political Theory of a Compound Republic: Designing the American Experiment.* Rev. ed. Lincoln: University of Nebraska Press.

Rousseau, Jean-Jacques (1978) *On the Social Contract.* Roger D. Masters, ed. New York: St. Martin's Press. First published in 1762 as *Du contrat social.*

Tocqueville, Alexis de (1945) *Democracy in America.* Phillips Bradley, ed. New York: Vintage Books. First published in 1835.

Wade, Robert (1986) "Common-Property Resource Management in South Indian Villages." In National Research Council, *Proceedings of the Conference on Common-Property Resource Management.* Washington, D.C.: National Academy Press, 231–257.

Williamson, Oliver E. (1979) "Transaction-Cost Economics: The Governance of Contractual Relations." *Journal of Law and Economics,* vol. 22, 233–261.

6

David Feeny

The Demand for and Supply of Institutional Arrangements

Introduction

The analysis of the effects of institutions on economic performance lies at the heart of economics. Yet institutional analysis frequently remains implicit and important issues are left unaddressed. There is, however, a growing realization within the discipline of economics of the importance of institutions and the need to analyze them rigorously. The traditional three pillars of economic theory—endowments, technologies, and preferences—are incomplete. The fourth and implicit pillar is institutions. Institutional arrangements inform decision makers about their standing and about the consequences of their behavior. It is institutions that assign authority in relation to the endowments of land, labor, and capital. Institutions matter.

The author acknowledges the many helpful comments of Vincent Ostrom on earlier drafts of the paper. Helpful comments were also received from Syed Ahmad, Daniel W. Bromley, Peter George, Yujiro Hayami, Stuart Mestelman, Elinor Ostrom, Hartmut Picht, Vernon W. Ruttan, T. W. Schultz, and Dan Usher.

That they do matter is recognized indirectly throughout the discipline of economics. Numerous lines of inquiry are based on this premise. Examples include comparative economic systems, the property rights school, theories of contract choice, investigations of alternative market arrangements in experimental economics, and public finance. Yet in many of these subdisciplines the importance of institutions is seen in the somewhat narrow context of particular issues or problems. The broader conclusion that institutions matter in general rather than just in specific contexts is generally left unstated. That institutions matter is a conclusion that has been reached deductively (see, for instance, Arrow, 1985; Solow, 1985). It has also been reached inductively by economic historians attempting to explain the process of economic growth and development (see, for instance, Hicks, 1969; North, 1971, 1978, 1979, 1986; North and Thomas, 1970, 1971, 1973; Davis and North, 1970, 1971; Matthews, 1986).

The prominence of institutional change in the economic history and development literature has several foundations. First, unlike most economists, economic historians and development economists have typically examined the functioning of economies whose institutional endowments have differed markedly from the daily reality of the investigator. For the economic historian the movement backwards in time confronts the scholar with an economy that differs in endowments, technologies, and institutions. Preferences too may have differed, but economists have generally maintained that the basic structure of human wants has remained stable even as the specific items that cater to those desires may have changed. While the economic historian's journey has been through time, the development economist often makes a similar journey across space.

A second path that has led to the realization of the importance of institutions has been that explanations of the factors accounting for growth and development that omit institutions and institutional change are incomplete and unsatisfactory. Growth in factor endowments has clearly contributed to growth in the material standard of living. Yet per capita input growth can account for only a small fraction of per capita output growth. This realization has focused attention on technological change as a mainspring of economic growth. Careful investigations of the process of technological change have revealed that institutions matter both in the generation of technological change and in people's ability to realize the potential gains from such change. Of the former, patent systems, systems of publicly funded agricultural research and development, and investments in human capital are examples. Joint-stock companies, limited liability, and legislation widening access to incorporation have facilitated the accumulation of sufficient capital to realize the economies-of-scale embodied in new technological processes of production and exchange. Studies in economic history, demonstrating a clear interaction between technological and institutional change, have led some investigators to focus on institutions and institutional change in a broader context than that of technological change alone.

If institutions matter—if they affect the performance of an economy—then, to be complete, a theory of economic change must include a theory of institutional change. A simple outline of a framework for the analysis of institutional change is the subject of this essay. The microeconomic theory of exchange presumes ethical, social, and legal foundations that inform parties about how they are expected to act and what kinds of agreements they can enforce (see chapters 11 and 12 of this book). Many macroeconomic models presume a central monetary authority, fiscal authorities, the existence of product and input markets, and a host of supporting institutions. Even though economic theory contains basic approaches of wide generality and generalizes relatively well within major institutional paradigms, it is still conditioned on institutions (Solow, 1985).

The prominent roles of both technological and institutional change in economic growth and development are high on the research agenda of economic historians. The close intellectual relationship reflects the fact that new technologies have often generated incentives for the creation of new institutional arrangements. Several investigators first approached institutional change largely as a by-product of technological change that permitted the potential gains of technological change to be realized (see Hayami and Ruttan,

1971; North and Thomas, 1973). In order to introduce the theory of institutional change then, it is appropriate to begin by briefly reviewing the demand-and-supply approach to the analysis of technological change. This approach serves as a metaphor for organizing our thinking about technological and institutional change. The analysis of technological change is more familiar and provides an analogy for beginning the exploration of institutional change.

The Demand for and Supply of Technological Change

There are several complementary approaches to the specification of the demand for technological change. John Hicks in his *Theory of Wages* ([1932] 1963) proposed that technological change is induced by changes in relative factor prices. As the cost of a factor of production rises, firms substitute, within the existing technology, cheaper factors of production for the now more expensive one. Hicks extended the argument to hypothesize that firms would respond to the trends in relative factor prices by focusing their search for new technologies on new methods that would permit them to substitute the increasingly cheap factors for the increasingly expensive ones. When interpreted within the economic history of modern industrial economies, the rise in real wages was then seen as a driving force behind the inducement of a stream of labor-saving technologies. Hicks did not argue that all technological change was the result of such an inducement mechanism. Firms had an incentive to develop and utilize any technology that reduced cost and increased profit. The argument was, however, that the search was biased toward finding substitutes for increasingly expensive factors of production.

There is in fact abundant evidence linking trends in relative factor prices to directions in the factor-saving bias of technological change (see, for instance, Hayami and Ruttan, 1985; Binswanger, 1974a, 1974b, 1977; Binswanger and Ruttan, 1978). Thus a land-scarce, labor-abundant Japan developed a stream of biological technologies that permitted the substitution of fertilizer and labor for land and raised crop yields. Contemporaneously in the United States, which possessed a land-abundant, labor-scarce economy, a stream of mechanical agricultural technologies were innovated in the nineteenth and twentieth centuries that permitted the substitution of capital and land for labor.

The evidence suggests strongly that the direction and pace of technological change respond to forces that shape expectations about the profits of innovation (additional evidence is discussed in Rosenberg, 1972; Griliches, 1957, 1960). Yet a demand-induced model of technological change is incomplete. High harvest-labor costs and the importance of timeliness in harvest operations created a market in nineteenth-century U.S. agriculture for machines to harvest small grains. The development and diffusion of the reaper and subsequent technological developments are consistent with the demand-induced model. Yet the same incentives existed for the development of machines such as the corn picker, cotton picker, and milking machine. Viable machines for these tasks, however, appeared in the early twentieth century rather than in the mid-nineteenth. What accounts for the delay? An important insight is offered by William Parker (Davis, et al., 1972: 379–389). While the reaper imitated the simple motion of the arm, the other innovations required much more sophisticated devices, ones able to imitate the actions of the human hand. In sum, these innovations were difficult and costly and their emergence was constrained on the supply side (see also Rosenberg, 1972, 1982; Ruttan, 1982; Hayami and Ruttan, 1985; Bogue, 1983).

Extending the Metaphor: The Demand for and Supply of Institutional Change

Just as much of the early investigation of technological change focused on the mechanisms of demand inducement, so a number of prominent works on institutional change employed a Coaseian perspective (Coase, 1960) in which institutions were seen to be altered when the benefits from change exceeded the costs. The approach explicitly recognized the importance of transaction cost in affecting the choice of institutional arrangements. Unfortunately, the political economic aspects of the supply of institutional change were, in general, implicit.

An example might be useful. Douglass C. North and Robert Paul

Thomas (1973) characterize the origins of the feudal system of 900-1500 in Europe as the result of an exchange of protection and justice, supplied by military elites, in return for labor services and other in-kind payments, provided by peasants. The classic manor is seen as a viable institutional arrangement in a land-abundant, labor-scarce economy in which there was a high demand for protection and a military technology with rather limited economies-of-scale. The low population density in conjunction with a lack of security and transportation infrastructure meant that there were only rudimentary product markets. In such an economy, rulers could not rely on the collection of money taxes and instead utilized a portion of the serf's labor services to produce the ruler's consumption bundle. The abundance of land and scarcity of labor implied a system of property rights in man; the high costs of supervising slave labor and lack of a market for the output of large-scale slave-agricultural production implied the choice of serfdom instead of slavery as the form of human property rights (see also Domar, 1970; Engerman, 1973). In North and Thomas's account of economic change in Western Europe, it was population growth, changes in military technology, and the rise of commerce that created the incentives for altering feudal institutions and, in England and the Netherlands in particular, resulted in a set of commercial and private property institutions that contributed to economic development.

A number of additional examples of the demand-induced approach to institutional change could be provided (they would include some of the case studies considered in Anderson and Hill, 1975; Davis and North, 1971; Hayami and Ruttan, 1971; Libecap, 1978; Dennen, 1976; and Umbeck, 1977). The accounts of the evolution of institutional arrangements in these works are insightful and correct up to a point, but the analysis is still incomplete. Although the authors do not, in general, explicitly state that change will occur whenever the marginal social benefits exceed the marginal social costs (including transaction cost) the lack of attention to the supply side of institutional change leaves that impression. In each of the examples given above, institutional change is seen as promoting the growth in efficiency and as being efficient. There is an implicit assumption, with some explicit exceptions, that the fundamental constitutional arrangements afforded a broad choice set, and that a particular set of institutional arrangements was chosen on the basis of its efficiency characteristics. Just as Jacob Schmookler (1962) explicitly suggests that the supply of technical change was highly elastic, and that therefore the direction of embodied technical change responded to the trend in the demand for capital goods, so institutional change is viewed in the earlier literature as being induced by trends in relative prices and the size of the market. It is as if it were being assumed that institutional innovation took place in a perfectly competitive political arena guaranteeing that only efficiency-improving innovations would be selected.

Yet it is not difficult to provide counterexamples either of the adoption of innovations for which the net social benefits were negative, or of the failure to adopt innovations with positive net social benefits. At a more subtle level, it is also possible to provide examples in which the timing of the adoption was affected by the more narrow interests of government officials (see, for instance, Kikuchi and Hayami, 1978a, 1978b; Hayami and Kikuchi, 1978; Hayami, et al., 1976).

An example of the failure to adopt an innovation with positive net social benefits is found in the case of pre-World War II irrigation policy in Thailand (Feeny, 1979b, 1982a, 1982b, 1983a). A divergence of elite net benefits and social net benefits led to failure of the induced public-investment mechanism. The integration of the Thai economy into the international economy in the nineteenth century and appreciation of the price of rice led to a boom in rice exporting, so that the area under paddy cultivation and exports of rice increased dramatically. An important repercussion of these trends was an appreciation in real land prices that in turn focused attention on interventions to increase the productivity of land: agricultural research and irrigation investments. The demand for land-productivity-increasing technical and institutional change was strengthened in the early twentieth century as officials became concerned with the apparent decline in land productivity.

Because of the physical characteristics of the Central Plain of the

Chao Phraya River valley, the region that accounted for the overwhelming bulk of rice exports, a large dam and extensive system of canals were required in order to provide irrigation services for the Central Plain.[1] The broad river valley with its gentle slope precluded effective small-scale projects or piecemeal development. The indivisibility of the facilities and need for coordination over a large geographic area indicated a role for central government as opposed to provincial or local government or local collective-action groups. The latter had been important in the provision of irrigation services in northern Thailand, where the small mountain valleys were conducive to effective small-scale projects.

A proposal for a dam on the Chao Phraya River at Chainat was forthcoming in late 1902. The project was designed by a noted Dutch irrigation engineer, J. Homan van der Heide, who had previously worked in Java. From 1902 through 1909 he repeatedly articulated his proposal and supported his arguments with a detailed plan that included estimates of the pecuniary costs and benefits (increased land taxes, charges for water) to government. Subsequent analysis (Feeny, 1979b, 1982b, 1983a) using the social cost-benefit analysis framework corroborates arguments made by van der Heide that the project offered Thailand substantial positive net social benefits. It would have generated an internal rate of return of 19 to 22 percent, a rate that compared favorably to those earned on other infrastructure investments made in the period, such as railroads. In addition, by the later 1910s or early 1920s, investing in irrigation would have been a cheaper way to expand paddy production than expanding the area under cultivation (Feeny, 1983a). Counterfactual ex ante estimates that utilize only information available at the time of the policy debates on irrigation also indicate a high social rate of return on irrigation investments.

In spite of the cogent arguments by van der Heide and other advocates of investment in irrigation, evidence of the high potential social rate of return on such investment, and the familiarity of Thai officials with the benefits of canal development, irrigation proposals were repeatedly rejected until the post-World War II period when, with the support of the World Bank, the van der Heide project was finally undertaken.

What accounts for the delay? Two divergences were crucial in affecting irrigation policy. First, there was a conflict between the goals of national security and economic development. Thailand was faced with an imperialist threat throughout most of the period. The threat implied high returns in national sovereignty to investments in public administration and the military, and related infrastructure investments, such as railroads. These, in fact, were the investments that Thailand chose to pursue during the period. Such investments were also in the interests of the central government in Bangkok, enhancing its security with respect both to foreign powers and domestic regional elites. A unitary bureaucratic form of government was gradually developed; Bangkok was increasingly able to exert its control over the provinces (Battye 1974; Brown, 1975, 1978; Bunnag, 1968; Holm, 1977; Ramsay, 1971).

The imperialist environment also had important implications for Thai public finance. Treaties signed with the Western powers and Japan in the mid-to-late nineteenth century froze rates of taxation on exports, imports, and land at relatively low rates (and also provided for extraterritoriality). It was not until 1926 that Thailand was able to renegotiate the unequal treaties and regain fiscal autonomy. Thus the ability of Thailand to raise government revenue to support public investment was highly constrained. Thailand was also reluctant to go heavily into debt and risk foreign interference. Irrigation investments that would require foreign loans were therefore unattractive; continuing to rely upon privately financed expansion of the area under cultivation, on the other hand, involved fewer public resources and minimal risk of foreign interference.

The second important divergence was between the private interests of elite government officials and the economic interests of the nation. If the van der Heide project had been undertaken and most of the Central Plain provided with irrigation, tenants would have left the Rangsit area, where many government officials and members of the royal family owned land, to migrate to newly irrigated lands. The largest irrigation investment made in the Central Plain in the pre-World War II period was the Pasak project, designed to benefit the

Rangsit area. Rangsit was also the site of the first rice experiment station in Thailand, established in 1916–1917. Thus when government officials were to be the main beneficiaries of public investments, the demands for interventions to improve land productivity were met; when such interventions would have been harmful to the interests of important officials, the demands were left unmet. This failure had important repercussions for Thai agricultural and economic development.

Thus the supply of institutional change is important; trends in the demand, although necessary, are not sufficient for understanding the path of change. Elements of political economic analysis are crucial; the political and economic costs and benefits to the ruling elites are a key to explaining the nature and scope of change. These inductive insights have been incorporated into more recent analytical thinking about institutional change and reflected in the on-going evolution of thought. Vernon W. Ruttan and Yujiro Hayami (1984; see also Hayami and Ruttan, 1985; Kikuchi and Hayami, 1980; Ruttan, 1978a, 1978b, 1981) have extended and broadened their previous work on induced institutional change, with particular emphasis on the factors affecting the supply of it. Their framework is based on four variables of fundamental importance: resource endowments, technology, institutions, and cultural endowments.

Cultural endowments include not only tastes and preferences but dimensions of culture that structure relationships that have been transmitted from the past. Thus the framework provides scope for the influence of religion and beliefs on the supply of institutional change. It also allows for changes in technology, resource endowments, and institutions to affect culture and thus the cultural endowment in subsequent periods. Institutions are viewed as "the rules of a society or organizations that facilitate coordination among people" (Ruttan and Hayami, 1984: 204). Institutions reflect conventions of behavior that have evolved in societies.

Ruttan and Hayami suggest that their framework be used to analyze the interrelationships between changes in each of the four major variables in a recursive general-equilibrium approach. The framework specifies direct and feedback relationships between changes in each pair of the variables. The demand-and-supply model of technical and institutional change is then seen as being nested in this larger framework.

The important role of net gains to elite decision makers is reflected in Hayami and Ruttan's characterization of the supply of institutional change. They argue that

> the supply of major institutional innovations necessarily involves the mobilization of substantial political resources by political entrepreneurs and innovators. It is useful to think in terms of a supply schedule of institutional innovation that is determined by marginal cost schedules facing political entrepreneurs as they attempt to design new institutions and resolve the conflicts among various vested groups (or suppression of opposition when necessary). We hypothesize that institutional innovations will be supplied if the expected return from the innovation that accrues to the political entrepreneurs exceeds the marginal cost of mobilizing the resources necessary to introduce the innovation. To the extent that the private return to the political entrepreneurs is different from the social return, the institutional innovation will not be supplied at a socially optimum level. Thus, the supply of institutional innovation depends critically on the power structure or balance among vested interest groups in a society. (Ruttan and Hayami, 1984: 213)

North (1981) argues that a theory of institutional change requires three basic components: property rights, the state, and ideology. The state is viewed as an organization with a comparative advantage in violence (North, 1981: 21). Because the essence of property rights is the right to exclude, the state—with its comparative advantage in violence—is able to specify and enforce property rights.

North analyzes the state within the framework of a wealth-maximizing ruler who trades services (protection, justice) for revenue. The state, in this view, attempts to act as a discriminating monopolist, devising property rights for separate constituents in order to maximize state revenue. The state is constrained by the potential for rivals in the form of other states, or of individuals in the same state who could offer constituents better terms. Economies-of-scale in the provision of law, justice, and defense are seen as a basic source of civilization.

North stresses the fundamental tension between social efficiency and the maximization of revenue to the ruler. The ruler has the incentive to maximize the rents from the property rights system that accrue to him. Within that objective, the ruler has the incentive to reduce the transaction cost to maximize the output of society, and thus the base for tax revenues. Both the threat of potential rivals and the transaction cost of collecting tax revenues imply that the ruler tolerates inefficient property rights. In North's view, therefore, inefficient property rights are likely to be widespread; the challenge of economics is to explain the aberrant emergence of efficient property rights that, North argues, contributed to the economic rise of Western Europe (especially in the Netherlands and England).

Inefficient property rights persist because the free-rider problem inhibits the organizational development necessary to alter the institutional arrangements. The free-rider problem is thus important in accounting for the stability of states. By the same logic North argues that institutional innovation "will come from rulers rather than constituents since the latter would always face the free-rider problem" (North, 1981: 32). Thus, North argues that adjustments will be undertaken when private benefits to rulers exceed private costs to rulers.

Another key component in North's framework is ideology. Ideology is seen both as a normative system and as a comprehensive worldview that orders, interprets, and legitimizes beliefs. North argues that organizations (including the state) invest heavily in socialization in order to provide ideological convictions to constrain maximization of self-interest. Successful ideologies must be capable of accommodating changing circumstances—retaining the loyalty of older groups while capturing the loyalty of new ones. North further argues that

> most crucially, any successful ideology must overcome the free-rider problem. Its fundamental aim is to energize groups to behave contrary to simple, hedonistic, individual calculus of costs and benefits. This is the central thrust of major ideologies since neither maintenance of the existing order nor its overthrow is possible without such behavior. (North, 1981: 53)

Changes in ideology—both in terms of a conventional wisdom

concerning why and how relationships are to be organized and in terms of providing a basis for equity judgments—are therefore a fundamental component of economic change. Yet analytical tools to examine and explain ideological change are poorly developed. This point, made by North, is similar to points made by Ruttan and Hayami concerning the lack of adequate theory for explaining changes in cultural endowments. Such factors, however, are seen as being fundamental to the explanation of institutional change and economic growth and development.

The Demand for and Supply of Institutional Change: Beyond the Metaphor

In what follows I shall provide the sketch of a heuristic framework of the demand for and supply of institutional change, a sketch that builds directly on previous work. Components of the framework will be introduced and motivated. The framework will be presented in a simplistic but general form; one major lesson of the analysis of institutional change (and of economic history in general, see Feeny, 1987) is the importance of specifying the details of the situation that is being analyzed. Thus, the framework identifies general categories of variables that must in turn be given concrete form relevant to the particular historical or contemporary institutional change being considered.

Definitions. The presentation of a heuristic framework of institutional change should include a definition of "institutions." The definitions and usage of this term in the works of Lance Davis, Yujiro Hayami, Douglass North, Ronald Oakerson, Elinor Ostrom, Vincent Ostrom, and Vernon Ruttan are basically compatible, perhaps reflecting the direct and indirect influences of John R. Commons. For our purposes the definition provided by North will be adopted.

> Institutions provide the framework within which human beings interact. They establish the cooperative and competitive relationships which constitute a society and more specifically an economic order. . . . Institutions are a set of rules, compliance procedures, and moral and ethical behavioral norms designed to constrain the behavior of individuals. (North, 1981: 201–202)

It is useful to delineate categories of institutions. North (1981: 203) distinguishes among constitutional rules, operating rules, and normative behavioral codes while noting that in practice they overlap. Davis and North (1971: 6–9) distinguish between the institutional environment and institutional arrangements while delineating certain related concepts: the primary action group (makes decisions/initiates change); the secondary action group (established by the primary action group to further its interests); and institutional instruments (documents or devices employed by action groups). Vincent Ostrom (see, for instance, chapter 15 of this book) distinguishes among levels of choice, from the constitutional level to the level of collective action to the operational level. Similarly, in the context of the analysis of decision-making arrangements for the management of common property resources, Oakerson (1986: 17–19) specifies three categories of rules: rules that govern the conditions of collective choice within the group; operational rules used to regulate the use of the commons; and external arrangements (the rules that govern the relationship of the group to other groups and authorities).

The common thrust of these typological systems is that it is essential to distinguish basic and fundamental rules about how society is organized (the constitutional level) from actions taken within that constitutional framework or paradigm. A constitution can be defined as specifying the terms and conditions of governance (collective choice). Governance includes the setting of rules, the application of rules, and the enforcement and adjudication of rules. The constitution includes oral and written traditions; it refers to more than documents as such. The constitutional order is therefore the first category of institutions; it specifies the fundamental rules that establish the conditions of collective choice. These are the rules for making rules. The category includes, "the set of fundamental political, social, and legal ground rules that establishes the basis for production, exchange, and distribution" (Davis and North, 1971: 6). These rules are meant to be costly to modify and change more slowly than the operational rules that are derived from them. The focus in the first category of institutions is on the terms and conditions of collective choice.

The second category of institutions refers to the institutional arrangements (borrowing from Davis and North, 1971) created within the framework of the constitutional order. This category includes the operational rules in the typologies provided by North and Oakerson. It includes laws, regulations, associations, and contracts.

Following North, the third category of institutions refers to normative behavioral codes. Like the constitutional order, these behavioral codes evolve more slowly and are more costly to modify than institutional arrangements. Codes of this sort are important in legitimizing both the constitutional order and the institutional arrangements; indeed, they provide the basis for normative inquiry in the society. This concept of institutions includes the "cultural endowments" described in the framework of Hayami and Ruttan and "ideology" in North's framework.

In addition to providing definitions of the categories of institutions, it is necessary, in a heuristic framework of the demand for and supply of institutional change, to specify what is endogenous and what is exogenous. The endogenous variables in this framework include institutional arrangements and the degree of their utilization. The constitutional order and the normative behavioral codes are taken as exogenous.

A heuristic framework of endogenous institutional arrangements represents a compromise. It is a major advance relative to conventional economic analysis, in which all institutions are explicitly (or implicitly) taken as exogenous. Yet by considering two major categories of institutions (the constitutional order and normative behavioral codes) to be exogenous, the heuristic framework is not capable of analyzing all and, in particular, the most dramatic institutional change. The framework is not meant to address the more fundamental and important analysis of constitutional choice: choosing the conceptions and rules for making rules. Yet I argue that the compromise is warranted. The analytic logic of the theory of endogenous institutional arrangements would apply to a more ambitious model of institutional change. Refinement in theory and empirical testing is, however, facilitated by the less ambitious approach.

In the more ambitious framework the investigator can make important contributions by weaving consistent stories of the evolution of institutions that are analytically sound and empirically accurate. A good example of the approach is given by North (1981). The ability to tell a consistent story is an important test of the analytical framework; yet more rigorous and demanding empirical tests of the model are not facilitated by the broad sweep of the argument.

On methodological grounds, the less ambitious approach, in which only institutional arrangements are endogenous, offers both advantages and disadvantages relative to an approach in which all institutional change is endogenous. First, the less ambitious approach is analytically more tractable; the analysis is considerably simplified by taking the constitutional order as given. Second, more rigorous and quantitative testing of analytical frameworks is facilitated in the less ambitious approach. Models of institutional change can be tested through story telling (for more on methodology and argument in economics see McCloskey, 1983; see also Field, 1979, 1981, 1984; Grabowski, 1988). Yet at least parts of the story and some major hypotheses need to be subjected to more rigorous empirical tests. The results of such investigations may then be incorporated into modifications to the analytical frameworks, thus improving theory. The ability to reject hypotheses is enhanced.

A further advantage of the less ambitious approach is the relatively shorter duration of the time period suitable for subjecting models derived from the heuristic framework to empirical testing. Normative behavioral codes evolve slowly. Similarly, the constitutional order evolves slowly but occasionally is subjected to major discrete changes in the form of revolutions. Thus the investigator seeking to test empirically a model of institutional change that views the constitutional order as endogenous will need to use a long period of time for the sample frame and/or focus on shorter but less typical periods of major change. In the former approach, a great many other factors (technology, population) are also likely to have changed substantially over such a long period of time that it is difficult to analyze the effects of the changes in institutions separate from the effects of other changes. The latter approach poses special problems of separating the general from the idiosyncratic.

The advantages of simplification and facilitation of empirical testing come, however, at considerable cost. By taking the constitutional order as given, the investigator is invited to invest intellectual effort into providing better answers to less important questions. An approach in which institutional arrangements are endogenous and the constitutional order and normative behavioral codes are taken as exogenous needs to be complemented by other approaches, ones in which all categories of institutions are endogenous. The latter are both more difficult and more important. The framework here is designed to explain the creation and dissolution of institutional arrangements. It is also designed to explain the level of utilization of existing institutional arrangements.

All institutional arrangements have the potential to affect both the distribution of income and the efficiency of resource allocation. Much of the early demand-induced model of institutional change focused on the evolution of institutional arrangements, primarily in terms of their effects on efficiency. Models of rent-seeking (see, for instance, Bates and Rogerson, 1980; Krueger, 1974) explicitly explore the incentives to create institutional arrangements to redistribute income, and the resulting implications for efficiency. These positive models of government policy reflect the same kind of thinking that is emphasized in the analysis of the supply of institutional change.

Thus the institutional arrangements that are endogenous in the framework may be redistributive or allocative arrangements in their intent. The distinction between the two is, however, not particularly meaningful to the agents involved in changing institutional arrangements. The distinction reflects the viewpoint adopted by the analyst. The viewpoint typically adopted in economics is that of society as a whole with a basic assumption that all persons receive equal weight in considering changes in income distribution. Thus the focus is on the allocative effects of institutional arrangements. Institutional arrangements that create opportunities that more than offset their costs are viewed as providing net gains; arrangements that create costs that exceed benefits generate net losses. The approach is neutral to whoever receives the income.

This normative criterion of efficiency (see also chapter 11 of this book) is a useful analytical device. Yet the agents involved in change have their private criterion of personal gains and losses and are not indifferent to the income distribution effects of institutional arrangements. Positive modeling of change in institutional arrangements needs to take income distribution into account.

Although the framework is designed to explain change in institutional arrangements of both a distributional and an allocative character, it may be useful to focus research on the latter. The incentive to use the rules of collective choice to create institutional arrangements that will shift the income distribution toward oneself always exist and can be expected to be opposed by the potential losers. The results of the struggle change over time as demographic, technological, and other changes affect the relative power of various groups. Perhaps the more interesting puzzle is to explain efficiency-improving institutional change against the constant background of redistributive struggle.

Institutional arrangements and their level of utilization are the endogenous variables in the framework. Exogenous variables are classified into either demand or supply factors. The framework builds explicitly on the previous work of Davis, Hayami, North, Ruttan, and Thomas. (For related approaches, see also de Janvry, 1973, 1977; Guttman, 1978, 1980, 1982, 1987; La Croix and Roumasset, 1984; Otsuka, Kikuchi, and Hayami, 1986; Posner, 1979, 1980; Roumasset, 1978; Roumasset and La Croix, chapter 10 of this book; Schultz, 1968).

The Demand for Institutional Change. The basic source of the demand for changes in institutional arrangements is the recognition that existing arrangements leave potential gains uncaptured. Agents realize that by altering existing arrangements they could capture gains that cannot be obtained under the institutional status quo. The incentive to alter institutional arrangements to shift the income distribution toward oneself and away from others is obvious. The demand for institutional change is, however, not exclusively redistributional in character. New forms of property rights creating new production opportunities that enhance efficiency while, of course, affecting the distribution of the gains, are also examples of the demand for institutional change.

The logic of the framework is that agents will demand new arrangements when the net expected benefits to them of creating and utilizing the new arrangements are positive. The viewpoint is that of the individual or a group of individuals for whom the expected benefits exceed the expected cost. Naturally, the expected net benefits for other groups and for society as a whole may differ—in many cases quite dramatically. Although the statement of the motivation behind the demand for new institutional arrangements provides a useful generalization, its high level of generality may serve to obscure as well as illuminate the issue.

This heuristic framework of institutional change combines the comparative static analysis of equilibrium with an evolutionary perspective through iterative application. Thus change in one period becomes part of the endowment and status quo in the next, in turn affecting the subsequent demand for and supply of change. This heuristic framework postulates an initial equilibrium in institutional arrangements that is then shocked by a change in one or more exogenous factors. Comparative static analysis is then used to analyze the effects of the exogenous shock on the equilibrium set of institutional arrangements.

In this framework a number of factors, exogenous in the heuristic framework of institutional change (but perhaps endogenous in a model of economic development), are the factors that affect the demand for new arrangements, the factors that change the expected net benefits of altering institutional arrangements and therefore shift the demand for institutional change. Important demand-side factors are relative product and factor prices, the constitutional order, technology, and the size of the market.

Demographic and technological change have frequently been important sources of changes in relative product and factor prices.

Examples in the contemporary world include the effects of mechanization, the introduction of fertilizer-responsive varieties of rice, and the effects of population growth on labor-market institutions for the recruitment and supervision of rice-harvesting labor in Indonesia and the Philippines. Yujiro Hayami and Masao Kikuchi (1981) provide an analysis of the evolution of the harvest-labor institutions. Traditional arrangements provided access to harvest labor employment for all village members at a fixed share of the paddy harvested by the laborer (for instance, one-sixth or one-eighth). Hayami and Kikuchi demonstrate that, given rice yields on native varieties and the prevailing level of wages, the harvest-share wage was in equilibrium with the level of wages in the local economy. The harvest-share wage had a further advantage from the point of view of the cultivator: it reduced supervision cost with respect to the alternative of paying a daily wage for agricultural workers.

The equilibrium of the harvest-share wage with daily wages was shocked by several trends in the 1960s and 1970s. Population growth exerted a depressing effect on the level of real wages; in some localities real wages did in fact decline, while in others the increase in the supply of labor was offset (or more than offset) by shifts in the demand for labor. In addition, technological change in agricultural machinery (sometimes reinforced by credit policies that favored the acquisition of modern equipment) lowered the cost of machines as a substitute for harvest labor. Finally and more importantly, new rice varieties dramatically altered yields. Thus while there were downward pressures on real wages (population growth and reductions in the cost of mechanical harvesting) there was a dramatic growth in paddy yields, implying that the traditional share of the harvest exceeded substantially the local daily agricultural wage. It should also be noted that the new rice varieties increased the demand for agricultural labor both by increasing the amount of work involved in raising a particular crop and by facilitating double cropping. Double cropping in turn increased the demand for timeliness in agricultural operations, thus further increasing the advantages of mechanization, especially in irrigation, plowing, harvesting, and threshing.

From the point of the view of the cultivator, the old share wage exceeded the cost of labor and assigned too much of the gains from adopting the new technology to harvest laborers. Naturally the harvest laborers resisted attempts to reduce the share toward a new equilibrium. A variety of new arrangements emerged. There was, however, a choice of three primary responses: mechanization of harvest operations, the hiring of extravillage harvest labor teams, or the innovation of a new share-harvest arrangement with an implicit reduction in the share wage. Hayami and Kikuchi argue that the response adopted depended on the relative bargaining power of harvest laborers and cultivators. In villages with little social cohesion (often in regions that were frontier settlements in the late nineteenth to early twentieth century) the cost to the cultivator of breaking with custom was low. In these situations mechanization was often adopted if the topography of the land and existing water control system facilitated it. If not, standing crops were often sold to persons from outside the village (who had no traditional share-harvest rights), and they then recruited extravillage workers to harvest the crop.

In villages with higher degrees of social cohesion the costs of breaking with custom were more substantial. In some cases cultivators were able to negotiate a reduction in the harvest share; more commonly the rights to access to harvest-labor employment were restricted to those who had performed "free" weeding labor on the field during the growing season. Hayami and Kikuchi demonstrate that the amount of paddy received, according to the traditional harvest-share rule, divided by the hours of weeding labor plus the hours of harvest labor are roughly equivalent to the prevailing daily wage for agricultural labor. Thus the new institutional arrangement restored the equilibrium in wages in the harvest-labor market while preserving the substance of local custom. New institutional arrangements were innovated in response to changes in both technology and relative factor prices.

Changes in the constitutional order, the basic rules of government, can affect profoundly the expected costs and benefits of creating new institutional arrangements and thus the demand for them. The early history of the United States provides a useful case study. Among the important trends in the constitutional order was an extension of voting rights from a more exclusive group of property-owning adult white males to virtually universal adult-white male suffrage by 1865 (Davis and North, 1971: 64–73). From the point of view of the framework, the changes in voting rights are taken as exogenous. Davis and North speculate that the emergence of political parties, the influence of the French republic on democratic ideals, and the entry of new trans-Appalachian states that had granted universal manhood suffrage were part of the pressure for changes in the rules of suffrage. Because votes mattered, each political party had the incentive when in power to extend suffrage to its potential supporters; because voting rights are hardly ever taken away once granted, over time the franchise was broadened.

The effects of the broadening of suffrage are seen in the evolution of U.S. federal government policy with respect to the disposal of public lands (see Davis, et al., 1972: 100–109; Davis and North, 1971: 83–93; Hughes, 1983: 94–104; North and Rutten, 1987). As the suffrage was broadened, the political benefits of favoring large land speculators decreased while the political benefits of favoring the interests of small-scale investors increased. The result was a dramatic decline in the size of the individual parcel of land sold by the federal government over the period extending from 1787 to the Homestead Act of 1862. While in 1787 Congress authorized the sale of a 1-million acre tract in Ohio, by 1832 the minimum tract for sale was 40 acres. The Homestead Act in turn opened up the disposal of the remaining public lands on terms of occupation and development for tracts of 160 acres or less. Thus a change in the basic rules of government had an important impact on institutional arrangements concerning property rights in land and the disposal of public lands. These in turn affected the structure of economic and political activity in the trans-Appalachian states.

Another important demand-side exogenous factor is size of market. The logic is straightforward; as the size of market increases, fixed costs may be recovered on a large number of transactions rather than being focused on a relatively few. Thus fixed costs will represent less of an impediment to innovations in institutional arrangements.

The innovation of general laws of incorporation by state governments in the United States in the nineteenth century provides an example. Limited liability provided expected benefits to investors in enterprises even when shares were closely held. Limited liability also greatly facilitated the participation of the large number of investors needed to accumulate sufficient capital to capture economies-of-scale. These advantages became more important over time as growth in the transportation sector expanded the size of the market, and as technological change increased the importance of scale economies.

The corporate charter in the form of a special grant of limited liability to an individual firm was well known in colonial America, having been used in Europe from the seventeenth century (Davis and North, 1971: 136–139, 168–171; Hughes, 1983: 145–146, 363–367). With the exceptions of New York (1811) and Connecticut (1837), state governments in the ante bellum period required a separate charter for each new corporation. As the national transportation system developed, and in particular as the rail network expanded, firms had the opportunity to serve a national market. New technologies (the Bessemer process for steel, Hungarian reduction techniques for grain milling, new fractional distillation methods in petroleum refining) further underscored the advantages of organizing large firms and thus the advantages of limited liability. In the years after 1845, and in particular in the 1860s and 1870s, most states outside the South passed general laws of incorporation. The laws allowed for registration of new corporations according to a standard set of rules, thus dramatically reducing the cost of incorporating. The results included a shift in income distribution away from legislators who had required payments for the passage of special charters and toward the owners of capital who sought limited liability. In addition, general laws of incorporation reduced the transaction cost of governance and congestion in legislative calendars. The change in institutional arrangements was in response to growth in the size of markets and in the importance of economies-of-scale.

Thus far the historical and contemporary examples of changes in institutions and institutional arrangements have illustrated the effects of changes in important demand-side factors: relative product and factor prices, the constitutional order, technology, and the size of market. Although case studies were described briefly to illustrate a particular factor, the nature of the natural experiments drawn from history is such that each case involves a mix of factors, even if one figured prominently. In particular, technological change was an integral part of the case studies involving changes in harvest-labor arrangements (along with changes in relative factor prices) and the introduction of general laws of incorporation (along with changes in market size).

In addition to discussing the demand-side factors that shift the demand for institutional change, it may also be useful to reflect on important sources of the benefits expected from innovations in institutional arrangements. These sources include the capture of capital gains, risk sharing, the achievement of economies-of-scale, the reduction of transaction cost, and the amelioration of incomplete markets, externalities, and market failure. Appreciation in the prices of assets creates capital gains that can be more reliably captured through changes in institutional arrangements that provide for more precision in property rights. Share contracts ameliorate incomplete markets in risk and information (Newbery and Stiglitz, 1979; Feeny, 1983b). The provision of limited liability allows for the capture of economies-of-scale. Organized commodity exchanges and stock markets reduce transaction cost. The growth in the importance of externalities in land use created the gains from the amelioration of these externalities through new arrangements such as zoning. A great many additional examples could be provided. These sources of gain imply that new arrangements will allow agents to capture gains previously uncaptured, thus increasing their income. This list also reflects the focus on cases in which efficiency may also be improved through innovation in institutional arrangements, situations in which institutional change is not wholly redistributive in character.

The Supply of Institutional Change. The demand for institutional change is derived from the perception that new arrangements will allow for the capture of gains that cannot be appropriated under existing arrangements. The supply of institutional change depends on the capability and willingness of the political order to provide new arrangements.[2] In this framework, because the constitutional order is taken as exogenous, the existing set of such basic rules of the political order, as well as the existing set of institutional arrangements, will have a profound effect on both the capability and the willingness of the political order to respond to shifts in the demand for particular institutional arrangements.

Because the demand for institutional change is based on capturing the currently uncapturable, it is time- and place-specific; it depends on the circumstances of the status quo. This is also the case with the supply of institutional change. There are a number of important factors that affect the capability and willingness of the political order to provide new arrangements. These factors include the costs of institutional design, the existing stock of knowledge, the expected cost of implementing the new arrangements, the constitutional order, existing institutional arrangements, the normative behavioral code, the conventional wisdom, and the expected net benefits to powerful elite decision makers who exercise positions of dominance. The premise is that although the political order may or may not be a unitary one, it is characterized by hierarchy (whether unitary or decomposible), and that the political arena is not a perfectly competitive one. Such a premise reflects the recognition that the political order is in part concerned with organizing the provision of public goods, and may in turn have a monopoly on the legitimate use of coercive force (see V. Ostrom, chapters 2 and 13 of this book).

The supply of institutional change is characterized as depending on the capability and willingness of the political order to provide change as an analogy to the factors that affect the supply of goods in conventional product markets. In the conventional model of product markets, the prices of factors of production and technology define a marginal-cost schedule; the assumption of a behavioral rule, profit maximization by the firm, converts the marginal-cost schedule (above the minimum point of the average variable cost curve in the standard U-shaped short-run case) into a supply schedule:

In the case of the supply of institutional change, factors of production are used in institutional design; existing knowledge affects the innovation possibilities; and the motivations of the agents affect which changes are forthcoming. Examples may provide clarification.

The cost of institutional design depends on the factor prices of the human and other resources used in designing new institutional arrangements. Because we are accustomed to viewing institutional change as an evolutionary process, the role of the costs of design may often be obscured. In established legal systems, new arrangements usually require specific legislation, or judicial interpretation, or both. If the maintenance of the legislature and/or judicial system is costly, then the design of institutional arrangements will tend to be more costly. More generally, if the environment in which a new arrangement might be supplied is such that highly skilled and sophisticated labor inputs are required, design will be more costly; if it is such that less skilled labor will suffice, design will be less costly. There is an analogy in the trends in nineteenth-century technological change in the United States (Rosenberg, 1972). The stream of mechanical innovation of the early and mid-nineteenth century relied on intuition and trial and error. Yeoman inventors could compete quite successfully with trained engineers in providing new mechanical technologies. Later in the nineteenth century, however, as advances in knowledge in electricity, magnetism, and chemistry became important sources of innovation, the design of new technologies required more sophisticated and trained labor inputs, contributing to the roles of the professional engineer and scientist and of the formal research and development department of the modern corporation.

The costs of the factors of production used in institutional design may differ in important ways, as we can see by comparing the regulation of groundwater use in California and Arizona (Blomquist and Ostrom, 1985; E. Ostrom, chapter 4 of this book). This example also illustrates the roles of the constitutional order and existing institutional arrangements. (As in the case studies used to illustrate the demand-side factors, evidence drawn from natural experiments tends to compound at least several analytically distinct factors.) Voluntary associations of water users and local public water districts are permitted under California law. In contrast, in Arizona, a state which is also located in an arid area, the regulation of water use is reserved to the state government. Thus, while ordinary citizens in California may engage in the design of institutional arrangements to regulate their water use and ameliorate externality problems associated with the pumping of groundwater, only government officials may engage in institutional design in the state of Arizona. We would thus expect that the cost of innovation of institutional arrangements for the regulation of water use would be much lower in California, and all other things being equal, the supply of institutional change larger and the regulation of water use more successful. The evidence is consistent with the crude predictions. The example reflects on more than the importance of factor costs in institutional design.

The ability to provide new institutional arrangements is affected by more than the factor costs of the factors utilized in institutional design. Just as the stock of existing scientific knowledge affects the cost of technological innovation, the stock of knowledge concerning institutional arrangements affects the innovation possibilities frontier for institutional change. The growth in interactions among economies that has taken place in the last five centuries, and at an accelerating pace in the last two, has affected more than the size of markets. It has also facilitated the spread of knowledge concerning a wide variety of institutional arrangements. In addition, research in the social sciences and law has contributed to growth in knowledge about institutions (Hayami and Ruttan, 1985; Ruttan, 1984).

An example that reflects the effects of new knowledge on the design of institutional arrangements is found in the development of more precise property rights in land in late nineteenth- and early twentieth-century Thailand (Feeny, 1982b, 1988). During the nineteenth century in Thailand, as the importance of rice exporting increased and as the price of rice relative to the price of manufactured goods appreciated, there was a dramatic increase in both the area under paddy cultivation and the relative price of land. As land became more valuable there were demands for more precise documentation of land rights. Disputes over ownership of particular parcels of land became endemic.

The government of Thailand responded in a series of legal and administrative changes. In 1892 a new land law was enacted with a provision for the issue of title deeds and the use of land as collateral for loans. There remained, however, an important deficiency in the set of arrangements; there was no mechanism for the unambiguous identification of the parcel of land that corresponded to the parcel described on the written document. Local government officials were frequently confronted with the situation in which two (or more) persons could present documents giving them ownership rights to the same parcel of land. The problem was especially important in the Rangsit, an area to the northeast of Bangkok that had been developed by a private canal company in the rice boom of the 1890s.

During this period the Royal Survey Department had engaged British surveyors (from the Indian Civil Service) to produce modern maps of Thailand and to train an indigenous staff of surveyors. In 1896, the department was diverted from map making to conduct a cadastral survey in Rangsit. This ad hoc arrangement was formalized in a 1901 land law that established a cadastral survey system for land titling, and also by an ambitious program of cadastral surveys in the most commercialized areas of the Central Plain in the period from 1901 to 1909. The land titling system that was applied in Thailand was the Torrens system, based on experience in Australia, knowledge of which became available in Thailand through the employment of foreign experts. Knowledge of systems used for land titling elsewhere affected the design of the institutional arrangements in Thailand.

The supply of institutional arrangements will also be affected by the expected cost of implementation. This expected cost applies to the administrative or physical infrastructure; political costs and benefits are considered later in the concluding paragraphs of this section.

An example of the effects of the expected cost of implementation can be found in the evolution of land rights on the range in the Great Plains of the United States (Anderson and Hill, 1975; Dennen, 1976; Libecap, 1986). In the 1860s, range rights were initially defined by prior appropriation. As long as land was in great abundance, cattlemen seeking entry to a range could readily find an area

Institutional Arrangements

in which no one had prior rights and occupy it. As cattle raising became more popular and more land came into use, voluntary associations in the form of stock growers' or cattlemen's associations were organized to convert open-access range into communal property by enforcing exclusion of nonmembers from it. The control of access to scarce watering sites and to roundups, an activity characterized by economies-of-scale, reduced the cost of enforcing exclusion. In an environment in which fencing material in the form of rock or wood was very scarce, the implementation costs of defining strictly private range rights were too high.

Barbed wire dramatically changed the cost of implementing privatization. Sales of barbed wire went from 10,000 pounds in 1874 to 80,500,000 in 1880 (Anderson and Hill, 1975: 175). As one would expect, fences were first erected around croplands and around prime grazing land with access to water. The cost of implementation affected the choice of institutional arrangements and the degree of their utilization.

The implications of the constitutional order for the supply of institutional arrangements are illustrated by the variation in regional taxation levels for agricultural land in British India (Kumar, 1986; McAlpin, 1983; Feeny, 1988). In general, land tax revenues were lower in regions settled under the *zamindar* system, beginning with the 1793 Permanent Settlement in Bengal. Under this settlement system, property rights of the land and the liability for land taxes were assigned to a cadre of indigenous tax collectors, *zamindars*, who became landlords to the mass of cultivators; land taxes were fixed in perpetuity at the time of settlement. The Permanent Settlement contrasted with the *ryotwari* system introduced in Madras in the 1790s, in which property rights were assigned to the peasant cultivator, *ryot*, using the land at the time of settlement. The *ryotwari* system allowed for periodic reassessment of land taxes. The example also illustrates the effects of implementation cost at both the political and administrative levels. The *zamindar* system co-opted the political loyalty of important indigenous officials; it also reduced the administrative cost for the government by requiring the documentation of land ownership rights for a relatively few instead of, as in the *ryotwari* system, a great many.

Existing institutional arrangements affect the supply of institutional change. Like the cost of implementation, this factor affects the ability of the system to provide new arrangements. (The effects of existing institutional arrangements on the demand for institutional change and on the political costs and benefits of change will be treated separately.) An example of the effects I have in mind can be found in the adaptation of the framework of regulation provided by the Interstate Commerce Act of 1887 to the regulation of airline services by the Civil Aeronautics Board in 1938 (Davis and North, 1973: 47–51, 157–166). While it took several decades to innovate the arrangements of the Interstate Commerce Commission, the airline industry was able to use that model to create a publicly enforced cartel very soon after the introduction of the DC-3 in 1937 made the provision of passenger service on a large scale viable.

Normative behavioral codes have the potential for profound effects on the choice of institutional arrangements. North (1981, 1986), Hayami and Ruttan (1985), and others (see, for instance, Axelrod, 1986; Chantornvong, chapter 3 of this book; Oakerson, chapter 5 of this book; Popkin, 1979) stress the importance of the congruence and legitimacy of institutional arrangements with cultural norms.

A comparison of social norms in Japan and Thailand provides an example. In Japan traditional norms placed a great deal of emphasis on conformity and compliance with community obligations (see, for instance, Cox, 1982; Hayami and Ruttan, 1985: 103–109, 320–326; Kikuchi and Hayami, 1978a; McKean, 1982, 1986; Ruttan and Hayami, 1984; Smith, 1959). These obligations included participation in constructing, operating, and maintaining local irrigation systems. In 1899 the national government, alarmed over Japan's loss of self-sufficiency in rice production, passed the Arable Land Replotment Law (revised in 1905 and 1909) in order to strengthen the ability of local groups to engage in collective action for investments in infrastructure. "The law authorized compulsory participation by farmers and landlords in an area of a land improvement project if consent were obtained from two-thirds of the landlords owning two-thirds of that area" (Kikuchi and Hayami, 1978b: 849). The effects of the traditional norms and enforcement mechanisms and the newer legislation are evident in the highly developed water control systems (and other local infrastructure facilities) that allowed Japan to realize the gains of biological technological change in the nineteenth and twentieth centuries. The realization of potential gains from the modern varieties of rice responsive to fertilizer has been delayed in many areas throughout South and Southeast Asia in part by deficiencies in local water control systems.

An example is the case of Thailand. In contrast to the tightly structured communities of rural Japan, communities in Southeast Asia and in particular in Thailand have been characterized as loosely structured (see, for instance, Evers, 1969; Hayami and Ruttan, 1985: 103–109, 320–326). Highly individualistic behavior is expected and tolerated; traditional norms of conformity and cooperation do not serve to reduce the cost of organizing local collective action. The normative behavioral code does not facilitate institutional arrangements that require collective action. In addition, village and other units of local government in Thailand have very limited fiscal authority and lack the right of eminent domain (Gisselquist, 1976; Feeny, 1982b: 121–123). Thus in Thailand it is difficult for groups of farmers to organize improvements in irrigation systems or the construction of local roads and other facilities that would contribute to growth in agricultural productivity. Both cultural norms and the constitutional order that defines the authority of local units of government serve to raise the cost of local collective action, and thus constrain the likely set of institutional arrangements. A lack of local infrastructure formation has been the result in Thailand, with deleterious effects on productivity and welfare in the rural sector. The experience in Japan in the Tokugawa and Meiji periods was quite different. Of course, important differences between Japan and Thailand include more than normative behavioral codes.

The final component in cultural endowments is conventional wisdom. As North (1981) argues, implicit and explicit models of how the world works affect views about the appropriate institutional arrangements. These effects are separate from the normative judgments discussed above.

An example of the effects of conventional wisdom on institutional arrangements for the disposition of public lands in the United States is the Homestead Act of 1862 (Davis, et al., 1972: 104–109; Hughes, 1983: 94–110; North and Rutten, 1987). It allowed settlers to obtain the title to public lands in the West on the condition of five years' continuous residence on and development of the land. The maximum claim allowed under the law was 160 acres, a farm size consistent with practice in the humid and forested areas of the East. For the more arid regions west of the ninety-eighth meridian, however, 160 acres was, in general, too small for a viable farm. Conventional wisdom based on Eastern U.S. ecosystems and farm practice was enshrined in the institutional arrangements and was inappropriate.

Settlers adopted a variety of legal and illegal strategies to overcome the 160-acre limitation. Subsequent legal changes—the Desert Land Act of 1877, the Timber Culture Act of 1871, the Enlarged Homestead Act of 1909, and the Stock-Raising Homestead Act of 1916—raised the maximum to 320 or 640 acres and imposed additional conditions on land development. Institutional arrangements were in part adapted to a new conventional wisdom based on experience in arid regions.

The final supply-side factor affecting institutional change is net benefits to elite decision makers. A number of examples already discussed illustrate the point. The Thai case is particularly instructive (see Feeny, 1979a, 1979b, 1982a, 1982b, 1983a, 1983b, 1987, 1988). The creation of more precise and secure property rights in land was in the interests of elite decision makers, who were also landowners and land speculators. Important new institutional arrangements for property rights in land were forthcoming. (In the case of Thai land rights, as in the case reported by Roumasset and LaCroix in chapter 10 of this book, rent-seeking and efficiency were not inconsistent.) However, investments in increasing land productivity through irrigation and agricultural research, although in the social interest, were not in the interests of the leaders of government.

Underinvestment was the result, except in a few selected localities where elites could readily capture the benefits.

The analysis of Lance E. Davis and Robert A. Huttenback (1982) of British imperialism provides another example in which it appears that policy conformed to the interests of the elite at the expense of the social interest. Davis and Huttenback compare the returns from imperial investments in excess of the domestic rate of return in the United Kingdom to the financial burdens of the empire, mainly defense expenditures. In these terms they find that on net the empire represented a burden to Britain. Ownership of firms with empire investments was, however, concentrated among financiers, large banks, and the gentry. These groups were well represented in government. Taxes in support of the empire, however, were borne by less well-represented middle- and lower-class citizens. Although the work of Davis and Huttenback cannot be considered to be a fully comprehensive accounting of the pecuniary costs and benefits of British imperialism, it does strongly suggest that the colonial empire involved an important redistribution of income from the middle class to the upper class in Britain.

The costs and benefits to various groups including the leaders of the political order need to be taken explicitly into account. Because the provision of public goods frequently involves an element of coercion (or the potential for its use), leaders are in a strategic position to affect the supply of institutional arrangements and ensure that innovations are congruent with their interests. The fewer the constraints on the ability of leaders to use coercion, the wider the potential for divergences between elite and social benefits and costs.

Dynamic Sequences. The heuristic framework is meant to be applied iteratively to examine the evolution of institutional arrangements. Starting from a particular point in time and space, innovations in the initial period become part of the endowments in subsequent periods, thus affecting both the demand for and supply of institutional change.

The innovation and subsequent development of institutional arrangements for the public funding of agricultural research and development provide an important example of dynamic sequences of institutional change (see Davis, et al., 1972: 391–393; Davis and North, 1971: 100–102; Evenson and Kislev, 1975; Grantham, 1984; Hayami and Ruttan, 1985: chs. 8–9; Ruttan, 1980, 1982: chs. 3–5; Schultz, 1964). Agricultural research is vulnerable to market failure for a variety of reasons. First, property rights in intellectual discovery are, in general, incomplete; thus it is very difficult for an innovator to capture much of the gains of the innovation that has resulted from the investment of resources in research. The limited appropriability of the gains from innovation may be especially important for biological technical change. New crop varieties may be duplicated in most cases without compensation to the original breeder. Disembodied technical change in the form of information, for instance new cultural practices such as a system of crop rotation, provide even less scope for appropriating payment for use of the innovation.

Second, over some range of output there are economies-of-scale in research. Thus for any particular geoclimatic zone, an experimental farm may achieve much more than a large number of isolated farmer-researchers.

Third, by its very nature research involves risk. The production of new knowledge is uncertain; if it were not, the knowledge would not be new. Mechanisms for risk spreading are thus of potential importance in eliciting investment in research activity.

Fourth, much of the benefit of agricultural research is ultimately transferred to consumers in the form of lower equilibrium prices for agricultural goods. The transfer reflects the effects of the innovations on the supply of such goods and the competitive markets through which the goods are supplied. Thus even if agricultural producers are able to organize effectively to provide agricultural research as a club good, the producers will still have the incentive to underinvest because much of the benefit is captured by consumers, not producers.

The nature of agricultural research, especially for biological and disembodied technical change, thus implies a divergence between the private and social rates of return. This gap grew larger in eighteenth- and early nineteenth-century Europe. Increased trade served to spread pests and parasites, raising the returns on innovations to combat the problems. Advances in science, particularly organic chemistry as reflected in the work of Justus von Liebig (1803-1873) also raised the expected benefits of research. Finally, the decrease in the price of nitrogen resulting from the import of Chilean nitrates, and in later periods from a series of technological changes in the chemical industry, again raised the expected returns from biological research.

The potential gains did not go unnoticed. In the United Kingdom voluntary associations were formed to conduct agricultural research. A notable example was the Rothamsted Agricultural Experiment Station, organized in 1843 and supported by private philanthropy. Yet the level of research activity relative to its potential returns remained very low. The first publicly supported (socialized) agricultural experiment station was organized in Mockern, Saxony, in 1852. It reflected the participation of farmers' groups and of the government of the principality. The environment was one in which science and the public policy of various German governments were being deliberately harnessed to foster development in Germany to catch up with the pioneer of the industrial revolution, Great Britain. The innovation in Saxony was imitated in other German principalities. It was adapted and extended in the United States, beginning in 1863 with the creation of the land-grant college system by the Morrill Act. In conjunction with the research program of the federal government's United States Department of Agriculture, the United States built a system of Federal- and state-level participation in agricultural research. The system allowed for research at the general level with a mechanism for local adaptation at the state level, and additional research on crops and activities of more parochial interest. The joint national-local framework was important because of the specificity of location of most biological technologies. This arrangement was imitated by the Japanese in the design of their publicly funded agricultural research system in the 1880s and 1890s.

These institutional arrangements were important in generating a stream of technological change in U.S. and Japanese agriculture that underwrote large gains in productivity. Yet the free-rider problem, although ameliorated, was not solved. Ruttan (1980) argues that state governments in the United States continue to underinvest in agricultural research because some of the benefits are captured by neighboring states. He proposes changes in the mechanisms for federal cost sharing to reduce the divergence between state and national rates of return on agricultural research.

The positive externalities of agricultural research are, however, not contained within the geographic boundaries of the country that supported the initial research. States in the United States have the incentive to underinvest because they do not capture all of the gains; each nation does as well. The institutional response has in part been to organize international agricultural research institutes. Early antecedents to recent developments tended to focus on colonial export crops; the colonial government, because it represented both the producer's interest (the colony) and the consumer's interests (the home country), was perhaps more willing to invest in agricultural research. Yet the potential to increase agricultural productivity in the major food grains in tropical countries was not being realized.

International attempts to ameliorate the free-rider problem are reflected in the organization of the International Rice Research Institute in the Philippines in 1960. Similarly CIMMYT (Centro Internacional de Mejoramiento de Mais y Trijo), organized within the Mexican Ministry of Agriculture in 1943 and then as the International Center for the Improvement of Wheat and Maize in 1963, represented an attempt to focus interdisciplinary applied research on two additional important crops. By the end of the 1970s, these institutional arrangements had been further imitated and adapted to create a network of twelve major international centers devoted to work on major crops or agricultural problems in a variety of major geoclimatic zones.

The evolution of institutional arrangements for publicly funded agricultural research, from voluntary to state-government to national-government to international-institute provision, reflects an attempt to weaken the incentives for underinvestment in an activity

Table 6.1
Summary of the Framework of the Demand for and Supply of Institutional Arrangements

Categories of institutions

    Constitutional order
    Institutional arrangements
    Normative behavioral codes

Endogenous Variables

    Institutional arrangements
    Degree of utilization of institutional arrangements

Exogenous variables: The demand for institutional change

    Relative product and factor prices (including demographic change)
    Constitutional order
    Technology
    Size of market

Exogenous variables: The supply of institutional change

    Constitutional order
    Existing institutional arrangements
    Cost of institutional design
    Existing stock of knowledge
    Expected cost of implementing new arrangements
    Normative behavioral code
    Conventional wisdom
    Expected net benefits to elite decision makers

Dynamic sequences

    Paths of change / Institutional evolution

with important public-good characteristics. It also reflects the increase in the potential returns from research embodied in advances in science. Institutional arrangements innovated in particular settings in particular periods have been used in subsequent periods as models for the design of new institutional arrangements. One theme in the evolution of the institutions for publicly funded agriculture research has been the innovation of new arrangements to reduce the importance of positive externalities. Another theme has been the creation of arrangements in which both producers and consumers share in the costs and benefits. Although underinvestment in agricultural research persists, there is a substantial body of evidence that indicates that the performance of publicly funded agricultural research institutes has contributed importantly to economic performance (see, for instance, Evenson and Kislev, 1975; Hayami and Ruttan, 1985; Ruttan, 1982).

Conclusions

A simple framework of the demand for and supply of institutional change has been elaborated in this paper. It is summarized in Table 6.1.[3] In the framework presented, institutional arrangements are endogenous; the constitutional order and normative behavioral codes are taken as exogenous. Thus the framework is appropriate for the analysis of important changes in institutional arrangements (and, of course, trivial ones) but inadequate for analysis of fundamental and profound changes in the institutional environment. It may be argued that the constitutional order and normative behavioral codes are more important than institutional arrangements in explaining relative economic and political success and the failure of different societies in different periods. Nevertheless, focusing on institutional arrangements instead of the broader institutional environment does reflect a methodological strategy postulating that problems sometimes need to be made more tractable if intellectual progress is to be made—even if, as a consequence, the less important problems are addressed first.

The framework then is incomplete. Even within that constraint, it is important to ask what can be accomplished with it. At one level of analysis it can be used to create a consistent story of institutional evolution. That such a story can be constructed does not mean that there are not other stories consistent with the same sets of qualitative and quantitative evidence. In addition, that such a story can be constructed does not imply that the model is correct. Yet the requirement that an empirically consistent story be constructed does provide an important methodological hurdle that serves the research community well by rejecting at least some models.

Although the testing of models derived from the heuristic framework is confined to tests based on interpreting evidence from historical and contemporary natural experiments, an explicit framework has several additional advantages over implicit approaches. First, although the presentation of the framework is deliberately general, its explicit specification serves to clarify the argument. The marshaling of counterargument and counterevidence are thus facilitated.

Second, even if testing of a complete model must rely primarily on story telling (see McCloskey, 1983), components of the model or implications of it may be tested more definitively. Assertions about the costs and benefits to particular groups of particular arrangements may be tested empirically (see, for instance, Feeny, 1982b). The association between rates of change of endogenous variables and exogenous ones implied by the model may be tested statistically (see, for instance, Hayami and Kikuchi, 1978; Libecap, 1978; Libecap and Wiggins, 1985; Otsuka, Kikuchi, and Hayami, 1986; Wiggins and Libecap, 1985).

The framework of analysis presented in the paper represents one important approach to constructing positive models of institutional change. Explicit models combined with empirical testing provide a mechanism for refining and improving institutional analysis in development. Institutional analysis remains, however, time- and place-specific. This characteristic is intrinsic according to the logic of the framework presented in the paper. In order to analyze institutional change, one must know the institutional endowments and other conditions of the status quo. The analyst is forced to describe concrete situations; thus some generality is immediately lost. Yet meaningful and important positive research on institutional analysis requires such concreteness. Virtue is created from necessity.

Finally, it is important to reiterate that further elaboration and, in particular, empirical testing of models derived from this and other frameworks for the analysis of institutional change should be high on the research agenda in the social sciences and law. The issues concerning how and why institutions change are of general relevance and provide great intellectual challenge. From a normative viewpoint, improvements in human welfare are intimately linked to improvements in institutional design and performance. Positive models of institutional change therefore have the potential to play an important role.

Notes

1. The general point here is that the nature of the good or service will affect the set of feasible institutional arrangements for its supply; the point is elaborated in Plott and Meyer (1975).

2. As a metaphor, "demand for and supply of institutional change" can be taken too literally. It applies in a relatively unqualified fashion to situations where one is considering the degree of utilization of an existing institutional arrangement. In this case, the unit of measurement of the institutional arrangment is relatively homogenous. In the case of the innovation of new arrangements, however, the "good or service" is discrete and often multidimensional. It is like the case of differentiated products considered in some models of imperfect competition. In addition, new arrangements are often provided in "markets" characterized by restricted entry, rivalry, or other elements of less-than-perfect competition—situations in which the standard supply curve derived from the theory of the firm in a competitive industry may not exist. Thus the supply of institutional arrangements should be understood to apply to contexts in which a variety of "market" structures may exist.

3. The list of factors affecting the demand for or supply of institutional change is lengthy. It could be shortened by distinguishing between basic and derived determinants of demand and supply. For

instance, in a small, open economy characterized by extensive economic intercourse with the outside world, the exogenously given terms of trade, technology, and domestic factor endowments would be viewed as basic. These factors in the context of a general equilibrium model determine the relative factor prices and size of market. Thus the framework could be made more compact by focusing on basic determinants. That advantage comes, however, at the price of a loss in concreteness and with a danger that the analyst may overlook derived determinants. Thus the list given in Table 6.1 includes both basic and derived determinants.

Works Cited

Anderson, Terry L., and P. J. Hill (1975) "The Evolution of Property Rights: A Study of the American West." *Journal of Law and Economics*, vol. 18, no. 1 (April), 163–179.

Arrow, Kenneth (1985) "Maine and Texas." *American Economic Review*, vol. 75, no. 2 (May), 320–323.

Axelrod, Robert (1986) "An Evolutionary Approach to Norms." *American Political Science Review*, vol. 80, no. 4 (Dec.), 1095–1111.

Bates, Robert H., and William P. Rogerson (1980) "Agriculture in Development: A Coalitional Analysis." *Public Choice*, vol. 35, no. 5, 513–527.

Battye, Noel Alfred (1974) "The Military, Government and Society in Siam, 1868–1910: Politics and Military Reform during the Reign of King Chulalongkorn." Ph.D. diss., Cornell University.

Binswanger, Hans P. (1974a) "The Measurement of Technical Change Biases with Many Factors of Production." *American Economic Review*, vol. 64, no. 6 (Dec.), 964–976.

——— (1974b) "A Microeconomic Approach to Induced Innovation." *Economic Journal*, vol. 84 (Aug.), 940–958.

——— (1977) "Measuring the Impact of Economic Factors on the Direction of Technical Change." In Thomas M. Arndt, Dana G. Dalyrmple, and Vernon W. Ruttan, eds., *Resource Allocation and Productivity in National and International*

Agricultural Research. Minneapolis: University of Minnesota Press, 526–550.

Binswanger, Hans P., and Vernon W. Ruttan, eds., (1978) *Induced Innovation: Technology, Institutions and Development*. Baltimore: Johns Hopkins University Press.

Blomquist, William, and Elinor Ostrom (1985) "Institutional Capacity and the Resolution of a Commons Dilemma." *Policy Studies Review*, vol. 5, no. 2 (Nov.), 383–393.

Bogue, Allan G. (1983) "Changes in Mechanical and Plant Technology: The Corn Belt, 1910–1940." *Journal of Economic History*, vol. 43, no. 1 (March), 1–25.

Brown, Ian G. (1975) "The Ministry of Finance and the Early Development of Modern Financial Administration in Siam, 1885–1910." Ph.D. diss., University of London.

——— (1978) "British Financial Advisers in Siam in the Reign of King Chulalongkorn." *Modern Asian Studies*, vol. 12, p. 2 (April), 193–215.

Bunnag, Tej (1968) "The Provincial Administration of Siam from 1892 to 1915: A Study of the Creation, the Growth, the Achievement, and the Implications for Modern Siam, of the Ministry of Interior under Prince Damrong Rachanuphap." Ph.D. thesis, St. Anthony's College, University of Oxford.

Chantornvong, Sombat (1988) "Tocqueville's *Democracy in America* and the Third World." In Vincent Ostrom, David Feeny, and Hartmut Picht, eds. *Rethinking Institutional Analysis and Development: Some Issues, Alternatives, and Choices*. San Francisco: ICS Press.

Coase, Ronald H. (1960) "The Problem of Social Cost." *Journal of Law and Economics*, vol. 3 (Oct.), 1–44.

Cox, Thomas R. (1982) "Commentary." *Environmental Review*, vol. 6, no. 2 (fall), 88–91.

Davis, Lance E., Richard A. Easterlin, and William N. Parker, eds. (1972) *American Economic Growth: An Economist's History of the United States*. New York: Harper & Row.

Davis, Lance E., and Robert A. Huttenback (1982) "The Political Economy of British Imperialism: Measures of Benefits and Support." *Journal of Economic History*, vol. 42, no. 1 (March),

119–130.
Davis, Lance E., and Douglass North (1970) "Institutional Change and American Economic Growth: A First Step Towards a Theory of Institutional Innovation." *Journal of Economic History*, vol. 30, no. 1 (March), 131–149.
_____ (1971) *Institutional Change and American Economic Growth*. London and New York: Cambridge University Press.
De Alessi, Louis (1988) "How Markets Alleviate Scarcity." In Vincent Ostrom, David Feeny, and Hartmut Picht, eds., *Rethinking Institutional Analysis and Development: Some Issues, Alternatives, and Choices*. San Francisco: ICS Press.
de Janvry, Alain (1973) "A Socioeconomic Model of Induced Innovations for Argentine Agricultural Development." *Quarterly Journal of Economics*, vol. 87, no. 3 (Aug.), 410–435.
_____ (1977) "Inducement of Technological and Institutional Innovations: An Interpretative Framework." In Thomas M. Arndt, Dana G. Dalyrmple, and Vernon W. Ruttan, eds., *Resource Allocation and Productivity in National and International Agricultural Research*. Minneapolis: University of Minnesota Press, 551–563.
Dennen, R. Taylor (1976) "Cattlemen's Associations and Property Rights in Land in the American West." *Explorations in Economic History*, vol. 13, no. 4 (Oct.), 423–436.
Domar, Evsey (1970) "The Causes of Slavery or Serfdom: A Hypothesis." *Journal of Economic History*, vol. 30, no. 1 (March), 18–32.
Engerman, Stanley (1973) "Some Considerations Relating to Property Rights in Man." *Journal of Economic History*, vol. 33, no. 1 (March), 43–65.
Evenson, Robert E., and Yoav Kislev (1975) *Agricultural Research and Productivity*. New Haven: Yale University Press.
Evers, Hans-Dieter, ed. (1969) *Loosely Structured Social Systems: Thailand in Comparative Perspective*. Southeast Asia Studies Cultural Report Series no. 17, Southeast Asia Center, Yale University.
Feeny, David (1979a) "Competing Hypotheses of Underdevelop-

ment: A Thai Case Study." *Journal of Economic History*, vol. 39, no. 1 (March), 113–127.

_____ (1979b) "Paddy, Princes, and Productivity: Irrigation and Thai Agricultural Development, 1900–1940." *Explorations in Economic History*, vol. 16, no. 2 (April), 132–150.

_____ (1982a) "Infrastructure Linkages and Trade Performance: Thailand, 1900–1940." *Explorations in Economic History*, vol. 19, no. 1 (Jan.), 1–27.

_____ (1982b) *The Political Economy of Productivity: Thai Agricultural Development 1880–1975*. Vancouver, B.C.: University of British Columbia Press.

_____ (1983a) "Extensive versus Intensive Agricultural Development: Induced Public Investment in Southeast Asia, 1900–1940." *Journal of Economic History*, vol. 43, no. 3 (Sept.), 687–704.

_____ (1983b) "The Moral or the Rational Peasant? Competing Hypotheses of Collective Action." *Journal of Asian Studies*, vol. 42, no. 4 (Aug.), 769–789.

_____ (1987) "The Exploration of Economic Change: The Contribution of Economic History to Development Economics." In Alexander J. Field, ed., *The Future of Economic History*. Boston: Kluwer Nijhoff, 91–119.

_____ (1988) "The Development of Property Rights in Land: A Comparative Study." In Robert H. Bates, ed., *Toward a Political Economy of Development: A Rational Choice Perspective*. Berkeley: University of California Press.

Field, Alexander James (1979) "On the Explanation of Rules Using Rational Choice Models." *Journal of Economic Issues*, vol. 13, no. 1 (March), 49–72.

_____ (1981) "The Problem with Neoclassical Institutional Economics: A Critique with Special Reference to the North/Thomas Model of Pre-1500 Europe." *Explorations in Economic History*, vol. 18, no. 2 (April), 174–198.

_____ (1984) "Microeconomics, Norms, and Rationality." *Economic Development and Cultural Change*, vol. 30, no. 4 (July), 683–711.

Gisselquist, David Phillip (1976) "A History of Contractual Relations in a Thai Rice Growing Village." Ph.D. diss., Yale University.

Grabowski, Richard (1988) "The Theory of Induced Institutional Innovation: A Critique." *World Development*, vol. 16, no. 3 (March), 385–394.

Grantham, George (1984) "The Shifting Focus of Agricultural Innovation in Nineteenth-Century Europe: The Case of Agricultural Experiment Stations." In Gary Saxonhouse and Gavin Wright, eds., *Technique, Spirit and Form in the Making of the Modern Economies: Essays in Honor of William N. Parker. Research in Economic History*, supp. 3. Greenwich, Conn.: JAI Press, 191–214.

Griliches, Zvi (1957) "Hybrid Corn: An Exploration in the Economics of Technological Change." *Econometrica*, vol. 25, no. 4 (Oct.), 501–522.

―――― (1958) "Research Costs and Social Returns: Hybrid Corn and Related Innovations." *Journal of Political Economy* (Oct.), 419–431, reprinted in Nathan Rosenberg, ed. (1971) *The Economics of Technological Change*. Baltimore: Penguin Books, 182–202.

―――― (1960) "Hybrid Corn and the Economies of Innovation." *Science* (July), 275–280, reprinted in Nathan Rosenberg, ed. (1971) *The Economics of Technological Change*. Baltimore: Penguin Books, 211–228.

Guttman, Joel M. (1978) "Interest Groups and the Demand for Agricultural Research." *Journal of Political Economy*, vol. 86, no. 3 (June), 467–484.

―――― (1980) "Villages as Interest Groups: The Demand for Agricultural Extension Services in India." *Kyklos*, vol. 33, no. 1, 122–141.

―――― (1982) "Can Political Entrepreneurs Solve the Free-Rider Problem?" *Journal of Economic Behavior and Organization*, vol. 3, 357–366.

―――― (1987) "A Non-Cournot Model of Voluntary Collective Action." *Economica*, vol. 54, no. 213 (Feb.), 1–19.

Hayami, Yujiro, and Masao Kikuchi (1978) "Investment Inducements to Public Infrastructure: Irrigation in the Philippines." *Review of Economics and Statistics*, vol. 60, no. 1 (Feb.), 70–77.

———————————————— (1981) *Asian Village Economy at the Crossroads: An Economic Approach to Institutional Change.* Tokyo: University of Tokyo Press.

Hayami, Yujiro, and Vernon W. Ruttan (1971) *Agricultural Development: An International Perspective.* Baltimore: Johns Hopkins University Press.

———————————————— (1985) *Agricultural Development: An International Perspective.* Rev. ed. Baltimore: Johns Hopkins University Press.

Hayami, Yujiro, et al. (1976) "Agricultural Growth Against a Land Constraint: The Philippine Experience." *Australian Journal of Agricultural Economics*, vol. 20 (Dec.), 144–159.

Hicks, John (1963) *The Theory of Wages.* Second ed. London: St. Martin's Press. First published in 1932.

———————— (1969) *A Theory of Economic History.* Oxford: Oxford University Press.

Holm, David Frederick (1977) "The Role of the State Railways in Thai History, 1892–1932." Ph.D. diss., Yale University.

Hughes, Jonathan (1983) *American Economic History.* Glenview, Ill.: Scott, Foresman.

Kikuchi, Masao, and Yujiro Hayami (1978a) "Agricultural Growth against a Land Resource Constraint: A Comparative History of Japan, Taiwan, Korea, and the Philippines." *Journal of Economic History*, vol. 38, no. 4 (Dec.), 839–864.

———————————————— (1978b) "New Rice Technology and National Irrigation Development Policy." In International Rice Research Institute, *Economic Consequences of the New Rice Technology.* Los Banos, Philippines: International Rice Research Institute, 315–332.

———————————————— (1980) "Inducements to Institutional Innovations in an Agrarian Community." *Economic Development and Cultural Change*, vol. 29, no. 1 (Oct.), 21–36.

Krueger, Anne O. (1974) "The Political Economy of the Rent-Seeking Society." *American Economic Review*, vol. 64, no. 3

(June), 291–303.

Kumar, Dharma (1986) "The Taxation of Agriculture in British India and Dutch Indonesia." In C. A. Bayly and D.H.A. Kolff, eds., *Two Colonial Empires: Comparative Essays on the History of India and Indonesia*. Dordrecht: Nijhoff, 203–225.

La Croix, Sumner J., and James Roumasset (1984) "An Economic Theory of Political Change in Premissionary Hawaii." *Explorations in Economic History*, vol. 21, no. 2 (April), 151–168.

Libecap, Gary D. (1978) "Economic Variables and the Development of the Law: The Case of Western Mineral Rights." *Journal of Economic History*, vol. 38, no. 2 (June), 338–362.

——— (1986) "Property Rights in Economic History: Implications for Research." *Explorations in Economic History*, vol. 23, no. 3 (July), 227–252.

Libecap, Gary D., and Steven N. Wiggins (1985) "The Influence of Private Contractual Failure on Regulation: The Case of Oil Field Unitization." *Journal of Political Economy*, vol. 93, no. 4 (Aug.), 690–714.

McAlpin, Michelle Burge (1983) *Subject to Famine: Food Crises and Economic Change in Western India, 1860–1920*. Princeton: Princeton University Press.

McCloskey, Donald N. (1983) "The Rhetoric of Economics." *Journal of Economic Literature*, vol. 21, no. 2 (June), 481–517.

McKean, Margaret A. (1982) "The Japanese Experience with Scarcity: Management of Traditional Common Lands." *Environmental Review*, vol. 6, no. 2 (Fall), 63–88.

——— (1986) "Management of Traditional Common Lands (Iriaichi) in Japan." In National Research Council, *Proceedings of the Conference on Common-Property Resource Management*. Washington, D.C.: National Academy Press, 533–589.

Matthews, R.C.O. (1986) "The Economics of Institutions and the Sources of Growth." *Economic Journal*, vol. 96, no. 384 (Dec.), 903–918.

Newbery, David M.G., and Joseph E. Stiglitz (1979) "Sharecropping, Risk Sharing and the Importance of Imperfect Information." In James A. Roumasset, Jean-Marc Boussard, and Inderjit Singh, eds., *Risk Uncertainty and Agricultural Development*. Laguna, Philippines: Southeast Asian Regional Center for Graduate Study and Research in Agriculture Development Council, 311–339.

North, Douglass C. (1971) "Institutional Change and Economic Growth." *Journal of Economic History*, vol. 31, no. 1 (March), 118–125.

―――――――― (1978) "Structure and Performance: The Task of Economic History." *Journal of Economic Literature*, vol. 16, no. 3 (Sept.), 963–978.

―――――――― (1979) "A Framework for Analyzing the State in Economic History." *Explorations in Economic History*, vol. 16, no. 3 (July), 249–259.

―――――――― (1981) *Structure and Change in Economic History*. New York: Norton.

―――――――― (1986) "The New Institutional Economics." *Journal of Institutional and Theoretical Economics*, vol. 142, no. 1 (March), 230–237.

North, Douglass C., and Andrew R. Rutten (1987) "The Northwest Ordinance in Historical Perspective." In David Klingaman and Richard Vedder, eds., *Essays on the Economy of the Old Northwest*. Athens: Ohio University Press.

North, Douglass C., and Robert Paul Thomas (1970) "An Economic Theory of the Growth of the Western World." *Economic History Review*, vol. 23, no. 1, 1–17.

―――――――――――――――― (1971) "The Rise and Fall of the Manorial System: A Theoretical Model." *Journal of Economic History*, vol. 31, no. 4 (Dec.), 777–803.

―――――――――――――――― (1973) *The Rise of the Western World: A New Economic History*. London: Cambridge University Press.

Oakerson, Ronald J. (1986) "A Model for the Analysis of Common-Property Problems." In National Research Council, *Proceedings of the Conference on Common Property Resource Management*. Washington, D.C.: National Academy Press, 13–30.

―――――――― (1988) "Reciprocity: A Bottom-up View of

Political Development." In Vincent Ostrom, David Feeny, and Hartmut Picht, eds., *Rethinking Institutional Analysis and Development: Some Issues, Alternatives, and Choices.* San Francisco: ICS Press.

Ostrom, Vincent (1988) "Cryptoimperialism, Predatory States, and Self-Governance." In Vincent Ostrom, David Feeny, and Hartmut Picht, eds., *Rethinking Institutional Analysis and Development: Some Issues, Alternatives, and Choices.* San Francisco: ICS Press.

────────── (1988) "Opportunity, Diversity, and Complexity." In Vincent Ostrom, David Feeny, and Hartmut Picht, eds., *Rethinking Institutional Analysis and Development: Some Issues, Alternatives, and Choices.* San Francisco: ICS Press.

Otsuka, Keijiro, Masao Kikuchi, and Yujiro Hayami (1986) "Community and Market in Contract Choice: The Jeepney in the Philippines." *Economic Development and Cultural Change*, vol. 34, no. 2 (Jan.), 279–298.

Plott, Charles R., and Robert A. Meyer (1975) "The Technology of Public Goods, Externalities, and the Exclusion Principle." In Edward S. Mills, ed., *Economic Analysis of Environmental Problems.* New York: Columbia University Press, 65–90.

Popkin, Samuel L. (1979) *The Rational Peasant: The Political Economy of Rural Society in Vietnam.* Berkeley: University of California Press.

Posner, Richard A. (1979) "Utilitarianism, Economics, and Legal Theory." *Journal of Legal Studies*, vol. 8, 103–140.

────────── (1980) "A Theory of Primitive Society with Special Reference to Law." *Journal of Law and Economics*, vol. 23, no. 1 (April), 1–53.

Ramsay, James Ansil (1971) "The Development of a Bureaucratic Polity: The Case of Northern Siam." Ph.D. diss., Cornell University, Ithaca, New York.

Rosenberg, Nathan (1969) "The Direction of Technological Change: Inducement Mechanisms and Focusing Devices." *Economic Development and Cultural Change*, vol. 18, no. 1, pt. 1 (Oct.), 1–24.

────────── , ed. (1971) *The Economics of Technological Change.* Baltimore: Penguin Books.

_____ (1972) *Technology and American Economic Growth*. New York: Harper & Row.

_____ (1976) *Perspectives on Technology*. Cambridge: Cambridge University Press.

_____ (1982) *Inside the Black Box: Technology and Economics*. Cambridge: Cambridge University Press.

Roumasset, James A. (1978) "The New Institutional Economics and Agricultural Organization." *Philippine Economic Journal*, vol. 17, no. 3, 331–348.

Roumasset, James A., and Sumner J. La Croix (1988) "The Coevolution of Property Rights and Political Orders: An Illustration from Nineteenth-Century Hawaii." In Vincent Ostrom, David Feeny, and Hartmut Picht, eds., *Rethinking Institutional Analysis and Development: Some Issues, Alternatives, and Choices*. San Francisco: ICS Press.

Ruttan, Vernon W. (1978a) "Induced Institutional Change." In Hans Binswanger and Vernon W. Ruttan, eds., *Induced Innovations: Technology, Institutions, and Development*. Baltimore: Johns Hopkins Press, 327–357.

_____ (1978b) "Institutional Innovations." In Theodore W. Schultz, ed., *Distortions of Agricultural Incentives*. Bloomington: Indiana University Press, 290–304.

_____ (1980) "Bureaucratic Productivity: The Case of Agricultural Research." *Public Choice*, vol. 35, no. 5, 529–547.

_____ (1981) "Three Cases of Induced Institutional Innovation." In Clifford S. Russell and Norman K. Nicholson, eds., *Public Choice and Rural Development*. Washington, D.C.: Resources for the Future, 239–270.

_____ (1982) *Agricultural Research Policy*. Minneapolis: University of Minnesota Press.

_____ (1984) "Social Science Knowledge and Institutional Change." *American Journal of Agricultural Economics*, vol. 66, no. 5 (Dec.), 549–559.

Ruttan, Vernon W., and Yujiro Hayami (1984) "Toward a Theory of Induced Institutional Innovation." *Journal of Development Studies*, vol. 20, no. 4 (July), 203–223.

Schmookler, Jacob (1962) "Economic Sources of Inventive Activity."

Journal of Economic History (March), 1–20. Reprinted in Nathan Rosenberg, ed. (1971) *The Economics of Technological Change*. Baltimore: Penguin Books, 117–136.

Schultz, Theodore W. (1964) *Transforming Traditional Agriculture*. New Haven: Yale University Press.

―――――――――――― (1968) "Institutions and the Rising Economic Value of Man." *American Journal of Agricultural Economics*, vol. 50, no. 5 (Dec.), 1113–1122.

Scott, James C. (1976) *The Moral Economy of the Peasant: Rebellion and Subsistence in Southeast Asia*. New Haven: Yale University Press.

Smith, Thomas C. (1959) *The Agrarian Origins of Modern Japan*. Stanford: Stanford University Press.

Solow, Robert M. (1985) "Economic History and Economics." *American Economic Review*, vol. 75, no. 2 (May), 328–331.

Taylor, John (1988) "The Ethical Foundations of the Market." In Vincent Ostrom, David Feeny, and Hartmut Picht, eds., *Rethinking Institutional Analysis and Development: Some Issues, Alternatives, and Choices*. San Francisco: ICS Press.

Umbeck, John F.A. (1977) "The California Gold Rush: A Study of Emerging Property Rights." *Explorations in Economic History*, vol. 14, no. 3 (July), 197–226.

Wiggins, Steven N., and Gary D. Libecap (1985) "Oil Field Unitization: Contractual Failure in the Presence of Imperfect Information." *American Economic Review*, vol. 75, no. 3 (June), 368–385.

Part III

Institutions and Development in Less Developed Countries

7

Susan Wynne

Institutional Resources for Development among the Kgalagadi of Botswana

In democratic countries the science of association is the mother of science; the progress of all the rest depends upon the progress it has made.
—Tocqueville*

Introduction

The concepts from which social organizations are constructed constitute an important part of the cognitive heritage of any group of people. This heritage represents generations of learning about how to organize productively and is thus one of the most valuable forms of "capital" any country has with which to pursue its economic

---

For their helpful suggestions in the preparation of this chapter, I wish to express my appreciation to the editors as well as to Ronald Oakerson, Gary Okihiro, Elinor Ostrom, Filippo Sabetti, Amos Sawyer, Jacqueline Solway, and Patricia Summerside.

*Tocqueville, [1840] 1945, vol. 2: 118

development. In his efforts to account for the character of the American political system of the 1830s, Tocqueville emphasized the significance of this cognitive heritage, which constituted an important dimension of what he referred to as the "customs" of a people.[1]

> I am convinced that the most advantageous situation and the best possible laws cannot maintain a constitution in spite of the customs of a country; while the latter may turn to some advantage the most unfavorable positions and the worst laws. The importance of customs is a common truth to which study and experience incessantly direct our attention. It may be regarded as a central point in the range of observation, and the common termination of all my inquiries. (Tocqueville, [1835] 1945, vol. 1: 334)

This position was echoed in the 1970s by Amilcar Cabral, who stressed the fundamental significance of culture in the process of liberation (Morgado, 1974).

> Culture is simultaneously the fruit of a people's history and a determinant of history, by the positive or negative influence which it exerts on the evolution of relationships between man and his environment, among men or groups of men within a society, as well as among different societies. Ignorance of this fact may explain the failure of several attempts at foreign domination—as well as the failure of some international liberation movements. (Cabral, 1973: 41)

What then is the nature of this stock of cognitive resources upon which all modern Africans can draw? Cabral suggests that a search in any particular modern African country for the "fruits of the past" will usually reveal the fact that culture there is not uniform. One is likely to find hierarchical conceptual principles or organizational norms, such as those used by the Fula of Guinea Bissau, as well as nonhierarchical conceptions, such as those of the Balante (Cabral, 1973: 44–45). Cabral also warns that the "multiplicity of social and ethnic groups complicates the effort to determine the role of culture in the liberation movement," and, presumably, in the design of institutions in independent countries as well (p. 45).

My inquiry into the social organizational heritage of three Tswana-speaking ethnic groups suggests that the nature of the cognitive heritage of many African ethnic groups is even more complex than Cabral suggests.[2] The "traditional" organizational norms of these groups, which now live in central Kweneng District, Botswana, are based upon hierarchical principles, yet these people have had extensive experience with the autonomous organization of communities in which decision making among adult males was consensual. The conceptual heritage of *each* of these groups is thus quite complex.

Historical events suggest that this degree of complexity is probably widespread in Africa. We know that numerous societies described as "stateless" or "acephalous" existed in Africa prior to the European colonial period (Murdock, 1959; Schneider, 1979). We also know that hierarchical principles were widely used prior to the European colonial era to organize units ranging in size from small chiefdoms to large empires. However, virtually all Africans have had some recent experience with hierarchically organized colonial and independent regimes.

Long-standing resistance to centralized governmental control by groups such as the Nuer, the Balante and the Putu, whose social organization Amos Sawyer describes in chapter 8 of this book, is evidence that nonhierarchical organizational norms still constitute an important part of the cognitive heritage of these peoples. The fact that the social world of most Africans has not crumbled despite the significant levels of violence inflicted on it strongly suggests that consensual patterns of interaction did and still do exist, even in hierarchically organized groups.

In this paper, I argue that the nineteenth- and twentieth-century history of the Kgalagadi of central and western Kweneng provides an example of consensual interaction among people with a long tradition of hierarchical organization. In Kweneng, "Kgalagadi" (the people of the desert) is the name given persons who belong to one of three distinct but closely related Tswana-speaking ethnic groups. Many of these people were originally incorporated as low-status members of the Kwena chiefdom, located in the southeastern part of what is now modern Botswana. In the 1820s, in the midst of civil war and external invasion, they fled or were forced, in conditions of servitude, into the arid desert of western Kweneng. Coping effectively with harsh, uncertain circumstances requires flexible, cooperative social relationships. The survival of these people and their significant economic success in a harsh environment was, in large part, a result of relationships among the primarily kin-based social units of the Kgalagadi called *kgotla*, which were not hierarchical.[3] Over time, their normative conceptions about how people should be organized have been adapted to incorporate nonhierarchical principles.

I begin this account of the adaptation of Kgalagadi principles of social organization with a consideration of a type of small social unit, of which the *kgotla* is an example, that appears to be a promising place to begin a systematic search for the locus of productive behavior responsible for at least minimal survival in formally hierarchical systems. I then provide a description of the contrasting sets of rules that structured the social organization of the Kgalagadi before and after their flight into the desert in the nineteenth century. In the last two sections, I summarize the conditions that permitted the productive operation of Kgalagadi *kgotla*, and characterize the nature of the remaining social organizational challenges that face the Kgalagadi and other residents of Botswana.

Primary Local Units of Collective Action

While the polygamous or monogamous family is the basic social unit in all African societies, families never exist independently of one another. The smallest social unit that is capable of operating with considerable autonomy is an aggregation of families. Structured in a wide variety of different ways, this larger unit is ubiquitous in human society because all people confront tasks requiring joint effort with others, and also because they prefer to live "in society" with others. The *kgotla* of Botswana is an example of such a unit, as is the early nineteenth-century New England township described by Tocqueville. In chapter 5 of this book, Ronald Oakerson refers to such units as "primary local units of collective action."

Tocqueville begins his study of American political life with the township because, after the family, it represents the first or "primary" level of social organization. "The village or township is the only association which is so perfectly natural that, wherever a number of men are collected, it seems to constitute itself. . . . [It] exists in all nations, whatever their laws and customs may be" (Tocqueville, [1835] 1945, vol. 1: 62). The term "primary *local* units of collective action" (my emphasis) distinguishes a social unit such as the *kgotla* from a larger ethnic or religious group that individuals might, in some circumstances, identify as their "primary" affiliation.

Despite their ubiquity and central social significance, these small-scale social units have only rarely been recognized as an embodiment of social capital of considerable value, or been subject to systematic comparative study by political scientists. Most political leaders of independent African countries have regarded them as either quaint anachronisms or as dangerous remnants of earlier, inegalitarian societies. In Botswana, formal governing authority has been withdrawn from them in an effort to rid the political system of its patrimonial features. Accounts of *kgotla* operation by foreign observers (Kuper, 1970; Odell, 1985; Richards and Kuper, 1971) have stressed the continuing social significance and productive potential of the *kgotla*. These, however, are rebutted by authentic accounts of arbitrary behavior by *kgotla* headmen. Undoubtedly the behavior of headmen, supported, as they were by the authority of the larger structure of a hierarchical chiefdom, could be most undemocratic. Neither supporters nor detractors of the *kgotla* have been sufficiently aware, however, of the *circumstances* under which "traditional" hierarchical principles of social organization yielded more consensual social relationships. No systematic study has been made to determine the extent to which hierarchical norms of social organization have been adapted to include nonhierarchical principles.

"Traditional" organizational arrangements have been studied by ethnographers and political scientists alike primarily as unique organizational forms.[4] Scholars have focused largely on differences rather than on attempting to understand what commonalities underlie the obvious differences. Without an effort to examine commonalities as well as differences, little can be learned about older forms of social organization that is useful in present-day circumstances. The rules used to constitute these units embody the organizational experiences of people in particular ecological environments. These organizational forms deserve to be the subject of serious comparative analysis. Their internal organization, as well as their role in larger political structures, needs to be sympathetically understood in the way that Tocqueville sought to understand the organization of the New England township of the 1830s and its relationship to state and national institutions in American society (Tocqueville, [1835] 1945, vol. 1: 61–101).

Important first steps in the comparative study of these institutions are to identify a unit of analysis and to specify a set of categories of rules that can be used to define the structure of the unit. The Kgalagdi *kgotla* will be examined here as an example of a primary local unit of collective action. Such a unit is characterized by a membership that is largely self-organizing; consists of an aggregation of families (the lower bound of group size is two families); shares some sort of "kinship" (possibly from common experiences) that is the basis upon which they distinguish themselves from others; and occupies a defined territory.

In this chapter, I contrast the different sets of rules that structured the internal organization of the Kgalagadi *kgotla* and the relationships between *kgotla* before and after the flight of the Kgalagadi into Kweneng's western desert. The analytic descriptions of these two different *kgotla* structures will, for the purposes of this discussion, consist principally of the rules that regulate entry and exit from *kgotla* and delimit the authority of *kgotla* members and leaders.[5]

A cross-cultural study of local units of collective action should yield a diverse array of structures. The structures that have provided a basis for productive endeavor should, however, have common features that, once identified, will contribute to the fuller development of a theory of collective action. In the fourth section of this chapter, I summarize the conditions that have played an important role in the productive operation of the Kgalagadi *kgotla* in the later nineteenth and twentieth centuries.

Table 7.1
Organizational Principles of Kwena and Kgalagadi *Kgotla*, Early Nineteenth Century

Within each family and each *kgotla*:

- A father exercises absolute authority over the assets of a son until his marriage, and over family assets until his own death. A son must obey his father and elder male kin.
- The birth order of sons determines the rank order of their decision-making ability, and is a legitimate basis for the unequal distribution of decision-making authority among brothers. Younger brothers must obey older brothers.
- A man's heir is the first son of his first-ranked wife.
- Only adult males authorized to form a new *kgotla* may leave the *kgotla* into which they were born.

Among *kgotla*:

- Only the senior son of each wife (other than the first-ranked wife in a polygynous family) is authorized to establish a separate *kgotla*.
- Each new *kgotla* must be located nearby that of the new *kgotla* leader's father (see note 11).
- Leaders of new *kgotla* retain their genealogical rank order and must obey senior male kinsmen.
- A superior ethnic group should not be subject to outside control, but culturally inferior groups must acquiesce in the leadership of superior groups.

Hierarchical Principles of Organization

I turn now to a description of the "traditional" hierarchical norms for the regulation of relationships within and among *kgotla* as used by groups attached to the Kwena chiefdom at the beginning of the nineteenth century (see the summary in Table 7.1). The larger social structure was built up from the hierarchical principles of family organization that gave a father significant authority over sons, and elder brothers significant authority over younger brothers (Okihiro, 1976; Schapera, 1977). Hierarchical relations among brothers were maintained as new associational units were added over time. The conception and the language of superior-subordinate status that characterized the relationship between older and younger brothers was also applied to relationships among different ethnic groups (Okihiro, 1976). The subordination of one cultural group to another was justified by the presumption on the part of the dominant group that cultural differences were evidence of cultural inferiority. During much of the nineteenth century, relationships among the three major cultural groups in Kweneng were distinguished by personal relationships of domination that approximated serfdom.

Authority Relationships within the Family. Polygyny was common in Kweneng through the 1920s. In a polygynous household, the male head managed several semiautonomous production/consumption units composed of an adult woman and her children (Schapera, 1966). The family head built a separate homestead and cleared a field for each of his wives.[6] Each woman controlled the use of the produce of her own field. The wives and children of each household could personally own livestock that were distinguished from animals owned by the other households and by the male head, who usually owned the largest number of animals.

Each member of a polygynous family held a place in a well-specified hierarchy of authority. The male head exercised a high level of authority over all his wives and children. A man's wives were ranked according to the order in which he had married them.[7] The rank of sons and daughters was determined by the rank of their mother and the order of their birth within their mother's household. In general, women deferred to men of their own or higher status. From the level of a wife's household to that of the larger cultural group, subordinates were expected to obey their superiors.

In order to ensure his and his wives' security in old age, the head of the household retained control of the livestock (cattle and goats), the household's principal store of wealth, until his death. The eldest son of the first-ranked wife was the father's heir. He inherited the bulk of his father's livestock as well as principal responsibility for the well-being of all his father's surviving wives and children. Ownership of the remainder of the herd was distributed among the younger sons. Somewhat larger portions were given to the eldest sons than to the younger sons of the second and third wives. The eldest son of each wife inherited most of her livestock upon her death and assumed responsibility for the well-being of his younger brothers and their families. Sons often kept inherited livestock together in one herd after their parents' deaths, so that even those brothers who inherited few animals had access to animals for milking and plowing purposes (Henderson, 1980).

The family was not, however, simply a production and consumption unit. Indeed, orderly production and consumption were possible only because it was also the elemental unit of government. The childhood recollections of a young man recorded by I. Schapera describe the type of deference that was expected of younger brothers toward older brothers in a headman's family in about 1920.[8] It also demonstrates the rule-making and rule-enforcing role of the family and extended family.

> While I was still growing to the age of discernment, I was a lad who loved to herd livestock. I had an older brother, whom I used to slight; in the afternoon, on coming home (from the pastures), when he wished to suck a goat, I would push him away from it. When we got home we went to the forum (*kgotla*) and slept there; then after dark we went to pass the time in my mother's homestead, and when we were given food, if he helped himself first I became sullen and took and spilled it, I really did so. It once happened that my father gave us some porridge; my brother took a handful, and as he was breaking it up I took and threw it (the porridge) to the ground, and my father almost killed me. The next day three big he-goats were slaughtered. This day we did not go out to herd, but stayed at home. The blood (of the goats) was cooked, and after it was done my brother and I were given some in a little pot; I took and put it before him, he helped himself, and I lifted up the pot and poured out its contents. My father asked me (why I had done so), and I told him that my spirit had

taught me I was senior to my brother. My father then spoke to my maternal uncle, saying: "Take a lash and whip him"; but my uncle refused, saying, "He is my nephew, and perhaps I have spoiled him." My father replied, "Take some ash and dust him with that, but you must also whip him." I tried to run away from him (the uncle), but he took a cane from the veranda of the hut and pursued me, and I ran with all my might. As I was still running, I looked back at him, and I found that he was close to me. As I ran there was close to me a hole from which the women used to dig out earth, and when I tried to jump over it I fell in, and he caught and beat me. When my mother heard me crying, she also cried. In the evening, after the sun had set, when I came from the cattle-kraal I went to my mother's homestead; and after dark she gave me porridge, saying that I should eat it with my brother, but when he helped himself first I became sulky, and my father almost killed me. From now on I ceased entirely from slighting my older brother. (Schapera, 1938: 186)

Disputes that could not be resolved at the individual family level were passed to successively more senior relatives. As the story illustrates, maternal kin also played a role in family dispute resolution.

The Rules of *Kgotla* Formation. Rules regulating *kgotla* formation in the early years of the nineteenth century determined: (1) which adult males were authorized to form a separate residential and decision-making unit; and (2) where, with respect to their father's homestead, leaders of new *kgotla* could build their own. The way in which new *kgotla* were generated in a growing population organized as polygynous families can best be explained if I begin with what might be considered an "original" polygynous household composed of a man and his three wives (see Table 7.2). The household head's heir was the eldest surviving son of his senior wife. While all of the male head's sons were expected to acknowledge the seniority of this son, it was recognized that men would always feel closer to the brothers born into their own mother's household. Each wife's sons were also expected to show deference and loyalty to their elder brothers in their mother's household.

As sons reached adulthood and were married, they could choose from several associational options. All the sons could elect to remain within the existing social unit. In this case, the original polygynous

Table 7.2

Formation of *Kgotla* from Original Polygynous Household, Early Nineteenth Century

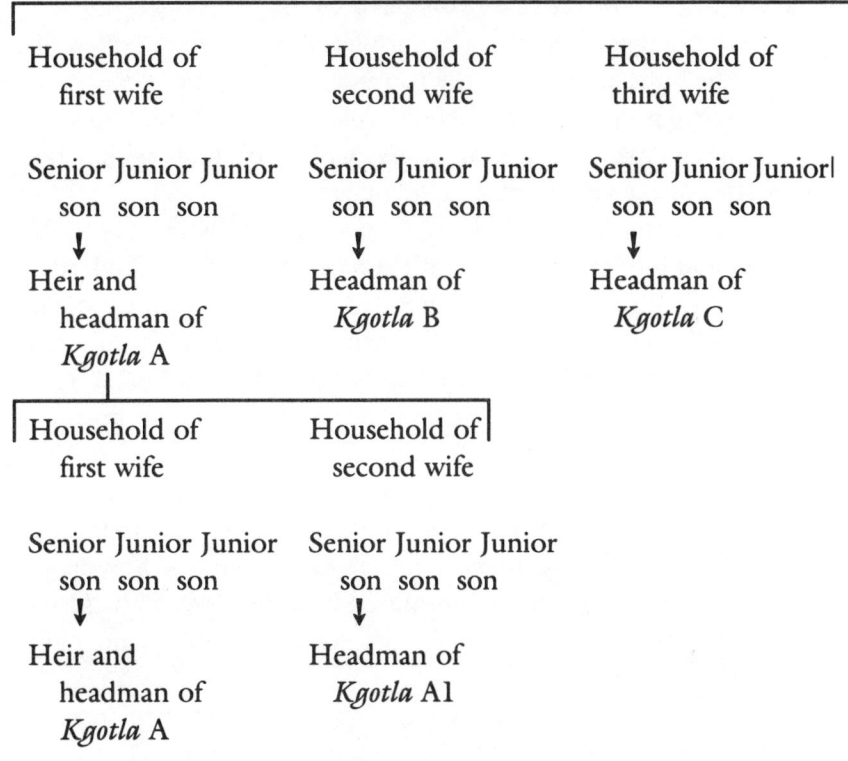

household would simply expand into a larger social and political unit—*Kgotla* A in Table 7.2—under the leadership of the father's heir. It was also possible for the senior sons of the second and third households to form their own *kgotla*. In this case, three *kgotla* would be formed, *Kgotla* A, *Kgotla* B, and *Kgotla* C. Each of these would constitute a separate social unit comprising the household of the senior son and those of his two younger brothers. Each new *kgotla* would acquire the rank of its headman. The relative seniority of these *kgotla* would be maintained through successive generations as new *kgotla* were formed. In the third generation, the rank order of *kgotla* would be A, A1, B, B1, C, C1. The rule permitting the formation of new *kgotla* offered individuals with different maternal kin the opportunity of exercising greater independence without breaking completely with their paternal kin (Okihiro, 1976).

If two new *kgotla* were to be formed, new homesteads would normally be built separate but not too far away from the homesteads of the original polygynous household. All new homesteads, whether or not they constituted a new *kgotla*, had to be built within the boundaries of the chiefdom settlement site.

An individual male stranger with or without his own family could be integrated into this structure as a junior "brother" of the leader of *Kgotla* A, B, or C. A larger extended family group of strangers might be allowed to establish their own separate *kgotla* under the leadership of any married son from any of the three original households. Leadership of the new *kgotla* would be passed down through the descendants of this son. Occasionally, a larger group led by a highly competent and trustworthy stranger would be given status as an additional junior "*Kgotla* D" in this system under its own leader. Gary Y. Okihiro (1976) provides a detailed account of how large numbers of strangers were incorporated into the Kwena chiefdom during the nineteenth century in the wake of great population dislocations in southern Africa.

These organizational norms were adapted in practice to take account of important economic considerations relevant to the viability of a *kgotla*. Both adult male Kwena and strangers, if they had few or no livestock, had to establish their homestead in the *kgotla* of a man wealthy enough to be able to loan them livestock with which to support their families (Duggan, 1986). Because most of the livestock went to the eldest son of the senior wife, elder sons in other houses might not have had sufficient livestock to form their own independent *kgotla*. This economic constraint helps to explain why fewer new *kgotla* were established among the Kwena than the rules would lead one to predict.[9] It also meant that, occasionally, an entrepreneurial younger brother in a household was able to establish his own *kgotla*.

Rules of Ethnic Inequality. Since the settlement of the Kwena in what is now Kweneng in about 1650, political life there has been characterized by inegalitarian relationships among three cultural groups—the Kwena, the Kgalagadi, and the Sarwa (Okihiro, 1976; Schapera, 1952). The core of the Kwena chiefdom was composed of descendants of Kwena as well as a small number of people from related groups who had become thoroughly integrated into the chiefdom. This well-organized group has occupied the highest position in the ethnic hierarchy. Culturally and physically the most distinct from the Kwena, the people referred to collectively in Tswana as the Sarwa have occupied the lowest position in the ethnic hierarchy. These people, sometimes referred to as Bushmen, are descendants of the aboriginal populations of southern Africa. In the nineteenth century, most of them lived as hunters and gatherers in small dispersed population groups in the isolated northern and western regions of Kweneng. The Tswana-speaking Kgalagadi groups have occupied the middle position in this ethnic hierarchy.

Civil war among the Kwena and attacks by succeeding waves of foreign invaders who swept into eastern Botswana in the early nineteenth century sharply increased the deprivations to which population groups living in Kweneng but not fully integrated into the Kwena chiefdom were subjected (Okihiro, 1976). By about 1824, both newly arrived refugees and groups who had lived with the Kwena for a long time had either fled or been forced out into the western desert to become the Kgalagadi. The Kwena needed guns to combat well-armed invading groups. Kgalagadi were expected to collect for the Kwena large quantities of the wild animal skins, ivory, ostrich feathers, and other desert products that traders sought in exchange for rifles. Family groups of Sarwa were attached, sometimes forcibly, to Kgalagadi families whom they assisted in hunting and in preserving skins and meat (Schapera, 1938: 169–170). For the next forty years, Kwena patrols periodically tracked down Kgalagadi groups, confiscated any animal skins, meat, ivory, livestock, or grain they could find, and killed anyone who resisted.

In 1853, warfare among Kwena factions and between Kwena and external invaders ended. Kgalagadi, most of whom had been controlled by the leader of the rebel Kwena faction during the civil war, were distributed more widely among individual Kwena of high rank. Entire ethnic groups were still characterized as servants.[10] But the relationship now paired individual household heads in one group with heads in another; each Kgalagadi household head was personally attached to a Kwena. When the son of a Kwena married, he was given control of the household of one of the sons of the Kgalagadi attached to his father. In turn, each Sarwa household head was attached to a Kgalagadi household head. Kgalagadi paid tribute directly to their own Kwena master, who was expected to send a portion to his senior kinsmen.

In the second half of the nineteenth century, the brutality of these relationships was gradually reduced and the personal and property rights of Kgalagadi gradually restored. The institution of servitude was formally abolished in 1892 by the Kwena chief in order to direct Kgalagadi tribute, relabeled as a tax, to himself alone. Tribute payments to former masters continued, however, until the protectorate administration, under the 1934 Native Administration Proclamation No. 74, outlawed receipt of any form of tribute (Bechuanaland Government, 1934a). Kgalagadi have now regained most of the economic ground they lost in the nineteenth century, but they remain social inferiors (Solway, 1980). Most Kweneng Sarwa are now only part-time hunters and gatherers who also work as field laborers or herders for Kgalagadi and Kwena (Vierich, 1981).

Nonhierarchical Organizational Principles of Kgalagadi *Kgotla*

The conditions of life that Kgalagadi groups encountered in the arid western Kweneng made it impossible for them to organize in accordance with norms still recognized among the Kwena. Political and environmental factors, in addition to the demise of polygyny, helped make the Kgalagadi *kgotla* a different kind of social unit organized on different principles (see summary in Table 7.3). The result has been the development in central and western Kweneng of small scattered autonomous settlements containing fragments of ethnic groups formed into one or more *kgotla* . Until the past few decades, family groups could move at little cost to join kin in other settlements or establish a new settlement. Beginning in the 1920s, access to the opening of wage-labor opportunities for men with, at the same time, the increased significance of male labor in plow cultivation of croplands, gave younger brothers more bargaining power within the family. These factors have had a leveling effect on hierarchical relationships among brothers.

The Kgalagadi Pattern of *Kgotla* Organization.[11] From 1824 to 1853, Bolaongwe and Shaga moved incessantly in *kgotla* or individual family groups to find food and water and to evade Kwena and Ndebele raiders. During this period, members of the two Kgwatheng *kgotla* were able to remain in the vicinity of Kwena cattle-post wells at Letlhakeng. The Kwena made fewer tribute demands on them, apparently because they were not good hunters.[12]

When the fighting ended in 1853, only two Kgwatheng *kgotla*, two Bolaongwe *kgotla*, and probably about ten Shaga *kgotla* remained on the fringes of the Kwena chiefdom territory. The Kwena routinized the tribute system, reducing somewhat the uncertainty of the Kgalagadi. This encouraged the establishment of more permanent settlements. As populations increased, the size of settlements remained small; often a settlement contained only a single *kgotla*. Individuals and individual families also moved independently for portions of the year, rejoining larger groups at reliable water sources for the dry winter season when group hunting was carried on.

This organizational form facilitated hunting and gathering that provided food as well as the tribute demanded by the Kwena. The Kwena, therefore, had no incentive to force Kgalagadi to settle down in a few large settlements. Since any livestock that Kgalagadi managed to accumulate could still be confiscated, there was little family wealth that could be inherited. In such circumstances, younger brothers unhappy with their treatment could easily leave their *kgotla* and attach themselves to other kin.

In the third quarter of the nineteenth century, the Kwena allowed trading relationships to develop. Kgalagadi could now exchange any animal skins that were not needed for tribute payments for cattle. The

Table 7.3
Organizational Principles of Contemporary Kgalagadi *Kgotla*

Within each family and each *kgotla*:

- Fathers share authority over assets of sons until the sons marry, and control family assets until they die.
- The order of birth of brothers is recognized as conferring on older brothers superior wisdom and knowledge acquired through their greater experience. Younger brothers must respect older brothers but need not obey them.
- A man's principal heir is the first son of his first-ranked wife. Younger brothers are entitled to a considerable share of family wealth at the death of the father.
- An adult male may settle anywhere he chooses.
- The genealogically most senior male in a settlement is the legitimate leader of the *kgotla*.

Among *kgotla*:

- Any adult male can establish a new *kgotla*.
- A new *kgotla* can be located anywhere, although fathers prefer that sons settle near them.
- Genealogically senior males have no authority over junior kin in other *kgotla* except when they have been sought out as mediators of conflicts.
- Individuals may appeal judgments of a Kgalagadi *kgotla* court to Kwena *kgotla* courts, including the court of the Kwena chief.
- Kgalagadi should not be subject to Kwena, but Sarwa should acquiesce in the leadership of Kgalagadi.

expanding cattle herds required larger amounts of water, increasing the dependence of the Kgalagadi on the perennial water sources in the valleys of central Kweneng. Gradually families that brought cattle to Letlhakeng, Kgesakwe, and Khudumelapye during the dry winter months began to remain in the area. Newly arrived family groups built houses near kin already established there, and the genealogical senior was recognized as the common leader.

Over the course of the century, the nature of the social group that constituted the principal social and residential unit in the central and western part of Kweneng gradually changed. This group did not consist of a neat, well-defined branch of a family tree but was, in many cases, a small community composed of fragments of more traditionally organized *kgotla*. Occasionally these new communities included a few family heads from different ethnic groups. Some intermarriage occurred among Bolaongwe, Shaga, and the Ngologa who lived west of Kweneng.

The *kgotla* currently found in the villages of Letlhakeng and Khudumelapye were formed in 1945, when *kgotla* scattered around the wider central Kweneng region were asked to move together to form a densely structured village. These official *kgotla* represented the major divisions in the three major ethnic groups. They also included family groups belonging to immigrant Kwena, refugees from the wars who had settled with the Kwena and then decided to move west. Population increase resulting from the continuing immigration of kin fragments has not resulted in the formation of any new *kgotla* in Letlhakeng since 1945. New *kgotla* formation within established settlements among the Kgalagadi appears to have ended for the same reasons as among the Kwena. The monogynous marriage pattern and the withdrawal of recognized governing authority from the leaders of *kgotla* removed both the traditional reason and the incentive for new *kgotla* formation within an existing settlement. Existing *kgotla* have simply continued to expand in size.

Neither the Kgalagadi as a whole nor any of the three ethnic groups individually recognized a single "chief" with authority over *kgotla* in all settlements.[13] Individuals know how they are related to others in their ethnic group. They may approach senior kin for help in resolving a dispute, but senior kin living outside their settlement have no impact on their daily lives. A man's younger brothers are still expected to remain close to him. Little can be done, however, to stop them from setting out into the desert on their own if they choose to do so.

The populations of *kgotla* in the major Kgalagadi settlements have fluctuated considerably since their founding. Family groups have moved in and out in search of better hunting, better pasture, better water for livestock, a better place in which to cultivate crops, or more agreeable neighbors or leaders. The low cost to any household head, whose wealth was in livestock, of exit from a given *kgotla* has encouraged restraint in the extent to which senior members attempt to dominate junior members in a *kgotla*. The dispersed settlement pattern has created multiple associational options for the heads of households.

The Kwena did not aspire to control the way in which Kgalagadi organized their own affairs except to ensure the collection of tribute and taxes. Kwena *kgotla* courts were occasionally used as courts of appeal for Kgalagadi unhappy with the judgments of their own courts. Kgalagadi, however, tended to avoid paying taxes when possible and to resolve disputes with minimal contact with the Kwena. Protectorate administrative reforms in 1934 removed the independent judicial authority of almost all *kgotla* headmen (Bechuanaland Government, 1934b). The chief's representative sent to Letlhakeng as a judicial officer for all Kgalagadi of central and western Kweneng was, from the point of view of Kwena and Kgalagadi, principally a tax collector. However, because Kgalagadi *kgotla* headmen constituted the council that advised the chief's representative on all cases brought to the court, they continued to have a direct role in judicial matters. This common local court has become a useful institution. Unfortunately, without the assistance of *kgotla* courts, it has become overburdened and frequently refuses to hear civil cases.

Wage Income and Increased Equality within the Family. Hierarchical relationships and more authoritarian management styles have survived the longest inside the family. From the point at which Kgalagadi began to rebuild their livestock herds until the late 1920s, when men began to go to work in the mines of South Africa, control of household resources by the family head kept the cost of disobedience, which was disinheritance, high—particularly for the eldest son in each household. Initially, fathers demanded that mine wages be turned over to the family head to meet consumption needs or for investment in livestock (Schapera, [1938] 1977: 220-221).

Wage-employment opportunities provided young men with a source of income that was not controlled by their senior male relations. Younger sons could, if they chose, break with their families and keep their wages for themselves. The threat of this break and the loss of wage income and scarce male labor from the family inspired many fathers to give sons greater control over their wages and over the livestock in which their wages were invested. A gradual alteration of inheritance rules, which had closely approximated primogeniture, has also occurred. Today, a father's estate, primarily in the form of cattle, is distributed more evenly among his sons (Henderson, 1980). Daughters also may now inherit from their fathers. This change has encouraged younger sons to remain a part of the family production team.

Genealogically senior males still have leadership prerogatives, but they are no longer assured. Reduction in the official authority of the *kgotla* headmen only partially explains the fact that a mere one in seven of the *kgotla* in the village of Letlhakeng is now led by the genealogically senior male member. As early as the 1850s, when *kgotla* headmen wielded considerable formal authority, some Kgalagadi who were entitled to leadership positions chose not to take them because they disliked the responsibilities involved. Personal qualities including literacy skills are increasingly important in the selection of leaders.

New *Kgotla* Near Cultivation Areas and Boreholes. Kgalagadi are not the only cultural group in Kweneng that has demonstrated the ability to adapt the conception of the *kgotla* and create new kinds of communities. Survey research by R. M. K. Silitshena (1979) indicates that in the 1960s the Kwena began moving away from the main body of the chiefdom established in the large village of Molepolole located in eastern Kweneng to form new settlements in cultivation areas previously inhabited only during the growing season. Accelerated development of underground water in the 1950s and the declining influence of the Kwena chief since Botswana's independence in 1966 were principally responsible for this new *kgotla* formation in eastern Kweneng.

The development of deep-bored wells has also been associated with the process of new *kgotla* creation in the central and western parts of the district. Former residents of the first larger permanent settlements such as Letlhakeng, Dutlwe, and Takatokwane, as well as family groups that had not yet joined a large permanent settlement, have established new *kgotla* at places that were originally isolated cattle posts (Kramer and Odell, 1979). Although the opportunity costs of moving away from established villages have increased because of the development of schools and clinics, population movement continues.

This remarkably vigorous community-generating process continues even though *kgotla* headmen have no formally recognized governing authority. The district administration does recognize the leaders of villages of some minimal size as subordinate judicial authorities. But neither *kgotla* nor villages have independent lawmaking or taxing authority. Botswana's political leaders have been of two minds about these new communities. On the one hand, they realize that the productivity of agriculture will be increased if people live near their fields and animals. On the other, the multiplication of small settlements, makes it more difficult to fulfill promises about providing social services. Some of the new settlements in the east and west have been officially accepted as villages and their headmen have been recognized as official judicial authorities. Even in those settlements where the headmen are not so recognized, they arbitrate disputes and organize local affairs (Silitshena, 1979). Difficult cases are forwarded to authorized judicial officials of recognized village courts. Residents of unrecognized settlements do not, however, take part in the selection of representatives to the Kweneng District Council, the only subnational representative body with any lawmaking authority.

Table 7.4

The Successful Operation
of Primary Local Units of Collective Action:
Some Prerequisites

1. *Common understanding.* A common understanding among members about the rights and duties of membership. Reaching a common understanding about the operation of a unit is facilitated by a common (or similar) language(s) as well as by common experiences.

2. *Group interaction characterized by reciprocity.* Members must understand reciprocity and consider reciprocal behavior the proper way for group members to interact.

3. *Some autonomous authority.* Some autonomy from superior administrative units (possibly as a result of geographical isolation) that allows the making and enforcing (possibly only with social sanctions) of rules, and enables the group to marshal group resources and to limit the authority of leaders.

4. *Small size.* When the upper bound of group membership is considered relatively small (perhaps 20-30 adult household heads in illiterate societies), groups can more easily monitor each other's behavior thereby discouraging shirking and free-riding.

5. *Reasonably priced exit option.* The existence of other autonomous groups, attempting to achieve similar objectives, to which a group member might, at a reasonable cost, move, enhances the effectiveness of any one member's voice within the organization and increases the likelihood that leaders will be sensitive to the views of others.

Conditions for the Productive Operation of Primary Local Units of Collective Action

The history of Kgalagadi *kgotla* in the nineteenth century illustrates conditions for the successful operation of local units of collective action in a way that confirms the importance of certain theoretical elements that are not widely recognized (see the summary in Table 7.4). Theories of teamwork begin with the observation that there are numerous tasks, such as group hunting, whose accomplishment enhances life and that could not be managed as successfully or as cheaply by individuals acting alone (Alchian and Demsetz, 1972). Successful teamwork, however, depends crucially on the characteristics of the participants and their attitudes toward each other. Vincent Ostrom (1987) has stressed the significance of the cognitive requirements of sustained, productive, coordinated group activity. Members of productive groups share a similar language and other cultural characteristics that have reduced the costs to them of reaching agreement about organizational rules.

Ronald J. Oakerson in chapter 5 of this book and John F. A. Taylor in chapter 12 emphasize the significance of reciprocity for the success of coordinated efforts. Members must be willing to continue to cooperate with others even when the short-term costs of membership outweigh immediate benefits. Cooperation is sustained by a confidence that the long-term benefits of cooperation will outweigh costs, and that consistently uncooperative people will not be allowed to benefit from the joint efforts of others. It follows that local units of collective action can be most easily organized among kin, to whom reciprocity is the normal pattern of behavior. But they need not be composed only of kin.

Logically, members of such units must have some autonomous authority to make and enforce rules, which is necessary for the marshalling of the resources to carry out common tasks, and to limit the authority of leaders. The authority exercised to this end may or may not be legal in the sense of being embodied in a code of laws. Because larger-scale hierarchical organizations suffer from loss of information and control (Simon, 1965; Tullock, 1965), one would expect to find opportunities for small-scale organization to operate even within systems that grant little or no autonomy to small social units, such as Kgalagadi *kgotla* . Human beings have self-organizing capabilities that even the most repressive regimes cannot thwart entirely.

In voluntary, self-organizing collectivities, members must rely upon organizational features other than the threat of criminal sanctions in order to discourage fellow members from shirking or free-riding. It is easier to discourage undesirable behavior and safeguard group cohesion in small-scale organizations in which all members can easily monitor each other's activities than in large-scale organizations (Hardin, 1982; Olson, 1971; E. Ostrom, 1985). The fact that a group is defined as being self-organized implies an upper limit on its size. The exact size of a group that can self-organize and operate successfully over time is, however, an empirical question; literate persons, for example, may be able to manage a larger group than illiterate ones.

Albert O. Hirschman (1970) and Vincent Ostrom and his colleagues (1961) have pointed out that the existence of alternative groups to which individuals can defect, if membership in one group imposes high deprivation costs, serves to enhance the voice of each group member and to discourage group leaders from the arbitrary use of authority. This feature also encourages leaders of one group to learn from the successes of other groups in order to avoid losing members to them. The cost of exit faced by an individual is a crucial issue here. Ronald J. Oakerson and others (1987) and Harold K. Schneider (1979) have emphasized that exit costs are lowest for persons, such as nineteenth- and early twentieth-century Kgalagadi hunter-gatherer cattle keepers, whose capital accumulation is highly mobile. Together, the last three conditions listed in Table 7.4 help to guard against majority tryanny inside the group without the assistance of outside authorities.

The Continuing Challenge of Institutional Analysis and Design

The significance of the Kgalagadi experience in the desert is ignored by others in Kweneng because it is the experience of people who are still considered not very "civilized." Its significance is also discounted by some Kgalagadi, in part because their ancestors were forced into the harsh circumstances that required them to adapt their social organization so that it more closely resembled that of the "uncivilized" Sarwa. Some Kgalagadi have accepted the views of others that this pattern of social organization is indeed part of what makes them less "civilized." The fact that aspects of the Kgalagadi social organizational heritage are contradictory also creates confusion. Frustrated Kgalagadi elders occasionally contend that a return to "traditional" practices, that is, to conceptual norms of hierarchy, is all that is needed in order to solve modern social problems. These same men, however, are deeply resentful of headmen or government officials who attempt to "rule" over them. Older Kgalagadi are especially likely to take off for the cattle post or some small western settlement in order to avoid tax collectors or other persons asking for contributions for local development projects that appear to promise few benefits for them.

The complexity of the organizational dimension of the Kgalagadi's cognitive heritage increases both the difficulty of diagnosing the structural sources of a social problem and the likelihood that the resulting diagnosis will be correct. Conclusions about the institutional sources of past successes and failures depend in large part on which theory one brings to the analysis. If one's understanding of institutional principles is limited to those of hierarchy, problems can only be addressed simplistically by attempting to perfect hierarchical organization. Even for people who can draw upon a more varied repertoire of design principles, diagnosis is a difficult task. Problems such as overgrazing of pasture land or juvenile delinquency could be due to the degree to which community organizations have moved away from the strictly hierarchical control of genealogical or bureaucratic "seniors." Conversely, they could be due to residual hierarchical features or to some inappropriate combination of hierarchical and nonhierarchical principles.

Ultimately, only experimentation can confirm the accuracy of a particular diagnosis. Learning on the part of any group of people is enhanced when they are able to conduct their own experiments based upon their own heritage of conceptual principles and experiences in light of an awareness that other principles of organization are available. Opportunities for experimentation with institutional design have, however, been sharply curtailed by Botswana's central government leadership, which has insisted upon preempting all major institutional reforms. In the interest of fairness to all groups, the leadership has insisted on uniformity in organization design. To permit the expression of ethnically based experiences in organization is thought to be an invitation to "tribal" conflict and civil war.

That any significant devolution of authority to subnational social units is associated with chaos demonstrates what surely is the most serious challenge in designing institutions for the people of modern Botswana. This is the absence, from both the conceptions and experiences of the Tswana-speaking population, of principles, other than those of hierarchy, by which *kgotla* might be linked for the purpose of addressing problems affecting larger communities in Kweneng and Botswana. In the past, Kgalagadi required access to the wider community beyond their *kgotla* only for the purposes of judicial appeal. Officially they had access to the courts of the Kwena *kgotla* to which they had been attached as servants; informally they sought out senior relatives to act as mediators. Increasing population density and new technologies are generating new problems that have widespread effects and require the attention of people living in many *kgotla*. The absence of an understanding of nonhierarchical means of organizing collective choice among *kgotla* ensures that the hierarchical principles of the institutions of government in Botswana cannot be supplanted. Despite repeated "reform" efforts, the fundamental "form" will remain the same.

The cognitive heritage of other groups inside modern Botswana, such as the Kalanaga, whose conceptual principles of organization are nonhierarchical, may well provide some assistance. So little serious *analytic* attention has been given to the political theories of "traditional" African societies that it is difficult to know what in the way of conceptual heritages there is to be drawn upon for the construction of multicultural, self-governing societies. The concepts and computational logic that people use to order their ways of life are the ingredients of their political theory. In Africa, these heritages are undoubtedly rich. To identify and analyze the cognitive heritage of the peoples of Africa is therefore a research task of the greatest significance for understanding the social capital that is available for African development.

Notes

1. "I here use the word customs with the meaning which the ancients attached to the word mores; for I apply it not only to manners properly so called—that is, to what might be termed the habits of the heart—but to the various notions and opinions current among men and to the mass of those ideas which constitute their character of mind. I comprise under this term, therefore, *the whole moral and intellectual condition of a people*" (Tocqueville, [1835] 1945, vol. 1: 310, my emphasis).

2. Much of this chapter is based on oral historical material I collected in Letlhakeng and other villages in central Kweneng. My own understanding of population movements in western Kweneng is derived from oral histories of the Bolaongwe and the Shaga collected by Jacqueline Solway. The interpretation of these materials is my own.

3. In standard Tswana, the term *kgotla* (pl. *dikgotla*) refers to the meeting place in which members of a social unit, the *lekgotla* (pl. *makgotla*), gather for discussions. In everyday usage, Tswana speakers frequently shorten the word *lekgotla* to *kgotla*. In order to simplify the discussion, I use the term *kgotla* to refer to one or more of these social units.

4. Extensive comparative research has been done on kinship systems. Kinship rules are frequently what constitute primary local units in traditional societies. Of particular importance here are the pioneering efforts of Schneider (1979) to associate kinship systems with other characteristics of East African societies including the structure of authority.

5. Elinor Ostrom (1986a, 1986b) has suggested the following classification categories for rules that, in configural relationship with one another, can be used to describe the analytic structure of institutions.

1. *Boundary rules*, which set the entry, exit, and domain conditions for individual participants.
2. *Scope rules*, which specify which states of the world can be affected and set the range within which these can be affected.
3. *Position rules*, which establish positions, assign participants to positions, and define who has control over tenure in a position.
4. *Authority rules*, which prescribe which positions can take which actions and how actions are ordered, processed, and terminated.
5. *Information rules*, which establish information channels, state the conditions under which they are to be open or closed, create an official language, and prescribe how evidence is to be processed.
6. *Aggregation rules*, which prescribe formulae for weighting individual choices and calculating collective choices at decision nodes.
7. *Payoff rules*, which prescribe how benefits and costs are to be distributed to participants in positions given their actions and those of others.

6. Some Kwena men also cleared a field for themselves. In good years, the grain harvested from this field represented a surplus used for investment in livestock (Schapera, 1943). Income invested by Kgalagadi in livestock was generated primarily by hunting and wage labor.

7. Among the most genealogically senior families whose marriages had considerable political significance, the wife whose eldest son would be considered heir was sometimes not the first wife married.

8. This story was told by Gaoonwe Seloilwe, who was the headman of the Bolaongwe *kgotla*, Goo-Modimo, in the Letlhakeng area when Schapera recorded it. Josefa, the older brother mentioned in the story, died before his father, so the leadership position had passed to the storyteller. Deference toward genealogical seniors, which is such an issue in this story, was probably viewed with somewhat greater seriousness in a headman's family than in other families because the heir would become *kgotla* headman.

9. If each of the nine sons of the founder of *Kgotla* A married three wives and each of these wives produced three sons, eighteen new *kgotla* could be formed in the next generation.

10. The Tswana-language terms that are translated in the text as "master" and "servant" are *mong* (pl. *beng*) and *motlhanka* (pl. *batlhanka*). *Motlhanka* has been used in Kweneng to refer to the subordinate party in two types of asymmetrical relationships that have involved some form of servitude (Okihiro, 1976: 132). As it has been most commonly used, the term refers to the subordinate in relationships between persons of different economic status who belong to the same cultural group and enjoy the same personal and property rights—a man and his son, an older brother and his younger brother, or a wealthy man and a poorer one. Used in this way, the term has been translated as "servant" (Schapera, 1943) and "client" (Tlou, 1977). As it is used in this chapter, *motlhanka* refers to the subordinate party in relationships between persons of radically different economic status who belong to different cultural groups and enjoy radically different personal and property rights. Used in this way, *motlhanka* has usually been translated as "serf" (Schapera, 1943; Silberbauer and Kuper, 1966; Tlou, 1977). Similar conditions of servitude involving Sarwa, however, were characterized as "slavery" by British administrators and missionaries (see Gadibolae, 1985; Hailey, 1953; Hitchcock, 1987). Because the terms "slave" and "serf" have not been used consistently to refer to specific conditions of servitude, and because the conditions of servitude experienced by Kgalagadi and Sarwa in Kweneng have varied considerably over time, I have chosen to retain the more general term "servant" to describe the subordinate party in both types of relationship. This requires that the conditions of servitude in any particular

asymmetrical relationship be specified for each time period.

11. Because collection of the oral histories of the Kgwatheng, the Bolaongwe, and the Shaga of Kweneng has only just begun, this generalization must be qualified. The rule that a new *kgotla* had to be built near existing *kgotla* was almost certainly shared by the Kwena, the Kgwatheng, and the Shaga in the early nineteenth century. Kgwatheng oral historical accounts of this period indicate that this group, which lived with the Kwena for more than a century and a half prior to their expulsion into the desert, used the same rule the Kwena used for some time after they moved west (Okihiro, 1976: 130). Phitsane, the second-ranking son of Moiphisi who established the Kgwatheng *kgotla* in Letlhakeng, killed one of his younger brothers who had moved away from the *kgotla* settlement at Mhateng and refused to come back when ordered to do so. Moiphisi's eldest son, Dire, who was not interested in being headman, also left the settlement soon after his father died. Dire's genealogical seniority made it possible for him to leave without consequence. (These examples come from my Letlhakeng interviews.) Three of the five groups among which modern Shaga are divided—the Moriti, the Sekgalo, and the Motsoto—lived with the Kwena and Kgwatheng for a considerable period of time (Okihiro, 1976: 176–178). The other two Shaga groups—the Panyana and the Monyemane—which arrived much later at the Kwena settlement, had fled from settlements destroyed by invaders located immediately east or southeast of the Kwena (p. 133). These groups probably also shared settlement rules similar to those of the other three Shaga groups. The settlements of Tswana chiefdoms both large and small of this period were distinctive among southern African livestock-keeping people for their densely clustered settlement pattern (Legassick, 1969; Wilson and Thompson, 1969: 153). Their prior experience in the desert probably meant that, among the Kgalagadi groups, the Bolaongwe experienced the least change in their norms of social organization in the course of the nineteenth century. Okihiro (1976: 130–131) indicates that the Bolaongwe arrived in the vicinity of the Kwena in the early nineteenth century after extensive travels lasting perhaps a century and a half in the southwestern and western part of what is

present-day Botswana. Their population, having hived off from a larger group, was quite small, so the question of how many settlements they should have may not have been relevant to their circumstances.

12. Kgwatheng did not escape entirely from the predations of the Kwena during the period of warfare. Modern-day *kgotla* informants describe elaborate techniques developed during this period for hiding grain from Kwena and Ndebele raiders.

13. After the village of Letlhakeng was formed in 1945, the district officer of the protectorate administration appointed the genealogically senior Bolaongwe in Kweneng, who was at that time headman of Goo-Modimo *kgotla* of Letlhakeng, as "chief" of the Kgalagadi. The appointment had no effect, since this chief was given no governing authority of any kind. Today the headman of this *kgotla* acts as assistant to the chief's representative, who is president of the village court, but excercises no official authority.

Works Cited

Alchian, Armen A., and Harold Demsetz (1972) "Production, Information Costs, and Economic Organization." *American Economic Review*, vol. 62, 777–795.

Bechuanaland Government (1934a) *Native Administration Proclamation No. 74*. Cape Town: The High Commissioner of South Africa.

_____ (1934b) *Native Tribunals Proclamation No. 75*. Cape Town: The High Commissioner of South Africa.

Cabral, Amilcar (1973) *Return to the Source: Selected Speeches of Amilcar Cabral*. Africa Information Service, ed. New York: Monthly Review Press.

Duggan, William R. (1986) *An Economic Analysis of Southern African Agriculture*. New York: Praeger.

Gadibolae, Mabunga (1985) "Serfdom (*Bolata*) in the Nata Area 1926–1960." *Botswana Notes and Records*, vol. 17, 25–32.

Hailey, Lord William M. (1953) *Native Administration in the*

British African Territories, Part V: The High Commission Territories—Basutoland, the Bechuanaland Protectorates and Swaziland. London: Her Majesty's Stationery Office.

Hardin, Russell (1982) *Collective Action.* Baltimore: Johns Hopkins University Press.

Henderson, Willie (1980) "Letlhakeng: A Study of Accumulation in a Kalahari Village." Ph.D. thesis, School of African and Asian Studies, University of Sussex, Brighton, England.

Hirschman, Albert O. (1970) *Exit, Voice, and Loyalty: Responses to Decline in Firms, Organizations, and States.* Cambridge: Harvard University Press.

Hitchcock, Robert K. (1987) "Socioeconomic Change among the Basarwa in Botswana: An Ethnohistorical Analysis." *Ethnohistory,* vol. 34, no. 3 (summer), 219–255.

Kramer, A., and M. J. Odell, Jr. (1979) "Planning for Development: Western Kweneng District—A Spatial and Development Plan." Rural Sociology Report no. 6. Gaborone, Botswana: Rural Sociology Unit, Ministry of Agriculture.

Kuper, Adam (1970) *Kalahari Village Politics.* Cambridge: Cambridge University Press.

Legassick, Martin (1969) "The Sotho-Tswana Peoples before 1800." In Leonard Thompson, ed., *African Societies in Southern Africa.* London: Heinemann, 86–125.

Morgado, Michael S. (1974) "Amilcar Cabral's Theory of Cultural Revolution." *Black Images,* vol. 3, no. 2 (summer), 3–16.

Murdock, G.P. (1959) *Africa: Its Peoples and Their Culture.* New York: McGraw-Hill.

Oakerson, Ronald J. (1983) "Reciprocity: The Political Nexus." Working paper, Department of Political Science, Marshall University, Huntington, West Virginia.

——— (1985) "The Meaning and Purpose of Local Government: A Tocquevillist Perspective." Working paper, Advisory Commission on Intergovernmental Relations, Washington, D.C.

Oakerson, Ronald J., Roger B. Parks, and H. Aaron Bell (1987) *How Fragmentation Works.* Washington, D.C.: Advisory Commission on Intergovernmental Relations.

Odell, Malcolm J., Jr. (1985) "Local Government: Traditional and Modern Roles of the Village Kgotla." In Louis A. Picard, ed., *The Evolution of Modern Botswana*. Lincoln: University of Nebraska Press.

Okihiro, Gary Y. (1976) "Hunters, Herders, Cultivators, and Traders: Interaction and Change in the Kgalagadi, Nineteenth Century." Ph.D. diss., Department of History, University of California, Los Angeles.

Olson, Mancur, Jr. (1971) *The Logic of Collective Action: Public Goods and the Theory of Groups*. New York: Schocken Books.

Ostrom, Elinor (1985) "The Rudiments of a Revised Theory of the Origins, Survival, and Performance of Institutions for Collective Action." Working Paper W85-32, Workshop in Political Theory and Policy Analysis, Indiana University, Bloomington, Ind.

─────────── (1986a) "An Agenda for the Study of Institutions." *Public Choice*, vol. 48, 3-25.

─────────── (1986b) "A Method of Institutional Analysis." In F. X. Kaufmann, G. Majone, and V. Ostrom, eds., *Guidance, Control, and Evaluation in the Public Sector*. New York: de Gruyter, 459-475.

Ostrom, Vincent (1987) "Constitutional Foundations for a Theory of System Comparisons: An Inquiry into Problems of Incommensurability, Emergent Properties, and Development." Paper presented at the Radein Research Seminar, Redagon, Italy, February 14-25.

─────────── , Charles M. Tiebout, and Robert Warren (1961) "The Organization of Government in Metropolitan Areas: A Theoretical Inquiry." *American Political Science Review*, vol. 60, no. 4 (Dec.), 831-842.

Richards, Audrey, and Adam Kuper (1971) "The Kalahari Lekgotla." In Audrey Richards and Adam Kuper, eds., *Councils in Action*. London: Cambridge University Press.

Schapera, I. (1938) "Ethnographic Texts in the Boloongwe Dialect of Sekgalagadi." *Bantu Studies*, vol. 12, no. 3 (Sept.), 157-187.

─────────── (1943) *Native Land Tenure in the Bechuanaland Protectorate*. Alice, Republic of South Africa: Lovedale Press.

_____ (1952) *The Ethnic Composition of Tswana Tribes.* London School of Economics and Political Science Monographs on Social Anthropology no. 11. London: Lund Humphries.

_____ (1966) *Married Life in an African Tribe.* Evanston, Ill.: Northwestern University Press. First published in 1940.

_____ (1977) *A Handbook of Tswana Law and Custom.* London: Cass. First published in 1938.

Schneider, Harold K. (1979) *Livestock and Equality in East Africa: The Economic Basis for Social Structure.* Bloomington, Ind.: Indiana University Press.

Silberbauer, G. B., and A. J. Kuper (1966) "Kgalagari Masters and Bushmen Serfs: Some Observations." *African Studies,* vol. 25, no. 4, 171–179.

Silitshena, R.M.K. (1979) "Changing Settlement Patterns in Botswana: The Case of the Eastern Kweneng." Ph.D. thesis, Graduate School in Arts and Social Studies, University of Sussex, Brighton, England.

Simon, Herbert (1965) *Administrative Behavior: A Study of Decision-Making Processes in Administrative Organization.* New York: Free Press. First published in 1947.

Solway, Jacqueline (1980) "People, Cattle and Drought in Western Kweneng: Report on Dutlwe Village." Rural Sociology Report No. 16. Gaborone, Botswana: Rural Sociology Unit, Ministry of Agriculture.

Taylor, John F.A. (1966) *The Masks of Society.* New York: Meredith.

Tlou, Thomas (1977) "Servility and Political Control: *Botlhanka* among the BaTawana of Northwestern Botswana, ca. 1750–1906." In Suzanne Miers and Igor Kopytoff, eds., *Slavery in Africa.* Madison: University of Wisconsin Press, 367–390.

Tocqueville, Alexis de (1945) *Democracy in America.* Vols. 1 & 2. Phillips Bradley, ed. New York: Vintage Books. First published in 1835 & 1940.

Tullock, Gordon (1965) *The Politics of Bureaucracy.* Washington, D.C.: Public Affairs Press.

Vierich, Helga I.D. (1981) "The Kua of the Southeastern Kalahari: A Study in the Socio-Ecology of Dependency." Ph.D. diss., De-

partment of Anthropology, University of Toronto.
Wilson, Monica, and Leonard Thompson, eds. (1969) *The Oxford History of South Africa*. Vol. 1. Oxford: Clarendon Press.

8

AMOS SAWYER

The Putu Development Association: A Missed Opportunity

Introduction

Efforts to use community organizations as instruments of development have usually failed because of the way that development programs are designed and implemented. Participation is a crucial element in the generation of capabilities for development. Where genuine participation takes place in designing and implementing development efforts, such efforts become self-organizing and self-sustaining—essentially, they become exercises in self-governance. Using the experience of the Putu Development Association of Putu, Liberia, this chapter shows how traditional institutions can be deployed to achieve development objectives within a framework of local self-organization. The Putu experience also shows what can

---

This chapter has benefited from the helpful comments of Elinor Ostrom, Vincent Ostrom, Susan Wynne, and other colleagues at the Workshop in Political Theory and Policy Analysis, Indiana University.

happen when such efforts toward self-governance are initiated within the framework of a larger political autocracy.

The Role of Participation in Development

One of the crucial questions that has always confronted development specialists has to do with the role of participation in development. Both concepts have undergone considerable transformation since the era of Third World independence was ushered in at the end of World War II. In the 1950s and 1960s, development was perceived as the improvement of the economic and social well-being of a society. These required economic growth (Hirschman, 1958; Cairncross, 1962) and social mobilization, that is, increased potential for socially efficacious behavior (Deutsch, 1971). Participation was perceived as the mobilization of people to perform functions of interest articulation and legitimation of authority (Nettl, 1967; Nettl and Robertson, 1968; Huntington and Nelson, 1976).[1]

Typical of how the modernization process was perceived was the perspective of Warren Ilchman and Ravindra C. Bhargava that it depended "on securing a central polity, its penetration into various spheres of life, and obtaining for the polity free-floating resources unattached to any ascriptive group to pursue further modernizing goals" (1971: 268).[2] Most development programs of the 1950s and 1960s revolved around the establishment of strong administrative systems for planning and implementing development programs. It was assumed that in the absence of viable political and social institutions, a strong and efficient bureaucracy would not only serve as an instrument of economic development but as a significant contributor to "political growth and development" (Braibanti, 1971).

Operating on this logic, development programs were dominated by cooperatives organized by governments and funded by external donors, public corporations, and rural-based projects operated by central governments and donor agencies in accordance with predetermined blueprints with well-defined targets and largely quantifiable goals.[3] Participation was reserved for the political realm.[4]

Economies-of-scale required such arrangements for some of these projects such as irrigation works, dams, highways, bridges, and electrical generation capacity.

Irma Adelman and Cynthia T. Morris (1973), among others, have effectively pointed out that the approach often failed to have a positive impact on the poor. The new approach to development that evolved in the 1970s slightly altered the concepts of development and participation and established a direct link between the two. Development was now defined as economic growth with equitable distribution of the fruits of growth (World Bank, 1981); participation was to be the nexus where people and government met in the process of development. This nexus was to be located at the implementation stage of development projects.[5] Decentralization was the new strategy introduced to ensure participation.

Experiments with decentralization through the 1970s have produced uneven results, in part because the concept has been used in many different ways in the design and implementation of development programs.[6] In some cases, decentralization has only meant attempts to operate development schemes through village development committees appointed by government or supervised by the political party, as in the case of Lesotho (Thoahlane, 1984), Malawi (Addai, 1984), and most of Africa. In other instances, it has meant the shifting of intractable problems to ill-equipped, quasi-autonomous agencies as a strategy to absolve central government of responsibility, as apparently is the case with the Central Tunisia Development Project (Nellis, 1983). In still others, it has become a device for inducing a shift in peasant production away from the local staples to export crops, as in the cases of the Societe d'Amenagement et d'Exploitation des Terres du Delta du Fleuve Senegal (SAED) and the farmers of Jamaane, Senegal (Adams, 1980).[7] Perhaps uneven results should be expected not only because of differences in the design and implementation of development programs but also because of the nature of such undertakings. Decentralization involves adaptation in institutional arrangements to fit specific circumstances and, as such, cannot produce universal solutions.

After a review of decentralization projects in Asia, Africa, and Latin America, G. Shabbir Cheema and Dennis A. Rondinelli (1983) concluded that if decentralization is perceived as the incremental building of institutional capacity, then, on balance, the experiments in decentralization as undertaken in the 1970s can be judged as "moderately successful." It is not clear how that judgment emerged in such a short time frame despite considerable evidence of minimal local participation.[8] David C. Korten (1980) is more circumspect in his review of decentralization schemes; he was disappointed at their lack of participatory opportunities. In his review of decentralization projects in Asia, he can identify only a few successes.[9] Every one of the successful projects he identifies grew out of the experience of the local community, involved local people in their planning and implementation, and was driven by the dedication of one or more highly respected local individuals.

Community Development as Self-Governance

Limiting participation to implementation is a serious shortcoming of current decentralization approaches. In addition, a more serious conceptual problem is the failure of such approaches to appreciate the predatory tendencies inherent in the relationship between local communities and central governments. Even with an abundance of good-will on the part of a national leadership, the temptation to recentralize in the face of seemingly difficult circumstances is always present.

The alternative perception of nongovernmental organizations (NGO's) as a substitute for central government—that is, in situations where central government is weak, permissive, or indifferent—is also problematic. In many such situations, local communities stand precariously close to developing a patron-client relationship with NGO's. Sometimes both central government and community organizations become highly dependent on them.[10]

There is no substitute for genuine participation in the planning and implementation of community development efforts if they are to achieve their purposes. Participation cannot be seen as a strategy or a means; it must be an integral part of the ends to be accomplished. It is a major factor of empowerment, and an indispensable element in self-generated, self-organized, and self-sustained development.[11] The ability of individuals in a community to take full advantage of a wide range of institutional possibilities made available through processes of constitutional choice—of individuals who are seeking solutions to individual and collective problems and pursuing both individual and collective aspirations—cannot be only a function of participation; more importantly, it is a demonstration of capacity for self-governance (V. Ostrom, 1987).

From perceiving development as self-governance, a different perspective emerges. Not only does this perspective put individuals as they interact with others in their community at the center of the development process; it also puts greater emphasis on the generation of self-reliance, as opposed to strategies for positioning a community to receive spin-offs from the top. A community now becomes preoccupied with the use of institutions as "social technologies" for building complex arrays of relationships and linkages—including linkages with other communities in pursuit of mutual interests—and vertical relationships with the center. With the use of various forms of institutions, an appropriate structure of incentives, and the benefits of past experience and the experiences of others, a community may make available to itself a variety of possibilities for production, distribution, appropriation, and consumption of goods and services (V. Ostrom and E. Ostrom, 1977; E. Ostrom, 1986a, 1986b). A different type of relationship is also perceived with NGOs: their inputs become supplementary, and require adaptation and integration.

Finally, with development perceived as self-governance, the level of social efficacy generated in the local community is independent of the requirements of central hierarchies. This is a source of tension and a major threat to independent local initiatives in developing countries. Such was the case in Putu, Liberia, where the Putu Development Association, with the assistance of a Liberian NGO, organized a community-wide effort leading to self-governance that was legitimized by traditional authority.

Background: Putu Society

The people of Putu belong to the Krahn ethnic group. This group is one of six that make up the Kwa-speaking people, most of whom are found in southeastern Liberia. The acephalous social organization of Kwa societies sets them apart from the two other ethnic-linguistic groups (Mel- and Mande-speaking) found in northern and western Liberia. These three linguistic groups together constitute more than 90 percent of Liberia's population. Putu Chiefdom is located in Konobo District in the heart of the tropical rain forest in southeastern Liberia. It is one of five chiefdoms in Konobo District. Konobo is one of the poorest districts in Liberia; and Putu is one of the poorest chiefdoms in that district.

At the beginning of the twentieth century, when the Liberian government extended its control over the wider territory that now constitutes Liberia, the people of Putu stiffly resisted incorporation. They organized armed resistance and refused to pay taxes to the central government. In the 1930s and 1940s, they refused to be conscripted into the military or to work as wage labor on rubber plantations.

Two factors seem to have enabled Putu to engage in such sustained resistance. One was Putu's remoteness from the center of government authority. The second was the incompatibility of Putu's internal institutional arrangements with those of hierarchical organizations. There are about four thousand inhabitants of Putu Chiefdom. They live in thirteen villages and towns dispersed throughout the forest and connected mainly by footpaths. The largest town, Penoken, is situated on the main highway and is the chiefdom's major link with outside groups.

After the establishment of central government authority, Putu remained marginal because it had resisted the central government. In the early 1960s, the government granted concessions to a number of private firms to exploit the vast timber resources of the area. Putu still has not experienced many benefits from its dwindling timber resources. Roads bypassing villages have been built deep into the forest by logging companies, and employment is minimal and seasonal because of the nature of logging operations.[12]

Putu Social Organization

Prior to the establishment of central authority over Putu, a large village or a cluster of villages constituted an autonomous political unit. Given the high level of ethnic homogeneity in this region, as well as the small size of settlements, most villages consisted of hardly more than the extended family or lineage segment. Quite frequently, a village consisted of "quarters" that were nothing more than the households of the adult children of one person. The polygynous household was the basic social unit. Economic production took place largely in the household. The father of the household exercised control over the fruits of production.

While a village or cluster of villages constituted an autonomous political unit, other configurational relationships existed that created special jurisdictions. For example, several villages or autonomous political units would organize to use the services of artisans such as blacksmiths and weavers, or to participate in public works projects. These special jurisdictions usually crosscut hitherto autonomous political units and served specific purposes.

Structure of Authority

Authority within the household resided in the father or husband; adult children were expected to leave the household and establish households of their own. The eldest son of the senior wife was the heir to the household property and the authority of the father, but he had to demonstrate leadership ability in order to be respected. Enterprising younger brothers were not infrequently treated informally as de facto family heads.

The elders of the households constituted the "quarter council," whose purpose was largely to resolve disputes within the quarter. The greater the diversity of kinship or lineage in the village, the more important the authority of the council. Elders who exercised influence in such bodies were usually those who had demonstrated considerable skills in some form of production.

The village Council of Elders, which was composed of elders selected from the quarter councils, was the body that exercised ultimate authority over the village. Elders were selected from the various quarters to be members of the council. Selection to such a body was determined by age as well as by performance over the years. An elder must have excelled by exceptional merit in a particular endeavor to be nominated from the quarter and accepted by the Council of Elders as a member of that body. Some of the areas in which demonstrated excellence was recognized were in farming, hunting, oratory and debate, drumming, dancing, fine arts, and warfare.

The most important function of the Council was to supervise the use of community land. This function was of crucial importance, not only to ensure the availability of farmland to all villagers, but also to provide control of land in view of the ease and frequency with which new settlements were formed by individuals who, for any reason, desired to move away from existing villages.[13] Disputes not resolved within the households and quarters were also submitted to the Council. The Council of Elders was headed by a chief who was elected by the council from among its members. His authority was derived from the council and not from paternal descent. In effect, the chief in Putu society was very similar to a coordinator—the presiding officer of the council.

Beyond the chief and Council of Elders of the village, a higher council of limited authority existed called the Owners of the Land. This was a group of the most prominent and distinguished elders from all the autonomous political units throughout Putu society.[14] Only elders who had attained celebrity, if not legendary, status and commanded the respect of the entire society were selected as owners. The Owners of the Land had exclusive jurisdiction over land disputes involving persons or agencies outside Putu society. In addition, they had jurisdiction over disputes between villages, and in matters that involved custom, traditions, and values of the society, and that required the imposition of sanctions by Bleah Kwee.

Bleah Kwee was the ultimate authority in Putu society, the embodiment of its moral and legal authority. It combined spiritual connection to the ancestors with other magico-religious beliefs, and was symbolized by a mask dancer. The intervention of Bleah Kwee in a dispute signified that the matter was of enormous gravity or involved failure to meet a very important civic responsibility. While Bleah Kwee represented the moral and legal authority of the society, its sanctions were endorsed and enforced by the Owners of the Land.

One of the most prominent among the elders was chosen by the Owners of the Land as chairman. His responsibilities were limited to convening meetings and seeing that they were properly conducted. The chairman needed to be known for his judiciousness, even-tempered manners, and stately comportment. Another official of this council was the Speaker, who acted as spokesman of the Owners of the Land. He had to be an eloquent and articulate person with an exceptional command of language, logic, and parables. His knowledge of the history of the society and vision of its future needed to be inspiring. The position of Speaker was especially important in circumstances requiring serious discussion of an issue critical to the well-being of the society. Then there was the bodio. He was the high priest of the society, in charge of its religious affairs.

Principles of Association in Putu

A basic principle of association in Putu hinged on age. Many social activities were organized on the basis of age-sets. Age criteria also defined the limits of what could be expected from an individual. Size of farm, physical prowess, and mental agility were all evaluated with reference to age.

While association based on age-sets was the most common form of association, individualism and independence were highly prized. Their exercise, however, did not excuse failure to meet family and community obligations or to observe established authority relations. Competition within age-sets was a hallmark of association in Putu. This practice was maintained throughout all age levels. It was in this context that characteristics such as courage, fortitude, and endurance were highly valued, serving to ensure status and recognition.

Beside the criterion of age and the prescribed structure of authority, performance was another important basis for respect. A father exercised authority over his household, and a son was obliged to respect and obey his father. However, the esteem and social status that accrued to an individual in the larger society depended upon public evaluation of his performance. The social status accorded an individual was determined more by achievements than by descent.

Contemporary Operational Pattern of Authority in Putu

In the early 1920s, the Liberian government imposed on Putu and other interior areas a system of interior administration very similar to the British colonial system of "indirect rule" (Lugard model). This arrangement organized indigenous authority into hierarchies in which villages were brought together into clans, and clans into chiefdoms. A paramount chief was selected for each chiefdom and a clan chief for each clan. For quite some time, the government appointed clan and paramount chiefs. Bogus elections were organized for these positions after the practice of direct appointments ended.

Paramount chiefs are responsible to the district commissioner who reports to the superintendent of the county. The superintendent, in turn, reports to the minister of internal affairs, a cabinet officer who reports to the president. The "election" of paramount chiefs provides for the selection of leaders by a new set of criteria that are largely external to Putu society. Access to financial and other resources and to a support base outside Putu has become as important in "winning elections" in Putu as it is elsewhere in Liberia.

The imposition of the new authority structure radically transformed authority relations in Putu as it did elsewhere among the acephalous societies of southeastern Liberia. By installing a paramount chief, who was responsible to an authority outside the society, the status of the Council of Elders and Owners of the Land was reduced to that of advisory bodies. In such a situation, the position of paramount chief, too, was usually untenable. On some occasions he had to rely upon the military force of the central government to ensure his effectiveness. Many times, a crafty paramount chief would seek to walk the tightrope of invoking local support through the

Council of Elders and Owners of the Land in order to ensure greater compliance. More often than not, the relationship between the people of Putu and the local authorities of the central government was laden with conflict.

This conflict led to the central government's decision to withhold key infrastructures from Putu. The first medically qualified person, a physician assistant, was assigned to Putu only in the early 1970s. The nearest doctor was at a hospital more than a hour's drive from Penekon on the main highway and several days' walk along footpaths from all the other villages. A dilapidated elementary school built by the community with three teachers and 150 students was located in Penoken. Only one of the teachers was paid by the government. About 800 children awaited turns to attend some classes.

Until 1980, a hut tax in the amount of ten dollars per hut and a development tax in the amount of five dollars per adult were collected annually from the people of Putu as they were from all citizens in rural Liberia. In addition, numerous official "contributions" were exacted for "county development" or "national development" projects. Putu has rarely been a beneficiary of these resources. Although the hut tax was abolished in 1980, official and unofficial requests for "contributions" have increased.

Most essential commodities not available to local villages have had to be obtained from the county seat under conditions of great hardship. Life in Putu is rugged and austere. Although the people have reached an uneasy accommodation with the imposition of central government authority, they have remained proud and undaunted.

A History of the Putu Development Association

In the early 1970s, a few professionals who were or had been associated with the University of Liberia organized a consortium in an effort to address some of the social and economic problems of the society. The ending of the twenty-seven-year rule of William Tubman as president of Liberia in 1971 deepened their desire to explore ways of developing institutional capacities for democratization. This multidisciplinary group was called SUSUKUU and was legally incorporated as a nonprofit agency designed to study problems of urban and rural poverty.[15] Konobo District became one of SUSUKUU's target areas because of the documented indices of extreme poverty in Konobo that appeared in national economic surveys.

Upon hearing of the existence of SUSUKUU and its interests, the Youth Association of Putu invited it to Putu in July 1976. The association consisted of two groups of young men from the age-set of about 15 to 25. One group was resident in Monrovia; many of its members were students of various schools or employees in low-paying clerical and service jobs. The other group resided in Putu and consisted largely of part-time farmers, hunters, and seasonal employees of timber companies that operated in the area.[16] SUSUKUU was introduced to Putu by a respected local association. This enabled it to be perceived without suspicion.

The principal of the school and the president of the local youth association proved indispensable in organizing the approach to community-wide decision making and participation. These two organized a meeting with the Speaker of Putu and a later meeting among the Speaker, the paramount chief, and SUSUKUU representatives. As a result of the latter, a general meeting of the chiefdom's people was organized by the paramount chief. Such a meeting could have been called by the Owners of the Land and would have been considered a significant one, about grave internal matters; however, it would have lacked official sanction or aroused suspicion.

Representatives of every sector of the population were present at the general meeting. Among the represented were three female age-sets, two men's age-sets, and a number of social clubs and artisan groups. In addition, a number of town chiefs and the entire Council of Elders of Penoken and all the Owners of the Land were present. The meeting brought together the official leadership of the chiefdom as well as the traditional leadership. The youth organization and the principal of the local school played important and catalytic roles.

It was clear from the discussion that while there was a unanimity in the perception of the problem, there were significant differences in how the problem should be resolved. The lack of educational, health, and employment opportunities was the major concern of all of the people. The paramount chief attributed these problems to the laziness of the people. The women blamed the lack of internal cohesion. The youth blamed the government. General, but unspoken, agreement existed that the central government was the chief cause of Putu's poverty.

The Owners of the Land remained silent throughout most of the discussions. Occasionally an elder would intervene to correct an erroneous statement or to provide some information. The Speaker, who shared the presiding officer's role with the paramount chief, would occasionally ask a question or seek clarification of a point. Much of the debate involved the paramount and clan chiefs, the youth, women, and others such as the owner of a local retail shop who was a district officer assigned elsewhere in Konobo.

The paramount chief was enthusiastic about the prospect of cooperation with SUSUKUU and proposed the formation of a community consultative body to work with him on a development project for which SUSUKUU would provide funding. The youth objected. The idea of organizing a unit of collective choice to undertake community development projects was welcomed by all sectors of the community for different reasons. After several hours of vigorous discussion, the participants agreed to organize the Putu Development Association to devise a scheme for improving the conditions of life for the people of Putu Chiefdom.

Organizing the Putu Development Association

About two weeks after the first general community meeting, a second meeting was held for the purpose of organizing the Putu Development Association. As a result of prior consultations among influential members of the community, a proposal was made and accepted to organize a board of directors and a local management team that would be in charge of day-to-day implementation of the association's projects.

As soon as the institutional framework was agreed upon, officers were elected. The paramount chief presided over the elections. A nine-man board of directors was elected consisting of all nine members of the council referred to as Owners of the Land. The chairman of the Owners of the Land was elected chairman of the board and the paramount chief was requested by the board to serve as its chief advisor.

The Speaker was elected to be president and chief executive officer of the association. As executive officer, he was head of the management body that would supervise the day-to-day activities of the association. Four other members were elected to the management team. These included a representative of the youth association, the leader of the middle age-set women's association, and the principal of the primary school.

The types of officers that were elected demonstrated the resurgence of traditional institutional structures as a vehicle for collective action. The election of the Owners of the Land as a board of directors indicated that the association would be clothed with the full legitimacy and moral authority of the people of Putu. It was considered a genuine outgrowth of their own initiatives, one that would proceed in accordance with their own wishes.

The chairman of the Owners of the Land, Elder Mehngee, who was now chairman of the board of directors, was a stately man of about seventy. As a young man, he had displayed valor in the resistance of the 1920s and 1930s. He was considered to be a fervent protector of the land and the integrity of the society. His calm and deliberate manners inspired confidence. He was highly respected throughout Putu society.

Dugbe Saydee Parue, the Speaker of Putu, who had been elected executive officer of the association and a member of the board, was eloquent and articulate. He was respected as a courageous spokesman who could be relied upon to convey the opinions and sentiments of the elders. He treated his colleagues with respect, actively seeking their views and engaging in dialogue and debate with them. He had traveled widely throughout southern and southeastern Liberia and was aware of and sensitive to the impact of external influences on local society. He had been an excellent hunter. Parue, in short, was a flamboyant personality. He was barely literate—the only literate member among the Owners of the Land. He was about sixty-five years old.

The election of the principal of the school as a member of the management team was also of strategic importance. Principal Jedo was about forty-five years old. He had completed high school in the county headquarters in the 1950s and had attended the Zorzor Teacher Training Institute in northern Liberia when it was first opened in the early 1960s. Jedo could have made a higher salary elsewhere, but he had returned to Putu to take over the school that had been built as a self-help project. Over the years, he had won the confidence of the Owners of the Land and was immensely popular among the people of the chiefdom. He wrote and read letters for them and undertook most of their transactions that required literacy. He had been co-opted as secretary to the Owners of the Land and had won the confidence of members to the extent that he was allowed to attend their meetings. When the central government decided to establish the position of justice of the peace in Putu Chiefdom, the people recommended Principal Jedo for the position. His selection for such an important position had reduced the potential for conflict between official and traditional legal jurisdictions that would otherwise have certainly developed among the people of Putu. Jedo, as both school principal and justice of the peace, was the single most important catalyst. He was knowledgeable about local culture, commanded the total confidence of the people, and was committed to innovation and change without alienating local institutions.

Martha Paye was the representative of the middle age-set women's organization on the management team. She was a widow of about fifty years old and was respected for her skills as a farmer and as an organizer. She was not gifted as a public speaker but was extremely effective in small groups and persuasive in interpersonal discussion. She owned one of the most productive farms in the chiefdom.

Pyne Wollo, who represented the youth, was about twenty-six years old. He had completed four years of schooling but had lapsed into illiteracy. He was an excellent farmer and was respected for his physical prowess. He had lived in the mining community of central Liberia for a period and had also travelled to Monrovia on many occasions. He worked on and off with local logging companies. He was somehow an associate of Kwee and, as such, was close to the Owners of the Land.

The combination of people who formed the board and the management team provided the appropriate mix for authentic and forward-looking community development. The board of directors consisting of the Owners of the Land provided the institutional legitimacy and authority, while the management team that enjoyed the full confidence of both the Owners of the Land and the people understood technology sufficiently to organize the introduction of innovations into the society without arousing fear and apprehension. This arrangement provided the framework for introducing and legitimizing change through traditional institutional channels while maintaining stability. The interfacing of this arrangement with the central government was the one unknown factor.

In summary, it seems that at least three elements were important in the formation of the Putu Development Association as a local unit of collective choice. First, there was a legitimate, latent, indigenous, institutional framework that may have had other objectives but could constitute the basis for the undertaking of a new endeavor. Second, there was the availability of innovative influences such as the external animating influence of SUSUKUU and the catalytic role of such internal agents as Principal Jedo and the Youth Association. Third, there was a significant issue or need that was the center of concern for most people in the community.

Formulating a Program and Mobilizing Resources

At the next general meeting of the association, projects were selected. The needs of the society were quite obvious. The major debate revolved around priorities. The first project agreed upon was the construction of an elementary and junior high school capable of accommodating 600 students with facilities to train them in the fundamentals of a liberal education as well as in the crafts and skills that are essential for life in the rural area. A health center was the second project agreed upon. Health facilities were needed that could provide out-patient care for many of the public-health-related diseases, a maternity ward, and sleeping accommodations for a limited number of referral cases. The third project identified at the meeting was a community shop. The women of the middle age-set lobbied for this facility, which they proposed to operate as a project of their organization.

The management team was requested to explore certain long-range possibilities. These included a trunk road to be built with community labor and equipment of the logging company. Fuel costs were to be paid by the association, and electricity was to be provided for Penoken, the chiefdom headquarters.

Community labor was to constitute the major resource in the development of these projects. Not a single proposal was made to collect financial contributions locally. In order to mobilize capital, a community farm was to be developed. Rice and other food products were to be the major products, and cash crop production was to be undertaken later. The emphasis on food production was perceived to be important to this association; it demonstrated that community self-interest is always at the core of genuine community decision making. Putu and all of southeastern Liberia had always experienced shortages of food—especially rice, the staple, during certain times of the year. It was only logical that an association whose decision making was intrinsically democratic would focus on the food problem first. This differed from the experience elsewhere in Liberia where, in spite of food shortages, "self-help" projects that were government-guided or politician-inspired were forced to produce a cash crop even in the face of severe food shortages.[17]

The Role of SUSUKUU. Early in the development of the association, SUSUKUU had informed the community that it was not a donor agency, or an organization with ready-made answers. Its basic interest had been to study the problems of poverty first and then make some suggestions. It was, however, prepared to work with the community as long as the projects retained their communal character both in decision making and in implementation. SUSUKUU was now requested to serve in an advisory capacity to the management team. SUSUKUU's immediate task was to devise means by which funds could be mobilized to procure a pickup truck and substantial quantities of farm implements (machetes and portable power saws), and to provide technical assistance in the cultivation of swamp rice.[18]

Within three months, SUSUKUU had secured grants from international agencies to procure a used pickup truck and an assortment of simple farm tools.[19] The community was encouraged by SUSUKUU to send two young men to an eighteen-month agricultural training program near Monrovia so as to immediately begin developing self-sustaining technical capabilities.

The procurement of both tools and a truck within such a relatively short period by SUSUKUU, with the constant presence of SUSUKUU representatives in the villages, reinforced the commitment of the association. The people of Penoken had already begun to see new possibilities. Women talked of expanding backyard gardens to produce more pepper for sale in the county seat. Others talked of importing saltwater fish for sale in the community. Already increased purchasing power and increased possibilities were being perceived.

Organizing Production. According to an arrangement worked out by the management team and the leaders of the various villages and approved by the Owners of the Land, each village was to contribute a full day's work on the community farm on a rotational basis twice a month. A schedule was worked out so as not to disrupt work on individual farms. Every social group of the village was to fulfill the usual role assigned to it in the farm preparation and production cycle. The leaders of age-set groups were to ensure that members of their groups were in full attendance at the appropriate times. Their authority as leaders of the groups would be reinforced by support of the village Council of Elders and, ultimately, by the authority of the Owners of the Land.

Enforcing Sanctions. Compliance on the part of each individual in these undertakings relied fundamentally on the value of honor that was entrenched in Putu culture. The esteem of an individual who did not honor his commitment was diminished in the eyes of his peer group and others in the society. This shame reflected on his father and household. Considerable moral pressure was available to promote a sense of duty and a sense of integrity.

Kwee, a mask dancer, was another important instrument of moral pressure. Its function was to extol the virtues of the upright and decry the vices of the slothful through songs, skits, jokes, and other art forms. Every self-respecting member of the society tried to avoid becoming the subject of ridicule and shame by Kwee.[20]

An individual who remained undeterred by Kwee's sanctions and continued to be uncooperative or to break rules would be sanctioned by the village Council of Elders upon the recommendation of the leader of his age-set group. Such sanctions could involve the payment of fines in labor or cash, denial of participation in age-set group activities, or expulsion from the village.

If the issues involved bore upon the well-being of the larger community (Putu society), the sanctions of Bleah Kwee might be invoked with the full authority of the Owners of the Land. Because the boundaries of the Putu Development Association were coterminous with the boundaries of the chiefdom, and membership in the chiefdom was perceived to be coterminous with membership in the association, all of these sanctions that were available in the wider society were available in support of the association.

Conflict and Conflict Resolution

The resurgence of traditional institutions as instruments of social change within a society dominated by external institutions, when added to the new sense of efficacy, was bound to produce conflict. Two types of conflict arose. The first type was conflict originating within the association as a result of the introduction of technology, and by the internal dynamics of the association. The second type of conflict was the result of the impact of external authority on the association.

Internal Conflict. As a result of the introduction of the pickup truck, portable power saws, and hand tools for agricultural production, the people began to develop a broader perspective of what was considered attainable. This, by itself, was a potential source of conflict. For example, the availability of a pickup truck was a much-welcomed relief to expectant mothers and traditional midwives.

Formerly, preparations for a delivery involved considerable mobilization of financial and other material resources, causing emotional strains. The availability of a pickup truck changed this situation. However, competition for use of the vehicle developed, especially at night, from enterprising young men who ventured far out from the village to near the main highway to collect discarded pieces of logs that they prepared for sale as firewood in the county seat. Considerable conflict also ensued over the private use of tools, especially portable power saws.

Conflict over access to resources also developed between the management team and the paramount chief. Paramount Chief Kai Farley felt entitled to special privileges including the use of the pickup for official and other purposes. Other local officials of the district government, such as the local revenue officer, assistant district commissioner, and the physician assistant, threatened to invoke central government intervention unless privileges to which they felt entitled were granted. Although many of these officials were resident in Putu, they were not originally from Putu and did not feel constrained by the moral and legal authority of traditional institutions. Although the Putu Development Association had been legally registered as a nonprofit community association, it could not escape such harassment.

Most of the internal conflicts were resolved through discussions among the management team, the leaders of age-set groups, and representatives of the Council of Elders of the particular village. In situations of enduring conflict, the chairman of the board of directors would be asked to intervene. On one occasion, a conflict about the quality of participation of one village required not only a meeting of the full board of directors but also a general meeting of all groups within the chiefdom, much like the earlier meetings during which the association was organized.

External Conflict. The major conflicts that hindered production and almost destroyed the association were a series of conflicts with the central government. The three sources of conflicts were: the tradition of resistance to central authority; the desire of local representatives of central government to "enjoy the spoils"; and central government's perception of SUSUKUU. As progress with the project became visible, the resurgence of social efficacy in Putu seemed to revive memories of the resistance. At the level of the district and county headquarters, the view was that the people of Putu were arrogant and disrespectful to "constituted authority." This view was fueled by district and county officials who were either resident in Putu or had reasons to travel there regularly. Since most of the activities of the association involved transactions internal to Putu and SUSUKUU, county officials were never seriously involved with the association. They could neither claim credit for the success that was experienced in Putu nor enjoy the privileges. Their attitudes spawned hostile reactions to activities in Putu.

The reaction from Monrovia grew increasingly hostile. A factor that influenced the government's reaction was the involvement of SUSUKUU. That many of SUSUKUU's members were associated with the University of Liberia, perceived to be a base of antigovernment activities, invoked an automatically negative reaction from the central government. The late 1970s were a period of fermentation in urban Liberia. Student agitation was high, strikes by workers were frequent, and an urban-based pressure group successfully registered as the first opposition party in twenty-five years. In 1979, as a result of the government's attempt to break up a demonstration against proposed increases in the price of rice, riots broke out in Monrovia in the course of which about 200 people were killed and millions of dollars' worth of property was destroyed.

The Putu Development Association began production in 1978 and was mid-way into the second farming season when the rice riots broke out. Many students of the university who were associated with SUSUKUU were arrested during the demonstrations. SUSUKUU was accused of instigating trouble in Putu. As a result, the government arrested about 400 men and boys in Putu and transported and detained about 30 of the men in prisons around the country. This conflict took place at the beginning of the farming season when 43 acres of land were being cleared for cultivation. The women of Putu took charge of the farm and, under special dispensation from the Bodio, the "high Priest," were permitted to fell trees and cut through very thick vegetation, tasks normally reserved strictly for men.

SUSUKUU was obliged to withdraw from Putu. The government ordered stronger supervision of activities in Putu by the superintendent of Grand Gedeh County. County officials created county administrative machinery under which the Putu Development Association was to operate. Under the new military regime in 1981, a new management team consisting of local politicians was organized, and the association virtually faded away about a year later.

Lessons from Putu

Achievements in Putu. Given the short active life of the Putu Development Association, not many material successes can be claimed for it. Only one harvest of 20 acres of rice was produced. Income from sale of firewood and other activities was applied to commence construction of the school. The land clearing for the health center was completed and about 6,000 sun-dried bricks were made to begin construction. A rice milling machine had been purchased to reduce the cost of rice preparation by about 30 percent. The involvement of nursing and medical students in Putu had led to improved health education and improved public health practices. For example, breast-feeding, which was being discontinued in favor of feeding with a homemade porridge, was widely resumed, and better waste disposal practices were introduced.

The primary success of the Putu Development Association, however, was the resurgence of self-organizing capabilities and the renewal of a sense of social efficacy. The people of Putu had used their traditional institutions as basic infrastructure, and had adapted innovations that enabled those institutions to constitute a viable framework for genuine participation in the pursuit of modern values. This development defied those theories of modernization that assume that traditional institutions are always preoccupied with primordial considerations that are anti-modern.[21] Moreover, the Putu Development Association demonstrated that, by taking advantage of possibilities for self-organization, a community, no matter how poor, can undertake capital formation once it is left relatively free to do so. Putu showed that important as money is, the organizational ingenuity of a community and the work that it can mobilize are more important forms of capital. In particular, the committed leadership and entrepreneurship of individuals such as the school principal appear to have been crucial in furthering Putu activities.

Dilemma of Self-Governance within Hierarchical Orders

The Putu Development Association was put together in a way that made it internally viable as an instrument for collective action in developing common-property resources and public facilities. It had established a system of rules that defined the local community of interest, identified what it might accomplish, established the rights and duties of participants, and arranged for the enforcement of those rules. The Putu Development Association was so constituted that it was internally adaptive by modifying rules over time. The Putu people had put together instrumentalities for collective action that were viable arrangements for undertaking a communally organized program of collective action.[22]

The basic tension that destroyed the infrastructure that the Putu people had developed was their relationship to the larger structure of authority relationships in the government of Liberia. A critical problem that affected the association had to do with the demands of individuals such as second-level county and district officials who, by virtue of their residency in Putu, were perceived by the association as having legitimate claims to the use of resources. These individuals apparently perceived themselves as having greater proprietary rights than others. Such a situation obviously requires a mechanism capable of disposing of such claims either within the organization or elsewhere, in the more extended system of government. In the case of the Putu Development Association, no such mechanism was available within Putu. Those making claims for priority did not perceive the internal mechanisms of the association to be competent to dispose of their demands; they sought remedies outside the boundaries of the association within a larger hierarchy with which the association already had a tenuous relationship.

The survival of local units of collective action depends upon their being nested in a larger system of federated authority relationships. Elinor Ostrom stresses the need for "effective communication" with those organizations and authorities that are beyond the boundaries of the local organization, and the need to seek the "nesting of organizational arrangements in federated structures of various kinds" (1985: 27). This suggestion poses a tremendous challenge for local organizations that strive to survive within the confines of large and predatory hierarchies. The predatory character of hierarchies takes an official as well as an unofficial form. Officially, it takes the form of legal demands for taxes and for restricting and regulating behavior promoting its own interests. Unofficially, individuals who occupy positions in such hierarchies take the liberty from time to time to harass, intimidate, extort resources, and claim private privileges. In such situations, it is most difficult, if not impossible, to establish effective communication that ensures the resolution of conflict while preserving the integrity of local units of collective action. It is essential that the larger system, within which such local collectivities are nested, should see the survival and efficient performance of these organizations as important in the development of society.

One method sometimes used by local organizations involves making informal payments to local, regional, and national officials in return for their support. The problem with this approach is that it directs capital resources away from production and is therefore a bad bargain, since a false sense of autonomy is being bought at the expense of those same objectives for which autonomy was perceived to be necessary and desirable. Autonomy now becomes meaningless. Moreover, the payment of such protection money results in the development of a de facto unitary authority structure.

The effective nesting of local units of collective action in a larger system to ensure their survival can facilitate the formation of other similar units in other communities. By helping others to develop self-organizing capabilities, a collectivity can eventually transform a situation that had been perceived by the larger hierarchy as a special case into a common feature of the society. This is one way that innovation occurs.

There is another possibility to be explored. When a donor agency is involved, it may reduce the predatory impact of the larger hierarchy. The risk is that a new dependence on the external donor agency is created. There are interlocking relationships among government and nongovernment donor agencies. The provision of assistance by such agencies to specific endeavors within a given society makes the agencies interested parties and implies a commitment to the encouragement of certain trends in social development in the recipient society. Too often donor agencies are silent partners of predatory states.

The general situation in most developing countries is that development is perceived to consist of activities organized in various local communities by central government and donor agencies. Local people are usually called upon to participate in the implementation of those projects. Although some projects have successfully improved the lot of some local people, the general case is that the lot of most people in local communities has not been improved. Among the important elements missing from this approach to development is the opportunity for genuine participation of local people in the design and implementation of the activities. The Putu Development Association departed from this pattern and indicated considerable self-organizing capabilities that increased the potential for self-governance at the community level.

The tension between the development of self-organizing capabilities in local communities and the imposition of control from larger national hierarchies is one of the fundamental conflicts underlying the development process in African societies. The United Nations Research Institute for Social Development (UNRISD) has recognized both the existence of this problem in the wider context of the Third World and the indispensability of community self-governance for the development of society. UNRISD has asserted that:

> authentic participation heightening the participants' awareness of values, issues, and the possibility of making choices, influencing the content of development, generating new ways of doing things, and also safeguarding the participants' right to an equitable share in the

fruits of development remains an elusive aspiration. But the conversion of this aspiration into reality may well in the end prove the central requisite for a style of development enabling a society to function over the long term for the well-being of its members. (in Machooka, 1984: 60)

If freedom of association is considered to be a fundamental human right, there could not be any better evidence of its exercise than in the freedom of a community of people to organize and improve themselves through self-governance. This problem deserves greater attention.

Notes

1. Huntington and Nelson discovered from a review of several studies of participation in the Third World that the nature of participation in these societies is influenced more by the attitude of the political elites than by any other factor.

2. The word "modernization" is generally used interchangeably with the word "development" (see, for instance, Ilchman and Bhargava, 1971).

3. For an excellent example of how a top-down approach can be made more efficient, see Glynn Cochrane (1986).

4. The claim was that the three central values that drove society were national unity, economic development, and political stability, and that the quest for these required a minimum of internal dissension. It is no coincidence that the perpetuation of leaders in office also requires a minimum of internal dissension (see Weiner, 1966: 208).

5. Scholars concerned with modernization had persistently asked what the impact of large-scale political participation on economic development in developing countries might be, but they remained equivocal on the issue. Myron Weiner (1966) had suggested, rather tentatively, that there was no direct relationship between the two.

6. Four types of decentralization have been identified from a review of several decentralization projects: deconcentration, or the redistribution of administrative responsibilities within central government; delegation to semiautonomous agencies such as public

corporations; devolution, which in its purest but rarely used forms has to do with the creation of independent local authorities; and the involvement of nongovernmental organizations, or NGO's (see Cheema and Rondinelli, 1983).

7. There are cases where decentralization has been used to promote experimentation in technology transfer and other forms of social engineering by research agencies (see Jedlicka, 1977; Langley, 1982).

8. The major problems of decentralization pointed out by Cheema and Rondinelli have to do with the lack of administrative capabilities, of political commitment, and of an orientation promoting decentralization in bureaucracies. They also mention problems of design deficiency and inadequate human and financial resources. Most of these problems relate to management activities at the top.

9. Korten asserts that in order to be considered successful, a project must have achieved a high degree of "fit" between program design, beneficiary needs, and the capabilities of assisting organizations. The concept of "fit" is taken from a theory of organizational design that explores the critical relationships between task, strategy, and structure (see Chandler, 1962; Galbraith and Nathanson, 1978).

10. Writing about a development project in Cameroun, Philip Langley has dramatized the behavior of the authorities vis-a-vis donor agencies: "The picture that emerges from the discourse of institutional representatives in this study is closely akin to the prayers made in the Cargo Cult, going so far in one case to inform European donors of their 'prayerful interest for greater things to come'" (see Langley, 1984: 196).

11. Bryant and White have conceived of participation as empowerment and as a value in its own right; however, they quickly prescribe it as an "antidote for the psychological pain of colonization," thereby marginalizing its importance for all peoples (1982: 211).

12. The poverty-stricken condition of the area can be judged from the fact that its average income is below the estimated national rural income of $70 and its literacy rate is under 10 percent—well below the national average of 30 percent. Over half of its population is under 18; infant mortality is about 137 per 1,000, and average life expectancy is below 45 years. Malaria, diarrhea, tuberculosis, and

other communicable diseases that result from poor public health conditions are common.

13. While land was communally held, usufruct rights were observed and farms were owned by households or individuals. The slash-and-burn method of clearing and a rotation pattern of five to eight years were employed.

14. Putu is the name of the mountain that dominates the region. It is also the name of the area in the immediate vicinity of the mountain where the group of autonomous villages that constitutes the subject of this discussion is located. Putu is also a political concept that refers to the association of autonomous political entities. For details of Krahn ethnography, see Seibel and Schroeder (1974).

15. The word SUSUKUU is coined from a combination of two words, *susu* and *kuu*. *Susu* is an indigenous loan association to which members contribute and for which in turn they are eligible to borrow. *Kuu* is an organization for collective clearing of the bush for farms of individual members. Information on the Putu experience and the SUSUKUU's role was compiled by the author, who was a participant observer of these developments. I am grateful to Togba Nah Tipoteh, director of SUSUKUU, for sharing his reflections about Putu with me. See also Kamara (1983).

16. This extension of a rural, community-based peer group association into urban areas is not uncommon. Such relationships form an important link for the infusion of material resources and value-orientations from urban areas into rural areas and vice versa.

17. For an excellent analysis of food production and availability in Liberia, see Kamara (1987).

18. Although efforts are sometimes made to introduce swamp rice, upland rice cultivation is the type of rice production widely known in this region of Liberia.

19. Grants were received for the project from a West German ecumenical foundation, a Dutch international agency for cooperation with non-governmental development organizations, and a Canadian development-oriented agency.

20. Kwee is not to be confused with Bleah Kwee. The latter represented a deeper source of authority and more severe forms of sanctions than Kwee.

21. For an excellent rebuttal of this view, see Gusfield (1971).
22. The conditions specified in this paragraph have been developed by Elinor Ostrom (1985).

Works Cited

Addai, G. K. (1984) "People's Participation in Development at Grassroot Level: A Case Study of Malawi." In A. C. Mondjanagni, ed., *People's Participation in Development in Black Africa*. Douala, Cameroun: Pan African Institute for Development (PAID), 203–218.

Adams, Adrian (1980) "The Senegal River Valley." In Judith Heyer, Pepe Roberts, and Gavin Williams, eds., *Rural Development in Tropical Africa*. New York: St. Martin's Press, 325–353.

Adelman, Irma, and Cynthia T. Morris (1973) *Economic Growth and Social Equity in Developing Countries*. Stanford: Stanford University Press.

Braibanti, Ralph (1971) "Administrative Reform in the Context of Political Growth." In Fred W. Riggs, ed., *Frontiers of Development Administration*. Durham, N.C.: Duke University Press, 227–246.

Bryant, Coralie, and Louise G. White (1982) *Managing Development in the Third World*. Boulder, Colo.: Westview Press.

Cairncross, A. K. (1962) *Factors in Economic Development*. London: Allen and Unwin.

Chandler, Alfred D. (1962) *Strategy and Structure*. Cambridge, Mass.: MIT Press.

Cheema, G. Shabbir, and Dennis A. Rondinelli, eds., (1983) "Decentralization and Development: Conclusions and Directions." In *Decentralization and Development: Policy Implementation in Developing Countries*. Beverly Hills: Sage, 295–315.

Cochrane, Glynn (1986) *Reforming National Institutions for Economic Development*. Boulder, Colo.: Westview Press.

Deutsch, Karl W. (1971) "Social Mobilization and Political Development." Second ed. In Jason L. Finkle and Richard W. Gable, eds., *Political Development and Social Change*. New York: Wiley, 384–405.

Galbraith, Jay R., and Daniel A. Nathanson (1978) *Strategy Implementation: The Role of Structure and Process.* St. Paul, Minn.: West.

Gusfield, Joseph R. (1971) "Tradition and Modernity: Misplaced Polarities in the Study of Social Change." In Jason L. Finkle and Richard W. Gable, eds., *Political Development and Social Change.* New York: Wiley, 15–26.

Hirschman, Albert O. (1958) *The Strategy of Economic Development.* New Haven: Yale University Press.

Huntington, Samuel P., and Joan M. Nelson (1976) *No Easy Choice: Political Participation in Developing Countries.* Cambridge, Mass.: Harvard University Press.

Ilchman, Warren, and Ravindra C. Bhargava (1971) "Balanced Thought and Economic Growth." In Fred W. Riggs, ed., *Frontiers of Development Administration.* Durham, N.C.: Duke University Press, 227–246.

Jedlicka, Allen D. (1977) *Organization for Rural Development: Risk Taking and Appropriate Technology.* New York: Praeger.

Kamara, Siapha (1983) "Popular Participation in Rural Development in Post-Colonial Africa: The Case of PUDECO in Liberia." M.A. thesis, Institute of Social Studies, The Hague.

―――― (1987) "Food Production and Availability Trends in Liberia." M.Phil. thesis, Institute of Social Studies, The Hague.

Korten, David C. (1980) "Community Organization and Rural Development: A Learning Process Approach." *Public Administration Review,* vol. 40, no. 5 (Sept./Oct.), 480–511.

Langley, Philip (1982) *ZOGID: Zone of Guided Integrated Development, A Research Contribution to Rural Development.* Douala, Cameroun: Pan African Institute for Development.

―――― (1984) "Wapi Participation: Integrating Development Rhetoric as a Cargo Cult Practice." In A. C. Mondjanagni, ed., *People's Participation in Development in Black Africa.* Douala, Cameroun: Pan African Institute for Development, 171–201.

Machooka, S. M. (1984) "People's Participation in Rural

Development." In A. C. Mondjanagni, ed., *People's Participation in Development in Black Africa*. Douala, Cameroun: Pan African Institute for Development, 53–74.

Nellis, John R. (1983) "Decentralization in North Africa: Problems of Policy Implementation." In G. Shabbir Cheema and Dennis A. Rondinelli, eds., *Decentralization and Development: Policy Implementation in Developing Countries*. Beverly Hills: Sage, 127–182.

Nettl, J. P. (1967) *Political Mobilization: A Sociological Analysis of Methods and Concepts*. London: Faber.

Nettl, J. P., and Roland Robertson (1968) *International Systems and the Modernization of Society*. London: Faber.

Ostrom, Elinor (1985) "The Rudiments of a Revised Theory of the Origins, Survival, and Performance of Institutions for Collective Action." Workshop in Political Theory and Policy Analysis, Indiana University, Bloomington, Ind.

———— (1986a) "A Method of Institutional Analysis." In F. X. Kaufmann, G. Majone, and V. Ostrom, eds., *Guidance, Control, and Evaluation in the Public Sector*. Berlin and New York: de Gruyter, 459–475.

———— (1986b) "An Agenda for the Study of Institutions." *Public Choice*, vol. 48, 3–25.

Ostrom, Vincent (1986) "Constitutional Considerations with Particular Reference to Federal Systems." In F. X. Kaufmann, G. Majone, and V. Ostrom, eds., *Guidance, Control, and Evaluation in the Public Sector*. Berlin and New York: de Gruyter, 111–125.

———— (1987) *The Political Theory of a Compound Republic: Designing the American Experiment*. Rev. ed. Lincoln: University of Nebraska Press.

Ostrom, Vincent, and Elinor Ostrom (1977) "Public Goods and Public Choices." In E. S. Savas, ed., *Alternatives for Delivering Public Services: Toward Improved Performance*. Boulder, Colo.: Westview, 7–49.

Rondinelli, Dennis A., and G. Shabbir Cheema (1983) "Implementing Decentralization: An Introduction." In G. Shabbir Cheema and Dennis A. Rondinelli, eds., *Decentralization and Development: Policy Implementation in Developing Countries.* Beverly Hills: Sage, 9-34.

Rondinelli, Dennis A., John R. Nellis, and G. Shabbir Cheema (1984) *Decentralization in Developing Countries: A Review of Recent Experience.* World Bank Staff Working Paper no. 581. Washington, D.C.: World Bank.

Seibel, Han Dieter, and Guenter Schroeder (1974) *Ethnographic Survey of Southeastern Liberia: The Kran and Sapo.* Newark, Del.: Liberian Studies Association.

Thoahlane, Thoahlane (1984) *A Study of Village Development Committees: The Case of Lesotho.* Institute of Southern African Studies, National University of Lesotho, P.O. Roma 180, Lesotho.

Weiner, Myron (1966) "Political Participation and Political Development." In Myron Weiner, ed., *Modernization: The Dynamics of Growth.* New York: Basic Books, 205–217.

World Bank (1981) *Accelerated Development in Sub-Saharan Africa: An Agenda for Action.* Washington, D.C.: World Bank.

9

Amos Sawyer

The Development of Autocracy in Liberia

Introduction

Since the end of World War II, and the transformation of the former colonial territories of Africa and Asia into independent countries, scholars have used a variety of approaches to explain and predict patterns of political development and modernization in these societies. Many of these scholars have assumed that political development and modernization in Africa should proceed in stages. In the early stages traditional and communal institutions would be dominant. After a "transitional" stage the countries would be transformed into modern polities (Lerner, 1958; Pye, 1966; Palmer, 1985). This pattern of development implies a process of political integration in which diverse ethnic groups are brought together into unified nation-states (Weiner, 1965; Cohen and Middleton, 1970). Traditional political

---

Comments by Carl Burrowes, Elinor Ostrom, Vincent Ostrom, Hartmut Picht, Susan Wynne, and Tai-Shuenn Yang have been most helpful.

arrangements, it is thought, will be superseded by modern political structures characterized by "structural differentiation" and "functional specificity" (Almond and Powell, 1966; Almond, 1970).

Another approach has seen development largely as the institutionalization of political organizations and procedures to ensure stability. Huntington, for example, argues that national development is signified by the centralization of authority in recognized national law-making institutions, the development of complex and disciplined administrative hierarchies, and broad-based political participation. Failure to achieve these conditions induces, he argues, a process of deinstitutionalization and political decay (Huntington, 1968).

Evidence abounds that political order in Africa has not evolved patterns of structural differentiation or functional specificity, nor have the structures, which were intended to be "institutionalized," been capable of achieving national integration or socioeconomic progress.[1] The process of modernization and nation-building in Africa should be perceived within a broader framework of comparative historical analysis free of preconceived, culture-bound notions of what a "developed Africa" should look like.[2] In this respect, the problem of unstable regimes and socioeconomic stagnation and decline, which is evident in Africa, should be perceived as related to the larger problems bearing upon the constitution of order in African societies.[3]

Any heuristic that seeks to explain the constitution of order in Africa would need to take into account the nature of the precolonial political order in African society, the impact of colonialism, the nature of the process of decolonization, and the strategies adopted by African governments as they have striven to formulate and implement their socioeconomic programs. When considered all together, these factors have resulted in the development of highly centralized structures of authority. Authority has been concentrated into fewer and fewer hands. Personal and autocratic rule has evolved instead of democracy and self-determination. These developments retard the capacity of societies to enhance their social well-being.

Using Liberia as the point of reference, the purpose of this paper is to examine the process by which centralized authority, as established and constituted in modern African societies, has led to the development of autocracy. This is the first step in exploring alternatives to autocratic rule in Africa. The analysis delineates factors that have resulted in the centralization and concentration of authority in African societies. This pattern is then examined in the specific case of Liberia, which shows the development of autocratic tendencies that have stifled the possibilities for self-governance and socioeconomic development in one of Africa's oldest examples of centralized modern government.

Foundations of African Political Order

Several scholars have previously attempted comparative analyses of African political orders by taking into account the historical processes and cultural experiences that have both resulted from and contributed to their development. Aristide R. Zolberg (1966), for example, posits that four factors have interacted within African societies to create political orders that are highly centralized, predatory, and without much legitimacy in their wider societies. These are: (1) the colonial political arrangements that were characterized by authoritarian structures, (2) independence movements that were largely urban-centered and not broadly supported, (3) mass-based political organizations whose organizational coherence and efficiency were much exaggerated, and (4) Western-educated, organization-minded, Pan-African-oriented leaders who had been deeply affected by the social, cultural, and economic changes that began after World War I. Zolberg further argues that African leaders were being highly motivated by the challenges and opportunities of independence, especially the challenge of integrating disparate ethnic groups into one "nation-state." They adopted a one-party ideology and attempted to transform the political organizations, which had been instrumental in gaining independence, into the dominant instrument for pursuing national unity and social progress, even though their societies were largely dominated by ethnic loyalties and social ties that militated against one-party centralization. This pursuit created tension between centralized authority, exercised through a single-party and a government bureaucracy, and the larger society.

Tension was further exacerbated by the pressure of international politics to adopt either "socialist" or "capitalist" economic strategies, and to build alliances in a competitive bipolar world system. Not only did this pressure raise the general sense of crisis and insecurity, it strained the Pan-Africanist orientations that had been at the foundation of the anti-colonial struggle. International pressure also made for fierce competition among neighbors, deepened territorial nationalism, and reinforced the tendency toward strong, centralized rule.

Confronted with rising expectations and enormous claims from many sectors of society, by efforts to politicize disparate ethnic loyalties, and by tremendous setbacks in achieving economic and social progress, African regimes moved toward modifying party and government so as to further concentrate authority in the hands of an already powerful leadership. African regimes employed methods of co-optation, intimidation, manipulation and control that eventually ensured the achievement of personal rule (Zolberg, 1966: 66–92). Zolberg concludes that although differences in style, emphasis, ideological pronouncements, and patterns of alliances exist, the process of constituting political order in Africa has strayed far from the direction of broadened political participation and the institutionalization of structures rooted in the society. Instead, the process has been dominated by the creation of centralized, authoritarian and personalized political orders whose major purpose is the "self-maintenance of incumbents" (pp. 124–125).

Zolberg's analysis is supported by the work of J. P. Nettl and Roland Robertson (1968), Sheldon Gellar (1973), and Robert H. Jackson and Carl G. Rosberg (1982). Nettl and Robertson argue that the creation of the modern African state is similar to an (inheritance situation) in which the granting of independence by the colonial powers corresponded to the bequeathing of ownership to beneficiaries (inheritance elites) who assumed control of the instruments of colonial authority. This analogy is employed to describe the decolonization process in the majority of African states, and to provide a basis for understanding the nature of the "neocolonial" arrangement that developed between the inheritance elites and the metropolitan powers. The perception of political authority as an inheritance also speaks to the nature of the relationship between the inheritance elite and the society. The character and constraints of the inheritance situation have dominated societies irrespective of the ideological preferences and international sympathies of the regimes that govern them. It is the manipulation of authoritarian structures bequeathed to inheritance elites by colonial authority, and the utilization of instruments of control such as the police, army, and legal system, that have established patterns of order in African societies.

Gellar's use of the concept of "neopatrimonialism" is meant to explain the character of centralized authority that, with limited resources and little legitimacy, seeks to penetrate and control the society through a system of clienteles and through the instrumentality of a central bureaucracy (Gellar, 1973). Patrimonial rule in Africa has many personal styles and forms. Jackson and Rosberg provide a useful discussion of personal rule in Africa. They argue that a pertinent condition leading to the development of personal rule is the absence of a "relevant and viable institutional tradition in the political life of a state" (Jackson and Rosberg, 1982: 21). They stress that in newly formed, modern political systems, whose members have not shared a common political tradition and political culture as was the case in Europe, personal rule takes the place of institutional rule. In the case of Africa, the territories of the new states were not congruent with traditional African political systems. As a result, there was no opportunity to resurrect and build upon traditional political institutions at independence. In the absence of such unifying and authoritative political institutions, rulers rule on the basis of their skills, craftiness, fortunes, and ability to monopolize instruments of coercion. Law becomes "a license of unrestricted command." Personal rule is, therefore, by definition arbitrary and vulnerable.

Jackson and Rosberg identified four types of personal rule systems that have emerged in Africa. They include the "princely" type, in which a ruler rules by manipulating clients, lieutenants and other subrulers to cultivate their loyalty, cooperation and support. The "autocrat" is described by Jackson and Rosberg as one who deploys the instruments of authority directly, and does not share authority with sub-rulers. His rulership resembles that of absolute monarchs. A third category, called "prophetic," has more to do with the purpose of rulership than with its style. Prophetic rulers are autocrats or princely rulers with a vision, usually a radical vision of society, who seek to transform society accordingly. "Tyranny" is the fourth type of personal rule, and one into which any of the other forms may deteriorate. In such situations, the moral constraints on the use of force are removed. Tyranny is marked by "particularly impulsive, oppressive, and brutal rule that [lacks] elementary respect—and has sometimes shown complete disdain—not only for the rights of persons and property but also for the very sanctity of human life" (1982: 80).

In summary, the pattern of political order that has emerged in Africa is the result of the dynamic interplay of such forces as: (1) the pre-colonial social formations whose tendencies, though dominated by colonialism, were not extinguished by it; (2) the nature and structure of colonial authority; (3) the nature of the process of decolonization; and (4) the objectives of national policy since independence and the strategies devised to achieve those policy objectives. Each of these factors has contributed to the emergence of overcentralization and personalization of authority as the mode of "government" in modern Africa. In its domination of African societies for a century, colonialism imposed authoritarian control over traditional political cultures of diverse types. The resurgence after independence of these diverse political cultures posed a serious problem for the new system of political authority, which was fashioned at independence in the mold of the authoritarian colonial arrangements it replaced. The new leaders, being bounded by certain perceptions of national unity and strategies for social development, and confronted with growing local and international pressures, sought solutions by centralizing control and imposing personal rule. This pattern of political order constitutes a general pattern that is also observable in many former colonies in Asia as well (Wriggins, 1969).[4]

I will not attempt here to elaborate a theory of constitutional choice for self-governance in Liberia. I will, however, take the first step in showing how centralized authority was constituted, consolidated, and transformed into personal and autocratic rule in Liberia. I will then critically reflect upon the conceptualization used to constitute the system of governance in Liberia and the relationship of this conceptualization to the emergence of personalized autocratic rulership.

Creating the Liberian Political Order

The individuals who were repatriated to Africa at the beginning of the nineteenth century to organize the Republic of Liberia were products of American slavery. The exigencies of the repatriates' situation did not allow tendencies toward democratic development to take firm root. Instead, environmental conditions, a quest for cultural homogeneity, the persistently hostile attitude of the native African communities, and the intervention of European imperial powers constrained the desire for equality and liberty; a higher priority was assigned to security than to justice, and to a hierarchy of authority rather than to democratic self-governance. The Liberian experience reveals the paradoxical situation of a group impelled by democratic ideals but employing the colonial methods of the day in an attempt to establish a republican form of government in Africa.

I will begin by discussing the conceptual foundations of Liberian national political arrangements. Then I will turn to a brief investigation of the African societies within whose midst repatriation took place and Liberian national institutions developed. I will then look at the process by which centralized authority, once established, was consolidated into personalized authority, thereby impairing the potential for democratic development and fostering the development of an autocracy. I will conclude with some thoughts on the problem that confronts Liberia and other African countries in identifying the foundations for self-governance.

The Idea of Repatriation. The repatriation of slaves was one of the earliest and more enduring proposed solutions to the American dilemma.[5] The first plan for repatriation was that of a prosperous black trader from Massachusetts called Paul Cuffee. In 1815 Cuffee, largely at his own expense, repatriated thirty-eight blacks to Sierra Leone. Cuffee's initiatives were not approved by all blacks. Black Americans remained divided on the question of repatriation as a solution to their plight in the Western Hemisphere. The majority, including Frederick Douglass, agreed with the "radical" abolitionists that repatriation was a conspiracy to deny blacks the right to live freely in the land of their toil (Douglass, 1859). Others, such as the Reverend Martin Delaney, maintained that black progress in America was linked to the demonstration abroad, particularly in Africa, that black people were capable of developing a major civilization (Delaney and Campbell, 1969).

The repatriation movement appeared to be driven by objectives that had been expressed in a letter of February 1816 to John P. Munford of New York from the Reverend Robert Finley of New Jersey, the leading organizer of the American Society for Colonizing the Free People of Color of the United States, later known as the American Colonization Society (ACS).

> The state of free blacks has very much oppressed my mind. Their numbers increase greatly, and their wretchedness too as appears to me. Everything connected with their condition, including their color, is against them; nor is there much prospect that their state can ever be ameliorated, while they shall continue among us. . . . Our fathers brought them here, and we are bound, if possible, to repair the injuries inflicted by our fathers. Could they be sent back to Africa, a three-fold benefit would arise. We should be cleared of them; we should send to Africa a population partially civilized and Christianized for its benefit; our blacks themselves would be put in a better situation. (in Wickstrom, 1958: 22)

The removal of free blacks thus represented mixed motives of questionable integrity. The opportunity to extend Christianity and Western civilization to Africa, the search for better opportunities for blacks elsewhere, and a desire to get rid of blacks seem to have been among the major motives behind repatriation as sponsored by the ACS.[6]

One may conclude that repatriation of blacks to Africa was a problematic concept from the start. The twin objectives of "Christianizing and civilizing" were moral justifications that contained a latent tension in a dominant African environment. This inherent tension was never resolved. It was destined to pose a perennial problem for Liberian society and to become a major factor in the development of a highly centralized and autocratic structure of authority. The repatriation scheme, being flawed as it was in concept and design, was bound to produce a false start. Black Americans were, accordingly, never enthusiastic about it. Only a small number of them were prepared to be repatriated to Africa.[7] I will now look very briefly at the region and the African societies into which the repatriates were introduced.

The Indigenous African Setting. The area that later became Liberia was located on the edges of what was known in the nineteenth century as the Western Sudan, the savanna region from which the empires of Ghana, Mali, and Songhai sprung between the eleventh and sixteenth centuries. This portion of the Western Sudan, which ran along the Atlantic coast, was considered part of the so-called Grain Coast, a sub-region of the Lower Guinea Coast.[8]

A dominant geographic feature of the Grain Coast subregion was an extensive tropical rain forest (Mabogunje, 1976). Except for a few salt factories along the coast and wild kola nuts in the forest, there was little that connected this region with the center of economic and political activities in the savanna region to the northwest. Occasionally, a group seeking refuge would take sanctuary in the rain forest. For centuries, only scattered human communities existed in this region in virtual isolation from the interior. As a result, no major societies had ever developed there.

Two major events took place in the late fifteenth and early sixteenth centuries that had a tremendous impact on the region. The first was the disintegration of the Mali Empire. The second was the arrival of European traders along the coast. The breakup of the Mali Empire created disturbances in the savanna region that had a sustained ripple effect, pushing peripheral groups deeper into the tropical rain forest. As a result, small autonomous political communities, based on ethnic lineages, were formed and had to work out an accommodation among themselves.

The conflict and competition among these groups intensified when European traders, especially slave traders, entered the region. Several confederacies and alliances were organized largely to ensure control and use of trade routes. These alliances were tenuous and short-lived because of the changing circumstances and variable fortunes of individual political communities.[9] This situation still characterized the arena into which the repatriates entered in the early nineteenth century. Although the political environment was rife with conflict, competition, and tenuous alliances, there were stable social institutions with clear and discrete patterns of order within each ethnic autonomous political community.

African Social Organization. Carl Burrowes (1986) has estimated that by the year 1700 the population of the coastal belt of this region was about 143,000. This population covered an area extending some 300 miles east from what was known as the Gallinas, in present-day southeastern Sierra Leone, to the Cavalla River, the current border with the Ivory Coast. While it is not known how many people lived in the rest of the region, it is known that the population consisted of some sixteen ethnic groups, the product of three ethnolinguistic stocks: the Mel-, Mande-, and Kwa-speaking peoples.[10] The Mel and Mande groups are to be found in the western and northern sections of the region, while the Kwa groups are generally located in the southern (coastal) and eastern sections.[11]

Although the Mel- and Mande-speaking groups were part of two larger and distinct linguistic groups, the close association among their constituent ethnic groups over some five centuries had, by the nineteenth century, made them similar in their social organization and authority relationships. The Kwa-speaking groups, on the other hand, employed a pattern of social organization and authority relationships different from the Mel and Mande. Nonetheless, some key features of social organization were common to all three groups.

In all of the African political communities, the household is the basic unit of social organization. The core of the household is the nuclear polygamous family that is derived from a patrilineal descent line. The household is both the physical structure (the main house and its satellite house or houses), and a domestic social unit. It is the most important unit for production, especially agricultural production. The status of individuals in the household depends upon their relationship to the head of the household, so that the senior wife is the most deferred to, and the oldest son of the senior wife is the immediate heir. The social status of the household depends upon the status of the head of the household in the larger social unit, the "quarter."

The "quarter" consists of related households. Among the Mel and Mande it is a lineage segment and, as such, it is more than the physical cluster of households. It embodies a sentimental attachment of relatives bonded by a presumed kinship derived from a common patrilineage, real or fictive. Among the Mel and Mande, the political community consists of a number of lineage segments, or quarters, ranked in order of relation to the lineage segment of a founding ancestor. Social status is determined on the basis of a relationship to that core lineage. Among the Kwa, the equivalent of the quarter is the "panton." The panton is a cluster of related patrilineal households with sentiments, allegiances, and history that may connect with clusters of related patrilineal households in other political communities based on the myth or reality of a common odyssey. The quarter or panton is the most important political and social unit. The eldest male of the quarter who is the nearest kin to the founder of the quarter is its leader. He governs the quarter in consultation with elderly male relatives, who constitute a council.

The village or town and its adjoining service "half towns" (the actual cites of production) constitute the political community. Among the Mel and Mande, the head of the quarter of the founding ancestor has to be the chief or head of the political community. Decisions are made by consensus by the chief and council of elders, which consists of prominent elders of the quarters. Among the Mel and Mande, in case of a failure to reach consensus, the matter is taken to the Poro, a secret society, for resolution. Among the Kwa, there is a tendency, when the elders have failed to reach a consensus, to place the issue before a broader constituency that includes the women and young people of the community. Only matters relating to war or the negotiation of peace would be discussed by a forum limited to males. The ascriptive nature of political leadership is particularly strong among the Mel and somehow less so among the Mande. It is virtually nonexistent among many Kwa-speaking groups on the southern coast and in the eastern section.

There is a greater tendency among the Kwa to encourage achievement and individualism. This tendency has induced a higher degree of competitiveness, smaller social organizations, and more conflictual relationships than are found among the Mel- and Mande-speaking peoples. In Kwa societies people live in small, scattered communities; quite frequently, disgruntled people may opt out of a political community and establish one of their own.

Poro Authority. The Poro and Sande societies are important features of life in the region of western and northern Liberia among the Mel and Mande peoples. The Sande is a rites-of-passage organization for women. In addition to being a rites-of-passage organization for men, the Poro is also a secret society that provides a deeper basis for order in the political community. It is the Poro that legitimizes the political order, guards the belief system, sets rules of conduct and brings sanctions to bear, and unites the secular and religious elements of the society. It ensures a common socializing experience for all members of the numerous micro political communities of western and northern Liberia. It is the final authority in interethnic and intercommunity disputes.

The Poro society is a panethnic institution that has existed in all of the Mande and Mel societies in Liberia, Sierra Leone, and Guinea since the fifteenth century. Only communities that are Islamized do not have Poro institutions. This is because Islam forbids participation in organizations that are not Islamic. Each political community has its Poro authority structure, which is linked to other such societies in a panethnic and transethnic configuration in the region.

The Poro also exercises a supervisory and restraining role vis-a-vis the hierarchical authority structure headed by the chief. In some ways, this role seeks to prevent arbitrariness and to ensure conformity within a deeper constitutional order. The widespread existence of Poro societies in the northern and western areas of Liberia accentuates the difference between these areas and the southern and eastern areas in which the Kwa live and where there is no Poro or any equivalent institution.[12]

Land, Property, and Commodity Production. The political communities of the region have been largely agricultural, producing grain and tubers for local consumption. Until the coming of European traders, the major commercial commodity items were wild kola nuts from the rain forest and salt from the coast. With the appearance of the Europeans, a market was also created for spices and tropical fibers. By the eighteenth century, however, slaves had become the most important trade item. The introduction of slaves as a commercial commodity in the seventeenth century intensified hostile interaction among the political communities and encouraged confiscatory raiding.

Although commodity production was important, land remained community property under the control of the chief and the elders. Land was apportioned to quarters, which in turn made assignments to households. While certain internal arrangements readjusting the assignment within or between quarters were possible, use of land, no matter how consistent, did not confer ownership upon the user. The products of the land, however, were considered the personal property of the producer. Therefore, individual heads of households could accrue substantial resources as a result of the skillful organization of household production, supplemental entrepreneurship, and control over other factors affecting production.

Artisans also enjoyed considerable influence in the community. The blacksmith was the most important of these. His craft was considered to be on the frontier of technology. He did not farm, but received support from the tribute given to the chief as well as from individuals for whom he made tools. The skills of the blacksmith, like those of most artisans, were transferred through hereditary descent. His products were essential tools for both agricultural and military purposes.

Among the coastal Kwa political communities, there were some differences. The development of a seafaring culture showed differences in the nature and organization of production in that area. Not only was fishing the major production activity along the coast, but control of the trade with the Europeans was also very important. The seafaring Kwa communities had long established commercial relationships with Europeans and were already engaged in long-distance seagoing travel before the arrival of the repatriates. Their control of seaports and access to Europeans, both of which were independent of the political community established by the repatriates, eventually constituted a significant source of conflict.

In summary, before the introduction of the Liberian state, the region now called Liberia was replete with numerous autonomous micropolitical communities, defined by the ethnic lineage of their leaderships but consisting of a heterogeneous population. These autonomous political communities were at varying levels of social development by the early nineteenth century. Some had developed strong orientations toward individualism and achievement while others showed a greater tendency toward reliance on ascription. Linkages among them were weak and rather tenuous. In the case of the Mande and Mel, the Poro provided a common basic value system, and a higher level of authority. Nonagricultural production was neither very extensive nor complex. As a result, artisans and other specialists including merchants had not developed as groups capable of significantly influencing the structure of authority or social organization.

As was the case generally in West Africa, the slave trade intensified the conflict in the region and produced an enormously unstable environment. By the turn of the nineteenth century, European presence had become a permanent factor in the region. Europeans had established strong commercial links with the Kru, Grebo, Bassa (Kwa-speaking), and Vai (Mande-speaking) along the coast. This was the nature of the environment in which the repatriates (settlers) from the Western Hemisphere were to attempt to develop a new society, Liberia.

Forming the New Society

If the conception and planning of repatriation were one source of tension, the manner of acquiring territory in West Africa was another. On December 15, 1821, U. S. Naval Captain Robert F. Stockton and Dr. Eli Ayres, agent for the U. S. government, met with Dei and Bassa, (Kwa-speaking) chiefs whose territories would become the site of the first settlement. Captain Stockton, in a move to speed up the "negotiations," pulled out his pistol, put it to the head of one of the chiefs, and obtained a favorable agreement to the Doukor Contract, as the "agreement" is sometimes called.[13]

The permanent ceding of land through purchase was alien to local African practice despite previous contacts with Europeans. The establishment of a permanent alien settlement along the coast was unanticipated, as was the expansionist character of the alien society once established. The establishment of repatriate settlements under such conditions required a permanent state of vigilance and mobilization on the part of the repatriates. In such circumstances it was easy for the repatriate society to develop a centralized authority system.

Conceptualizing the Constitutional Order. Even before land had been acquired, the ACS had formulated a constitution for the settlement that was to be established. The Constitution for the Government of the African Settlement, as it was called, was adopted by the ACS on June 26, 1821. The constitution as formulated prescribed what amounted to an ideal Hobbesian model of governance.[14] It centralized legislative, judicial, and executive authority in the hands of the ACS. In doing so, the constitution established the ACS as the sovereign authority. The ACS was not accountable to the repatriates.

Problems of unfriendly relationships with the surrounding African societies and growing economic difficulties quickly began to strain the settlers' relationship with the ACS. Also, in the course of their normal daily interaction as they sought to cope with their situation, the repatriates began to develop an alternative pattern of order. Periodic town meetings were one of the institutions that emerged. From 1823, the town meeting became an important institution in settler society and remained so throughout the nineteenth century and well into the twentieth. The concerns of town meetings were broad. They ranged from organizing for public works purposes to considerations regarding the role of the communities in matters of constitutional importance such as the appointment of magistrates, formulation of rules governing distribution of land, and relations with the surrounding African societies. As authority was continually being centralized, the town meeting became less important as a framework for community decision making. Its value in promoting community esprit de corps was its major achievement.

Three issues required effective local authority to resolve. The first was the persistent occurrence of skirmishes with the surrounding African societies. These skirmishes not only resulted from conflicts over the settlers' acquisition of African territory but also from their intervention in the continuing transactions in slaves between European slave traders and some African chiefs. The second issue was internal to the new society. It related to the inability of the ACS to meet the challenges caused by the expansion of repatriate settlements. The transfer of authority from the ACS to the settlers was now a necessity. Fundamental problems involved control over land and the settlement of recaptured African slaves. The insistence of the ACS on maintaining control over large tracts of land in and around the major settlements was a major bone of contention between it and the settlers.

The third issue that required effective local authority for resolution was the continued incursion of the British and French into territory claimed by the Liberian government. British and French merchants continued to establish trading posts and to maintain trade relationships in the area in total disregard of Liberian claims. With the support of their governments, the merchants refused to pay customs levies and to recognize Liberian authority. Both powers claimed that Liberia was not a sovereign state and, therefore, was in no position to exercise sovereign prerogatives. A legal declaration of independence and the transfer of sovereign authority internally were perceived by the settlers to be the most appropriate measures.

A new constitution was drafted by a Constitutional Convention that met in Monrovia in July 1847. The new constitution established a centralized authority system with separation of powers among three branches of government: the legislature, the executive, and the judiciary. It assigned strong appointment powers to the president. Except for the members of the bicameral legislature, all public officials, including judges, were to be appointed by the president. With the exception of judges, all appointed officials were to serve at the president's pleasure.

The constitution seemed to have only transferred authority from an external source, the ACS, to a national triumvirate located high above the society. No provisions were made for the exercise of local authority. In doing this, the designers seemed to have expressed a preference for an arrangement facilitative of centrally mobilized action against external forces rather than of democratic growth and development. It would appear that the incursions of the British and French, and the persistent skirmishes with the surrounding African societies in whose galaxy the settler republic was now one of the major actors, had led the drafters to perceive a need for strong centralized leadership above all else.

One of the ironies of the Liberian experience is that in spite of the assignment of total authority to national structures, the capacity to resolve the pressing issues of the society did not increase as was anticipated. Relations with the surrounding African societies remained tenuous, at best, for the next century. Relationship with the British and French did not improve until both powers had consolidated their empires a half century later. The internal desire for local participation remained unfulfilled. The constitutional arrangements had centralized authority in three branches of government. As this arrangement evolved, authority would become increasingly concentrated in the executive branch of government. This process can be seen as the government of Liberia sought to consolidate its hold over the region.

The Consolidation of Authority. The national government sought to consolidate its authority over the territory by two methods: pacification, and co-optation of the indigenous African societies. These strategies involved the use of military force and the conclusion of treaties of amity and commerce.[15] There were two exploratory missions to the interior (Anderson, 1971).[16] Despite this, it was not until the British and French made significant incursions at the turn of the century that the Liberian government formulated a plan for the interior.[17]

In an effort to achieve effective control over the interior, President Arthur Barclay's government, in 1904, announced a new interior policy known as the Barclay Plan. The plan was a scheme for "indirect rule" over the interior much like the British "indirect rule" plan of colonial administration in Africa and Asia (Gopal, 1963; Kirkwood, 1965; Hatch, 1969). It called for the grouping of villages into districts. The chiefs and councils of elders who had governed autonomous political communities would henceforth report to district commissioners. Over the next thirty years, the scheme would evolve as a hierarchical grouping of villages and towns into clans, clans into chiefdoms, chiefdoms into districts, and districts into provinces. At each level in the hierarchy, executive and judicial functions were merged and exercised by "native" authorities holding their positions by grace of the secretary of the interior, who presided over the entire machinery and reported to the president.

A second part of the plan was the creation of the Liberian Frontier Force, supposedly a standing professional military force on the order of the Sierra Leone Frontier Force created by the British in the late 1800s for pacification purposes. The new interior policy marked a significant shift in authority relations within the Liberian government. Never before had there been a permanently organized machinery for interior relations. Nor had there been a standing military force. Relations with the interior had been sporadic and confined to efforts to secure new sources of trade. Both the new interior bureaucracy and the Frontier Force were responsible to the president. By vesting the interior administration with both judicial and executive powers, the presidency grew stronger. In addition, the opportunities allowed the executive to revise the plan through executive orders, and "departmental regulations" significantly expanded the legislative authority of the presidency.

By 1930, as a result of serious abuses in the system of interior administration, Liberia was investigated by the League of Nations and found to be indulging in forced labor practices. These charges emanated from contracts signed between Spanish plantation owners on the island of Fernando Po and officials of the Liberian government acting in a private capacity, but with the approval of the government, to supply workers to Fernando Po cocoa plantations. The supply arrangement degenerated into raiding indigenous communities and pressing people into forced labor under harsh conditions and low wages. Similar measures were employed by the government to recruit workers for the Firestone Plantations Company, which was in its infancy in Liberia, and other private rubber plantation owners. The League's findings produced expressions of moral outrage. The president and vice-president of Liberia were forced to resign. The authority of the national government was severely shaken. The new president, Edwin Barclay, nephew of the author of the Barclay Plan, used stringent means to restore presidential authority. Some of the most repressive laws on sedition, treason, and press restrictions were passed during this period (League of Nations, 1930).

The concentration of authority in the presidency was reinforced as competition in party politics declined. The True Whig Party (TWP), which ascended to power in 1869, became the only party to control the government. Until the ascendency of the TWP, the Republican Party, which was the party of the Monrovia trading interests and coastal mulatto political leaders, controlled the government. The TWP mobilized the support of the agriculturally based settler communities outside Monrovia and the immediate coastal strip, and combined that support with lower-class urban support from Monrovia. These groups together constituted the majority of the settlers and provided a major transformation in power alignment. The Republican Party, which had held power until it was defeated by the TWP in 1868, proved to be an ineffective rival after about ten years of TWP rule. A number of sporadic challenges were made to the TWP during the first half of this century, but none materialized into sustained opposition.

Having consolidated its position as the only party to control the government, the TWP underwent internal transformations at the turn of the nineteenth century. Between 1900 and 1920 the position of party chairman, which was the most powerful position in the party, lost considerable clout. The president or standard bearer became institutionalized as the center of power in the party. This development coincided with the formation of the interior bureaucracy and its capacity to mobilize votes and determine elections (Liebenow, 1969).

The Personalization of Authority. When William Tubman succeeded Barclay in 1944, he inherited a presidency that towered over all other national institutions. The presidency had also become a source of fear for most Liberians in the interior.[18] Tubman introduced two policies that were radical departures from Barclay's policies: the open door policy and the unification policy.

The open door policy, which was his strategy for the economic development of Liberia, was designed to attract foreign investment and respond to the advances of multinational corporations that were now the major source of international investment. This strategy differed markedly from that of his predecessor, whose approach to economic development had relied largely on attempts to expand commerce. Firestone had been the only major foreign investor prior to 1945. In the next twenty-five years, mining became the dominant form of investment capital in Liberia through the creation of joint-venture companies with the Liberian government. The transition to capital-intensive production during this period required sophisticated technical skills that, in turn, required an expanded educational system. The result was in a shift from subsistence farming to wage labor that intensified the rural-urban drift. All of this put more stress on the social infrastructures.

The unification policy was meant to adjust the social situation, particularly in light of the new demands placed upon the society by the economic policy. Suffrage was extended to all hut-tax-paying individuals in the interior;[19] physical and social infrastructure was expanded, and an ongoing dialogue with chiefs was instituted through a series of Unification Councils. Like his predecessor, Tubman also sought to regulate the Poro and Sande organizations (Department of Interior, 1962).

In 1964 the government created four new counties and, for the first time, established a uniform system of local administration for the entire country. This was an exceedingly popular move in the interior. It created a psychological presumption of equality and provided bureaucratic sinecures for professionals from the interior who found it difficult to compete with their coastal counterparts for public offices.

Other measures were taken by Tubman that led to the personalization of authority. In 1951, upon approaching the end of the single eight-year term of office allowed by the constitution, he pushed through the legislature a bill amending the constitution so that he could run for an indefinite number of terms. Through this amendment, he remained in office until his death twenty years later. He built an elaborate security network that included a personal network of informants, called Public Relations Officers (PRO's), financed by the public treasury.

Tubman also developed a personal system of patronage and clientelism that was supported by public funds. Public accountability broke down as he encouraged personal loyalty and sycophancy and destroyed efforts to build a civil service. The person of the president became indistinguishable from the institution of the presidency. His personal resources were also indistinguishable from the public treasury. Thus, while Edwin Barclay had made the presidency an exceedingly strong and dreaded institution, Tubman transformed it into an instrument of personal power. He developed a system of personal rulership that vacillated between princely and autocratic rule.

In the early 1970s, the prices of Liberia's major export commodities began to decline at the same time as the price of oil rose dramatically. The economic boom that had begun with the establishment of the iron ore economy in the early 1950s and peaked in the mid-to-late 1960s was now in sharp decline. It was at this time that Tubman's vice president of nineteen years, William Tolbert, succeeded him. In his haste to stamp his own imprint on the presidency, Tolbert embarked on a series of expensive projects that included the construction of a village for a summit conference of the Organization of African Unity (OAU).

By temperament, style, and taste, Tolbert was unwilling and unable to fit into Tubman's mode or to develop his own mode of personal rule. The declining economic situation also denied him the resources to establish his own personalized regime. More importantly, seeds of social change had been planted by the expansion of educational opportunities in the 1950s and 1960s by the development of a large mining labor force, and by the alienation of peasant land through the expansion of agribusiness and the timber industry. All of these forces posed powerful challenges that became ready to be articulated in the early 1970s as Tolbert took office. Other national institutions, having been stripped of what residual legitimacy they had had, were unable to respond to the challenges. The result was the total collapse of the authority of the national government and a military takeover on April 12, 1980.[20] Over the next six years, military rule degenerated into brutal tyranny.

Conjectures and Conclusions

The Republic of Liberia, when it was founded diverged markedly from nineteenth-century patterns of European imperialism. The motives that inspired development of the Liberian venture in human governance were provided by a philanthropic group organized as a voluntary association rather than an imperial power bent on conquest and the exercise of imperial hegemony. Yet the result is very similar to what has occurred among other African states with distinct colonial heritages. Are there humanitarian motives that have yielded similar results?

The humanitarian impulse in the resettlement of former slaves in Liberia involved mixed motives. The motive to extend Western civilization and to advance Christianity were easily transformed into imperial impulses. The motive of getting rid of blacks was less than humanitarian. Perhaps the most critical aspect was to presume that the ACS could exercise ultimate authority over the governance of affairs among the settlers in Liberia and thereafter create a democratic society by transferring authority to centralized structures. This is the same basic conception that is used in all imperial ventures. It has usually resulted in the creation of autocracies in which coercion is the principal motor driving society. There is a basic presumption in any such conception that governments govern and that states rule over society.

The struggle in achieving democratic systems of government has been to constrain the exercise of governmental prerogatives so that they are exercised with the consent of the governed; so that taxation does not occur without representation, the prerogatives of government are subject to a rule of law and exercised by a due process of law; so that the basic integrity and fundamental rights of human beings are recognized as inalienable; and so that citizens exercise a fundamental voice in the conduct of government. The ACS bequeathed the foundations of an imperial heritage to an "inheritance elite" who, through pacification of local populations and the development of a system of indirect rule, put into place a system of control similar to the patterns of imperial control that existed among the other colonial domains of Africa.[21] As a result, this system of control has produced the same predatory strategies as in other African states. The system, as is evident since the military takeover of Liberia in 1980, now operates irrespective of the backgrounds or origins of the rulers. A minority group of Krahn (Kwa-speaking) soldiers, having installed themselves in authority, acquired the same levers and prerogatives and pursued the same predatory strategies that had been entrenched in the system of control (Liebenow, 1987).

One such strategy is reflected in the patterns of economic development in Liberia.[22] These derived from changes in the constitutional order and in world circumstances. The establishment of the interior bureaucracy created entrepreneurial opportunities for the president and his associates and agents who ran the government as their proprietary domain. World War II and economic reconstruction in Europe after World War II created new opportunities for economic development. The involvement of multinational corporations in Liberia's economy became more intensive. While the major infrastructural development that took place at this time was related to the economic activities of multinationals, considerable improvement also took place in the development of the general social and physical infrastructure of the country.[23]

Since that period, however, there has been an alarming decline in real wages and a persistent rise in unemployment. This decline has intensified since 1980—especially in rural Liberia, where about 70 percent of Liberians engage in traditional agriculture.[24] Most striking of all, regarding the problem of agriculture, is the government's monopoly control over the distribution of the agricultural products.[25] Against the declining economic situation of the rural areas, there exists the ever increasing demand for taxes and other "contributions."[26]

Even those economists who are noted for being charitable to the Liberian government over the years have observed intensive predation. While they consider this predation to be a problem stemming from the lack of planning and deficiencies in technology, one can perceive a more serious problem associated with economic decline. This problem is related to the enduring constraints upon opportunities to engage in productive enterprise, a condition that parallels the concentration and personalization of authority in the society. The opportunities for gainful central employment are reduced by the predatory tendencies of governmental authorities. The government has become the major employer.

What we have seen in Liberia, as is the case elsewhere in Africa, is how improperly institutionalized central authority has given way to personalized and autocratic rule that, in turn, has had serious consequences for Liberian society. Not only has personalized rule made the institution of the presidency indistinguishable from the person of the president; it has greatly restricted social space and circumscribed social institutions through the overwhelming presence of the person of the president throughout the society. It has undermined respect for rules because rules are sporadically and selectively applied and, more importantly, because the ruler and those associated with him live outside the rules and are known to be doing so. Social prestige accrues to those who demonstrate an ability to avoid paying taxes, drive cars without license tags, and run though red traffic lights with impunity.

What we have seen is the use of the instrumentalities of government by a few or, perhaps, by a single individual to make decisions that are generally construed to be collective decisions. Collective action is then exacted largely through coercion and disincentives. This presents a situation that is always tense and on the brink.

Collective action depends upon people acting in accordance with decisions taken. This cannot always be done on the basis of command alone. Although coercion may affect people's calculations, instruments of coercion cannot be relied upon to make everyone do what a policy requires. Collective action requires that those who are to undertake it develop shared understandings and common interests. People must have an understanding of the decision—the policy—and perceive an incentive for themselves in taking collective action with others to implement it. It is collective action that constitutes a deeper form of participation than participation in the form of voting. Voting is too easily manipulated by those who run the government. Where government is conducted with the consent of the governed, both voting and collective action must be grounded in institutions that are consonant with principles of self-government.

Notes

1. More than 80 percent of African societies are under military or militarized rule. Economic stagnation and social degeneration have been well documented by the OAU (1980) and the World Bank (1983, 1984).

2. See Sheldon Gellar's (1973) excellent critique of many of the theoretical approaches now applied to Africa.

3. The view that the development of human societies turns upon the conception and design of their system of ordering, so that self-governance is essential to political development, is a perspective I have adopted from the work of Elinor Ostrom and Vincent Ostrom and the Workshop in Political Theory and Policy Analysis, Indiana University.

4. For an interesting case study on Burma, see U. Maung Maung (1969).

5. In 1691, the Legislature of Virginia enacted a law prohibiting the emancipation of slaves unless for purposes of deportation. Between this time and the early nineteenth century, several such proposals were made, one by Thomas Jefferson in 1777 to the Legislature of Virginia. See G. B. Stebbins (1853: 5), Kathrine Harris

(1982: 29), and Tom Shick (1977: 4–5).

6. It should be stated here that an economic motive has also been advanced. T. L. Spraggins has stated that some supporters of repatriation argued that it would have provided an economic foothold in the tropics by creating a pool of black U.S. workers potentially trainable by U.S. businesses there. It was also argued, according to Spraggins, that the removal of free blacks from the U.S. labor force would have made room for more rapid absorption of immigrants from Europe. See T. L. Spraggins (1957). For another aspect of the economic motive argument, see also Phil S. Sigler (1969, esp. ch. 2).

7. It is estimated that in 1821 there were about 500,000 free blacks and more than 3 million slaves. Only 18,700 blacks were repatriated from 1821 to 1865. Of these, 5,000 were free black men, women, and children; 8,000 were slaves manumitted purposely for repatriation; and 5,700 were Africans who had been recaptured from slavers by antislave patrols. See Sigler (1969: i).

8. In the sixteenth century, the Portuguese designated the region from Cape Blanco to Sierra Leone the "Upper Guinea Coast," and from Sierra Leone to Cameroon the "Lower Guinea Coast." Subregions of the Lower Guinea Coast were designated by their principle exports: thus, the area now known as Liberia was called the Grain Coast because of the large quantities of "grain of paradise" (malagueta pepper) found there. Also, European ship captains sometimes referred to the coast of the subregion as the Windward Coast because of the direction of the prevailing winds in that part of the Atlantic. See J. D. Fage (1969: 57) and Basil Davidson (1977: 252).

9. One of the most important during the early nineteenth century was the Condo Confederation organized by Sao Boso; see Svend Holsoe (1966).

10. Taken together, these groups account for about 96 percent of Liberia's current population. The Mel ethno-linguistic stock consists of two ethnic groups: the Gola and Kissi. The Mande consists of eight: Vai, Mandingo, Loma, Gbande, Kpelle, Mende, Dan, and Mah. There are six ethnic groups that comprise the Kwa

ethno-linguistic stock; they are the Belle, Dei, Bassa, Kru, Krahn, and Grebo. For latest population figures, see Ministry of Planning and Economic Affairs (1974). The population of recaptured Africans that numbered about 5,700 in 1865 had been totally assimilated into the ranks of the American settlers by the second decade of the twentieth century.

11. This discussion of African social organization has drawn from the works of Warren L. d'Azevedo (1959, 1962a, 1962b, 1969), H. Scudder Mekeel (1937), James L. Gibbs (1960, 1965), George Brooks, Jr. (1972), Jane J. Martin (1968), and William Siegmann (1969).

12. Some Kwa-speaking societies that border Mande-speaking societies, for example, have adopted Poro institutions. These are exceptions.

13. "Doukor" is the name given Monrovia by the Vai.

14. Reference is made to Hobbes's concept of sovereignty as discussed in his *Leviathan*, Michael Oakeshott, ed. ([1651] 1960).

15. The pacification campaign of the Liberian government against the "uncooperative" African societies predated 1847. In 1822, for example, the first major hostilities broke out between the repatriates and the Gola. The hostilities were ended with a treaty of friendship and commerce. However, hostilities broke out again in 1838. In 1841, there were skirmishes with the Bassa after which Bassa chiefs were held to a treaty of peace in which indemnity was exacted. In 1852, there were more conflicts with the Bassa. Four years later, there was a major outbreak of fighting against the Kru. In 1875 and 1893, two campaigns were waged against the Grebo. From 1898 to 1900, there were violent uprisings in the northwestern region. More hostilities against the Grebo took place in 1910 and 1915, against the Gola in 1918, the Kpelle in 1920, and against the Kru in 1936. The history of the relationship between the settlers and the African societies is replete with hostile encounters that span more than a century. See Raymond Buell (1928, vol. 2: 704–889), M. D. Akpan (1973), and H. Abeodu Jones (1962). A few major efforts at incorporation through inducements are recorded. The first was before independence in 1842 when then Governor Roberts, upon

touring the interior, attempted through a treaty of friendship and commerce to induce certain African leaders to put their territories under the jurisdiction of the Liberian government. In a similar move in 1879, before the British annexed the Gallinas to Sierra Leone, the Liberian government invited Ibrahim Sesay and other chiefs of the area to take seats in the Liberian legislature. The government had already passed an act permitting nonvoting representation from surrounding African societies upon payment of a charge of one hundred dollars. See Akpan (1973: 220–224) and Charles Henry Huberich (1947, vol. 1: 149).

16. In 1868 and 1874, the Liberian government commissioned the noted Liberian naturalist and surveyor, B.J.K. Anderson, to explore the interior as a basis for formulating an interior policy. Anderson's two trips took him as far north as Musardu in the kingdom of the Western Mandingo. He signed numerous treaties of amity and commerce. Upon his return, he expressed concern about the activities of the French in the northern region and recommended that an intensive program involving commercial relationships and educational opportunities be developed for the area. See his *Narrative of a Journey to Musardu* (new edition, 1971, first published in 1870.)

17. In the colonial "scramble" during the latter part of the nineteenth century, Britain, which had recognized Liberia's independence in 1849, now asserted that the Liberian government had not established effective control over the territory it claimed. In 1885, Britain annexed the Gallinas to its colony in Sierra Leone. In 1891, the French annexed the littoral to the east of the Ivory Coast. In 1892, Liberia was constrained to sign agreements with the French ceding a large section of the land in the north and east. It was not until 1911 that last treaties were concluded with these European powers, treaties that defined Liberia's current borders.

18. In his attempt to strengthen the administrative capacity of the government, Barclay had sought to rationalize the civil service, further centralize interior administration, and enhance government's penetration of the Poro and Sande by requiring government oversight of those institutions. He had crushed an uprising on the Kru

coast in 1936, and executed some chiefs. By the end of the decade, not only was it clear that the government had established control over the territory; it was equally clear that the presidency was the supreme authority.

19. The hut tax was later enforced as if it were a head tax paid by each male adult in the interior. It was abolished in 1980 after the military takeover.

20. The military takeover in 1980 was not the first arbitrary use of force to effect a change of government in Liberia. The first was in 1871, when supporters of the Republican Party, through mob action, overthrew the government of President E. J. Roye and imprisoned him.

21. One grim episode in the pacification campaign occurred in 1912, when eight Gbande chiefs (Mande-speaking) were deposed for "treasonable practices." They had opposed the high-handed methods of two district commissioners. The two district commissioners were recalled but not before they had hanged the eight chiefs and installed new hand-picked replacements. When unrest broke out after the new paramount chief was murdered by a rival who was a relative of the former chief, the Liberian Frontier Force was sent in. See Akpan (1973).

22. For a discussion of the political economy of Liberia before 1940, see George Brown (1941). See Robert Clower, et al. (1966) for developments since World War II. Elliot Berg (1982), J. Gus Liebenow (1987), and Togba-Nah Tipoteh (1987) have provided current perspectives relevant to the period of military rule. C. E. van Santen's (1974) excellent study focuses on agricultural problems. Ministry of Planning and Economic Affairs (1971–1980, 1974) provides data on social and physical infrastructural development.

23. The first major road system that was begun in 1909 by the Liberian Frontier Force consisted in little more than a trunk road of some 45 miles (see Brown, 1941). By 1940, 1,200 miles of road had been built. By 1980, there were at least 7,000 miles of all-weather roads. There are four deep-water ports, constructed largely to accommodate the mining and timber industries (see Ministry of Planning and Economic Affairs, 1971–1980). Regarding social

infrastructure, literacy rose from less than 3 percent in 1920 to about 15 percent in 1950 and about 30 percent by 1980. School enrollment, which was less than 20 percent of school-aged children in 1950, had risen to about 66 percent by 1980. There were two hospitals in 1940; there are more than twenty today. While these indices suggest remarkable progress, there is still a chronic shortage of qualified teachers, and of equipment and supplies in schools and hospitals. The form of progress most often noted was the tremendous economic growth of nearly 6 percent annually experienced in the 1960s and the accompanying expansion of wage employment. About one-third of the adult male population was said to be in wage employment. This placed Liberia among the high-income economies of the Less Developed Countries (LDC's) in the 1960s.

24. From 1970 to 1979, agricultural workers experienced a 52 percent decline in real wages; mining workers, a 36 percent decline; and government salaried employees a decline of 25 percent. Since 1980, there has been an annual decline of 4.5 percent in real gross domestic product and close to a 50 percent decline in real income. Per capita income, which was $160 in 1970, is less than $100 today (see Tipoteh, 1987). There is only one agriculture extension officer for every 10,000 people in the rural area and, according to the United Nations Food and Agriculture Organization (FAO), they are handicapped in the performance of their work by lack of transportation and by demands for preferential treatment by "government officials" and others with connections (see van Santen, 1974).

25. The Liberian Produce Marketing Corporation (LPMC), which was established in the early 1970s with an initial capital of $250,000, declared a profit of 100 percent after its first year of operation. In 1979, it contributed $7 million to the government for the hosting of the summit conference of the OAU. In addition to the enormous profits being reaped by the LPMC, there are at least two levels of middlemen between the farmer and the agency. As a result, in spite of world market prices, prices paid to farmers remain constantly low (see Tipoteh, 1987).

26. Until 1980, there existed a regressive hut tax that was a levy of $10 to $15 annually on every household in the rural area.

Although the hut tax has been abolished, there remain numerous exactions in cash and kind as contributions to the president, proposed "development" projects, or a show of rural hospitality to visiting government officials.

Works Cited

Akpan, M. D. (1973) "Black Imperialism: Americo-Liberian Rule over the African Peoples of Liberia, 1841–1964." *Canadian Journal of African Studies*, vol. 7, no. 2, 217–236.

Almond, Gabriel A. (1970) *Political Development: Essays in Heuristic Theory.* Boston: Little, Brown.

Almond, Gabriel A., and G. Brigham Powell (1966) *Comparative Politics: A Developmental Approach.* Boston: Little, Brown.

Anderson, Benjamin, J. K. (1971) *Narrative of a Journey to Musardu* together with *Narrative of The Expedition Despatched to Musardu.* London: Cass. First published in 1870 and 1912, respectively.

Berg, Elliot (1982) *The Liberian Crisis and an Appropriate U.S. Response: Report to USAID.* Washington, D.C.: U.S. Agency for International Development.

Brooks, George, Jr. (1972) *The Kru Mariner in the Nineteenth Century.* Newark, Del.: Liberian Studies Association.

Brown, George W. (1941) *Economic History of Liberia.* Washington, D.C.: Associated Publishers.

Buell, Raymond (1928) *The Native Problem in Africa.* Vol. 2. London: Cass.

Burrowes, Carl P. (1986) "A Demographic Profile of Pre-Liberian Coastal Societies: 1660–1747." Glassboro State College, Glassboro, N.J. Mimeo.

Clower, Robert, et al. (1966) *Growth without Development: An Economic Survey of Liberia.* Evanston, Ill.: Northwestern University Press.

Cohen, Ronald, and John Middleton, eds. (1970) *From Tribe to Nation in Africa: Studies in Incorporation Processes.* Scranton, Pa.: Chandler.

Davidson, Basil (1977) *A History of West Africa, 1000 to 1800.*

London: Longman.

d'Azevedo, Warren L. (1959) "The Setting of Gola Society and Culture: Some Theoretical Implications of Variation in Time and Space." Kroeber Anthropological Society Papers no. 21., 43–125.

─────────────── (1962a) "Some Historical Problems in the Delineation of a Central West Atlantic Region." *Annals of the New York Academy of Sciences*, vol. 96, 512–538.

─────────────── (1962b) *The Gola of Liberia*. New Haven: Human Relations Area Files.

─────────────── (1969) "A Tribal Reaction to Nationalism." Part 1. *Liberian Studies Journal*, vol. 1, no. 2, 1–21.

Delaney, Martin and Robert Campbell (1969) *Search for a Place: Black Separation and Africa*. Ann Arbor: University of Michigan Press.

Department of Interior (1962) *Regulations Governing Poro and Sande Societies*. Government of Liberia, Monrovia. Mimeo.

Douglass, Frederick (1859) *Douglass Monthly*, vol. 1, no. 9 (Feb.) Rochester, N.Y., 19–20.

Fage, J. D. (1969) *History of West Africa*. Cambridge: Cambridge University Press.

Gellar, Sheldon (1973) "State-Building and Nation-Building in West Africa." In S. N. Eisenstadt and Stein Rokkan, eds., *Building States and Nations: Models, Analyses, and Data across Three Worlds*. vol. 2. Beverly Hills: Sage, 384–426.

Gibbs, James L. (1960) "Some Judicial Implications of Marital Instability among the Kpelle." Ph.D. diss., Harvard University.

─────────────── (1965) "The Kpelle of Liberia." In James L. Gibbs, ed., *Peoples of Africa*. New York: Holt, Rinehart & Winston, 197–240.

Gopal, Ram (1963) *British Rule in India: An Assessment*. London: Asia Publishing House.

Harris, Kathrine (1982) "The United States, Liberia, and Their Foreign Relations to 1847." Ph.D. diss., Cornell University.

Hatch, John (1969) *The History of Britain in Africa: From the Fifteenth Century to the Present*. London: Deutsch.

Hobbes, Thomas (1960) *Leviathan or the Matter, Forme and Power* of a Commonwealth Ecclesiasticall and Civill. Michael Oakeshott, ed. Oxford: Blackwell. First published in 1651.

Holsoe, Svend (1966) "The Condo Confederation in Western Liberia." *Liberian Historical Review*, vol. 3, no. 1, 1–28.

Huberich, Charles H. (1947) *The Political and Legislative History of Liberia.* vol. 1. New York: Central Book.

Huntington, Samuel P. (1968) *Political Order in Changing Societies.* New Haven: Yale University Press.

Jackson, Robert H., and Carl G. Rosberg (1982) *Personal Rule in Black Africa: Prince, Autocrat, Prophet, Tyrant.* Berkeley: University of California Press.

Jones, Hannah Abeodu (1962) "The Struggle for Political and Cultural Unification in Liberia, 1847–1930." Ph.D. diss., Northwestern University, Evanston, Ill.

Kirkwood, Kenneth (1965) *Britain and Africa.* Baltimore: Johns Hopkins University Press.

League of Nations (1930) *Report of the International Commission of Enquiry into the Existence of Slavery and Forced Labor in the Republic of Liberia.* Vol. 6. The Hague.

Lerner, Daniel (1958) *The Passing of the Traditional Society.* New York: Free Press.

Liebenow, J. Gus (1969) *Liberia: The Evolution of Privilege.* Ithaca, N.Y.: Cornell University Press.

———————— (1987) *Liberia: The Quest for Democracy.* Bloomington: Indiana University Press.

Mabogunje, Akin L. (1976) "The Land and Peoples of West Africa." In J.F.A. Ajayi and Michael Crowder, eds., *History of West Africa.* vol. 1. Second ed. London: Longman, 1–32.

Martin, Jane J. (1968) "The Dual Legacy: Government Authority and Mission Influence Among the Glebo of Eastern Liberia, 1834–1910." Ph.D. diss., Boston University.

Maung, U. Maung (1969) *Burma and General Newin.* London: Asia Publishing House.

Mekeel, H. Scudder (1937) "Social Administration of the Kru: A Preliminary Survey." *Africa*, vol. 10, 75–96.

Ministry of Planning and Economic Affairs (1971–1980) *Economic*

Survey of Liberia. Monrovia: Government of Liberia.

——————————————————————————— (1974) *Household and Population Census of Liberia.* Monrovia: Government of Liberia.

Nettl, J. P., and Roland Robertson (1968) *International Systems and the Modernization of Society.* London: Faber.

Organization of African Unity (1980) *The Lagos Plan of Action.* Addis Ababa: OAU.

Ostrom, Vincent (1987) *The Political Theory of a Compound Republic: Designing the American Experiment.* Rev. ed. Lincoln: University of Nebraska Press.

Palmer, Monte (1985) *Dilemmas of Political Development: An Introduction to the Politics of Developing Areas.* Third ed. Itasca, Ill.: Peacock.

Pye, Lucian W. (1966) *Aspects of Political Development.* Boston: Little, Brown.

Shick, Tom (1977) *Behold the Promise Land: A History of Afro-American Settler Society in 19th Century Liberia.* Baltimore: Johns Hopkins University Press.

Siegmann, William (1969) *Report on the Bassa.* Robertsport, Liberia: Tubman Center of African Culture.

Sigler, Phil S. (1969) "The Attitudes of Free Blacks Towards Emigration to Liberia." Ph.D. diss., Boston University.

Spraggins, T. L. (1957) "Economic Aspects of Negro Colonization During the Civil War." Ph.D. diss., American University, Washington, D.C.

Stebbins, G. B. (1853) *Facts, Opinions Touching the Real Origin, Character and Influence of the American Colonization Society.* Boston: Jewett.

Tipoteh, Togba Nah (1987) "Crisis in the Liberian Economy 1980–1985." *Liberian Studies Journal,* vol. 11, no. 2, 125-143.

van Santen, C.E. (1974) "Notes on Small Holder Rice Production in Liberia." FAO, Rome. Mimeo.

Weiner, Myron (1965) "Political Integration and Political Development." *Annals of the American Academy,* vol. 358 (March), 52–64.

Wickstrom, Werner (1958) "The American Colonization Society and Liberia: An Historical Study in Religious Motivation and Achievement, 1817–1867." Ph.D. diss., Hartford Seminary, Hartford, Conn.

World Bank (1983) *Sub-Saharan Africa: Progress Report on Development Prospects and Programs.* Washington, D.C.: World Bank.

―――――― (1984) *Toward Sustained Development in Sub-Saharan Africa: A Joint Program of Action.* Washington, D.C.: World Bank.

Wriggins, W. Howard (1969) *The Ruler's Imperative: Strategies for Political Survival in Asia and Africa.* New York: Columbia University Press.

Zolberg, Aristide R. (1966) *Creating Political Order: The Party-States of West Africa.* Chicago: Rand McNally.

10
J. Roumasset and S. J. La Croix

The Coevolution of Property Rights and Political Order: An Illustration from Nineteenth-Century Hawaii

Introduction

Throughout much of economic intellectual history, property rights have been treated as exogenous. Economists concerned with property rights have focused their attention on the consequences of those rights. Recently, however, some economists have begun to treat property rights as endogenous. Harold Demsetz, for instance, asserts "that property rights arise when it becomes economic for those affected by externalities to internalize benefits and costs" (1967: 353). Numerous economists have analyzed the evolution of property

---

We wish to thank the editors and John Joseph Wallis, Torben Andersen, and D. Bruce Johnsen for their helpful comments.

rights within this "efficiency tradition" (e.g., Davis and North, 1971; North and Thomas, 1971, 1973; North, 1981; Cheung, 1970; Pejovich, 1972; Anderson and Hill, 1975). Several authors, including Terry L. Anderson and P. J. Hill, have complained that the assertion that private property rights are efficient is vague, ad hoc, and tautological. Most discussions of the evolution of private property rights are suggestive of an investment problem. Borrowing language from the "new institutional economics" (Williamson, 1985), we can restate Demsetz's proposition as follows: Investment in governance structures to define and enforce property rights will proceed until the marginal social benefit of such investment is equal to the marginal social cost.

There are two difficulties with this formulation. First, it cannot be made operational without an explicit model of governance structures. (On this point see especially Baumol's (1986) discussion of the new institutional economics.) More importantly, it inappropriately assumes that private property is always more efficient than common property.[1] This backs the proponents of private property into a corner and forces them to resort to unspecified costs of change in order to explain the existence of common property.

In this paper we assume instead that the relative efficiency of economic institutions depends on the economic and political environment in which they exist. We also assume that the evolution of institutions is driven both by efficiency and by rent-seeking and other political considerations. The divergence between costs and benefits from the viewpoint of society as a whole and the divergence from the viewpoint of elite decision makers leads to rent-seeking behavior; as the divergence approaches zero, self-interested behavior by decision makers becomes consistent with efficiency. As we illustrate in our discussion of nineteenth-century Hawaii, the effect of rent-seeking behavior on the evolution of institutions should not be prejudged.

There is also a long intellectual history in economics that views governmental institutions as analytically exogenous and focuses on the consequences of governmental intervention. More recently, this tradition too has been challenged. In the "new economic history" (North, 1981) and in "neoclassical political economy" (Colander,

1984), both governmental institutions and economic policies are treated as endogenous to analysis. In this paper we argue that both property rights and government institutions are endogenous and that their evolutionary paths are highly related.

The plan of this chapter follows. The coevolutionary perspective is developed in the second section with a reference to the English enclosures. In the third section the perspective is illustrated with an application to the Hawaiian case. Concluding remarks are offered in the fourth section, including comments on the relevance of the coevolutionary perspective for economic development.

The Coevolution of Property Rights and Political Order

The presupposition of the new institutional economics is that the performance of institutions should not be prejudged according to the structure of institutions (Coase, 1937, 1960; Williamson, 1975, 1985; Roumasset, 1974, 1978). There is a long history of violations of this rule. In industrial organization there has been a tradition (Bain, 1951) of condemning industries containing a few firms on the grounds that small numbers facilitate collusion and the extraction of monopoly rents. William J. Baumol, John C. Panzar, and Robert D. Willig's (1982) analysis of contestable markets has helped to reverse this tradition by treating market structure as the endogenous product of more fundamental economic variables.

A similar tradition exists in the economic development literature of condemning the activities of landlords, middlemen, and foreign investors as both exploitative and inefficient. Hired labor has been regarded as a symbol of proletarization and the exploitation of labor. More recently, labor-market structure has been effectively analyzed as an endogenous institutional arrangement (Stiglitz, 1974, 1986; Feeny, 1983). When institutions are modeled as the endogenous creations of more fundamental economic variables, it is not meaningful to rank hypothetical alternative institutions according to their performance apart from the environment affecting their structure and performance. Following Ronald H. Coase's (1960) emphasis on comparative institutional analysis, we conclude it is competition that drives performance and that efficient performance manifests itself in different forms in different economic environments.

Curiously, many authors of the property rights school, while enamored with the comparative institutions approach, seem to lose sight of it when they come to evaluating private property and market institutions. Demsetz's (1967) assertion that private property is more efficient than common property is at variance with his emphasis on comparative institutional analysis in other contexts (Demsetz, 1969). It is a common presumption that private property and markets are necessarily more efficient than either communal organizations (e.g., feudalistic institutions and pre-market agriculture) or central control by the state. We take the more fundamental position that there are some environments wherein communal organization may be more efficient than market organization.

Instead of asking when the net benefits of market institutions—always alleged to be positive—justify the transition costs of changing institutional regimes, we ask what is logically the prior question concerning what confers positive net benefits to market institutions. By judging the nonmarket organization of economic activity to be inefficient *a priori*, the property rights school has departed from the central principle of comparative institutional analysis, namely, that the relative efficiency of alternative institutions depends on the environments in which they are found.

Under very plausible assumptions, competitive market pricing, the hallmark of market organization, is infeasible. In the early stage of economic development, as described by Adam Smith, labor productivity increases as the growth of population and declining transportation costs open up new possibilities for a division of labor. The increasing returns to scale afforded by specialization produce a nonconvexity in the aggregate production function such that marginal product pricing would more than exhaust output (Day, 1982). Only when the land frontier is closed and diminishing returns to labor set in does marginal product pricing become feasible. On the basis of this fundamental assumption about returns to scale, Richard H. Day develops a theory of the transition from one type of common-property regime, manorialism, to a private-property regime based on the use of markets to transfer rights in land. He argues further that the transition to competitive markets could only be accomplished following a lag, given that this institutional change requires a redistribution of income toward landowners. This fundamental analysis of nonconvexity, produced by increased coordination and specialization, provides a fresh perspective on the causes of the English enclosures. If we define efficiency to include transaction costs, then what is not feasible cannot be efficient.[2] Accordingly, private property would not have been more efficient than the communal property regime based on the manor in the early stages of development.

On the other hand, we would not expect immediate transformations of extant economic organizations into the institutions of private property and market exchange at the instant they become technically feasible. In the labor market, neoclassical exchange becomes feasible when the marginal product of labor declines to its average product. Rather, we would expect that, as the marginal product of labor fell below its average product, the nobility (landlords) would have had increasing incentives to invest in governance structures that tied the peasants to their own manor, thereby extracting some monopsony rents. If population pressure continues to increase in this scenario, then the marginal product will eventually fall to the point where it is the landowner who gains from switching to market pricing. Both the prospect of a lower "wage bill" and investment in land improvements and intensive cultivation practices, which private property protects, increase the potential rents that can be captured under private property. Peasants will resist transformation to private property, thereby imparting inertia to manorialism, but eventually the potential gains will be sufficiently attractive for landlords to invest resources to overcome that resistance.

This scenario leads one to hypothesize that by the time a parcel of land is actually transformed to private property, its rental value under the new institutions will be substantially higher than under manorialism. The hypothesis is borne out by evidence presented in Robert C. Allen (1982), who shows that English enclosures in the eighteenth and nineteenth centuries conferred rents on landlords that were two to three times as high as those they were able to garner through the traditional feudal institutions.[3] This was not generally typical of the earlier enclosures, however, when lords occasionally overcame political resistance and were able to capture rents even before it was efficient to do so (Allen, 1986).

It appears then that the evolution of property rights is driven by rent-seeking behavior. That this behavior is frequently consistent with efficiency leads us to reject the more pessimistic conclusions of the rent-seeking literature, that such behavior is always destructive.[4] Population pressure and other changes increase the benefits of governance structures that exploit greater specialization and exchange. The prospect of private property and appropriable rents induces investments in obtaining those rents, including investments in more centralized governance structures to enforce specialization and exchange over a broader spectrum of agents (Wallis and North, 1986).

Government power *per se* does not stimulate markets. It is the functions of the commonwealth articulated by Adam Smith (defense, standards of contracting, law enforcement, and public works) that facilitate market growth, not governmental activities that replace markets. In general, while the development of property rights and the growth of markets have often spurred the growth of central government, the converse of this proposition does not hold. Central governments can grow for a variety of other reasons such as changes in military and police technology, variations in the outside forces posing challenges to the state, movements in relative factor prices and the terms of trade, and variations in the ability to collect taxes.

The development of central government in Russia provides an example where the evolution of markets and the central government did not go hand in hand. While the Czars were consolidating their reign in the sixteenth and seventeenth centuries, service obligations were being imposed on all holders of land (Pipes, 1974: 93–95). This contrasts with the development of central government in France and England during the fourteenth and fifteenth centuries; centralization corresponded with the decline of traditional feudal institutions and passing of fiefs into outright ownership. Royal monopolies, internal tolls and tariffs on commerce, prohibitions on peasant trading, and restrictions on foreign merchants were present until the reign of Peter the Great in the early eighteenth century (pp. 207–211). In both Russia and Hawaii (see the discussion below) the rise of a central government corresponded with an initial repression of the market. In Russia, market institutions evolved in response to new pressures on the central government; changes in military technology (pp. 116–121) and outside pressure by Charles XII of Sweden prompted a recognition that for the Czar's government to endure, additional tax revenues for the military had to be generated. In Hawaii, the introduction of new military technology, the threat from imperial powers, changing relative factor prices and movements in the terms of trade prompted a demand for additional revenue by the central government and resulted in a drain on its treasury. In both cases, for additional taxes to be generated, the economy had to grow at a faster rate, and, given changes in the underlying economic environment, a movement toward market institutions provided a solution to this problem. The analysis by David Feeny (1982) of the evolution of property rights in nineteenth-century Thailand parallels this discussion.

The traditional view, that markets and governmental institutions are alternatives, fails to recognize a distinction between institutions that execute resource allocations, production, and exchange, and institutions that support such exchange.[5] In the coevolutionary view, the same forces that drive the creation of private property and market exchange also drive the evolution of governance structures to support broader contracting and exchange. However, the story does not end there. In a more centralized government, the potential for enforcing a solution that deviates from the competitive outcome also increases, that is, the incentives for rent-seeking behavior increase. In this way, governance structures that have been largely induced by efficiency become the primary cause of inefficiency. This is the fundamental dilemma of economies based on market exchange and private-property rights.

An Application to Nineteenth-Century Hawaii

When Captain Cook's ships came to anchor off the village of Waimea on January 20, 1778, it was not long before the Hawaiians realized life would never be the same. New visitors from Europe and the United States quickly introduced Hawaiians to the potential gains from trade with other countries, to new production technologies that would change traditional ways of life, and to Western diseases that would affect Hawaii more severely than the Black Death affected fourteenth-century Europe.

At the time of contact, Cook encountered four competing political entities bound together by a common culture.[6] Hawaii's 250,000–400,000 people lived on all eight major islands and were sharply divided into three social classes: *ali'i* (chiefs), *maka'ainana* (common people), and *kahuna* (priests). Each political entity was ruled by an *ali'i nui* (ruling chief), who owned all land and material goods. He gave temporary land grants to his *ali'i* retainers, who in turn gave land grants to *konohiki* (landlords who managed the land), who then sublet the land to *maka'ainana*. A ruling chief could in principle confiscate or redistribute material wealth at any time, but in practice redistribution occurred most frequently when a ruling chief assumed power or when the kingdom was conquered.

Most of the population consisted of *maka'ainana* who generally worked the land or engaged in a variety of other occupations such as canoe building, house building, bird catching, and fishing. *Maka'ainana* who worked the land owed labor dues to the *ali'i nui* and to their *konohiki*. During the 1820s, Protestant missionaries noted that the *ali'i* were able to appropriate approximately two-thirds of an individual's output. During earlier periods, the percentage appropriated may have been lower, as early historians of Hawaii have generally concluded that commoners were able to live above subsistence levels. Unlike serfs in medieval Europe who were bound to the soil, *maka'ainana* were free to migrate to other districts or islands. This ability to respond to better opportunities placed constraints on the transfers *ali'i* could exact from *maka'ainana*. In addition, the Stone Age status of weaponry in precontact Hawaii implied that large numbers of *maka'ainana* could overwhelm a small number of *ali'i*. David Malo's writings (1951: 195) on precontact Hawaii detail specific instances in which commoners revolted against oppressive *ali'i* and *ali'i nui*.

Hawaii's religion was much intertwined with the political order. Although *kahuna* (priests) led the people in a variety of rituals to the major gods, the *ali'i nui*, thought to be a direct descendant of the gods, was the religious leader of the kingdom. He supervised the building and rebuilding of large stone temples by *maka'ainana*. Malo (pp. 141–176) made careful note of the large quantities of food and livestock used in the rituals. A system of religious law (known as the *kapu*) helped to make up for the government's lack of a comparative advantage in violence. Since the *ali'i nui* was associated with the gods, violation of the *kapu* or a command of the *ali'i nui* could make one susceptible to punishment by the gods.

At this point, it may be useful to caution that the use of religion by rulers to reduce enforcement costs is not a free good. Significant resource expenditures to establish and to preserve the vitality of the doctrines are necessary. More importantly, the system of religious law may create an ethical standard which in turn places constraints on the ruler's actions and/or may create obligations that the ruler must fulfill. In Hawaii, *ali'i* and *maka'ainana* were alike bound by the prohibitions of the *kapu* system. Similar considerations apply to Douglass C. North's (1981) discussion of the role of commonly held values in reducing free-riding in communal activities.

Competition reigned in the political arena as well as in the labor market. Constantly waging war with other kingdoms, *ali'i nui* derived their power from the number (and quality) of *ali'i* warriors in their armies. A larger army was difficult to raise, however, as marginal land was very unproductive. While the balance of power was, therefore, difficult to disturb, that did not stop the *ali'i nui* from waging war on each other.

This equilibrium was upset by the arrival of Cook's ships. Contact with the remainder of the world altered several constraints for the *ali'i*. First, the prospects of trade raised the present value of the rents generated by the economic system. Since additional rents were available for extraction, the gains from being a member of the ruling coalition were enlarged. In addition, the gains that would accrue to one *ali'i* from conquering other kingdoms increased. Without any change in military technology, it would seem, however, that such wars would be as futile and ill-fated as in the precontact era.

Second, the introduction of modern weaponry changed this calculus. As trading ships began to visit the islands regularly, *ali'i nui* competed to purchase fighting ships, cannon, and muskets, as well as advice concerning their usage. It is debatable whether modern weaponry changed the cost of unifying the islands; if both sides acquired the new weapons, it is unclear whether it would be more or less costly to win a war. It is more certain that the new military technology: (1) conveyed a first-mover advantage to one ruling chief and (2) reduced the cost of maintaining a unified kingdom, that is, a cartel of chiefs. With the advent of large ships, an army of the central government could be quickly transported to islands that were experiencing unrest or where a chief was mounting a rebellion. In earlier times armies had to row log canoes across dangerous stretches of ocean to invade another island. Equally as important, modern arms reduced the importance of large numbers of warriors. Prior to contact large numbers would have sufficed to overthrow an *ali'i nui*. With the introduction of western weaponry, a small group of loyal supporters could hold off a large unarmed *maka'ainana* group. In effect, it became more difficult for a dissident group to mount a rebellion.[7]

It is not surprising that one *ali'i nui*, King Kamehameha I, began to wage war on other ruling chiefs shortly after contact. The cost of maintaining a coalition of chiefs had fallen, while the rents potentially available for extraction by governmental authorities had risen. Hawaii presents an interesting case of a centralized state that arose to extract rents created by the transition from autarchy to international trading. With the unification of the islands (except for distant Kauai) in 1795, the position of the *ali'i* was strengthened. *Maka'ainana* migrating to another island would no longer encounter a new political authority, only another of the king's retainers. The "wholesome fear of the people" on the part of their rulers that Malo (1951: 195) attributed to earlier *ali'i nui* was less necessary given the monopoly by the king (and his *ali'i* retainers) over modern arms. It was predictable that as *ali'i* became less and less constrained by the possibility of popular revolts and migration to other islands, appropriations (in the form of additional taxes or higher land rents) of income above the subsistence level would increase. Thus the first two decades of the nineteenth century can be characterized as an era in which property rights in the control over men were strengthened (Feeny, 1982). This change is consistent with archaeological evidence that land was sparsely utilized and that labor was the scarce resource.

The introduction of modern weaponry also affected the relationship between the political order and religion. In the absence of a comparative advantage in violence, the *ali'i* had invested substantial resources in the established religion in order to maintain the legitimacy of the political system. The introduction of Western arms reduced the benefits derived from popular support and increased benefits derived from the possession of Western military technology. Thus the resources devoted to building and maintaining the massive stone temples could be profitably reallocated to other uses. We do not mean to imply that economic factors were the only relevant ones behind the downfall of the traditional religion. Contact with European and American cultures surely challenged the ability of the religion to represent the people's experiences (Voegelin, 1952).

The 1819 abolition of the *kapu* system and the established religion (which occurred prior to the arrival of the protestant missionaries in 1820) by Kamehameha II can be usefully analyzed from the perspective of rent-seeking. A governing coalition can only extract rents if it has the power to exclude other potential claimants to the rents. When the costs associated with different methods of exclusion change, the adoption of the least-cost method is a condition for the long-term survival of the governing coalition. If the least-cost exclusion technique is not used, the coalition becomes vulnerable to defections and to competing groups who can promise to extract additional rents (net of exclusion costs).[8] That the elimination of the *kapu* system in 1819 occurred while the new king was acting to strengthen his ruling coalition is certainly consistent with this analysis. The redistribution of income from the *kahuna* who provided the outdated exclusion technology, to the *ali'i*, who provided the new one, lends some perspective to the subsequent revolt by traditional interests. Quickly put down by the superior firepower of government troops, the revolt emphatically proved the superiority of the new exclusion technology. More importantly, the decision by traditionalists to engage in a somewhat quixotic revolt against superior forces illustrates the size of the stakes associated with the process of rent-seeking.

The enforcement powers of the ruling coalition, enhanced by Western arms, allowed the king and his supporters to extract rents not only in the labor market but also in the product market. Trade in sandalwood with the United States and China grew to significant levels after the War of 1812 and continued through the late 1820s until the stock was virtually exhausted. King Kamehameha I had a monopoly on sandalwood sales, but turned over 40 percent of the gross proceeds to the chiefs. This arrangement prevented *ali'i*, who had limited tenure in the land, from indiscriminately harvesting sandalwood. Given their limited tenure, chiefs would then compete to supply Kamehameha's quantities with sandalwood from their lands. The exclusive marketing arrangement allowed Kamehameha (and his *ali'i* supporters) to reap monopoly rents while ensuring competition in the supply of the resource.

After the death of Kamehameha I in the spring of 1819, the structure of property rights evolved to reflect changes in the exclusion technology. Kamehameha II faced competition from traditional forces; given the new military technology, he was also more dependent on the support of his *ali'i* retainers, who had access to the new arms. To strengthen his ruling coalition, Kamehameha II gave up his right to market the sandalwood for export. With uncertain land tenure, the *ali'i* had incentives to sell sandalwood immediately without regard to future prices. The resulting surge in sandalwood sales surely helped the king remain in power, but just as certainly did not maximize the present value of sandalwood sales. In this instance, the king continued to share rents with the elite, but the tradeoff with efficiency indicates the rent-seeking nature of this transaction. Contrary to conventional wisdom, centralized political control over natural resources is insufficient to prevent rent-seeking and the dissipation of the resources' rents.

The opening of trade and the introduction of Western arms were the most important forces behind social change in the first fifty years after contact. However, by the late 1820s their effects were overwhelmed by the continual population decline induced by the introduction of western diseases (e.g., syphilis, gonorrhea, influenza, mumps, measles, and cholera, etc.) to the islands. Although there is much controversy over population estimates (250,000–400,000) for 1778, the first official census in 1850 revealed a native population of only 84,165, a remarkable decline regardless of the initial population estimate adopted. By 1900, the census showed just 37,656 Native (full or part) Hawaiians.

The population decline appears to have been one of two factors behind the transition in the 1840s to private property.[9] We postulate that as the stock of labor declined, land rents decreased and wage rates increased. Cursory supporting evidence for this assumption is that much land was abandoned in the decades after Western contact (Beechert, 1985: 29). The increased competition for labor effectively ended the *ali'i* labor cartel, but more importantly, it led to a crisis for the government and its *ali'i* supporters. Government revenue was derived from land rents, with the *ali'i* and *konohiki* serving as tax farmers.

Moreover, governance is a labor-intensive activity. The change in relative factor prices simultaneously reduced government's income and increased its expenditures. For the Hawaiian government to survive, it had to generate revenue flows sufficient to provide public goods of the same value as could be supplied by a competing domestic coalition or a foreign government. Indeed, cutting expenditures during an era of imperial expansion in the Pacific was not a viable option for the government to choose. Domestic borrowing was hampered by the primitive state of the financial system; international debts incurred by the chiefs had brought foreign warships to Hawaii's waters several times in the 1820s. The government acted to increase revenue by imposing additional taxes, e.g., a poll tax, but the revenue shortfall could not be made up by such measures alone.

Finally, the government did what individuals often do to meet revenue shortfalls: it sold a major asset, its land. In a process known as the *great mahele*, the king and the chiefs arranged for a division of land between the king, the government, the chiefs, and the common people. After the 1848 signing of the *mahele* agreement between the King and the *ali'i*, which specified the methods to be employed in dividing the land, a Board of Commissioners to Quiet Land Titles was appointed by the king to consider the rights and interest of individuals who filed claims to title in land. Testimony was taken and boundaries on claimed land were surveyed; if a claim was judged to be valid, then a Land Commission award was granted to the claimant. Upon payment of commutation, a monetary payment representing the interest of the government in the land, the applicant received a royal patent, a fee-simple title to the land. Although the casual surveying of the larger tracts of land led to much later litigation, the process proceeded remarkably smoothly and was completed by 1855.

Between 1846 and 1861 the government then proceeded to sell 31 percent of its total holdings, which amounted to approximately one-third of the islands' total land area. From 1849 to 1856, revenue from government land sales produced 8.5 percent of the government's annual revenue.

Land was only one of the valuable assets held by the "government" (which could not be distinguished from the king until the Constitution of 1839). Why did the Hawaiian government sell the land instead of following the example of the fifteenth- and sixteenth-century European governments that covered revenue shortfalls by selling long-term monopoly rights to the provision of various services and goods? North (1981: 28) has suggested that "the property rights structures that will maximize rents to the ruler (or the ruling class) are in conflict with those that would produce economic growth." North's theory implies that rulers will raise revenue from asset sales by selling those property rights that, for a given sales price, produce the lowest excess burden. However, Hawaii represents an interesting exception to this argument, as we argue below, in that the government's land sales did not detract from, but *encouraged* economic growth.

Feeny details a similar process for the evolution of land rights in nineteenth-century Thailand. He argues that formal property rights in land were established by the government because the elite (a group corresponding to the *ali'i* in Hawaii) shared in the gains resulting from a more secure property rights system. Declining real wages in Thailand also lessened opposition of the elite to "the abolition of slavery and *corvee*, actions which were in the interests of the monarch, who had a clear political incentive in seeking to abolish the control of manpower by his potential opposition" (Feeny, 1982: 98). In both Hawaii and Thailand, the establishment of large crown holdings of land under a formal system of property rights acted to secure a reliable source of income and wealth for the crown during a period of rapid social and economic change. These observations lead us to the conclusion that, in Hawaii and Thailand, rent-seeking by the elite during the mid-nineteenth century resulted in an efficient step in the evolution of property rights.[10]

The second factor behind the land reform was the change in terms of trade. With the advent of substantial economic activity on North America's west coast in the 1840s, the potential market for Hawaiian agricultural products expanded, thereby improving Hawaii's terms of trade. The new market was not for traditional Hawaiian agricultural products, such as taro and sweet potatoes, but for sugar. A crop usually grown most economically on plantations, sugar in Hawaii required for its efficient production that large tracts of land be assembled and that substantial capital investments be incurred. Prior to the 1840s, land could be rented only to foreign agricultural producers. As tenants, they were reluctant to incur expenses to prepare the land for sugar production, since the landlord could extract quasi-rents by breaking the lease or raising the rent. Conversion to private property enabled the requisite capital flows to take place and more efficient production techniques to be used.

Thus the Hawaiian example helps to generalize the theory of the coevolution of the political order and property rights. The history of Western Europe as well as the economics of Adam Smith suggest that technological change and population growth drive intensification and specialization. The new opportunities for capturing rents help to induce both private property and a stronger central government. In

Hawaii, a centralized state arose to extract newly created rents from international trade. Yet in later years continued rent-seeking by the *ali'i* and the king did not produce deadweight losses but, fortuitously, was consistent with the promotion of economic growth and efficiency.

Concluding Remarks

Institutional change is driven in part by individuals or groups investing in efforts to capture rents. Since efficiency is directly related to the potential rents that are available for capture, institutions often driven by rent-seeking behavior may be devised that respond to new opportunities for capturing efficiency gains. In the case of the English enclosures, increasing population triggered an evolution of private property that improved the efficiency of agriculture. Landowners were willing to invest in overcoming resistance to changing land-tenure institutions in order to appropriate the resulting higher land rents.

In Hawaii, population growth did not trigger the evolution of private property; in fact, the population was in decline. Instead, new markets for new agricultural products provided incentives consistent with efficiency to transform land-tenure institutions. The increased foreign demand for agricultural goods raised potential rents, and therefore increased the potential returns to investing in land improvements. Such investments were accelerated by the conversion to private property, which facilitated private capture of returns to investment.

Rent-seeking also played a significant part in the timing of the conversion to private property, as revenue from government land sales supplemented other tax revenues during a period when revenue (from the government's land rents) were falling. In this case rent-seeking was consistent with efficient economic growth, thus providing a case in which the usual tradeoff is absent. The divergence from the usual tradeoff may have been caused by the large changes in factor endowments and prices that occurred during the first half of the nineteenth century in Hawaii. Government, which maximizes tax revenue rather than national income, has incentives to expand beyond the point at which national income is maximized. One consequence is that, at the margin, additional increases in government taxes (and expenditures) will reduce national income, thereby generating a tradeoff between efficiency and government revenue. Large changes in factor prices or the terms of trade could, however, change the efficient size of government, that is, the level of expenditures that maximizes income. If optimal government size increases sufficiently, then the government that had "overexpanded" prior to the relative price changes may now be "too small." Marginal increases in taxes will then lead to rising incomes and tax receipts.

The Hawaiian case also nicely illustrates the coevolution of property rights and political order. Centralization of government shortly after contact was induced, in part, by the increased rents that could be captured by a centralized political order and, in part, by the decreased costs of maintaining a centralized political order. The establishment of an *ali'i* monopsony cartel in the labor market allowed rents created by the opening of trade to be extracted by the ruling elite. When the stability of the ruling coalition was threatened after the death of King Kamehameha I, his successor traded rights to participate in the sandalwood trade for support of his regime. This episode is more evocative of the European kings' sales of monopoly privileges than of Kamehameha III's dismantling of the feudal land tenure system.

As the sandalwood resource approached exhaustion, new opportunities for agricultural exports appeared (e.g., sugar to California) that increased the benefits of private property, and renewed the impetus for establishing governance structures supporting market exchange. In Hawaii this process was accelerated, since the central administration faced a revenue crisis and utilized land sales as an instrument of public finance. The evolution of the regime was soon transformed by the annexation of Hawaii to the United States (1898), the extension of territorial status (1900), and statehood in the American constitutional order (1959).

In contrast with the English enclosures, which were retarded by political pressure from the peasants, the development of market exchange and private property rights in Hawaii was accelerated by political pressures, thus illustrating that rent-seeking behavior by government is not necessarily contrary to efficiency. The pessimistic view that rent-seeking is always contrary to efficiency must therefore be modified. The efficiency of rent-seeking will be determined by the divergence between the costs and benefits of actions to society and those to the decision makers. That a divergence is often present and is frequently of significant proportions has been demonstrated by case studies presented by economists in the public choice tradition. We hope the cases outlined in this study will give public choice theorists and economic historians pause before they leap to the general conclusion that rent-seeking behavior is always at variance with efficient behavior.

Notes

1. See Dahlman (1980) for an excellent analysis of the system of property rights associated with the manor.

2. A similar notion, namely, the prohibitive information and enforcement costs of nondistortionary taxation, led Samuelson (1950) to distinguish the "feasibility frontier" from the conventional "Pareto-optimal frontier."

3. Allen obscures this interpretation, however, by assuming that the efficiency explanation and the income redistribution explanation of the enclosures are mutually exclusive.

4. Lee (1987) uses a similar approach; he examines the industrial and environmental interest groups that influence environmental regulation and questions whether the resulting legislation produces a resource allocation that can be significantly improved. Tullock (1967) presents a more pessimistic view of rent-seeking, arguing that it not only reduces gains from trade but often causes positive damage.

5. F. A. Hayek (1948) has, however, emphasized this point in his writings.

6. Kuykendall (1968) and Beechert (1985) provide in-depth reviews of the relevant historical materials. La Croix and Roumasset (1984, 1987) examine specific episodes in greater detail.

7. See La Croix and Roumasset (1984) for additional discussion of the role of violence in establishing state institutions.

8. In other words, even though a government may, almost by definition, be a natural monopoly, the monopoly may be contestable. See Baumol, Panzar, and Willig (1982) for a full discussion of contestability theory.

9. See La Croix and Roumasset (1987) for an extended discussion of the population decline, as well as a discussion of the background and mechanics of land reform (i.e., the Great Mahele).

10. Feeny (1982: ch. 5) also presents several episodes in Thai history in which the rent-seeking behavior of the elite led to institutional evolution that did not promote economic growth.

Works Cited

Allen, Robert C. (1982) "The Efficiency and Distributional Consequences of Eighteenth-Century Enclosures." *Economic Journal*, vol. 92, 937–953.

——————— (1986) "The Price of Freehold Land and the Interest Rate in the Seventeenth and Eighteenth Centuries." Department of Economics Discussion Paper no. 86-37, University of British Columbia.

Anderson, Terry L., and P. J. Hill (1975) "The Evolution of Property Rights: A Study of the American West." *Journal of Law and Economics*, vol. 18, 163–179.

Bain, Joe S. (1951) "Relationship of Profit Rate to Industry Concentration: American Manufacturing, 1936–1940." *Quarterly Journal of Economics*, vol. 65, 293–324.

Baumol, William J. (1986) "Williamson's 'The Economic Institutions of Capitalism.'" *Rand Journal of Economics*, vol. 17, 279–286.

Baumol, William J., John C. Panzar, and Robert D. Willig (1982) *Contestable Markets and the Theory of Industry Structure*. New York: Harcourt Brace Jovanovich.

Beechert, Edward D. (1985) *Working in Hawaii*. Honolulu: University of Hawaii Press.

Cheung, Steven N. S. (1970) "The Structure of a Contract: The Theory of a Non-Exclusive Resource." *Journal of Law and Economics*, vol. 19, 49–70.

―――――― (1976) "A Theory of Price Control." *Journal of Law and Economics*, vol. 3, 53–72.

Coase, Ronald H. (1937) "The Nature of the Firm." *Economica*, vol. 4, 386–405.

―――――― (1960) "The Problem of Social Cost." *Journal of Law and Economics*, vol. 3, 1–44.

Colander, David C., ed. (1984) *Neoclassical Political Economy: The Analysis of Rent-Seeking and DUP Activities*. Cambridge, Mass.: Ballinger.

Dahlman, Carl J. (1980) *The Open Field System and Beyond: A Property Rights Analysis of an Economic Institution*. Cambridge: Cambridge University Press.

Davis, Lance, and Douglass C. North (1971) *Institutional Change and American Economic Growth*. Cambridge: Cambridge University Press.

Day, Richard H. (1982) "Instability in the Transition from Manorialism: A Classical Analysis." *Explorations in Economic History*, vol. 19, 321–338.

Demsetz, Harold (1967) "Toward a Theory of Property Rights." *American Economic Review Papers and Proceedings*, vol. 57, 347–359.

―――――― (1969) "Information and Efficiency: Another Viewpoint." *Journal of Law and Economics*, vol. 12, 1–22.

Feeny, David (1982) *The Political Economy of Productivity: Thai Agricultural Development, 1880–1975*. Vancouver: University of British Columbia Press.

―――――― (1983) "The Moral or the Rational Peasant? Competing Hypotheses of Collective Action." *Journal of Asian Studies*, vol. 42, 769–789.

Hayek, Friedrich A. von (1948) "'Free' Enterprise and Competitive Order." In *Individualism and Economic Order*. Chicago: University of Chicago Press, ch. 6, 107–118.

Kuykendall, Ralph S. (1968) *The Hawaiian Kingdom*. Vol. 1, *1778–1854: Foundation and Transformation*. Honolulu: University of Hawaii Press.

La Croix, Sumner J., and James Roumasset (1984) "An Economic Theory of Political Change in Premissionary Hawaii." *Explorations in Economic History*, vol. 21, 151–168.

─────────────────────────────── (1987) "The Evolution of Private Property in Nineteenth-Century Hawaii." Unpublished manuscript.

Lee, Dwight (1987) "The Politics of Pollution and the Pollution of Politics." Paper prepared for Liberty Fund Conference on Institutions and the Environment of Liberty, June-July.

Malo, David (1951) *Hawaiian Antiquities*. Honolulu: Bishop Museum Press.

North, Douglass, C. (1981) *Structure and Change in Economic History*. New York: Norton.

North, Douglass, C., and Robert Paul Thomas (1971) "The Rise and Fall of the Manorial System: A Theoretical Model." *Journal of Economic History*, vol. 31, 777–803.

─────────────────────────────── (1973) *The Rise of the Western World: A New Economic History*. Cambridge: Cambridge University Press.

Pejovich, Svetozar (1972) "Towards an Economic Theory of the Creation and Specification of Property Rights." *Review of Social Economy*, vol. 30, 309–325.

Pipes, Richard (1974) *Russia under the Old Regime*. New York: Scribner.

Roumasset, James (1974) "Induced Institutional Change, Welfare Economics and the Science of Public Policy." Working Paper no. V-46, Department of Economics, University of California, Davis.

─────────────── (1978) "The New Institutional Economics and Agricultural Organization." *Philippine Economic Journal*, vol. 17, 331–348.

Samuelson, Paul A. (1950) "Evaluation of Real National Income." *The Oxford Economic Papers*, n.s. vol. 2, 1–29.

Stiglitz, Joseph E. (1974) "Incentives and Risk Sharing in Sharecropping." *Review of Economic Studies*, vol. 41, 219–255.

——————————— (1986) *Economics of the Public Sector.* New York: Norton.

Tullock, Gordon (1967) "The Welfare Cost of Tariffs, Monopolies and Theft." *Western Economic Review,* vol. 5, 224–232.

Turner, Michael (1986) "English Open Fields and Enclosures: Retardation or Productivity Improvements." *Journal of Economic History,* vol. 46, 669–692.

Voegelin, Eric (1952) *The New Science of Politics: An Introduction.* Chicago: University of Chicago Press.

Wallis, John Joseph, and Douglass C. North (1986) "Measuring the Size of the Transaction Sector in the American Economy, 1870–1970." In Stanley L. Engerman and Robert E. Gallman, eds., *Long-Term Factors in American Economic Growth.* Chicago: University of Chicago Press.

Williamson, Oliver E. (1968) "Economics as an Antitrust Defense: The Welfare Trade-offs." *American Economic Review,* vol. 58, 18–36.

——————————— (1975) *Markets and Hierarchies: Analysis and Antitrust Implications.* New York: Free Press.

——————————— (1985) *The Economic Institutions of Capitalism: Firms, Markets, Rational Contracting.* New York: Free Press.

Part IV

Market Institutions and Contingent Considerations

11
Louis De Alessi

How Markets Alleviate Scarcity

Introduction

Economics rests on the broad supposition that individuals desire many goods and seek many goals and that, for every individual, at least some goods are scarce. The inability of all individuals within a society to satisfy all their wants implies that they must compete with each other for a share of the resources available.

The fundamental economic problem within any society, therefore, is to evolve—whether by design, accident, or some combination of both—a set of rules for channeling competition and resolving the conflict. These rules, embedded in a framework of formal and informal institutions (laws and customs, for example), sanction the range of permissible behavior by specifying the nature of the rights that individuals may hold to the use of resources (including their own

---

The author has benefited from thorough and helpful comments by Vincent Ostrom, David Feeny, Hartmut Picht, and David G. Davies.

persons), to the income that the resources generate, and to the transferability of the resources to others. The resulting system of property rights determines how prices, whether explicit or implicit, are set and, thus, how the benefits and the harms resulting from a decision are allocated between the ones making decisions and others (Alchian, 1965, 1967).

The central insight of economics, first clearly articulated by Adam Smith ([1776] 1937), is that individuals respond predictably to opportunities for gain. Because different economic systems embody different structures of property rights, they confront decision makers with different opportunities for gain and thus affect their choices systematically. For example, the system of property rights affects such economic considerations as the quantity, quality, and prices of output; the quantity and combinations of inputs; the development and adoption of new production techniques; the structure of industries; and the allocation of resources between present and future consumption. It also affects other individual choices such as where to live and what sort of work to do, when and whom to marry, how many children to have and how to raise them, and when to die. In short, it affects *all* choices in which at least some of the options are mutually exclusive.

In a world of scarcity, individuals can increase their welfare through specialization and exchange. Specialization in production allows individuals to engage in those activities in which each has a comparative advantage, including participation in joint production within a firm, and thus results in a larger aggregate output. Exchange then allows each individual to obtain a preferred combination of goods and services, and thus provides the incentive to specialize. But even if there were no production and all individuals received identical baskets of goods at the beginning of each period, they would still gain from trade if the relative values they subjectively attached to these commodities differed at the margin (Bator, 1957; Radford, 1945). Trade expands consumption opportunities beyond those that would have existed without it, allowing each individual to obtain a consumption basket that is preferred (as the chooser sees it) and thus to enjoy a better standard of living.

How Markets Alleviate Scarcity

The market is simply a low-cost institution for facilitating specialization and exchange. It reduces scarcity by guiding the allocation of resources to their highest-valued uses by means of prices, which provide both consumers and producers with the information and the incentive to respond to changes in individual circumstances. The effectiveness of the market in relieving scarcity is closely tied to the extent to which property rights are fully allocated, privately held, and voluntarily exchangeable at relatively low transaction costs. Thus, the market both favors and is favored by a political environment of individual freedom.

At this point a caveat seems useful. Although economics provides the tools for analyzing the consequences of alternative economic systems, it does not provide the criteria for deciding which outcomes are preferable. Like any other positive science, that choice rests on normative (ethical) judgments. This statement, of course, does not deny that economics may be useful in explaining why certain ethical norms have evolved, or that considerations of the sort embedded in the Golden Rule ("Do not that to another, which thou wouldst not have done to thyself") may yield some generally acceptable criteria for making interpersonal comparisons (Ostrom, 1984).

Policies frequently would benefit if decision makers had a clearer understanding of how markets work and the consequences of using the market relative to some other control mechanism. Accordingly, this chapter addresses the main characteristics of a market system; the gains from specialization and exchange; how the market may be used to solve the economic problem; and some limitations of the market and of proposed alternatives, concluding with some general remarks regarding the choice of economic systems.

Characteristics of a Market System

Economic theory, although quite complex in its more rigorous formulations, rests on a few simple propositions (Bator, 1957). Briefly, these are that each individual desires many goods; that these are substitutable; that as the individual substitutes one good for another, keeping the level of satisfaction unchanged, the subjective value of an additional unit of the good being acquired falls relative to that of the good being given up; and that, for each individual, at least some goods are scarce. The postulate that goods are substitutable means that there is no hierarchy of wants; individuals, even the poorest, seek to satisfy a variety of wants.

These propositions apply to all individuals, regardless of the economic system in which they live and their role as decision makers (e.g., consumers, business managers, or government employees). If different individuals attach different weights to different goals (e.g., health, comfort, power, the welfare of others) including different means (e.g., persuasion, compulsion) of achieving them, then each individual has the incentive to advance those goals that he or she prefers. For predictive purposes, therefore, decisions taken within a family, a firm, a government bureau, a society, or any other group are best analyzed as the outcome of choices made by members of the group in pursuit of their own individual interests, including their view of what is best for other individuals and for the group as a whole. Thus, the individual is used as the basic unit of analysis not because of a normative judgement in favor of individual values but because this approach yields more accurate predictions (Blaug, 1980; De Alessi, 1983).

The ability of individuals to satisfy their wants is determined by the quantities of resources (including entitlements) available, their allocation, their productivity, and the system of property rights. The typical postulates underlying production functions are that inputs are substitutable; that increasing all inputs in the same proportion eventually results in total output increasing at a decreasing rate; and that, at the margin, the productivity of any input eventually decreases. These postulates apply to all productive activities, including those undertaken by households, firms, and government bureaus.

The framework just sketched, buttressed by more detailed specification of both preferences and constraints, yields the familiar implication that the lower the cost (whatever has to be foregone) of any good (whatever is a source of satisfaction to the chooser) or any input (whatever is used in production), the more the user will acquire; demand curves for both inputs and outputs are negatively sloped. Moreover, individuals respond to an expansion of the opportunities available to them (for instance, through an increase in productivity) by consuming more of all goods. And because inputs are costly and production functions have the characteristics that they do, additional units of output typically can be obtained only at higher cost; supply curves are positively sloped.

The hypothesis that individuals use more of a resource when its opportunity cost falls applies to all choices under constraints. Thus, it applies not only to the usual consumption and production decisions but to the entire range of choices among alternative pecuniary and nonpecuniary sources of satisfaction that an individual faces both on and off the job. For example, limiting the profits that a firm may earn lowers the cost to its managers of engaging in race or sex discrimination, and more of both will occur (Becker, 1957). Similarly, a subsidy to married couples for each additional child implies that individuals are more likely to marry as well as to marry earlier in life and have more children.

The economic principles discussed so far hold regardless of the system of property rights and whether trade takes place or not. Thus, the hypothesis that demand curves are negatively sloped implies that if a flood renders a river crossing more dangerous or time-consuming than another crossing, then, other things being the same, some individuals will shift from the higher-cost to the lower-cost crossing and, in the aggregate, fewer crossings will take place.

The structure of property rights found within a society typically is quite complex. For example, individual rights to the use of resources may be exclusive and voluntarily transferable (e.g., private), exclusive but not transferable (e.g., usufruct), or both nonexclusive and nontransferable (e.g., common-property with open access). Moreover, property rights in a particular good may be partitioned, so that different individuals may hold different rights to its use. For example, the private owner of a house may have the exclusive right to use it, sell it, or lease it; a lessor may have the right to use it but not to paint it or sublet it, and certainly not to sell it; a neighbor may have the right (easement) to run pipes under its front lawn; and everyone in the community may share in common the right to dump smoke and noise on it.

The spectrum of possible economic systems obviously is enormous.

Some of the archetypal arrangements found along the continuum include anarchy, in which individuals enforce their own rights; capitalism, in which individuals hold government-enforced private-property rights to consumption and production goods, including their own labor; socialism, in which individuals typically hold usufruct rights, assigned and enforced by government employees, to income-producing goods; and communism, in which central direction extends to the choice of jobs.

Different systems of property rights present individuals with different constraints, thereby altering the opportunities for gain and affecting choices systematically (Furubotn and Pejovich, 1972). Under a system of private property rights, future consequences are capitalized into current transfer prices and reflected in owners' wealth. In the limit when resources are fully allocated and transaction costs are zero, decision makers bear the full value consequences of their choices and thus have the incentive to take them fully into account; there are no external effects. Common ownership with open access, on the other hand, means that individuals lack exclusive, transferable rights to the use of resources. Because they cannot capture the full gains from any improvements they might undertake, they have less incentive to conserve the resources held in common (e.g., to postpone grazing) and to invest in them (e.g., build irrigation ditches on common pastures), and have more incentive to invest in the privately owned resources (e.g., sheep) used jointly in production (De Alessi, 1980). If private property is feasible (that is, if transaction costs are sufficiently low), then under common ownership resources are less likely to be assigned to their highest-valued use and output is smaller.

Gains from Specialization in Consumption. If the subjective rates at which individuals are willing to substitute one commodity for another differ at the margin, there will be incentive to trade. For example, suppose that A is willing to substitute 2 apples for 1 loaf of bread whereas B is willing to substitute 3 apples for 1 loaf of bread, each individual remaining at the same level of satisfaction. A would be just as well off with 1 less loaf of bread and 2 more apples, whereas B would be just as well off with 1 more loaf of bread and 3 less apples.

Thus, both gain if A gives 1 loaf of bread to B in exchange for more than 2 but less than 3 apples. The possibility of trade effectively has created an additional apple, the gain from trade, that A and B may share. Moreover, both A and B have the incentive to continue trading until their subjective rates of substitution become equal at the margin. This analysis applies to the choices of a primitive man as well as to those of a modern urban dweller. Trade evolved because it allowed individuals to become better off; although it may be severely limited in many parts of the world, it is ubiquitous.

Differences in the subjective rate of substitution may be due to differences in tastes or in the endowment of resources, including differences in natural skills, investment in human capital, wealth, and degree of control over various assets. For trade to take place, however, the reason why the subjective rates of substitution differ is irrelevant. All that matters is that they differ, thereby creating the possibility of mutual gain through exchange.

Although differences in the subjective rates of substitution are a prerequisite for trade, they are not sufficient. The extent of trade clearly depends upon the limits set by the system of property rights and by transaction costs, broadly defined as the costs of negotiating and enforcing contracts as well as of acquiring and processing information about alternatives. If A and B own the right to consume the apples and bread that they hold but are not allowed to exchange them, then the "extra" apples and bread made possible by trade will not be realized.

Depending upon the economic system, individuals may be allowed to own certain rights but not others, and some ownership rights may allow use but not exchange. Moreover, the rights that an individual is allowed to own and trade may be constrained by such variables as age (e.g., a minor may not have legal standing in certain matters), health (e.g., a cancer patient may have the right to own and use a particular drug but a healthy individual may not), time (e.g., a store may be open only during certain hours), place (e.g., zoning regulations may control land use), special qualifications (e.g., only a doctor of medicine may perform certain activities), and other considerations. To the extent that such limitations are agreed to voluntarily by the members of the community, they need not reduce welfare. Typically, however, trade restrictions are designed to protect specific groups from competition.

Transaction costs also inhibit exchange. Indeed, if transaction costs exceeded the gains from exchange, individuals would not trade. Thus, if transaction costs had been greater than 1 apple for each loaf of bread exchanged, A and B would not have traded.

Factors helping to determine the nature and mix of rights adopted within a society include the cost of defining and enforcing alternative property relations, preferences regarding the nature of the economic system, comparative advantage in the use of political power, and chance. If private property rights are too costly to establish and enforce relative to the benefits, then other arrangements, such as common ownership with open access, will evolve. If the costs of privatization fall or the benefits increase, however, there will be incentive to move toward a system of private property rights (Demsetz, 1967). The choice of property rights is also affected by preferences, which shape and are shaped by a society's moral code and view of justice; the activities of interest groups seeking to obtain special rights for their supporters (e.g., members of a business cartel or of a labor union); and chance, due to incomplete knowledge about the range of possible systems of property rights as well as about the full consequences of known arrangements.

Conceptually, in a market system, the role of the government is limited to helping decide who owns what rights and to helping protect those rights. Within this framework, individuals have the incentive to specialize in production, thereby increasing their income, and then spend this income to move outside the boundary imposed by their production possibilities and obtain a preferred consumption basket.

To maximize their welfare subject to an income constraint, individuals have the incentive to revise their consumption as long as, at the margin, the subjective rate of substitution between any two goods differs from the ratio of their prices. For example, if apples sell for $0.10 each and loaves of bread for $0.30 each, then individuals have the incentive to allocate their income between apples and bread so that, at the margin, they would be willing to substitute 3 apples for 1 loaf of bread. If the price of bread were to fall to $0.20, individuals would become better off if they shifted their consumption from apples to bread until, at the margin, they were willing to substitute 2 apples for 1 loaf of bread.

Thus, a decrease in the price of bread implies that individuals will consume more of it; demand curves are negatively sloped. They also consume more of those goods (e.g., cheese) that are complementary to bread, because the relative price of that combination has gone down, and less of those goods (e.g., rice) that are close substitutes for bread, because their relative price has gone up. And individuals will respond to an increase in income by consuming more bread, cheese, rice, and all other (noninferior) goods.

The prices that determine the choices of a user, of course, are not simply the nominal prices asked by the sellers. Rather, they are the full prices reflecting the full opportunity cost of acquiring the good. The full price includes time spent traveling and queueing up, other resources used up in getting to and from the store, bribes, tips, and all other explicit and implicit costs incurred by the consumer. In some societies the monetary payment made at the time of purchase is a trivial portion of the good's actual cost to the consumer and so plays a minor role in guiding the decisions of both users and producers.

In a market system, most costs are explicit and included in the nominal price. Buyers and sellers, however, are perfectly free to negotiate nonprice means of compensation, and frequently they do. For example, the transaction price may vary according to the dates at which the good is to be delivered and payment is to be made, the warranty that accompanies the good, and other factors, such as the promise of some future service (e.g., the owner of an apartment may accept a lower rent in exchange for the promise of better maintenance by the tenant). As the nonprice dimensions become more complex and extensive, however, monitoring, enforcing, and other transaction costs increase. The use of prices based on a generally accepted medium of exchange lowers transaction costs and facilitates specialization in both production and consumption.

Demand curves show the maximum price that individuals are willing and able to pay for each additional unit of a good rather than do without it. To the extent that the price individuals actually pay for each unit is less than the maximum they would have been willing to pay, the difference represents the gain from trade—the increase in welfare or consumer's surplus. This gain is maximized when consumers are able to buy as much as they wish of a good at the prevailing market price, a condition fostered by competitive processes. Moreover, if all individuals look at the same prices, then at the margin they attach the same relative value to all the goods they consume, and consumers' welfare is maximized in the Pareto sense that it is impossible to make someone better off without making someone else worse off (if production is also Pareto-efficient).

In practice, the equilibrium conditions of a market system, like those of any other economic system, never hold. Circumstances are always changing, and the system is always being buffetted toward a new equilibrium. The fundamental significance of a market system, however, is not as a set of equilibrium conditions, but as a process for channeling competition by providing both producers and consumers with the incentive to seek and exploit opportunities for gain.

Gains from Specialization in Production. Consider first an individual in isolation. If the marginal rate at which that individual is able to substitute one input for another in production varies among goods, then reallocating inputs from the uses in which they are relatively less productive to those in which they are relatively more productive allows more of all goods to be produced. For example, suppose that a farmer can substitute 3 units of land for 1 unit of labor in wheat production and 2 units of land for 1 unit of labor in corn production, leaving the output of both wheat and corn unchanged. Then reallocating 1 unit of labor from corn to wheat releases 3 units of land, only 2 of which are necessary to maintain the output of corn unchanged, yielding an "extra" unit of land that the farmer may use to increase the output of wheat, corn, or both. If the farmer can capture the full increase in output, he or she will have the incentive to reallocate inputs until the marginal rate of substitution is the same in the production of all outputs.

Exactly the same reasoning applies if the marginal rate at which inputs may be substituted in production differs among individuals. If the rights to the use of resources are transferable, owners will have incentive to trade until these differences are eliminated, allowing each individual to produce more of all goods.

Further gains from specialization and exchange, however, are still possible. Although the marginal rates of input substitution may be the same in all uses, some users may be more productive than others and some outputs may be more valuable than others. For example, suppose that the ratio of the value of the marginal products of land to labor in wheat is $1/$4 for farmer C but $2/$8 for farmer D. Then the output of wheat would be higher if both land and labor were reallocated from C to D. If the rights to the use of land and labor are privately held, their owners have the incentive to allocate each of the rights to the use with the highest-valued marginal product, whatever that might be.

Indeed, under a system of private property rights resources flow to the same uses regardless of their initial assignment, although the distribution of income would differ (Coase, 1960). Whoever attaches the highest value to a resource right would keep it, if initially given it, or acquire it, if initially assigned to someone else. The extent to which this process is carried out depends upon transaction costs.

If trade in either inputs or outputs is ruled out, individuals' consumption opportunities are strictly limited to those provided by their particular production possibilities. Trade in either inputs or outputs allows individuals to extend their consumption outside these limits, and trade in both allows them to extend it even further. For example, workers have the incentive to seek the highest compensation, including job-related nonpecuniary income, and thus gravitate toward those activities in which they are more productive. Similarly, employers have the incentive to minimize the cost of producing any given level of output and to choose an input-output configuration that maximizes profits. Thus, all owners of resources (whether employees or employers) have the incentive to specialize in those activities in which they have a comparative advantage. As a result, the value of the output is greater and all parties are better off.

Production functions, which specify how resources may be converted from one form to another, presumably vary from one producer to another within the same industry as well as from one industry to another. All production functions, however, share the general characteristics described earlier. In particular, production costs are positive and typically rise at the margin.

In a market system, producers have the incentive to increase output up to the point where marginal cost—the cost of producing an additional unit of output—is increasing and just equal to the revenue obtained from the sale of the additional output. Because competition forces price toward marginal cost, the value that consumers attach to a unit of output (measured by price) approaches the value of the goods that the resources could have produced in their next best use (measured by the marginal cost).

In order to survive and prosper, producers in a market system have the incentive to seek opportunities for profit. To the extent they are successful, they attract competitors, profits are squeezed out, and survivors earn the competitive rate of return on their capital. This rate, which bears little relation to accounting profits, represents the return that the owners could have earned if they had allocated their capital to its next best use.

The existence of transaction costs implies that property rights are not fully allocated to private users (e.g., some resources are held in common), fully enforced (e.g., some theft takes place), or exchanged (some mutually beneficial trade does not occur). Resources still flow to their highest-valued use, but that use is different for exactly the same reason that transportation costs affect the geographical distribution of goods (De Alessi, 1983).

Moreover, transaction costs explain why firms exist. Individuals have the incentive to work together as a team whenever the resulting output is greater than the sum of the outputs they could have produced separately. If transaction costs are positive, individuals have the incentive to shirk, enjoying the full benefits of their own shirking while bearing only a pro rata share of the resulting decrease in output. Thus business firms arise to lower the cost of monitoring exchanges and of directing the allocation of jointly cooperating inputs (Alchian and Demsetz, 1972).

In the case of privately owned firms, the dual problem of choosing the monitors and of providing them with the appropriate incentives is solved simultaneously, by assigning the monitoring function to the owners of the assets most specific to the firm and by giving them the right to the firm's residual earnings (Klein, Crawford, and Alchian, 1978). Similarly, firms have the incentive to integrate vertically in order to inhibit shirking, including both opportunistic (Williamson, 1983) and negligent behavior (De Alessi and Staaf, 1987) by agents outside the coalition.

Transaction costs also help to explain the evolution of business organizations. If monitoring costs are high relative to benefits, and if team production yields sufficiently more output relative to separate operation, then profit-sharing arrangements (e.g., partnerships in professional and intellectual work, some types of cooperatives, share contracts in agriculture) evolve to discourage shirking. If team size can be relatively large and monitoring costs are relatively low, then employer-employee contracts evolve (e.g., single proprietorships, corporations).

The historical record suggests that the modern corporation with limited liability and transferable shares evolved to lower the cost of raising large sums of capital when the investment in a firm's specific assets is substantial (De Alessi and Fishe, 1987). The transferability of shares in a corporation lowers the transaction costs to current and prospective shareholders of revising their investment portfolio, concurrently facilitating the realignment of ownership and the formation of coalitions to replace management (Ekelund and Tollison, 1980). Limited liability also lowers transaction costs by reducing the demand for information about current and prospective stockholders on the part of creditors and other stockholders (Woodward, 1985). Moreover, the indefinite life of the corporation allows it to exploit more fully those assets that are long-lived and specific to the firm.

Within the corporation, shareholders own the assets that are specific to the firm, bear the value consequences of exogenous events as well as of decisions made within the firm, and hold ultimate control over the managers. Debtholders specialize in the ownership of assets that are not specific to the firm (or, at least, not subject to moral hazard), and in monitoring the firm's compliance with the provisions of the loan agreements. Managers, acting as agents for the stockholders, specialize in day-to-day monitoring and decision making within the firm (Jensen and Meckling, 1976; Fama, 1980). The success of the coalition thus depends upon its success in choosing managers and other key personnel, in adopting contracts that provide a suitable incentive structure given the firm's circumstances, and in benefiting from unexpected events (Alchian, 1984).

Under open-market conditions, competition from other firms as well as from current and prospective members of the team (e.g., managers and owners) inhibits shirking and induces managers to seek to maximize owners' wealth. Competitive forces thus induce each firm to produce its output at the lowest cost and sell it at the lowest price. Indeed, competition encourages the evolution and adoption of contractual relations that enhance productivity.

A market system characterized by property rights that are fully allocated, privately held, and costlessly exchanged at mutually agreeable prices has the characteristic that no one can be made better off without making someone else worse off. All possibilities of mutually beneficial trade are exhausted. Although these conditions may not fully hold, the market process provides economic agents, whether producers or consumers, with the incentive and the opportunity to enhance their welfare by reducing scarcity.

The shirking-monitoring problem also explains government production, as distinct from provision, of certain goods (De Alessi, 1982). Thus, there is incentive to integrate activities into government when the costs of drawing and enforcing contracts with independent contractors become greater than the costs of monitoring inputs.

In concluding this section, it seems useful to note that the term competition has not been used to describe the perfectly competitive model of abstract economic theory, a model keyed to a large number of firms producing an identical product with each firm facing an horizontal demand curve. Rather, it has been used to describe the process for resolving the conflict among competing claimants to scarce resources. In a market system, competition means that both entrepreneurs and consumers adjust their activities in search of opportunities for gain subject to a private property constraint.

How Markets Are Used to Solve the Economic Problem

The task of any economic system is to channel competition for the use of scarce resources. In particular, it must provide institutions for deciding what and how much to produce, how to produce it, how to distribute it, how to allocate consumption over time, and who bears the risk associated with these decisions. How well these problems are solved depends in part upon the ability of the system to take account of individual circumstances of time and place; this knowledge, by its very nature, is dispersed and continually changing (Hayek, 1945).

Planning is unavoidable. Accordingly, the issue is not whether planning must take place, but who should do it, whether private individuals on their own behalf or central planners on behalf of everyone in the community. Central planners, like everyone else, maximize their own welfare, and their choices are affected systematically by the set of property rights (constraints) embedded in the relevant governmental institutions.

The distinguishing characteristic of a private property system is the use of the market to solve the economic problem through the free interaction of demand and supply on market prices. Prices transmit information cheaply and quickly while simultaneously providing users and owners of resources with the incentive to respond. Thus, an increase in the price of a good provides users with both the signal and the incentive to cut down on the good's consumption, while simultaneously giving producers both the signal and the incentive to increase output.

For example, suppose that there is a permanent increase in the demand for beef. As consumers buy more beef at existing prices, retailers exhaust their normal inventory more quickly than they had anticipated. Attracted by the prospect of higher profits from increased sales, they will order more beef from the wholesalers. As wholesalers fill the increased orders, their own inventories will fall and, spurred by the prospect of higher profits, they will instruct their agents to buy more cattle. As orders continue to run higher than anticipated, increased competition for the available cattle will drive their prices up, and the increased cost of beef to wholesalers and retailers will be reflected in higher prices to users.

The higher prices perform several crucial functions. On the demand side, they induce some users to reduce their consumption of beef. Not surprisingly, individuals who use relatively large amounts of beef or are more willing to substitute other goods for beef will be the first to cut back. Moreover, as time passes, individuals will have greater opportunity to adjust by taking advantage of lower search costs for finding lower-cost substitutes and other ways of economizing on the use of beef, further reducing the quantity demanded. That is, demand curves are more elastic in the long run.

On the supply side, the increase in prices provides new opportunity for profits, inducing producers to increase output and reduce the scarcity of beef. The increase in the price of beef means an increase in the value of the output produced by inputs in the beef industry, allowing producers to attract resources by offering higher compensation. Resources with a comparative advantage in the production of beef will flow to that industry, receiving a higher price, and other resources will be worth relatively less. As in the case of consumption, the response will be greater over time.

The shorter the time period considered for the adjustment, the higher is the opportunity cost of increasing output, and the greater is the uncertainty regarding whether the increase in demand is transitory or permanent. In the very short run, the increase in demand is reflected largely in higher prices. The prospect of higher profits will induce cattlemen to market younger cattle and shift some cattle from other purposes (e.g., breeding) to current beef output. All firms involved in the process of converting cattle into steaks have an incentive to lower the attrition of beef in the production process by providing better refrigeration, trimming cuts more carefully, and so on. The options available, however, are limited.

In the long run, more lower-cost alternatives for increasing output become available and increased confidence in the permanence of the demand change provides more incentive to take advantage of them. For example, cattlemen have the opportunity to increase the size of the herds and to grow beef faster by altering feeding practices. Similarly, wholesalers and retailers may be able to arrange faster transportation (reducing the inventory in transit) and take other steps, such as better packaging, to reduce losses from spoilage. Concurrently, other entrepreneurs may be expected to enter the market to raise beef, or import beef from other markets, or install better facilities for processing, storing, and distributing beef. Still other individuals will have the incentive to work on technological innovations to produce better strains of cattle, better diets, and other ways to increase output at a lower cost. As the quantity of beef supplied increases, prices begin to fall and profits are squeezed out. Supply curves, like demand curves, are more elastic in the long run than in the short run.

In the long run, both output and prices of beef generally will be higher than they had been before the increase in demand. In some cases, of course, technological breakthroughs stimulated by the higher profits or volume economies permitted by the extension of the market may actually result in lower prices.

The next task is to examine more carefully how a market system solves the central economic problems of any society.

What and How Much to Produce. These problems are solved through the interaction of the demand and supply curves for each good. If the highest price that consumers are willing to pay is less than the lowest cost at which the good can be produced, then output will be zero. For example, in today's market consumers are not yet purchasing their own private space shuttles. Thus, the observation that some goods are not produced does not imply some failure in the system to respond to consumer wants. More generally, the intersection of demand and supply curves determines the price and quantity of each good. Competition forces prices toward the corresponding marginal costs, and the value that consumers attach to each commodity approaches the value of the output foregone elsewhere.

Any event that affects the scarcity of a commodity will set the process of adjustment in motion. Thus, if a fire destroys part of a city, the decrease in the stock of housing will induce an increase in its price. At the higher price some individuals will reduce their use of housing (e.g., some renters will choose to shift to smaller apartments, some owners will rent part of their houses), encouraging a reallocation of the available housing to its highest-valued uses, and giving those displaced by the fire a better opportunity to find shelter and improve their welfare. Moreover, not only will the higher price of housing provide landlords with more incentive to restore damaged houses and build new ones, and do so more quickly, but it will also enable them to pay higher input prices and attract resources from other uses to help relieve the scarcity of housing.

Limits on private property rights inhibit the process of adjustment. Thus, rent controls discourage the reallocation of existing housing among competing users and reduce the incentive to repair damaged houses and build new ones.

How to Produce It. This problem is solved through the interaction of the demand and supply curves for each input. A firm's demand for each input is derived from the demand for the output, and is determined by the input's productivity. Thus, a firm will hire additional units of each input until the value of the additional output produced is just equal to the increase in the firm's total cost as a result of hiring the input.

The supply of an input, like the supply of any other good, typically is determined by its marginal cost. In the case of inputs whose supply is fixed (e.g., an individual's supply of his or her own labor, which is limited by the number of hours in a day), the supply is determined by the difference between the amount of stock held by each individual and the amount that he or she is willing to hold at all possible alternative prices. The market supply, of course, is the horizontal summation of the individual supply curves.

Under open-market conditions, producers have the incentive to adopt the technology and input combination that allows each alternative level of output to be produced at the lowest cost. For example, a ditch can be dug by men with shovels. The higher the cost of labor relative to the cost of capital, however, the more likely it is that men with shovels will be replaced by men using more sophisticated machinery, thereby reducing the cost of digging ditches and releasing resources for other purposes. Owners of rights to the use of resources have the incentive to allocate them to their highest-valued use; in particular, they have the incentive to rent or sell them to those who can employ them more productively.

Production, however, also entails the choice of institutions used to control inputs. The profitability of any business coalition depends largely upon its success in choosing team members and in adopting an organizational form with an incentive structure appropriate to the team and its productive activities. As discussed earlier, the market provides entrepreneurs with the incentive to evolve and adopt organizational forms that enhance productivity.

To consider an alternative institutional arrangement, suppose that individuals hold only nontransferable, usufruct rights to a resource. For example, under some programs of land redistribution, such as the *ejido* system in Mexico, the recipients can hold the land only as long as they use it themselves; legally, they cannot lease it or sell it to others. As a result, land may not be employed in its most valuable uses. Because owners of usufruct rights cannot capitalize future returns into current transfer prices, they have less incentive to plant longer-lived crops (the individual may not be around to collect the full compensation for having foregone consumption during the growing period), or to make specific investments in the land, such as irrigation works, to maintain or increase its productivity. Accordingly, output is smaller than if the rights had been transferable.

How to Distribute It. This problem is also solved through the interaction of the appropriate demand and supply curves. The income of each individual is given by the quantities and the prices of the resources that he or she owns. This income, in conjunction with the individual's preferences, then determines the individual's demand for various goods and services and, vis-a-vis the market prices of these goods, the individual's share of the community's output.

A characteristic of the market system is that individuals' incomes very directly, and closely, with the contribution to output of the resources they own. Accordingly, individuals have the incentive to acquire information about the alternative ways of employing the resources they own, including their labor, and to choose those that yield the highest compensation. Opportunities that yield sufficiently high returns provide individuals with the incentive to invest (e.g., to improve their land, or learn a trade) and enhance their productivity, increasing their own income while reducing scarcity.

As an alternative arrangement, consider nationally negotiated wages between an employers' association and an employees' union. Among other things, this rule prohibits variations in wages in response to changes in local conditions, inhibiting the flow of labor from lower- to higher-valued uses and shifting part of the adjustment from wages to employment. As demand and supply conditions change, unemployment of labor will increase in those regions where wages would have fallen, and shortages of labor will increase in those regions where wages would have risen. The rule also inhibits the ability of producers to compete in the output market, and affects the kinds, quantity, and prices of goods produced and their distribution.

The adoption of an economic system that inhibits use of the price system as an allocative mechanism shifts rewards from those characteristics that result in higher productivity, as measured in the market, in favor of other characteristics, such as a comparative advantage in using the political system as an allocative mechanism. Accordingly, measured output will be smaller.

Maintenance and Growth of the Economy. The interest rate is the price of the earlier availability of resources; in a market system, it is the key variable in determining the maintenance and growth of the economy. The interest rate, in turn, is determined by individuals' time preference, productivity, and uncertainty regarding the future. Thus, individual consumers whose preference for present over future consumption is greater than the market rate of interest borrow, and those for whom it is smaller lend. Concurrently, individuals have the incentive to invest in human and physical assets until, at the margin, the rate of return they receive is equal to the opportunity cost of capital. Finally, the greater the uncertainty regarding a project's payoff (e.g., the prize from investing in acting lessons and plastic surgery) the higher is the rate of return necessary to compensate those who are successful.

In a market system, the interest rate is the means for capitalizing (discounting) future consequences into current transfer prices. The interest rate provides individuals in the present generation with the incentive to take full account of the demand and supply conditions expected to exist in the future, guiding the allocation of resources to their highest-valued uses between the present and the future. The expected wants of future generations are thus taken into account. For example, as oil stocks are used up, the price of oil may be expected to increase. The price increase, among other things, will inhibit the consumption of oil, slowing its rate of depletion and increasing the profitability of alternative energy sources, thereby encouraging their development.

Alternative systems of property rights yield different solutions. For example, the salary of government employees typically increases with the size of the budget and staff that they supervise. If the agency is responsible for undertaking investment projects funded from special appropriations, then its managers have the incentive to use a low discount rate, increasing the present value of the returns (which occur in the future) relative to the present value of the costs (which usually are incurred in the present), and thereby justifying more and bigger projects. For example, the U.S. Army Corps of Engineers, whose responsibilities include building dams, for years used a zero discount rate in evaluating its projects. Thus, the corps built dams larger and earlier in time than market criteria would have indicated (De Alessi, 1969). When the corps was ordered to use a positive discount rate, its administrators sought to inflate benefits and take a longer time horizon into account, thereby continuing to justify more and bigger investments than market criteria would have allowed.

Who Bears the Risk. It should not come as a total surprise that this problem is also solved through the interaction of the relevant demand and supply curves. Individuals bear risk only to the extent that they own assets whose value is subject to fluctuation. Under a market system, individuals can specialize in risk bearing by choosing to own certain assets (e.g., human capital, homes) and not others (e.g., stocks of oil companies). Moreover, individuals can change their portfolio of risky assets by entering the market, selling the assets no longer desired, and acquiring others.

Under other systems of property rights, such specialization in ownership is inhibited or ruled out. Thus, all citizens hold nontransferable shares in all government-owned (political) firms within their community, and bear the full value-consequences of decisions taken by the firms' managers (and their political supervisors). Individuals who wish to change their portfolio of such assets can do so only by affecting the decisions of the firms' managers or by moving to a different political jurisdiction—both higher-cost alternatives than are found in a market system.

Citizens of centrally controlled economic systems bear the full value-consequences of the decisions taken by managers of political firms. Political firms simply are not subject to the same conditions for survival that apply in a market system to privately owned firms.

Limitations of the Market and of Some of Its Alternatives

The analysis so far has described how market institutions, relying on the incentive structure provided by a system of private property rights, may be used to harness individuals' self-interest to reduce scarcity. The market process is a powerful mechanism for the dissemination and utilization of knowledge, providing individuals with the incentive to search for and, through exchange, take advantage of opportunities to improve their production and consumption possibilities. Indeed, under ideal conditions, the market solution can be shown to be Pareto-efficient in the sense that it is impossible to make someone better off without making someone else worse off. In practice, of course, the conditions under which the market or any other economic system actually function are far from ideal.

Several factors limit the extent to which individuals may use the market. An important set of limitations is imposed by formal and informal institutional constraints on private ownership. Thus, within a society certain rights may be inalienable and other rights may be exchanged only under certain conditions. For example, individuals may not be allowed to sell themselves or others into slavery, work on Sunday, buy and sell certain drugs, eat certain foods, wear certain clothes, or hire someone to commit murder. These rules arise from a variety of considerations, such as enhancing the effectiveness of the market by defining and enforcing private property rights, promoting outcomes inhibited by the existence of positive information and transaction costs, benefiting special interest groups (perhaps by excluding competitors), and failing to understand how markets work.

An equally important and pervasive set of limitations is imposed by transaction costs. The higher these costs are, the greater is the extent to which they inhibit the establishment, enforcement, and exchange of private property rights. As a result, some rights may not be fully assigned (e.g., property rights in most migratory fish are held in common), enforced (e.g., not all trespassers are detected, tried, and convicted), or reassigned through exchange (e.g., the transaction costs may exceed the benefits of exchange). Resources still flow to their highest-valued uses, but the latter typically are different from and lower-valued than if transaction costs had been zero, and output is smaller (De Alessi, 1983). The cost of transacting, like gravity, is simply a fact of life that must be taken into account in comparing alternatives.

The existence of positive transaction costs implies that decision makers do not bear and, therefore, do not take into account, the full economic consequences of their actions. The resulting side effects, or externalities, may either harm others (e.g., air pollution) or benefit them (e.g., a beautiful home). The market undoubtedly provides the incentive to internalize many of these side effects. For example, shopping centers and housing developments are explicitly designed to capture beneficial side effects. Indeed, a developer planning the construction of a shopping center that will increase the value of adjacent land has the incentive to include some of that land in the initial purchase of the site or to make some other contractual arrangement for capturing at least part of the increased value (Demsetz, 1964). In many cases, of course, the external effects are simply too small to warrant taking into account. In still other cases, however, the external effects may be sufficiently great (e.g., substantial air or water pollution) that new property relations (e.g., pollution rights) may usefully be developed, providing scope for governmental action.

The existence of positive transaction costs also gives rise to the problem of Samuelsonian public goods (e.g., a radio or television signal), defined as goods or services whose consumption by one individual does not detract from anyone else's consumption (Samuelson, 1954). In the case of public goods, the market demand is obtained by adding the maximum price that each individual is willing to pay at all alternative amounts of the good (that is, individual demand curves are added vertically rather than horizontally). As in the case of any other good, production would then be determined by the intersection of demand and supply. Individual consumers, however, have the incentive to conceal information about their own demand curves, preferring to free-ride if possible. As a result, firms supposedly produce less than the "right" amount.

To solve this problem, it has been suggested that government provide some public goods, perhaps contracting with private firms for their production and, in some cases (e.g., where the exclusion of nonpayers is too costly), pricing them at zero to reflect the zero marginal cost of serving an additional user. It is not clear, however, how government planners would obtain information about individual demand functions or have the incentive to choose the "right" output. Indeed, constitutional arrangements may provide legislators and other government employees with the incentive and the opportunity to use public funds to win support from special interest groups; concurrently, individuals with common interests have the incentive to form coalitions to obtain benefits from government. Many goods have both private and public characteristics, and each consumer has the incentive to emphasize the public components and seek public subsidy for private consumption. As a result, government may frequently be expected to provide more than the "right" amount of public goods. More generally, the problem of monopoly power sanctioned or arrogated by government raises fundamental questions regarding the survival of self-governing societies (Ostrom, 1986).

In many cases, of course, the exclusion of nonpayers is feasible, and the problem of choosing the price-output combination can be solved under market or quasi-market conditions. Even if the goods were provided by a unit of government, however, pricing would still provide useful information. Although the cost of allowing an additional viewer to tune in a television signal is zero, setting the price at zero would not take account of the cost of producing the program being broadcast, which might be anything from a station signal to a sport event or a concert, and of viewers' preferences for one program relative to another. Thus, prices would assist in choosing what and how much to produce.

Positive transaction costs also imply that monopoly inhibits exchange. A monopolist, broadly defined as *any* firm facing a negatively sloped demand curve, must lower its price in order to sell more. If the cost of price discrimination is less than the resulting gains, however, the firm must lower the price on all the units it sells, not just on the additional ones, and charge the same price to all consumers. As a result, marginal revenue is less than price. It follows that, at the wealth-maximizing output where marginal cost is equal to marginal revenue, price is above marginal cost and all mutually beneficial trade is not exhausted. Consumers and producers do not exhaust all possible gains from trade because the cost of negotiating and enforcing contracts on marginal quantities of a good is prohibitively high. It follows that, if the market is open, monopoly does not necessarily imply a misallocation of resources.

Under open-market conditions, monopoly may arise from several sources. These include nonreproducible characteristics of a commodity (e.g., a singer's voice or a retailer's location), information costs (e.g., brand names become more important the greater is the cost of determining the quality of a product), collusion (typically short-lived without government sanction), and economies of scale (that is, the cost advantages of a larger planned volume output). The latter attract considerable attention because they occasionally result in the large, seemingly powerful firms that are popularly associated with the term monopoly.

If marginal cost falls over a sufficiently broad range relative to demand, then only a relatively small number of firms survive. In the case of so-called natural monopolies (the list typically includes electric power, gas, railroads, sewage, and water supply), where only one firm would exist in the industry, governments frequently control prices, investment, and profits, or own the firm outright, presumably to simulate a competitive solution. The existence of economies of scale, however, does not imply the existence of monopoly power (Demsetz, 1968). Among other things, firms can compete for the right to serve the whole market. Moreover, government regulation frequently is used to enforce collusion or cartelization within an industry (examples in the United States include electric utilities, airlines, and railroads) and thus thwarts rather than encourages market outcomes. The regulation and management of business enterprises by government employees—who, like everyone else, seek to maximize their own welfare—have introduced flaws of their own if judged by the same standards applied to market processes (De Alessi, 1980). Indeed, few monopolies with significant market power survive and prosper in the absence of government support.

At least in Western countries, much of the concern with private monopoly in open markets seems to be overstated. Empirically, in the United States and other market-oriented economies, the welfare loss from all forms of monopoly appears to be relatively small. To put the matter in perspective, in the United States welfare losses from monopoly have been estimated at less than 1 percent of gross national product (Harberger, 1954), whereas government programs adopted since the end of World War II to control the allocation of resources and the distribution of income have been estimated to have reduced gross national product by at least 25 percent (Brozen, 1986).

Under open-market conditions, monopoly may actually increase the welfare of consumers. First, the threat of actual or prospective entry inhibits deviations from marginal-cost pricing while allowing the provision of goods at prices below those that would prevail if maximum firm size were set by law and resulted in a larger population of smaller firms (Baumol, 1982). Second, many supposed barriers to entry, such as large outlays on advertising campaigns or on capital equipment, simply neglect the costs of creating and maintaining a good reputation, bearing the risk of innovation, and building a scale of operations appropriate to consumers' demand (Demsetz, 1982). Third, monopolies arising from such things as patents, copyrights, and trademarks contribute to economic growth or provide information and other benefits to consumers. Fourth, monopolies based on product differentiation arise from catering to the wants of specific groups of customers and thus enhance users' welfare and increase product variety, which is itself an economic good.

Under open-market conditions, the effect of monopoly on the allocation of resources is limited by actual or potential competition. To the extent that significant monopoly power may exist, government intervention to provide mechanisms for facilitating competition may appear useful. Even in these circumstances, however, government activities frequently are counterproductive. For example, there is growing evidence that much antitrust activity in the United States has been directed at practices that have enhanced rather than impeded competition (Haddock, 1982; Brozen, 1982), and that bureaucratic and political considerations rather than economic measures of monopoly power dominate the choice of antitrust suits brought by both the U.S. Department of Justice and the Federal Trade Commission (Long, et al., 1973; Asch, 1975; Siegfried, 1975). Moreover, if government regulation (e.g., public utility monopolies, licensing laws) is used to close the market, the process of competition is inhibited, and the deviations from the competitive solution will be more extensive and longer lasting than if market processes were allowed to work.

A closed market by definition limits entry, and thus allows the misallocation of resources to arise and persist. Indeed, the opportunity to earn monopoly rents provides organizations, including firms and labor unions, with the incentive to use the power of the state to exclude competitors. In the United States, government regulation of various industries typically evolved with the active support of the firms to be regulated. Indeed, government regulation of the electric power and other industries was first introduced in those markets in which competition was most active (Jarrell, 1978). The firms to be regulated correctly perceived regulatory agencies as low-cost devices (to the regulated companies, the cost being shifted to taxpayers) for establishing and enforcing cartel arrangements. Licensing of most activities typically serves the same purpose.

Monopoly has also been criticized on the distributive ground that it captures at least part of each consumer's surplus. On this issue, economics is silent. There is no ethically neutral judgment on how the gains from trade ought to be distributed among trading parties. The distribution of gains depends upon the system of property rights, and the choice of these rights is not value-free.

More generally, the market system has been criticized for generating an unequal distribution of income. If in-kind sources of income are taken into account, however, the inequality of income distribution appears to be less in market economies than in comparable centrally directed economies. Moreover, the level of income in market systems is substantially higher, reflecting the greater usefulness of the market in providing individuals with the information and the incentive to allocate resources to their highest-valued uses and produce more output. Indeed, government policies intended to reduce income inequalities can easily be counterproductive by reducing the opportunities for gain and lowering the general level of income.

Interestingly, the modern record of economic growth in open economies seems to suggest that income equality first falls and then rises (Fields, 1980), presumably reflecting the initial gains reaped by successful entrepreneurs followed by an increased demand for labor and broader-based investments in human capital.

The activities rewarded under alternative economic systems, however, differ. In a market system, the income of an individual is determined by the resources owned, including one's own labor, and by the use to which the owner chooses to put them. As a result, the welfare of individuals is closely related to the value consequences, both current and anticipated, of their decisions. In other systems, comparative advantage in the use of the political system may be rewarded. And competition for benefits through the political process not only consumes resources, but reduces the incentive to produce.

To examine more carefully the effects of different economic systems on the allocation of resources, the analysis will turn briefly to the consequences of alternative ownership arrangements in business firms. Recall that, in market systems, firms arise to solve the shirking-monitoring problem of joint production.

Worker Managed Firms. These are autonomous firms, owned and managed by the workers, whose wage payments include the return to capital. Although workers share in the current accounting income of the firm through their wages, they cannot liquidate their capital assets (not even when leaving the firm) and thus cannot capitalize future returns into current transfer prices. In effect, they share common rights in the capital goods used within the firm. Accordingly, a worker's decision to forego some current wages in favor of more capital investment depends not only upon the expected rate of return but also upon the expected payout period relative to the worker's expected tenure in the firm. Thus, workers have an incentive to choose higher wages and smaller investments with earlier payout profiles, a tendency emphasized the shorter is the expected tenure (e.g., workers who are older or who expect to change employment). These implications are supported by the evidence (Furubotn, 1974). In a competitive environment, there may be circumstances in which resource owners may choose to form a worker-managed coalition; for example, law firms typically are worker (lawyer) managed. The survival of the firm is then determined by its ability to compete in the market place, including its ability to provide on-the-job satisfaction. Requiring resource owners to combine under particular organizational forms reduces the opportunity to choose more suitable institutional arrangements, and to evolve new ones in response to changed conditions. It therefore results in smaller output with the same inputs.

Government Regulatory Agencies. The behavior of government employees responsible for regulating business activities is highly sensitive to the reward structures imbedded in the regulatory institutions. For example, consider regulation by government bureau or independent commission. Because the compensation of commissioners is less dependent upon the activities of their agencies, they have less incentive to regulate actively. Both theory and evidence indicate that, among other things, independent commissions are more likely to encourage monopolistic arrangements (Eckert, 1973).

Utilities typically are regulated by independent commissions who set the rate of return that the utility is allowed to earn and then approve the prices that the utility is allowed to charge. A profit constraint reduces owners' property rights in the firm's income, reducing their incentive to monitor managers and increasing the latter's opportunity for discretionary behavior. Evidence from the U.S. electric power industry suggests that regulation by independent commission results in higher prices, lower output, and higher owners' wealth. Moreover, stricter regulation is associated with lower rate structures that favor larger users, more fixed capital, and less expenditure on research and development (De Alessi, 1980).

Government-Owned Firms. The main difference between private and government-owned (political) firms is that ownership in the latter effectively is not transferable, ruling out the capitalization of future consequences into current transfer prices and specialization in ownership. As a result, the owners' incentive to monitor is reduced even more than in the case of regulated private firms. Moreover, consumers and other interested parties, such as producers of substitutable and complementary goods, have the incentive to use the political process to advance their own welfare at taxpayers' expense.

The evidence regarding the behavior of public firms is rich and varied. Data from the U.S. electric power industry suggest that, relative to regulated private firms, municipal firms charge lower prices, have greater capacity, spend more on plant construction, have higher operating costs, relate prices less closely to demand and supply conditions, change prices less frequently and in response to larger changes in their economic determinants, have prices that favor business relative to residential users and voters relative to nonvoters, offer a smaller variety of output, adopt cost-reducing innovations less readily, maintain managers in office longer, and exhibit greater variation in rates of return. Evidence from other industries suggests that, among other things, government-owned firms are less successful in satisfying consumer wants, incur higher costs, and emphasize the production of services more easily monitored by higher-level decision makers (De Alessi, 1980).

Conclusions

The system of property rights adopted within a society specifies the kinds of competition that may be used to resolve the conflict of interests arising from scarcity. Whatever the set of institutions (e.g., "capitalism," "socialism"), decisions regarding the allocation of resources entail the expression of a preference for more of some goods relative to some other goods. Decision makers somehow have to attribute relative values to both inputs and outputs, and these coefficients of choice, whether explicit in the form of market prices or implicit in the outcomes of the decisions, are simply prices (Schumpeter, 1934; Enke, 1954).

The question of choosing the "right" prices to reduce scarcity or to achieve some other objective is really a question of choosing the "right" institutions. That is, it is a question of choosing how society is to be ordered and what each individual may be allowed to do in a world of change and complex interactions (Alchian, 1967). Because prices provide both information and incentives to decision makers, the right prices must change with changes in circumstances. Accordingly, *the problem of choosing the right prices is the problem of choosing the right institutional processes for collecting, interpreting, and conveying information, and of providing incentives to the appropriate decision makers.*

Under a system of private property rights, market processes generate explicit prices that provide information and incentive to both consumers and producers. Market prices are a cheap and powerful mechanism for facilitating specialization and exchange as well as for solving the valuation problem. Thus, prices help to alleviate scarcity by guiding the allocation of resources to their highest-valued uses as judged by market criteria. Within such a system, the central role of the government is to help define, allocate, and enforce private rights to the use of resources.

The existence of positive transaction costs implies that not all rights to the use of resources are fully defined, allocated, and enforced. Pointing to natural monopoly, public goods, externalities, indivisibilities, and other supposed sources of market failure, economists have noted various circumstances in which, under equilibrium conditions, not all mutually beneficial trade is exhausted. In order to solve these apparent problems, a broad range of remedies has been proposed, including the public provision of public goods and suitably designed taxes, subsidies, and regulatory controls.

In assessing the desirability of any remedy, several caveats deserve note. First, some of the advantages of a market system should not be confused with possible limitations. For example, the existence of scarcity (including positive transaction costs) suggests that all possible goods would not be produced, that all public goods would not be zero-priced (pricing generates information about value), and that some private goods would be zero-priced (Demsetz, 1964).

Second, the importance of equilibrium conditions should not be overestimated. *In a world of change, equilibrium conditions seldom if ever hold, and what really matters is the process of adjustment.* As already noted, the market is a powerful mechanism for allowing individuals to choose and revise their consumption and production plans in response to changes in their own individual circumstances—circumstances that simply are unknowable to a central planner. Moreover, theoretical limitations may have little practical importance. For example, much of the concern with monopoly seems to be misplaced; in many instances, the allocative effects of monopoly are trivial.

Third, adequate consideration should be given to the consequences of government regulation, including the possible occurrence of unintended and undesired side effects. Our understanding of how economic systems actually work is still rudimentary, and the ramifications of a change in institutions on a complex web of economic relationships are more difficult to predict than a naive, one-product, partial-equilibrium analysis may suggest. For example, recent work on the nature of contractual relations indicates that many arrangements previously taken as anticompetitive in fact enhance competition (Williamson, 1979, 1983; Klein, 1980; Klein and Leffler, 1981; Haddock, 1982). And many governmental attempts at regulation demonstrably have made matters worse as a result of unanticipated and undesired consequences. For example,

U.S. programs in the 1970s designed to ease the oil "crisis" discouraged domestic oil production and generally disrupted adjustment. Similarly, stricter regulation of the drug industry apparently has resulted in more rather than fewer deaths, as the reduction in the number of deaths from defective drugs has been more than offset by the increase in the number of deaths from delays in the introduction of new drugs (Peltzman, 1974). Moreover, the longer time required for approval has lowered the profitability of introducing new drugs, and fewer of them are being made available.

Fourth, the relative usefulness of alternative economic systems should not be assessed by comparing the real-world solutions observed under one system with the theoretical outcomes of an alternative system under ideal conditions. Comparing the outcomes observed in a market system under positive transaction costs with the outcomes that an all-knowing planner would achieve under ideal conditions (including the ideal incentive structure) is pointless (Demsetz, 1969). *The real issue is how well do alternative economic systems work in practice.*

Fifth, it should be recognized that individuals have the incentive to exploit opportunities for gain whether these are offered in the private or the political realm. Individuals have the incentive to manipulate the power of government to their own advantage, and the alleged limitations of the market frequently provide the rhetoric for groups seeking protection from competitive forces. In the United States, for example, concern with the economic consequences of natural monopoly has provided public justification for federal, state, and local regulation of a broad range of goods and services (e.g., electric power, water, gas, telephone, railroads, trucking, airlines, communications, and the stock exchange). The evidence, however, suggests that—at least until the recent shift in political pressures—independent commissions and other regulatory agencies typically have acted to further the interests of those they are supposed to regulate, enforcing collusion among firms in the industry and protecting them from competition. Thus, regulatory agencies typically have enhanced monopoly power and reduced consumer welfare. Licensing of the professions, subsidies, fees, and taxes similarly have been advanced on the ground of improving the allocation of resources, while in practice they have simply been used to redistribute wealth from consumers and taxpayers to groups with a comparative advantage in the use of political power (Kalt and Zupan, 1984).

Government clearly has a fundamental role in helping to define, allocate, and enforce private property rights, and to provide alternatives when such arrangements do more harm than good. The extension of government activities beyond these limits, however, reduces the ability of individuals to respond to changes in circumstances, inhibiting entrepreneurial incentives and weakening the effectiveness of the market process in reducing scarcity (Kirzner, 1973). Understanding the economic consequences of alternative institutional arrangements should facilitate the choice of governmental activities, institutions, and policy instruments.

Works Cited

Alchian, Armen A. (1965) "Some Economics of Property Rights." *Il Politico*, vol. 30 (Dec.), 816–829.

_____ (1967) "How Should Prices Be Set?" *Il Politico*, vol. 32 (June), 369–382.

_____ (1984) "Specificity, Specialization, and Coalition." *Journal of Institutional and Theoretical Economics*, vol. 340, 34–49.

Alchian, Armen A., and Harold Demsetz (1972) "Production, Information Costs, and Economic Organization." *American Economic Review*, vol. 62 (Dec.), 777–795.

Asch, Peter (1975) "The Determinants and Effects of Antitrust Activity." *Journal of Law and Economics*, vol. 18 (Oct.), 575–581.

Bator, Francis M. (1957) "The Simple Analytics of Welfare Maximization." *American Economic Review*, vol. 47 (March), 22–59.

Baumol, William J. (1982) "Contestable Markets: An Uprising in the Theory of Industry Structure." *American Economic Review*, vol. 72 (March), 1–15.

Becker, Gary S. (1957) *The Economics of Discrimination*. Chicago: University of Chicago Press.

Blaug, Mark (1980) *The Methodology of Economics.* Cambridge, Cambridge University Press.

Brozen, Yale (1982) *Concentration, Mergers, and Public Policy.* New York: Macmillan.

_____ (1986) "The Economic Impact of Government Policy." Paper presented at the Symposium on Economic Policy in the Market Process: Success or Failure, Slot Zeist, Netherlands, Jan. 29.

Coase, Ronald H. (1960) "The Problem of Social Cost." *Journal of Law and Economics,* vol. 3 (Oct.), 1–44.

De Alessi, Louis (1969) "Implications of Property Rights for Government Investment Choices." *American Economic Review,* vol. 59 (March), 13–24.

_____ (1980) "The Economics of Property Rights: A Review of the Evidence." *Research in Law and Economics,* vol. 2, 1–47.

_____ (1982) "On the Nature and Consequences of Private and Public Enterprises." *Minnesota Law Review,* vol. 67 (Oct.), 201–219.

_____ (1983) "Property Rights, Transaction Costs, and X-Efficiency: An Essay in Economic Theory." *American Economic Review,* vol. 73 (March), 64–81.

_____ (1987) "Nature and Methodological Foundations of Some Recent Extensions of Economic Theory." In Gerard Radnitzky and Peter Berholz, eds., *Economic Imperialism: The Economic Approach Applied Outside the Field of Economics.* New York: Paragon House.

De Alessi, Louis, and Raymond P. H. Fishe (1987) "Why Do Corporations Distribute Assets? An Analysis of Dividends and Capital Structure." *Journal of Institutional and Theoretical Economics,* vol. 143 (March), 34–51.

De Alessi, Louis, and Robert J. Staaf (1987) "Liability, Control and the Organization of Economic Activity." *International Review of Law and Economics,* vol. 7 (June), 5–20.

Demsetz, Harold (1964) "The Exchange and Enforcement of Property Rights." *Journal of Law and Economics,* vol. 7 (Oct.), 11–26.

───────────── (1967) "Toward a Theory of Property Rights." *American Economic Review, Proceedings,* vol. 57 (May), 347–359.

───────────── (1968) "Why Regulate Utilities?" *Journal of Law and Economics,* vol. 11 (April), 55–65.

───────────── (1969) "Information and Efficiency: Another Viewpoint." *Journal of Law and Economics,* vol. 12 (April), 1–22.

───────────── (1982) "Barriers to Entry." *American Economic Review,* vol. 72 (March), 47–57.

Eckert, Ross D. (1973) "On the Incentives of Regulators: The Case of Taxicabs." *Public Choice,* vol. 14 (spring), 83–99.

Ekelund, Robert B., Jr. and Robert D. Tollison (1980) "Mercantilist Origins of the Corporation." *Bell Journal of Economics,* vol. 11 (autumn), 715–720.

Enke, Stephen (1954) "Some Economic Aspects of Fissionable Material." *Quarterly Journal of Economics,* vol. 68 (May), 217–232.

Fama, Eugene F. (1980) "Agency Problems and the Theory of the Firm." *Journal of Political Economy,* vol. 88 (April), 288–307.

Fields, Gary S. (1980) *Poverty, Inequality, and Development.* New York and London: Cambridge University Press.

Furubotn, Eirik G. (1974) "Bank Credit and the Labor-Managed Firm: The Yugoslav Case." In E. Furubotn and S. Pejovich, eds., *The Economics of Property Rights.* Cambridge, Mass.: Ballinger.

Furubotn, Eirik G., and Svetozar Pejovich (1972) "Property Rights and Economic Theory: A Survey of Recent Literature." *Journal of Economic Literature,* vol. 10 (Dec.), 1137–1162.

Haddock, David D. (1982) "Basing-Point Pricing: Competitive vs. Collusive Theories." *American Economic Review,* vol. 72 (June), 289–306.

Harberger, Arnold C. (1954) "Monopoly and Resource Allocation." *American Economic Review,* vol. 44 (May), 77–87.

Hayek, Friedrich A. (1945) "The Use of Knowledge in Society." *American Economic Review,* vol. 35 (Sept.), 519–530.

Jarrell, Gregg A. (1978) "The Demand for State Regulation of the Electric Utility Industry." *Journal of Law and Economics,* vol. 21 (Oct.), 269–296.

Jensen, Michael C., and William H. Meckling (1976) "Theory of the Firm: Managerial Behavior, Agency Costs, and Ownership Structure." *Journal of Financial Economics,* vol. 3 (Oct.), 305–360.

Kalt, Joseph P., and Mark A. Zupan (1984) "Capture and Ideology in the Economic Theory of Politics." *American Economic Review,* vol. 74 (June), 279–300.

Kirzner, Israel M. (1973) *Competition and Entrepreneurship.* Chicago: University of Chicago Press.

Klein, Benjamin (1980) "Transaction Costs Determinants of 'Unfair' Contractual Arrangements." *American Economic Review, Proceedings,* vol. 70 (May), 356–362.

Klein, Benjamin, and Keith B. Leffler (1981) "The Role of Market Forces in Assuring Contractual Performance." *Journal of Political Economy,* vol. 89 (Aug.), 615–641.

Klein, Benjamin, Robert G. Crawford, and Armen A. Alchian (1978) "Vertical Integration, Appropriable Rents, and the Competitive Contracting Process." *Journal of Law and Economics,* vol. 21 (Oct.), 297–326.

Long, William F., Richard Schramm, and Robert D. Tollison (1973) "The Economic Determinants of Antitrust Activity." *Journal of Law and Economics,* vol. 16 (Oct.), 351–364.

Ostrom, Vincent (1984) "The Meaning of Value Term." *American Behavioral Scientist,* vol. 28 (Nov./Dec.), 249–262.

_____ (1986) "Constitutional Foundations for a Theory of System Comparisons: An Inquiry into Problems of Incommensurability, Emergent Properties, and Development." Paper presented at the Radein Research Seminar, Redagon, Italy, Feb. 14–25.

Peltzman, Sam (1974) *Regulation of Pharmaceutical Innovation.* Washington, D.C.: American Enterprise Institute.

Radford, R. A. (1945) "The Economic Organization of a P.O.W. Camp." *Economica,* n.s. vol. 12 (Nov.), 189–201.

Samuelson, Paul A. (1954) "The Pure Theory of Public Expenditures." *Review of Economics and Statistics,* vol. 36 (Nov.), 387–389.

Schumpeter, Joseph A. (1934) *Economic Reconstruction.* New York: Columbia University Press.

Siegfried, John J. (1975) "The Determinants of Antitrust Activity." *Journal of Law and Economics,* vol. 18, 559–574.

Smith, Adam (1937) *An Inquiry into the Nature and Causes of the Wealth of Nations.* Edwin Cannan, ed. New York: Modern Library. First published in 1776.

Stigler, George J. (1961) "The Economics of Information." *Journal of Political Economy,* vol. 69 (June), 213–225.

Williamson, Oliver E. (1979) "Transaction Cost Economics: The Governance of Contractual Relations." *Journal of Law and Economics,* vol. 22 (Oct.), 233–261.

_____ (1983) "Credible Commitments: Using Hostages to Support Exchange." *American Economic Review,* vol. 73 (Sept.), 519–540.

Woodward, Susan E. (1985) "On the Economics of Limited Liability." Unpublished manuscript, University of California, Los Angeles.

12
John F. A. Taylor

The Ethical Foundations of the Market

Karl Marx supposed that all social institutions are grounded at last in economic institutions, namely, in institutions of production. He conceived all culture—all politics, all forms and manners and observances, all spiritual institutions—to be a superstructure established on economic foundations. Every social arrangement is the passive register of an economic distinction, every social transformation a mute obedience to the material conditions under which our lives are passed.

It is easy to disparage Marx. It is more difficult to answer him. The only secure path to an answer is to rediscover the moral foundations of society itself. What are the conditions essential to human community in any of its forms?

The analysis developed in this chapter is further elaborated in John F. A. Taylor, *The Masks of Society, An Inquiry into the Covenants of Civilization* (New York: Appleton-Century-Crofts, 1966); and John F. A. Taylor, *The Public Commission of the University* (New York: New York University Press, 1981).

We must be brought to see that the economic domain is not original but derivative, that it rests itself upon an ethical substructure, and that where that structure of moral covenant is wanting, we have not a society at all but only the illusion of one.

Where there is no vision, the people perish. We are as a people, even in our honeyed Canaan, in process of perishing. For we have grown blind to the moral premises of our simplest and most quiet acts. Therefore, I propose to describe the unborrowed ethic that is cognate to the business community itself—the ethic that is found in it, not an ethic that has been imposed upon it. For the task is not to produce an ethic where none was. The task is to articulate the implicit ethic that the business community uses but never states. Let it be confessed that the market is not the City of God. It is nevertheless a city, and unless marketers see it, the city will die. If a "market" is intended to mean not the place of the market—the stockyards and depots, the concourses and greengrocers' stalls—but an order of persons making exchanges, that is, of economic actors who, in the phrase of Adam Smith, truck and barter with one another, then I understand the market to be the compendious institution to which economic theory is finally addressed.

For ordinary purposes, among capitalist nations, that decision concerning the use of terms will excite no arrest. It is not, however, in point of consequence, so innocent as it may appear. For I do not intend by the use of the term "market" to restrict attention to any special form of it. In particular, I do not intend to restrict attention to that special form of it that economists are accustomed to describe as "the market system"—the system regulated by the competition of independent buyers and sellers in which, without interference from the state, the invisible hand is said to work. The community of exchange is more fundamental than the political agencies that historically have sought to regulate it. Exchange is the fundamental relation of any economic order—the relation by which economic actors are bound together in their distinctive form of community. That community is what I understand by the "market." The market will appear wherever the relation of exchange appears; the market system will not.

Traditionally, theory has viewed the exchange of goods in the market as a natural consequence of the division of labor in human productive activity. In any society whose labors are divided, each member must depend upon the efforts of those beyond him for the satisfaction of some of his needs. The market appears as the simple result of the inability of any one man to supply all of his private wants. The ascetic saint who subsists by his own labors, limiting his needs to those only that his own labors can supply, will frequent no market. He will draw directly from untenanted nature its free gratuity, without fee of return—for his meat the body of the locust and for his drink the honey of wild bee. He is party to no exchange, since he has no need that solicits an exchange; therefore he is party to no market, which is simply the community of exchangers. The market is the commerce of insufficient saints.

Such is the classical account of the origin of the market. Nor is it without its part of truth. The institution of the market is rooted in the reciprocal needs of men who traffic in the products of their divided labors. That fact is beyond question. Nevertheless, the belief that the division of labor adequately accounts for the bond of the economic community is one of the profoundest illusions of social theory.

The division of labor does not supply the bond of the economic community; it describes only the condition requiring it. For it does not follow, from the circumstance that two men may place a beam more easily than one, that they will join themselves together in placing it. They will join themselves together in placing it only on one condition, that each admits in the other a right to a part in the common shelter. Without that admission, their act will not occur. For the bond of their community, the tie that unites them, is not the physical beam that they have together lifted but the unspoken compact into which they have entered. The bond of community among men is measured by the mutuality of their acknowledgments, by the respect for claims that they acknowledge in each other, as parties to a common covenant.

The covenant may go unspoken. It is nevertheless essential and is always, wherever men have voluntarily contracted an exchange, mutually acknowledged to be binding on them both. For apart from their covenant, exchangers have no community; apart from their labors they may have it still. The right, the claim, outlives the act that earns it. That is why the economic community preserves its uninterrupted life even when the city sleeps. Its labors cease, its concourses are emptied, its goading needs are for a little time quiet or unfelt; yet all that potent mass of life slumbers beneath a common sky of its own making.

Economists are by profession disposed to study the factor of wealth in the economic community. I am concerned with the same community. But I attend to the factor of commonwealth. Where the economist sees in the behavior of the market a creation and a flow of goods, I see in it a transaction, an exchange of goods—in short, a commerce of persons. I shall be viewing the relation of the exchangers—not the ratio of exchange of bread and meat, but the conditions essential to the peace of the baker and the butcher. In order to provide the terms that will be found useful for this purpose, let me consider a simple limiting case, a community of two parties only, a community of two who contract an exchange with each other.

Ordinarily, men contract exchanges within an already established legal order that has defined in advance their relations to each other and supplied a constable to oversee their good behavior. We unheroic moderns suffer the illusion of supposing that the constable is essential to our community: we assume that where there is no constable there can be no contract. But that is an illusion of our positivist mentality. A constable may institute a jail; he is powerless to institute a society. He may by force protect a society that others have framed; he cannot by any act of force supply their omission in framing it.

Political science, as it is cultivated in our day, celebrates the constable. It forgets the community instituted by consent, which alone can ever justify his act or require it. That is why in our day we have no science of politics; we have only police administration. We live in the dispirited tradition of Thomas Hobbes, who wrote: "Covenants without the sword are but words, and of no strength to secure a man at all" ([1651] 1958: 128). It does not follow that the

The Ethical Foundations of the Market

sword without a covenant is a civility. Civility is the condition of peace under law that we have authorized, and no sword, no force in nature or heaven, can authorize it for us.

Therefore, for the sake of simplicity, let us be rid of the constable and of all of the adventitious securities of the legal order. When Martin Luther was asked where, if the ban were put upon him, he would go, he replied: "Under the sky." In the moral ambiguity of the twentieth century, we shall do well to imitate his example. Consider simply a community under the sky, the community constituted by two parties who have, out of the wilderness of the world, entered into a relation of exchange. Then, for any concrete analysis, certain elements will immediately present themselves as essential to that relation.

The two parties to the exchange I shall describe, borrowing a term from the law of contract, as "persons" *(personae)*: persons are the "subjects of exchange." These subjects contract their exchange with respect to certain objects: the "things" exchanged (*res*, in the language of the law) will then be technically described as the "objects of exchange." Thus, if Tom Sawyer trades with Huck Finn an apple core for a bent nail, Tom and Huck are persons, the subjects of exchange; the apple core and the bent nail are things, the objects of exchange.

For a discussion of the foundations of the American or any other economy, this exchange is hardly a translation of goods that shall have any appreciable effect on the destiny of nations or the economy of the Mississippi Valley. Nevertheless, for a philosophical purpose, that simplicity is precisely the thing wanted. It is possible, but it would be very unwise, to begin with an exchange in which the persons implicated were General Motors and the United States Government, and the things exchanged were trucks and tax dollars. I am interested for the moment less in the identity of the terms than in the structure of their relations to each other. Such dignity as marketers may ever claim will be found at last to depend upon their standing in that simple structure, related as Tom and Huck are related, as subjects of exchange, in the mutuality of a covenant into which they have freely entered.

Concretely, the topic of economics is a social fact, and we are forbidden to ignore the circumstance that this fact embraces persons as well as things. All of the men of little Lidice are dead in the ashes of their burned church. In a single stroke of Nazi vengeance, their village had been reduced to a desert of things. The village still stands; every market stall remains still stocked; but there is no market, and neither wealth nor commodity nor price.

Let me turn then to Tom and Huck, who were meditating, under the full afflatus of the profit motive, the exchange of an apple core for a bent nail. Tom examines the apple core, Huck the nail. Visibly, the objects have changed hands. An exchange has therefore occurred? No, the exchange waits upon an agreement, which is not yet. For the moment they simply meditate what it would be to make permanent this new distribution of the goods of the earth of which now, provisionally and experimentally, they make trial. The exchange does not consist of this merely de facto transfer of objects. The transfer essential to exchange is a transfer not of things but of rights. The objects may or may not pass between hands. But unless ownership passes, there has been no exchange de jure. The exchange, if it occurs, will consist in a transfer of titles, of rights which are held, and are commonly admitted to be held, by the two parties.

That common admission of rights is the curious invisible bond that unites Tom and Huck at this precarious and painful moment of decision in which each weighs the marginal advantage to himself of acquiring what the other owns. Tom and Huck stand related as persons for the one sufficient reason that each admits the other to be the bearer of a right: each admits in the other the right of governing the disposition of the object that he himself now holds. This, and never anything short of it, is what we mean by being a person: to be a person is to have standing and to be a subject of rights. To be a person—to be the subject of a right—is a fact necessarily and essentially involving, besides the person who has the right, another person who accredits it.

John Locke supposed a man's right to a nut, picked up from the forest floor, to be conferred by the labor expended in the act of picking it up. For, as Locke thought, in the act of picking it up the gatherer, as it were, congeals the labor of his own body into the nut, which belonged till then to nature's great common. That is an illusion. For it must then follow that if another may by force of seizure take from him his nut, the usurper then holds it by the same ground of legitimacy, having mixed his labor with it. On the contrary, no one can have property in anything except as others acknowledge it. My property in a thing is the consequence not of the labor that I have put into it but of your willingness to accredit it, your willingness to accredit the labor as the ground for a claim. And if you have not that willingness, then though I labor with all my heart, I have no property.

There lies the paradox of all property: my right of property in a thing depends not upon my claim to it but precisely upon your readiness to admit my claim as privileged. We here confront the fundamental condition of all peaceable intercourse among human beings in society. This is the radical sense in which all property is public. Private property is a public fact, or it is no fact at all. It is public for the reason that it depends quite abjectly on a public concern. It is always a reciprocal engagement, never a unilateral one.

Government, law court, and police may be invoked to preserve property. They are, however, powerless to originate it, and in fact they everywhere presuppose it as the social condition of any political arrangement.

For we have property only because first we consent to have community, and there is no greater mystification of human understanding than the belief of John Locke that men establish community in order to preserve rights of property which they have apart from it. Apart from it they have no property, and can have none. Outside of the bond of community a man owns nothing. He has only what he holds, and only for so long as he holds it or can by force unassisted prevent another from holding it in his place. That is the lesson of every revolution in all the world. The legal order is temporarily in relapse. Then men discover, in a precarious hour, the effective limits of their society. Their society extends as far as their mutuality extends, and can never by any political dispensation be made to extend further.

Rights can appear only where the demands of moral community have been acknowledged. There is never any point in asking whether A apart from B has any rights. A apart from B neither has them nor for that matter ever needs them. The only serious question is: Under what conditions will B admit rights in A? And to that question there is a direct and simple answer: On the one condition that A reciprocate by admitting rights in B. All rights are grounded in such reciprocity, in the solidarity of persons who, for the sake of rights that run against others, admit duties that run against themselves. Therefore, if you would know the limits of a community, look to the rights that it respects in practice. For wherever rights are admitted, there also there must be persons; and wherever there are persons, men stand under covenant in each other's presence.

It is not the business of social analysis to decide for mankind whether mankind wants civilization. But analysis can show, if mankind wants it, the terms of consent that are essential to the achievement of it, the terms that are prerequisite, in every domain of human activity, to the establishment of normal expectations among men, whether in a legal order, or a community of exchange, or a church, or a language, or a universe of inquiry.

That there are material conditions of human society no one doubts. But that there are, besides these material conditions, formal conditions as well, conditions of civility, the instituted restraints that human beings lay upon themselves and consent to honor in their acts, in order that they might have society at all—this falls beyond the ordinary contemplations of actors in society. Practical men of the world, they take simply for granted the social foundations of their intercourse with each other. They take them for granted exactly as the speakers of a language take for granted the conventions of syntax that are implicit in their community of discourse; or as practicing scientists take for granted the rules of proof and evidence that are essential to their community of inquiry; or as the buyers and sellers in a market take for granted the unspoken rules of the market that govern their peaceful interchanges. Such rules of consent, though they are not noticed or even alluded to until they have been violated or abridged, appear in every domain of civilized society. They are not matters of sentiment; they are the unexposed foundations of moral consent upon which our communities—such fragmentary communities as we have—are reared.

What are the conditions of the peace of the market? What rules are indispensably necessary if marketers are to frame, in spite of their competitions and divisions, normal expectations of each other? Certainly we cannot treat theft as the norm. The market is a community of exchange. The thief in the marketplace is party to the physical neighborhood, but not party to the community; the marketer in the marketplace is both. What are his assumptions? What articles of tacit civility must he subscribe to, if he is to enter upon that remarkable estate of marketer?

Every marketer must be able to assume, as falling within the general consent of all parties to the market, at least two rules: first, a "rule of reciprocal exchange," that for something given something shall be had in return; second, a "rule of voluntary bargain," that no exchange, no mutual transfer of rights, shall be accounted binding into which the parties to the exchange have not voluntarily entered. These rules will not prevent marketers from going broke. They nevertheless admit rights to reside in persons, and persons to be gathered under terms of peace in one society. They are the tacit but essential conditions of any market, without which there could be no market at all. An open market acknowledges the capacity of others freely to associate themselves with the shared community of understanding and mutual respect. Without them theft would be sufficient, and exchange superfluous. They are the unwritten constitution—what I describe as the *covenant*—of the economic community.

That there are such formal conditions of human community—conditions of peace accessible to understanding and amenable to positive construction—no one who has watched the deprivations of dignity in twentieth-century wars and Nazi concentration camps can any longer question. Many patterns of society are consistent with human dignity. Some, however, demonstrably prohibit it and abort its essential conditions. And to know those conditions, to know in every domain of civilized life the formal conditions of the dignity of persons, is in fact the study of all positive peace among men.

Immanuel Kant used to declare that two things excited his soul, the starry heavens above and the moral law within. The modern mentality shares his wonder, and has even studied to extend his wonder, before the first of these. There is no danger that a human being, born into the twentieth century, will take lightly the illimitable fact of the starry heavens above. But that same human being, if he has not learned to repudiate belief in the moral law within, has become nevertheless profoundly suspicious of it. He is apt to see in any profession of moral law in human affairs simply the poor profession of a time-entangled human soul, a piece of ideology inherited by historical accident and perpetuated by animal sloth. Kant thought otherwise. He formulated the moral law, or, as he called it, "the categorical imperative," as follows: "Act so as to treat man, in your own person as well as in that of anyone else, always as an end, never merely as a means" ([1785] 1949: 178).

A respect for the dignity of persons is the absolute demand of any community whatever. In the critical effort to "get the prices right," we encounter all of the great moral issues that arise out of the collisions and omissions of our inheritance: questions concerning human rights and our fundamental liberties; questions concerning freedom from want and freedom from fear; questions concerning the rights of women and minorities; child labor; apartheid; abortion; equal access to education, to the market, to courts of law; the demand for social security, peace, and the orderly resolution of international conflicts; the right to work, to sell one's labor for wages, to bargain collectively for the terms and conditions of labor.

I list these examples without attention to their order or completeness. All of them fall within the jurisdiction of the moral law, which Kant describes as "the realm of ends." There are for Kant technical and prudential imperatives that have not this measure of generality, that command only conditionally. "Whoever wills the end, so far as reason has decisive influence on his action, wills also the indispensably necessary means to it that lie in his power." Kant writes:

> In the realm of ends everything has either a price or *dignity*. Whatever has a price can be replaced by something else which is *equivalent*; whatever is above all price, and therefore has no equivalent, has dignity.

> Whatever is related to the general inclinations and needs of mankind has a *market price*.... But that which constitutes the condition under which alone anything can be an end in itself has not merely a relative value or price, but has an intrinsic value; it has *dignity*.... only good morals and mankind ... have dignity. ([1785] 1949: 182–183)

To have dignity is to be a subject of rights; to have price is to be an object of rights. The presiding peril of the system of free enterprise is the forgetfulness of men who treat the mechanics of the social process as their release from social obligation. Saint Augustine's "*Dilige et quod vis fac* [love and do as you please]" has shocked the ear of every generation since his day. That redoubtable old saint is the stoutest free enterpriser of us all. His dictum is not a counsel of anarchy. The meaning is: "So long as you preserve your concern for one another, you may do as you please: no other restraint may ever legitimately be put upon your act." A respect for the rights of persons is the absolute condition of any community whatever. The central problem of the free market is how to reconcile liberty with fraternity, freedom with mutuality.

Nothing in nature forbids that a man should be treated as a thing. Only men in community can forbid it. That is why Nigger Jim, who floats down the Mississippi on a raft, is so pathetic a revelation concerning the larger and formally more civilized adult community that lies beyond the community of Tom and Huck. In that adult community Nigger Jim is a man. But he lacks the status of being a person, of being party to that community. He is not a subject of rights; he is an object of rights. He may be bought: he is a chattel, a thing with a market price, a piece of capital or land according as you regard him as a producer's tool or as a raw natural resource. He has price, but not dignity. All communities are at last, like Tom's and Huck's, under the sky. And the sky is as wide as we make it—as wide and as narrow as men's sympathies, as benignant or cruel as the restraints we put upon ourselves.

When we press the conception of "getting the prices right" to consider more broadly the terms on which alternatives are available, including those terms and conditions on how human beings relate to one another, there is always the issue of human dignity and the way that human dignity gains expression in the structure of human institutions. The market as exchange must first meet the condition where human beings can relate to one another with respect for each other's dignity and allow choice as among the objects that are available. It is by such methods that human beings might strive to alleviate scarcity and contribute to mutually respectful relationships with one another in self-governing communities.

Works Cited

Hobbes, Thomas (1958) *Leviathan, or the Matter, Forme and Power of a Commonwealth, Ecclesiasticall and Civill*. W. E. Pogson Smith, ed. Oxford: Clarendon Press. First published in 1651.

Kant, Immanuel (1949) *The Philosophy of Kant: Immanuel Kant's Moral and Political Writings*. Carl J. Friedrich, ed. New York: Modern Library. First published 1764–1795.

13

Vincent Ostrom

Opportunity, Diversity, and Complexity

Complexities and the Conceptualization of Patterns of Order in Human Societies

Great complexities exist in modern societies. These complexities derive from pursuit of opportunities in diverse situations, posing a problem of how to think about circumstances in which opportunities are a function of both diversities and complexities.

K. Paul Hensel, in his *Grundformen der Wirtschaftsordnung* (Foundations of economic order), suggests that there are millions of different variations in economic goods. Each variation can be viewed as having a characteristic production process in which factors are being transformed into products. The way that human beings relate to one another in the production, exchange, and consumption of diverse goods and services requires recourse to an extraordinary

---

This chapter originated as a paper for the Conference on Multi-Actor Policy Analysis held at the University of Umea, Sweden, July 23–25, 1985.

variety in patterns of organization. Hensel suggests that the aggregate economic process in West Germany refers to a great number and variety of consumption units (*Haushaltungen*) and production units (*Betriebe*). Among the consumption units, Hensel refers to individuals, families, associations, and collectivities. He estimates that some 23 million collective economic units exist and that 3 million of these operate as producers. The 20 million collective consumption units range from the Federal Republic of Germany to single-family households. These 23 million units all require coordinated planning of jointly associated efforts. Actual numbers have certainly changed in the meantime, but the relative magnitudes have probably remained much the same.

Any particular joint effort depends upon the ordering of human relationships with reference to rules that apply to discrete individuals in terms of particular time and place variables. Each association is in some sense a polity that orders relationships according to mutual understandings that take account of discrete contingencies. Each association is nested into other configurations of associated relationships, so that human actions are coordinated through relationships of time and space that refer to societies as larger aggregate structures of social relationships.

Hypothetically, it is possible to conceptualize, aggregate, and disaggregate these relationships in many different ways. Some ways of doing so distinguish economic and political relationships. How such relationships might be distinguished turns upon the criteria used. One common criterion is to conceptualize the economic realm as being where relationships are organized by reference to monetary prices and where money is used as a medium of exchange. Government thus comes to be identified with the provision of goods and services that are not subject to exchange relationships. Economic relationships then implicitly refer to market orders, whereas governmental and other forms of organization refer to nonmarket orders.

Problems arise in such conceptualizations because some elements that are essential to market organization cannot be supplied under market conditions. Money as a medium of exchange has the characteristic, among others, of jointness of use for all who use it as a unit of account in establishing price relationships (see chapter 14 of this book). This jointness of use means that a monetary system viewed as supplying a medium of exchange is a public good. Similarly, while goods and services are exchanged in markets, there is a public-good aspect to market relationships in circumstances where the use of those arrangements by some buyers and sellers does not detract from their use by other buyers and sellers. There are mutual gains to be realized in alleviating scarcity by having more rather than fewer market participants. Market arrangements depend upon authority arrangements that have to do with property rights, and on contractual relationships that are not marketable commodities; rather, they are symbolically conceptualized ways of ordering human relationships so that agreeable exchange relationships can occur. Market systems are not exclusive social orders that exist apart from other institutional arrangements in human societies. They depend upon social infrastructures and facilities that require recourse to non-market decision structures.

Similar problems arise in conceptualizing something that might be characterized as a "state," referring to rule-ruler-ruled relationships in human societies. The traditional theory of sovereignty presumes that the coherence or unity of law depends upon there being a single source of law. The unity of law, in this view, depends upon a unity of power. The state might then be viewed as an autonomous actor that rules over society. The state is a pattern of subordination in a hierarchy of superior-subordinate relationships; it culminates in a single, ultimate center of authority that is the source of law, but that cannot itself be held accountable to law. The state is then a monopoly of the authority to govern, a monopoly that also exercises control over the lawful use of force in a society.

Drawing upon such a concept of the state and upon a contrasting pattern of organization associated with market systems, it is easy to conceptualize the nature of order in human societies as being constituted with reference to markets and states, or to markets and hierarchies as these conceptions are sometimes expressed. But using such simplified conceptions fails to clarify the contextuality of life in human societies as many of us experience it. Markets and states are not isolable autonomous realms that exist as mutually exclusive domains of life.

When I buy an automobile, for example, I enter into a contract as well as pay money to a dealer. The contract is a basis for establishing a legal title. Before I can operate the automobile, I must have a valid driver's license. I consummate the transaction through my relationship with an automobile dealer and with equivalent persons who register titles, issue vehicle and driver's licenses, and supply credit, insurance, and other contingencies that may be involved in becoming an owner and user of an automobile. I deal with private enterprises and public agencies. Some alternatives are available at each juncture, including which licensing branch to patronize.

I bring these relationships to a personal level not because of any special viewpoint about the diversity of institutions in modern political economies, but because I want to explore the relationship of social realities to the cognitive experience of individuals who exist in and have recourse to those and other institutions. I do so because I am concerned about the tendency to use labels such as "markets" and "states," or "socialism" and "capitalism," to address the multitudes of relationships that individuals pursue in human societies. These abstractions somehow achieve a sense of reality in our imagination and, depending upon our degree of attraction or aversion, may become either nirvana models or diabolical machines.

Karl Polanyi's *The Great Transformation*, for example, views market structures as diabolical machines. His term is "Satanic Mill" (Polanyi, 1957: vii, 33). Polanyi sees a market economy as "an economic system controlled, regulated and directed by markets alone" (p. 68). This is hard for me to imagine, because property rights cannot be established, maintained, and enforced by markets alone. Nonetheless, there are certain dynamics, including a proclivity among businessmen to form cartels, that are characteristic of markets, and some of them may have perverse effects in human societies. Polanyi has, in my judgment, overstated his case and not made adequate levels of comparison between, for example, life in what he refers to as a market economy and life in a feudal economy (which he idolizes). Yet there is some ring of truth about some of the costs

Polanyi has associated with the transformations that occurred in nineteenth-century industrial societies.

Similarly, Marx saw something that he labels as "capitalism" as having a competitive dynamic that yields a few large monopoly or monopoly-like enterprises that come to dominance in a market economy. It becomes possible in this environment for dominant capitalist enterprises to prevail in governmental decisions, exploit workers, and yield a revolutionary potential. What Marx was characterizing as "capitalism" is what Adam Smith would have labeled "mercantilism" (Smith, [1776] 1937, bk. 4). It is certainly possible for large-scale producers to collude with those who exercise rulership prerogatives and so to engage in predatory exploitation. That possibility exists in any state-dominated society where some single ultimate center of authority has a monopoly of the legally recognized instruments of coercion.

Allusions to "markets" and "states" or to "socialism" and "capitalism" do not take us very far in thinking about patterns of order in human societies. Some "market" economists in their allusions to "capitalism" even fail to distinguish between an open competitive market economy and a state-dominated mercantile economy. Socialists, in their propensity to label economies as "capitalist," often fail to recognize the relatively rich structures of communal and public enterprises that exist in societies with open and highly competitive market economies.

We thus might realistically expect to find some combination of market and nonmarket structures in every society. We might usefully think about combinations of private and public economies as existing side by side. Not all forms of public enterprise need to be state-owned and operated. Various forms of communal or public ownership may exist apart from state ownership. The options are much greater than we imagine, when we do not allow our minds to be trapped within narrowly constrained intellectual horizons.

Entrepreneurship in the Public Sector

My own inquiries in looking at quite a different vista of later nineteenth- and twentieth-century institutional development in the arid regions of the American West has given me a different understanding of the way that people confront opportunities in a market economy. Since water is a critical factor in an arid region, the focus of my concern was the way that institutional arrangements were used to shape development in the American West, with particular attention to California and especially to Southern California (see, for example, V. Ostrom, 1953, 1971).

Private profitable enterprises play only a relatively limited role in the supply of water services in California, especially in Southern California. Much more important are nonprofit cooperative enterprises (locally referred to as mutual water companies), a vast array of public water districts organized as limited-purpose public corporations with many of the characteristics of nonprofit cooperative societies. Just as important are a range of other specialized agencies of general units of government, including cities, counties, the state of California, and agencies of the United States such as the Corps of Engineers and the Reclamation Service (V. Ostrom, 1971). Thus the California water industry is comprised predominantly of nonprofit cooperative enterprises, public enterprises, and governmental agencies. Of the 5,000 or so enterprises, fewer than 300 are for-profit private enterprises subject to regulation by the State Public Utilities Commission. This configuration of institutional arrangements has made possible a course of economic development through which California has become the most populous state in the Union and enjoys a very high level of economic development. Yet this same state, with a very small population, experienced disastrous droughts in the 1860s that remind one of the African Sahel today.

People in diverse localities in California have worked out forms of collective enterprise that are highly sensitive to communal values while at the same time limiting opportunities for private water developers to extract a monopoly profit. These enterprises have allowed smallholder settlers to capture a significant share of the economic rent inherent in the opportunities for development in

California. The capital investments in water works and water supply systems are predominantly held as cooperative or public properties of one form or another. A competitive market economy, in a so-called capitalist society, has yielded a highly productive water industry composed predominantly of cooperative and public enterprises that some might be inclined to designate as "socialist" enterprises. In general, the social infrastructure of the California economy is a mixed economy composed of a great variety of profitable, nonprofit cooperative, and public enterprises that relate to one another in complex configurations of interorganizational arrangements.

How do we explain the circumstance that people in California did not allow water resource development to occur under circumstances where private developers could continue to extract a monopoly profit from their control over water supplies? Aspiring monopolists existed. Few, however, succeeded in dominating patterns of water resource development over an extended period of time. Most developments in California were initiated under circumstances of public entrepreneurship where control over water supply was vested in the local communities of users rather than in private monopoly suppliers.

The only explanation that I can offer is that the people of California developed an awareness that the incentives facing a supplier of water services who sought to maximize profits were not consistent with the interests of those being served. Both public and private ownership of property in land meant that profitable water utility companies were required to meet political terms and conditions pertaining to the granting of franchises and to exercising the power of eminent domain, so that rights-of-way might be acquired across intervening parcels of land. The essential leverage for invoking political processes came from private ownership of land by multitudes of private proprietors; the results yielded by the political processes prevailing in California through the course of time biased entrepreneurial decisions against profitable water utility companies and in favor of cooperatives and public enterprises. Political processes were themselves altered through constitutional decision-making processes to reduce the authority of the state legislature, to place greater reliance upon popular initiatives and referenda, and to enhance the constitutional authority of local communities (V. Ostrom, 1987, ch. 8).

The juxtaposition of property relationships with political processes, yielding the institutional characteristics associated with the California water industry, carries quite different implications than are yielded in Polanyi's or Marx's analysis. The property rights of individual persons, of mutual water companies, and of various types of public corporations gave standing to individuals and diverse communities of interest to sue and be sued. This power gave essential leverage for initiating potential veto capabilities in a political system characterized by strong emphasis upon a separation of powers among many independent units of government—units in a system that was highly federalized. A critical issue here is how diverse institutional arrangements, both market and nonmarket, get linked together. Public entrepreneurship that takes account of diverse communities of interest is facilitated by a combination of a highly differentiated system of property rights and the absence of monopoly power in the exercise of public authority. Systems of property in land rights, structures of governance, and forms of proprietorship in the California water industry developed in a evolutionary way that is analogous to the development of property rights in Hawaii (see chapter 10 of this book).

To explore these relationships further, let me shift the focus of inquiry away from California to some of the problems that arise in the so-called Third World. The contrast will enable us to indicate how different structures in human societies yield different opportunities to fashion diverse forms of enterprise and structures of relationships.

The Pursuit of Development Opportunities

Lord Bauer (1984), in his essay "Market Order and State Planning," provides us with some interesting speculations about the cognitive experience of individuals in relation to the pursuit of developmental opportunities. I wish to relate his observations to some by David Feeny (1984) about a demand-and-supply model for institutional change. I then wish to speculate about the implications of such a model where the supply conditions are dominated by a model of military dictatorship that has been espoused by American authorities concerned with maintaining stable regimes in the so-called Free World. These implications will give us some measure of understanding of the tenuous nature of market economies—so tenuous, in fact, that Polanyi's "Satanic Mill" comes to be little more than a paper tiger shredded by the repressive powers of the state.

Lord Bauer, in his discussion of market order in the Third World, indicates that major transformations occurred late in the nineteenth and early in the twentieth century. Rubber trees indigenous to South America were planted over millions of acres in Southeast Asia on plantations controlled by Western-owned companies and by many Asian smallholders. Much the same pattern occurred in West Africa with the development of the cocoa industry. This development, Bauer suggests, was made possible by the "establishment and extension of public security" (1984: 24). I assume that these conditions came about through the exercise of imperial authority by European powers.

The prodigious efforts undertaken by millions of people, Bauer argues, occurred without their needing to know the end use of the trees they planted and the crops they harvested; rather,

> they simply took advantage of the opportunities for improving their lot, which came to them as a result of complex processes which originated far way, and the outcome of which was transmitted to them by the market. All they needed to understand was the extension of their opportunities. (Bauer, 1984: 24)

The critical information was the opportunity represented by prices in the market.

But the success of the market order, Bauer also indicates, is everywhere challenged because it "provides no mechanism for its own survival." Success in the market, Bauer argues, "requires concentration on concrete problems of production and marketing." These problems require a devotion of time and energy that does not leave room for people to develop "sustained and perceptive interests in general issues and their analysis" (p. 36). This is much the same issue that Tocqueville raised when he expressed concern that the pursuit of wealth, in a democratic society, might come at the cost of citizenship (Tocqueville, [1835] 1945: see esp. vol. 2, bks. 2 and 4). Individuals who pay attention only to market prices in determining their choices become vulnerable to political argument that workers and peasants could achieve greater advantage by expropriating private property and instituting a socialist society—a society in which profits are eliminated and workers realize the full social product of their labor. The naive maximizer might select the option offered by those who make the biggest promises. This too would be to take advantage of perceived opportunities.

We are thus confronted, in choosing diverse types of institutional arrangements, with establishing the relative advantages or the relative prices that accrue to the alternatives that are available. Price in its most general sense can be defined as the terms on which alternatives are available. Some estimate of the terms on which alternatives are available, or might become available, is necessary before one can begin to estimate the demand for alternative institutional arrangements. Instead of money prices for discrete commodities, the choice is at a different level. It is the choice of configurations of rule-ordered relationships, or institutional choice, that is at stake. These are much more difficult to assess.

The supply of new forms of institutional arrangements depends upon procuring the necessary authorizations for establishing authority to act. This requires some form of legal standing, and legal standing depends upon legal processes associated with the exercise of governmental prerogatives. The supply of institutional arrangements may be controlled, as Feeny suggests, by "the elite decision makers of government" (1984). The tighter the elite and the more rigorous its control over the instrumentalities of power, the greater will be its dominance over the control of institutional arrangements that are available to the members of a society for organizing activities that reach beyond families, kinships, and secret societies.

In the case of European empires in Africa and Asia, we might anticipate that this price would come relatively high. While opportunities to pursue market options on the part of individuals and families within the constraints of imperial preference may have been readily accessible to subject populations, there would have been little chance of building up a network of institutions comparable to those of the California water industry. The less experience people have in dealing with diverse forms of enterprise and the less knowledge that is available to them about different institutional arrangements in other societies, the less opportunity they will have for articulating demands for institutional changes. Empires, given the combination of relatively simple structures of property rights with imperial structures of authority relationships, may have provided an adequate degree of public security to yield important economic opportunities in the development of rubber, cocoa, and other productive enterprises. But we have no reason to believe that such security would have facilitated the diverse forms of cooperative and public entrepreneurship that could have enabled the great variety of mutual water companies and public enterprises to support essential *public* infrastructures in a highly productive *market* economy. If political structures are organized as highly integrated monopolies, we would expect political elites to drive a more favorable monopoly bargain than might be expected from monopolists in other circumstances.

The British, Dutch, French, and Portugese empires have given way to a great number of new nations where formerly subject peoples are now concerned with undertaking their own course of development. This has provided them with an important opportunity to fashion institutional arrangements. Primary attention has been directed to building the apparatus of the state, on the assumption that the state is the essential foundation for supplying all other institutional arrangements that might be relied upon to undertake the modernization of those societies. What has occurred?

The experience is diverse; and what I have to say applies to only one pattern of development that is associated with coups d'état and military dictatorships. That pattern is sufficiently common in the Third World to give us some degree of understanding about the price of institutional innovation and change under strong monopoly conditions. In stating these conditions, I rely upon the analysis offered in Miles Copeland's *The Game of Nations* (see chapter 2 of this book). As we saw, the key instrumentalities of control are "a politicized police, a secret service, a happy army, an inflated bureaucracy, a mass movement organized as a one-party system, and a propaganda service to tell the people what to think." At the same time, "traditional institutions that have helped to sustain a way of life are subject to assault; and new ways that are amenable to mass appeals and maximization of the regime's control over society are put in their place. Revolutionary rhetoric about socialism is used to nationalize economic enterprises," as well as to expropriate property and control economic activity.

These are the conditions that can be expected to prevail in controlling the supply of institutional innovations governed by elites organized as military dictatorships. These opportunities can be highly lucrative for some. The *Washington Post* has reported the present private assets of a former African sergeant, currently a head of state, to be $4 billion. The change of government in the Philippines provides some superficial awareness of the opportunities for exploitation afforded to those associated with the Marcos regime. The private fortunes of Third World rulers are among the largest in the contemporary world. And the fortunes accruing to heads of state say nothing about the pervasive patterns of petty corruption and the accumulation of wealth by petty officeholders. Old-style imperialisms may have been relatively more benign than the new-style cryptoimperialisms of the contemporary world.

Since the price of supplying institutional innovations and change through "the elite decision makers of government" may come extremely high, we may want to consider some alternatives that may be available, alternatives for which people need not depend upon chance, coups d'état, or revolutions to fashion their systems of government. Such consideration requires a knowledgeable awareness of alternative terms and conditions that might apply to the creation and operation of systems of government. Lord Bauer's workers and peasants would be required to know much more than how to calculate the economic opportunities that were available to them on the world market. They would also need to know something about the opportunities afforded by market orders and alternative forms of economic organization. Markets themselves are never sufficient. Markets for different types of goods and services may take on quite different characteristics. Some may work well under the most impersonal conditions. Others may depend upon personal considerations involving high levels of trust among trading partners.

Further, Bauer's workers and peasants would need to know how to take best advantage of opportunities for teamwork, and how teamwork might be best organized so as to realize its advantages relative to pursuing economic opportunities with reference only to market-exchange arrangements. Great ambiguity exists, as H. G. Kruesselberg has indicated, about whether labor is to be appropriately conceived as a "commodity" to be bought and sold in markets, or whether the terms and conditions of employment are to be viewed as being "constitutional" in nature (see Kaufmann, Majone, and Ostrom, 1986: ch. 17, passim). In the latter circumstance the employment contract would be constitutive of institutional arrangements for the organization of teamwork in productive relationships. Different types of employment contracts could then yield types of productive relationships. Workers might create an enterprise and employ their own manager rather than let someone else become a proprietor and hire other workers as employees. In large-scale enterprises, workers might organize to bargain collectively with management. In turn, diverse cooperative and public enterprises might be organized to procure essential services like water supply or marketing facilities to gain access to more extended markets.

This range of opportunities always needs to be viewed against the possibility that Lord Bauer's workers and peasants might aspire to establish the terms and conditions of government so that they could exercise basic control over those who exercise governmental prerogatives. They would then realize that a naive faith in revolutionary appeals is extremely hazardous and is likely to yield increasing oppression and deteriorating conditions of life. Real revolutionary potential exists when people establish processes of decision making that specify the terms and conditions of government where citizens reserve to themselves fundamental authority that applies to the governance of society including the authority to set the terms and conditions of government.

A constitution can be viewed as the fundamental law specifying the terms and conditions of government. When people exercise the prerogatives of constitutional choice they can be conceptualized as exercising the authority to set the terms and conditions of government. When conditions can be set so as to maintain the enforceability of constitutional law and revise those terms and conditions through time, we can view people as citizens exercising, at the constitutional level, the basic prerogatives that control the other aspects of institutional choice that may be exercised by instrumentalities of government. When such conditions prevail we might think of people becoming self-governing.

I have elsewhere elaborated much more fully upon the terms and conditions that apply to the constitution of democratic societies, that is, societies where people can be said to exercise and control the prerogatives of rulership (Kaufmann, Majone, and Ostrom, 1985: ch. 5, passim; V. Ostrom, 1987). People are then not helpless victims of market systems as diabolical machines; they do learn to appreciate that markets afford important opportunities for them to order their relationships with one another in mutually productive ways. But markets do not suffice to yield the most favorable economic opportunities in all circumstances. Monopoly bargains may come at a very high price, and people may gain advantages in organizing natural monopolies as cooperative or public enterprises so as to constrain monopoly pricing, and share the inherent advantage of production technologies among the communities of users.

We need not think of "government" as occurring only with reference to states that govern over societies. Government may also occur within the context of families, kin, voluntary associations, villages, and other patterns of human association. It is the rules of association that are constitutive of human societies; and these can be constituted by communities of people who fashion their own systems of self-government. Rather than looking only to states and markets, we need to give much more attention to building the basic institutional infrastructures that enable people to find ways of relating constructively to one another and of resolving problems in their daily lives, but that also reach out to larger communities and configurations of relationships.

There comes a point where people can have recourse to self-help in arranging the supply of institutional arrangements rather than depend upon the price extracted by "the elite decision makers of government." Under such circumstances, alternatives become available; and the "state" is no longer in a position to extract its monopoly price. By relying upon principles of self-governance to apply to diverse units of government in fashioning a highly federalized system of governance, people can begin to alter, in a significant way, the price that applies to the supply of institutional arrangements in self-governing societies.

When the trader in the informal market of a local economy can help procure an infrastructure of communal services to develop public thoroughfares, provide for the security of persons and property in a local community, arrange effective sanitation facilities, fire services, healthful water supplies, etc., and at the same time extend the range of his or her own entrepreneurial opportunities to reach out to larger economic horizons, he or she has the potential of fashioning indigenous patterns of economic and political development. In such circumstances, each person can learn how both to serve his or her own interests and at the same time serve others who share the interdependent relationships that arise in human communities. Democratic societies cannot be fashioned without such roots. Nor can they survive in military struggles for power whether within nation-states or between nation-states. For this reason, the basic architecture of modern societies must, as Tocqueville has argued, draw upon a science of association to fashion rules of association that apply to diverse communities of relationships extending from villages to nation-states and beyond (Tocqueville, [1840] 1945, vol. 2: 102–124).

When people share in the exercise of the fundamental prerogatives of government through a properly constituted system of government, they can take account of different opportunities to fashion institutional arrangements for diverse productive and consumptive possibilities that occur in many different communities of relationships. Systems of public enterprise, as in the case of the California water industry, are as essential as systems of private enterprise in the operation of many other industries.

This implies that individual choice cannot be limited to prices in a market but should involve a much more extended range of calculations, a range extending to the terms on which alternatives become available in the context of diverse institutional arrangements, including both market and nonmarket systems of relationships. Human beings have the potential to take account of their own preferences and use their own cognitive and emotional facilities to come to a sympathetic understanding of what it means to be human and to relate in mutually productive ways to other human beings. But these relationships are always subject to tension because the maintenance of orderly relationships in human society depends upon the enforcement of rules, and enforcement involves potential access to instruments of coercion that can also be used to repress and exploit others. We can never escape from these tensions. Instead, we are required to find constructive ways of living with them in communities of relationships fashioned upon reciprocity and mutual respect for one another.

Conclusion

When human beings develop a sufficient level of understanding to become effective artisans in the production and use of diverse goods and services, to participate in taking collective decisions and pursuing joint opportunities with others, and to constitute systems of governance where those who exercise the prerogatives of government can be held accountable to the specifiable terms and conditions of a public trust, we should have a level of understanding sufficient to avoid becoming the victims of diabolical machines of our own making. Unfortunately, it is the vision of models of nirvana that serves to lead human beings to suppose an omniscience and omnicompetence that no one can realize. The most we can do is to act on the basis of choice in the light of discussion, reflection, and experience. Each of us needs access to diverse capabilities and to the opportunities afforded by diverse structures of relationships in our contemporary circumstance. Unfortunately, we can take advantage of and maintain those opportunities only when we learn how to do so.

Lord Bauer's workers and peasants, then, would need to know more than the prices that are available in markets. They would also need to know, as Tocqueville has suggested, the science and art of association to secure the many joint advantages that come both from working together in diverse types of joint enterprises, and from constituting systems of government where no one exercises unlimited authority, and where all officials can be held to account for the proper discharge of their public trust. Each individual would then be a knowledgeable actor in a self-governing society where opportunity is a function of organizational diversity and complexity.

A science and art of association that is appropriate both for understanding the nature and constitution of order in human society, and for engaging in those forms of association that are constitutive of mutually productive relationships, is the foundation for choice among the alternatives that are available. Since human beings, who are capable of innovation, cannot know what the future holds, there is an advantage to be gained by exploring diverse possibilities. Whether human beings can use methods of discussion, reflection, and choice to fashion the future course of human civilization remains to be determined. That civilization will be the richer as it becomes more diverse and more complex, provided that we strive to be cognizant of the basic "similitude" of thoughts, passions, and circumstances that characterizes all of mankind (Hobbes, [1651] 1960: 6).

Works Cited

Bauer, P. T. (1984) *Realities and Rhetoric*. Cambridge, Mass.: Harvard University Press.

Copeland, Miles (1969) *The Game of Nations*. London: Weidenfeld and Nicolson.

Feeny, David (1984) "The Development of Property Rights in Land: A Comparative Study." Center Discussion Paper no. 459, Economic Growth Center, Yale University.

Hensel, K. Paul (1974) *Grundformen der Wirtschaftsordnung.* Munich: Beck.

Hobbes, Thomas (1960) *Leviathan or the Matter, Forme and Power of a Commonwealth Ecclesiasticall and Civill.* Michael Oakeshott, ed. Oxford: Blackwell. First published in 1651.

Kaufmann, Franz-Xaver, Giandomenico Majone, and Vincent Ostrom, eds. (1986) *Guidance, Control, and Evaluation in the Public Sector.* Berlin and New York: de Gruyter.

Ostrom, Vincent (1953) *Water and Politics.* Los Angeles: The Haynes Foundation.

——— (1971) *Institutional Arrangements for Water Resource Development.* Springfield, Va.: National Technical Information Service.

——— (1987) *The Political Theory of a Compound Republic: Designing the American Experiment.* Rev. ed. Lincoln: University of Nebraska Press.

——— (forthcoming, 1988) "Some Developments in the Study of Market Choice, Public Choice, and Institutional Choice." In Jack Rabin, Gerald Miller, and W. Bartley Hildreth, eds., *Handbook on Public Administration.* New York: Dekker.

Picht, Hartmut (1985) "Monetary Arrangements for Economic Development." Paper prepared for Conference on Institutional Analysis and Development, sponsored by the U.S. Agency for International Development, Washington, D.C., May 21–22.

Polanyi, Karl (1957) *The Great Transformation.* Boston: Beacon Press.

Smith, Adam (1937) *An Inquiry into the Nature and Causes of the Wealth of Nations.* New York: Modern Library. First published in 1776.

Tocqueville, Alexis de (1945) *Democracy in America.* Phillips Bradley, ed. New York: Knopf. First published in 1840.

14

Hartmut Picht

Currency Competition: A Constitutional Perspective

Introduction

Since Benjamin Klein (1974) and Friedrich A. von Hayek (1976) raised the issue of a free market for currencies or currency competition, numerous articles and books have been published on the subject. Currency competition was seen by its original proponents as a radical alternative to current monetary regimes, which had brought about high rates of inflation and uncertainty, and as a consequence unemployment of labor and capital. It was thought that the alternative of a free market for currencies, in contrast, would preclude inflationary public finance, that is, the widespread practice of governments to turn to the money printing press in order to finance large public deficits notwithstanding the inflationary consequences. It would also guarantee that the money supply was out of reach of strong interest groups and central bank bureaucracies that stood to gain from monetary discretion (Wagner, 1984; Kane, 1980; Chant and Acheson, 1972).

The reaction to the proposal was mixed. Those who have argued strongly in favor of currency competition apparently conceived it more as a strategic device to constrain central bank bureaucrats and monetary politicians in an otherwise unaltered institutional setting (see, for example, Vaubel, 1984: 31; Brown, 1985: 27). Some qualifications were made even by its strongest proponents, since theoretical analysis and empirical evidence suggested that a free choice among currencies might not be viable in the long run because these were strong external economies (advantages) in the use of only one currency. In this view the time spent converging to the monopoly, however, might not be regarded as a wasteful aspect of competition since governments would not be in a position to know what the market process would have selected as most suitable (see, for example, White, 1983: 292–293).

Others have expressed concern that is quite inconsistent with currency competition as envisaged above. Milton Friedman (1962, 1984), for instance, has argued that any attempt to target the value of a currency by managing the money supply as implied by currency competition may cause severe macroeconomic instabilities, that is, cycles of boom and bust. He has made a case, therefore, for stabilizing monetary stabilization policies by implementing a firm money supply growth rule. Leland B. Yeager (1984: 104) has even talked about the absurdity of making the unit of account the supply-and-demand-determined value of the unit of the medium of exchange. Accordingly, he favors the so-called BFH system of monetary order in which the monetary unit would be defined by a government just as units of weight and measures are determined, and where no homogenous medium of exchange would exist as rival unit.[1] Still others consider monetary regimes based on irredeemable and exclusively paper monies to be inherently unstable from lack of confidence in the money suppliers—a danger that has even puzzled Klein, who opened the discussion on currency competition (Klein and Leffler, 1981: 624). Consequently some have argued that any viable monetary system, in order to bring about monetary stability and growth, would most likely be built upon money redeemable in a scarce commodity like gold (see, for example, Paul and Lehrman, 1982: 153; White, 1983: 293–295).

The institutional implications of the objections presented differ substantially from currency competition, but all suggestions have in common that the scope for governmental interference would be drastically reduced in comparison to existing arrangements. In all such cases monetary policy has been raised from the day-to-day level of decision making to the constitutional level, where the rules of the game are set. However, the market setting for currencies has been considered as the ultimate response to the historical experience of governmental abuse of monetary prerogatives, since seemingly no particular institutional provisions are necessary for the system to work (Brown, 1982: 35).

In this chapter an attempt is made to assess the attributes of a market for currencies as an apparently attractive system of monetary order. The focus is on competition among for-profit money suppliers, not on currency competition as a strategic device to constrain monetary policy makers in otherwise unaltered circumstances. The basic argument is that a successful implementation of currency competition as a system of order is largely dependent upon appropriate legal, administrative, and judicial provisions. In other words, the rules envisaged are seen as facilities supporting the market rather than as something opposed to its performance.[2] However, whether currency competition should actually be aimed at is an open question, since the risk of an uncontested monopoly as result of the competitive process is latent. In addition, it is pointed out that the costs of setting up the appropriate framework for currency competition at the international level in terms of time and effort may be quite high. For comparison, an alternative institutional arrangement, with attributes quite similar to currency competition, is advanced in the final section. The alternative avoids the latent risk of an uncontested monopoly that is associated with currency competition. It can even be incorporated without any international cooperation, but it involves in turn a number of other disadvantages. Apparently choice exists only among imperfect monetary regimes. Space limitations require that the critique of the BFH system and the commodity gold standard is largely left implicit in what follows.[3]

From Monetary Functions to Monetary Services

It is a well-established practice to introduce students to the world of money by referring to the functions money performs in an economy: money serves (first) as a store of value that is distinct from other assets in that it serves also (second) as a medium of exchange in numerous transactions, and in that the value of the unit of the medium of exchange is (third) the unit in which prices are quoted and debts and terms of other contracts are expressed (that is, the unit of account).

In history primitive monetary systems have emerged quite spontaneously on the basis of commodity monies, as the Austrian economist Carl Menger ([1892] 1984) convincingly argued at the end of the last century. Anthropologists as well as economists well read in history tell us that the productive usefulness of a good, or its capacity to satisfy directly human needs, or a combination of both, was regarded as a pledge for the functional usefulness of a good as money (Einzig, 1949: 140; Schneider, 1974: 172). Once established in this function, the intrinsic value of the good moved to the background without losing its function. The objects chosen for money were generally scarce, and showed attributes of physical durability, divisibility, and uniformity (Tucker, [1839] 1964: 6–10).

Apparently, however, there was something wrong with commodity monies: the intrinsic values of the objects chosen for money suffered from unpredictable changes in both aggregate supply and demand for those objects. In the process of cultural evolution, some crude procedures were developed to cope with these problems.[4] Yet central political powers have increasingly been substituted almost everywhere as the safeguarding device.[5] While governmental authority has often been abused, there are substantial benefits to be gained by shifting from a commodity standard toward a fiduciary one: productive efforts may directly be applied toward, first, servicing actors with stores of value that are free from arbitrary timely erosion; second, offering media as means of payment whose degree of acceptability is promoted to a varying degree; and third, supplying units of account whose real value does not impair economic calculation by excessive fluctuation (variance) and promoting their spread.

In addition, substituting paper monies for commodity monies has meant that scarce commodities like precious metal can be used for other purposes. Thus, a social saving of resources is associated with paper monies. However, in a free market setting investments in brand-name capital are necessary to establish confidence in the money supplier. They may take the form of sunk investments in the design of a firm logo and notably expensive promoting of the owner's reputation in general. In the case of cheating, the present value of the fall in the pecuniary returns depending on the reputation of an owner presumably active in other businesses needs to be higher than the extraordinary gains from choosing this option.[6] Such collaterals also function as constraints for the real volumes of the media of exchange issued. All efforts directed toward supplying the services described above stand, of course, for production costs.

In what follows the first category of services is combined with the third one because the activity of containing the uncertainty (variance) that results from fluctuations requires a reference to some expected mean value of the unit of account, which is—inter alia—the unit of the medium of exchange. The output is called "unit-of-account stabilization services." The second category is referred to as "payment" or "liquidity services." Unit-of-account stabilization services and liquidity services, taken together, are called "monetary services."

Jointness of Use and Feasibility of Exclusion

One standard approach to answering the question whether goods and services can be supplied in a market setting goes back to Paul A. Samuelson (1954). Jointness (nonrivalry or nonsubtractability) of use and feasibility of exclusion are advanced as two essential defining characteristics in distinguishing between private and public goods and services.

Exclusion has long been identified as a necessary, though not necessarily sufficient, characteristic for goods and services to be supplied under market conditions. Where use or consumption cannot be made contingent on the payment of a price, market competition is bound to fail. The other attribute of goods pertains to jointness of use. When no jointness of use applies, the use or consumption by one individual precludes its use or consumption by another individual. In turn, jointness of use implies that the use or enjoyment of a good or service by one individual does not foreclose its use or enjoyment by others; despite its use by one individual, the good or service remains available for use by others in undiminished quantity and quality (V. Ostrom and E. Ostrom, 1977: 11).

Only a few goods and services fit into the polar cases of feasible exclusion and nonjointness of use, on the one hand, and nonfeasible exclusion and jointness of use, on the other. In the extreme the attributes define pure private goods and pure public goods, respectively. Where exclusion is feasible and jointness of use applies, one talks about "toll goods," and where exclusion is infeasible and use is rivalrous, about "common-pool resources." Market competition as a system of order can be used to deliver either private goods or toll goods, where exclusion is feasible. Special problems arise where the conduct of one user may either detract from or add to the enjoyment of other users.

The question to be answered is: How do monetary services—that is, liquidity services and unit-of-account stabilization services—fit into the attributes of the goods and services scheme, and what are the institutional implications that can be drawn? Liquidity services seem to be characterized as private goods (White, 1983: 291–292). The standard argument goes as follows. "As long as one person holds a unit of money and benefits from its 'liquidity service,' nobody else can own it and benefit from it. If he gives it away, he increases his own risk of temporarily running out of cash. Therefore, he will ask for a quid pro quo—a good, service or some other asset" (Vaubel, 1984: 29). This interpretation misses the crucial point that one needs to slip into the position of a potential supplier of liquidity services. First, the liquidity characteristic refers to the degree of acceptability of a medium of exchange (Yeager, 1968: 67). The extent of acceptability granted to any one holder of one unit of a medium of exchange does also apply to any other person holding one unit at the same time. In other words, the use or consumption of this service is joint or nonrivalrous. Second, by choice of different quantities of a medium of exchange, individuals simply express to what extent they want to use the "network" provided, that is, they reveal preference intensities. But it is true that use or consumption of liquidity services is contingent on exchanging something in return for an amount of units of exchange (in other words, exclusion is feasible). Liquidity services, thus, fit into the category of toll goods rather than private goods. The irritation about the classification of the medium of exchange as a private good seems to stem from the circumstance that for the monetary asset the attributes of exclusion and rivalry apply—though financial assets are not produced like goods—while the characteristic liquidity service produced has the attribute of jointness of use. The toll-good character of a liquidity service reflects the condition that the enjoyment of the nonrivalrous liquidity service is contingent on holding an appropriate asset.

In absence of further complications, one basic requirement for the use of market competition is thus met. It is interesting to note that, in order to keep the value of a unit of a medium of exchange at a predetermined level (which is a matter referred to as a unit-of-account stabilization service), a potential supplier necessarily must service an additional customer. In other words, although he may charge him a price, he cannot foreclose the services, everything else being equal. This interpretation, of course, is equivalent to saying that a potential supplier needs to act in order to avoid price-level externalities (Friedman, 1969: 15; Kolm, 1972: 191–206).

The characterization of unit-of-account stabilization services has in part been subject to confusion as well (Vaubel, 1984: 29). Charles P. Kindleberger (1972: 434) and Leland B. Yeager (1983: 321) are correct in classifying this service type as a public good, at least in the current legal context. According to the definition advanced above, unit-of-account stabilization services refer to a production activity that is directed toward stabilizing the real value of the unit of account at a targeted level, toward keeping the variance (uncertainty) within limits, and toward inducing others toward using the very same unit. The enjoyment of this service indicated by using a unit in calculating an offer is not impaired if any other individual is using the unit in his calculations. Thus, the attribute of joint consumption prevails. At the same time, for a potential supplier it is, under current legal conditions, impossible to make use or enjoyment of the service contingent upon the payment of a price. The service investigated thus displays the attributes of a public good. In the absence of further considerations, it cannot be expected that private suppliers will offer the services in a market setting, since exclusion currently lacks a legal basis.

The conclusion to be drawn from the analysis presented so far is that market competition as a system of order is potentially applicable to the provision of liquidity services, but not to the provision of unit-of-account stabilization services.

Joint Supply and Synthetic Joint Use of Monetary Services

Apparently, special circumstances prevail in the current case because the services cannot be supplied independently of one another: the unit of account is the supply-and-demand-determined value of the unit of the medium of exchange. Both services are jointly made available to potential users; thus a case of joint supply prevails. In contrast to the classic Marshallian joint supply theory, however, the services do not meet the standard attributes of private goods and services, viz, exclusion and nonjointness in use.

The joint supply characteristic does not preclude the use of market competition for the provision of these services because the public unit-of-account stabilization service can be considered as a by-product of the liquidity service where exclusion is feasible. In present legal circumstances, the cost burden for the public unit-of-account service could be carried by the user of liquidity services. Before further conclusions can be drawn from the joint supply characteristic, however, a careful look at the demand side is necessary.

Theoretically and practically, the use or enjoyment of one service can be separated from the use and enjoyment of the other service. In other words, there is no apparent reason to assume that the unit of the medium of exchange used is necessarily used as a unit in which the sale prices are quoted, or in which debt and terms of other contracts are expressed. It may be conjectured, however, that there are to some extent gains for an individual, if the unit of the medium of exchange is also the principal unit of account (an example of economies-of-scope in use). Economically this pattern translates into synthetic joint use.[7] How large the advantages are nobody can say, but historically the joint-use pattern broke down in hyperinflationary settings even in the presence of massive governmental sanctions. The increasing substitution of the European Currency Unit (ECU) as the unit of account for units of national media of exchange, intended to denominate debts and claims in the international financial markets, is another indication of the fragile character of the joint-use pattern.[8] In a situation of free choice, the decision made with respect to joint or nonjoint use depends upon differences in the attributes of the services as supplied in the market, and the price to be paid upon the occasion of the use of liquidity services.

Suppose there are various suppliers in the market. One supplier, A, is assumed to raise the quality of the unit-of-account stabilization service; for example, he may offer one with a particularly low variance, but stay in line with other competitors, B, with respect to liquidity services. It may now become attractive for former customers of B to increase the demand for unit-of-account stabilization services supplied by A that are nonrivalrous in nature. In other words, the individual customers may at some juncture deliberately choose to give up the joint-use or consumption pattern.

Suppose further that the costs for the use of unit-of-account stabilization services—fixed with respect to the number of customers, but variable with regard to their attributes—are assigned on a per unit and time basis upon the occasion of the use of liquidity services as expressed by holding varying amounts of units of the medium of exchange (benefit pricing). For the moment, let us accept the implicit assumption that the holdings of different quantities of units of the medium of exchange are a suitable proxy of the preference intensity for unit-of-account stabilization services. In the standard case the supply level is expanded up to the level where the sum of marginal revenues equals the marginal costs of the service in question. In the scenario above, however, the consequence is that there is an additional demand for excellent unit-of-account stabilization services, but this demand is not directly translated into effective demand. Similarly, the withdrawal of demand from the use of unit-of-account stabilization services supplied by the competitors, B, does not translate into direct pecuniary consequences. In other words, no direct mechanism exists that rewards good and penalizes poor performance with respect to unit-of-account stabilization services to the extent that the joint-use pattern breaks down.

The conclusion to be drawn from this analysis is that, as long as no provisions are made to allow for charging a price for the use or enjoyment of unit-of-account stabilization services separately from the use or enjoyment of liquidity services, the functioning of market competition will depend upon the strength of the joint-use pattern. If the joint-use pattern breaks down, then there will be an undersupply of superior unit-of-account stabilization services, and an oversupply of inferior ones. While the joint-supply pattern is a technical characteristic, the joint-use pattern depends largely upon differentials in quality or quantity characteristics of the services supplied, as well as the charges. These are outcomes of the competitive process that cannot be known in advance. Thus an additional element of uncertainty exists about the properties of currency competition. A related inefficiency will be discussed below, in the section on the pricing pattern for cash media of exchange.

Economies-of-Scale External and Internal to Producers

We saw in the opening section of this chapter that complications may arise for the adoption of market competition as a system of order if economies-of-scale prevail. In the present case it is useful to distinguish between economies-of-scale that are external to a prospective supplier and those that are internal.

One of the most characteristic attributes of the subject investigated here is that transaction-cost externalities exist with respect to the use of media of exchange as well as to the use of units of account. The relationship may be expressed as follows: The more persons accept a medium of exchange, the higher is the liquidity characteristic, that is, the lower are the transaction costs one incurs as user in

Currency Competition: A Constitutional Perspective 417

completing transactions (Vaubel, 1984: 31–41). Transaction costs may take the form of time, trouble, or money.

The same applies to using unit-of-account services: The more frequently the same services are used by trading partners and competitors, the lower the transaction costs are. The spread of practice facilitates its further spread (Yeager, 1983: 314). By definition, transaction costs are lowest if only one medium of exchange is used, and if the unit of the sole medium of exchange is used as the unit of account.

But there are also economies-of-scale that are internal to prospective firms. A significant part of the productive effort of a supplier is directed toward promoting the spread of both the services supplied. As people have to be persuaded to use the services, the costs may be assumed to vary with the degree of competition. If there is no direct competitor, then the expenses incurred for that matter are lowest. They may not be zero, however, as long as parts of the economy are not monetized, or might fall back into barter, and as long as there is latent competition.

In addition, it is hard to assess whether there exists a permanently downward-sloping supply (decreasing cost) curve for performing payment functions on behalf of customers holding units of the medium of exchange in the form of checking accounts. However, the public-goods nature of unit-of-account stabilization services, notably the jointness-of-use attribute, is a clear indication that this service category displays substantial economies-of-scale. In absence of congestion effects (rather, the opposite holds in this case as indicated above), it is always advantageous to have one supplier servicing all customers. The threat of an emerging natural monopoly is thus reinforced by the finding that unit-of-account stabilization services have the attribute of jointness of use.

Further, it has already been mentioned that investments in sunk brand-name capital are necessary in order to grant confidence in the suppliers of paper money in a market setting. The general reputation of an owner has to some extent the character of an external collateral. The magnitude required in this particular case to beat cheating as an option may be assumed to be so high that, realistically, only large conglomerates may enter the market. Consequently, the barriers to entry will be quite high but, more important, as reputation capital is always limited, the size of the firm supplying monetary services in terms of real money balances outstanding will be limited as well. Rationing and related consequences might become possible at least in the short run.

A qualification, however, is necessary in talking about cost advantages with respect to monetary services. The implicit assumption made is that the services looked at are largely homogenous. This assumption is very restrictive. For example, as long as consumption and production plans among individuals differ substantially, one may not expect that the unit-of-account definitions, in terms of bundles of goods and services, used as a reference in the production of unit-of-account services, are equivalent (see, for instance, Brown, 1982: 29).

One may also envisage that there is a spatial dimension to the preferred spread of the services, since it is not only the number of persons per se that determines transaction costs but the standing the persons have with respect to the volume and frequency of transactions. Economies of density are an important aspect in the literature of optimal currency domains (Vaubel, 1977: 456–458). A similar differentiation may emerge along functional lines, that is, with respect to different purposes.

The usefulness of a unit of account and a medium of exchange is also a matter of learning: the more often it is used, the larger is the advantage related to its use (Brunner and Meltzer, 1971: 786). Another example of differentiation is the quantity or quality of the unit-of-account stabilization service as it pertains to the chosen level of price variability.

In essence, these qualifications mean that different forces are present that work against homogenization of the services offered. No one can translate these tendencies into opposing cost trends where costs would have to be conceived as opportunity costs. What one can probably expect is that there is no room for lasting competition among suppliers with largely identical services. The economies-of-scale internal to a supplier, in particular those associated with unit-of-account stabilization services, and those external to a supplier,

Currency Competition: A Constitutional Perspective

that is, transaction cost externalities, suggest that at best monopolistic competition will emerge. While in this case a supplier will have only a limited range for discretion, the worst outcome from the point of view of a customer would be a natural monopoly that is uncontested. The analysis presented has reinforced that this outcome cannot be precluded.

Pricing Pattern in the Case of Cash Media of Exchange

Another problem is that related to offering cash media for the discharge of liquidity functions. The use of cash—notes and coins—is preferred in some types of transactions, while deposits are preferred in others. For monetary stores of value, as well as for other assets functioning as stores of value, the payment of an interest rate can be expected. The interest rate being paid on a unit of a medium of exchange held may be assumed to be lower than the one paid on near-monies, or on nonmonetary assets, because the production of liquidity characteristics affords additional efforts. The costs may be so high that no interest rate is paid, or even that one is charged.

The likelihood of low interest rates being paid, or even of negative interest rates being charged on holdings of units of a medium of exchange, rises, as has been shown above, if the price for producing unit-of-account stabilization services is charged, on the occasion of holding units of the medium of exchange (and hence of enjoying liquidity services). One unfortunate aspect of this charging pattern is that the market for investable funds is distorted, because the enjoyment of unit-of-account stabilization services is something that is foreign to that market. The specific problem now with cash media of exchange is that the charge for the use of liquidity services (with unit-of-account stabilization services) cannot be levied directly as the difference between the interest rate being earned from holding the nonmonetary asset (which was acquired in return for issuing a certain amount of units of the medium of exchange), and the interest rate being paid to the holders of this amount of units of the medium of exchange. This is because paying an interest rate on cash media of exchange is difficult to arrange. Instead, for a supplier issuing notes and coins, a relatively convenient way of solving the charging problem is to deflate (or inflate) the real value of the unit of the medium of exchange that serves as a unit of account. The nominal interest rate paid to customers per unit and time of holding a nonmonetary asset, which will be equal to the sum of the real rate of return and the rate of change of the price level calculated in terms of the unit of account, will adjust to the actual rate of appreciation or depreciation of the unit of account. The nominal interest rate is an expression of the opportunity costs of holding units of the medium of exchange, or the price actually paid for the enjoyment of related services.

Whether an inflation rate or a deflation rate is chosen depends on the market situation. Suppose that the supplier is operating in a highly competitive environment where homogenous services are supplied (a situation that is considered to be nonviable in the long run because of economies-of-scale). The charge he takes depends not upon his discretion but solely upon the market. Consequently, the market would generate either uniform inflation or deflation rates, depending on the real rate of interest and the costs. In the absence of any costs, the outcome would correspond to Milton Friedman's (1969) argument that the optimal quantity of money is held when the deflation rate equals the real rate of return. If costs are positive, then the rate of deflation (inflation) is lower (higher). This outcome of competition is not consistent with the prediction of proponents of currency competition that a constant real value for the unit of the medium of exchange and, inter alia, the unit of account would result. If monopolistic competition prevails, instead, the magnitudes may differ (the charges may follow the limit pricing strategy), but the basic problem remains as long as cash monies are in use.

Some indirect incentives are provided not to overtax the issue, however. First, the rate of depreciation or appreciation of the unit of account, even if it is perfectly anticipated, may involve so-called shoe-leather costs (periodical changes of price tags, etc.), which reduce the attractiveness of the unit of the medium of exchange as a unit of account. An incentive is set, then, to deviate from marginal (benefit) cost pricing. For a supplier a propensity exists to prefer (discriminate against) other media of exchange (deposits) relative to cash media, depending on whether the actual marginal costs per unit and time with respect to cash media would have been higher (lower) than the interest rate earned from holding the nonmonetary asset acquired in return. Accordingly, instrumentalizing the rate at which the value of the unit of account is changing would not be very efficient for charging purposes, since the pricing pattern may lead to deviations from the optimal pricing rule, and subsequently to distortions. Second, any decision to select an inflationary or deflationary time pattern for the real value of the unit of account implies an uncertainty with respect to the use of this unit, since changing demand and supply (cost) conditions translate directly into shifts in this time pattern. Information has to be gathered and processed, which is costly (displacement-information costs), and errors are possible.

Only a firm commitment towards price level stability would avoid these problems. No shoe-leather costs and no displacement-information costs would exist, but distortions might result in the way just described. Note, however, that the term "optimal pricing" is somewhat ambiguous in this context, since the presence of shoe-leather costs and information costs indicates that the conditions for the application for standard pricing concepts for private and public goods are not met. The open question then is whether these costs would properly be internalized in a free market setting. No definite answer can be given.

Thus, given that there are certain advantages in using cash media of exchange rather than other media for which charging problems do not arise, a cynical observer might think primarily about discharging payments in the hidden or shadow economy. The use of competition as a system of order displays another unfortunate aspect that adds to the concerns already expressed.

Production Externalities with Respect to Unit-of-Account Stabilization Services

In the preceding analysis it has, for the sake of simplicity, been taken for granted that the value of the unit of account is stabilized by controlling the supply of units of the medium of exchange in relation to the demand for it. Unfortunately, the production of this service exhibits substantial negative external effects upon the market system as a whole.

The market for money is just a figure of speech, not a reality (Yeager, 1984: 104). Money is traded in all markets and has no specific market of its own. Just because money has no single price of its own to come under specific pressure if demand and supply imbalances arise, so monetary disequilibrium gets corrected only in a roundabout and often painful way. The question is not only what determines how much of the monetary asset people demand to hold, but in what way people go about giving effect to their demands.

An illustration of how monetary disorder may come about—for example, in the case of excess demand for units of the medium of exchange—may be helpful.

> [L]et us suppose that all prices are 'right' relative to each other but are 'too high,' in the same proportion, relative to the quantity of money. Everybody is willing to exchange his goods for other people's goods at the ratios implied by their existing money prices. Yet shortage of the medium of exchange interferes. Since people have been trying to build up their cash balances, they initially are failing to spend all the money received by selling their goods and labor. And since others are doing the same, the typical economic unit has trouble earning income. The depression of income is what chokes off the demand for cash balances below what it would be at full employment. (Yeager, 1968: 65)

Excess supply of the medium of exchange tends to remove itself in the very same distinctive and unpleasant way. Suppose the excess is brought about by the creation of new money. Then,

> the newly created money resides initially with those who create it. As these people spend this money, those who receive it will in turn find an excess demand for their products and services. This excess demand

leads to rising prices for these products and services. Eventually, the newly created money will become diffused throughout the economy, and the general level of prices will be higher than it was before the money creation. What is of importance, however, is that there is a temporal sequence to the receipt of the new money, and that the initial recipients are favored over those who occupy later positions in the chain of transactions. (Wagner, 1984: 251)

One may now recall again that aiming at a specific predetermined value of the unit of account means adjusting the money supply in just such a way that monetary equilibrium is brought about at the predetermined price level or trend. As adjustment takes place in a roundabout process that no one can predict, pervasive damage occurs to the market's performance in allocating resources efficiently: price changes are misunderstood as signaling changes in real scarcities, resources are put to wrong or no use, and erroneous junking of capital may occur. In other words, "noise" is introduced into the market.

There is nothing one can do with respect to the so-called non-neutrality of money. What one can do, however, is to keep the harmful effects within limits. In a competitive market setting, where suppliers are competing with respect to the degree of uncertainty (variance) of the unit of account offered, it may be assumed that it is just those suppliers who engage in sophisticated fine-tuning (stop-and-go), in order to keep the variations of the value of their unit of account within narrow limits, who do most damage to the functioning of the market. In other words, the extent of "noise" introduced into the market may be assumed to correlate positively with the performance in the market for unit-of-account stabilization purposes. Hence, if competition among rival suppliers leads to lower variances in the units of accounts, then it may also be assumed to lead to more damage to the market's ability to allocate resources efficiently. While the outcome on the one hand is highly welcomed by market participants, it would on the other hand create more rather than less damage to the market mechanism. Stabilizing the money's value itself destabilizes microeconomic relationships (O'Driscoll, 1983: 328).

Further, Friedrich A. von Hayek (1984) himself has implicitly made a strong case against currency competition recently. The argument goes as follows. Productivity tends to increase everywhere: in some industries the advances may be lower, in others they may be higher. On average, determined by supply and demand elasticities in both the goods and the factor markets, productivity increases will result in a general decline of some aggregate of all prices for goods and services. In order to secure a constant price level (constant value of the unit of account), the supplier of a medium of exchange needs temporarily to create an excess money supply. Monetary equilibrium is attained by the sluggish and painful process of adjustment in the markets for goods and services as described above. The argument now is that the external costs of producing unit-of-account stabilization services may be assumed to be lower, if the reference value for the unit of account in terms of a bundle of goods and services would rise (or the price index would fall) over time, according to the average effect of productivity advances on the prices for goods and services (Hayek, 1984: 34).

If monetary services are provided in a competitive market setting, then, as has been shown earlier, the rate of change in the value of the unit of account will be determined by other considerations. That is, no mechanism exists that would lead producers to account for the damages they may do to the functioning of the market system by the choice of a certain time pattern for the value of the unit of account.

Constitutional Implications for Currency Competition

The previous analysis suggests that there are serious doubts as to whether currency competition unsupported by institutional arrangements would help to bring about monetary stability and economic prosperity. One major result of this analysis is that monetary services would be misspecified if they were considered as private goods. Liquidity services display features of toll goods, while unit-of-account stabilization services have the attributes of public goods. Further, various externality problems exist. Several implications may be drawn.

First, as with all services that display the attribute of jointness in use or consumption, and where congestion is absent, a monopoly supply advantage exists in the present case. The traditional argument that a natural monopoly may arise because of transaction-cost advantages in the use of money has thus been reinforced. Risk considerations with respect to cheating set limits to the firm size, but these limits may not be unalterable. The threat of an emerging monopoly remains latent.

Second, the charging technique used with respect to unit-of-account stabilization services gives rise to serious inefficiencies. The supply of high-quality (low-variance) services may be expected to be too low (the quality should be higher), while the supply level of low-quality (high-variance) services would be too high (the quality should be lower). The inefficiencies arise when the joint-use pattern of liquidity services and unit-of-account stabilization services breaks down. This unattractive outcome can be avoided, if appropriate provisions are made that allow separate charging for the use of unit-of-account stabilization services independent of the use or enjoyment of liquidity services.

One way of solving the problem would be to draw upon information gathered already by the general tax revenue services on the denomination of incomes. These figures could be used as a proxy for the actual use of the unit of account, and hence for the use pattern of unit-of-account stabilization services. In addition, referring to one's relative income position with respect to others, and to the denomination of incomes in various units of account, may anyway be a more appropriate basis for measuring the actual use pattern of the unit-of-account stabilization services. In the light of given information-processing technologies, the costs of charging for the use of unit-of-account services may actually be low. From a legal point of view, the actual use of a unit of account needs to imply a legal right to claim the payment of a user charge on the part of a supplier, because only then an ordinary judicial process can be used to enforce payment.

Third, a major problem is posed by the use of the particular pricing pattern pertaining to cash media of exchange. It has been argued in this chapter that various inefficiencies may be expected to arise. In a competitive context as envisaged by proponents of currency competition, it must be expected that suppliers adopt the least costly charging techniques, no matter what the costs external to them are. As long as the indirect mode of charging by changing the value of the unit of account over time is less costly than any alternative with comparable characteristics in use, it will be applied. However, electronic media of exchange (so-called chip monies) are likely to gradually substitute for notes and coins, while having similar advantages. The likely result of this development is that the distortions resulting from the charging technique for cash media are reduced over time.

But avoiding shoe-leather and displacement-information costs has not been the sole concern with respect to the reference value chosen for the unit of account. As Hayek has argued, in order to avoid "noise" in the market, it may be advisable to stabilize the value of a unit of account at some rising trend (or falling price index) determined by the average impact of productivity increases on output prices. The impediment to the functioning of the market mechanism by stabilizing the value of the unit of account accordingly is considered to be lower than in any other case. How can a supplier be induced to internalize these costs? The only way out that can be seen is to prescribe some standard, or to prescribe some rule for choosing a standard. However, if one were to prescribe the latter, much of what has made currency competition an interesting subject over the course of the last decade, that is, its potential for fighting inflation and related adverse consequences, would then be made exempt from competition. But still, competition can evolve with respect to all other attributes of monetary services and with respect to prices.

Fourth, one of the features that still is subject to competition is the uncertainty problem involved in using a unit of account. If the conjecture is correct that currency competition would in this respect lead to a more predictable unit of account, and if it is correct that the production of this attribute of a unit of account requires more sophisticated operations, or stop-and-go, in the market for all goods and services, then currency competition must be equated with more "noise." No way is seen to internalize these costs. In order to limit "noise," one would have to restrict competition with respect to unit-of-account stabilization services.

While in principle, at least as long as the rules apply equally to all competitors, the market may nevertheless evolve in this tight rule-setting designed to cope with the major shortcomings of unsupported market competition, the question arises whether supported currency competition can serve normative purposes. An answer is attempted in the final section in the light of an alternative arrangement.

Currency Competition in the Light of Alternative Options

The conclusion drawn from the preceding analysis has been that currency competition needs to be supported by a set of legal, administrative, and judicial provisions in order to display quite attractive attributes irrespective of the risk of an uncontested monopoly. Severe additional problems arise, however, with respect to the implementation of currency competition as a quite complex system of monetary order. It would work only in a worldwide or at least a regional context involving a number of interdependent economies. In any case, latent competition needs to be present in order to constrain private suppliers of monetary services. The problem for a country wishing to introduce market competition is that the rules designed to supplement the market mechanism need to apply to all competitors. Competition from third countries may constrain the monetary discretion of a monopoly supplier, or a cartel of a few suppliers if this is the market outcome; but in the absence of equal treatment in the national (or regional) domain, the supplementary rules may become meaningless, since an external competitor to whom the rules do not apply may simply drive the national (regional) one(s) out of the market. Further cooperation with third parties would thus be required, but cooperation in the international setting poses difficulties. The costs in terms of time and efforts of setting up an appropriate framework for competition are high. They may even outweigh the potential benefits of currency competition as a system of order.

It would be inappropriate, however, to compare currency competition with some fictitious ideal standard that meets all demands. Probably such an arrangement does not exist.[9] A quite attractive alternative can instead been used for comparison. The alternative consists of two parts.

First, the option advanced as an alternative to currency competition is in part a variant of the well-known money supply growth rule proposed by Milton Friedman: The domestic money supply could be required to grow at an annual rate that allows for a secular fall in the price level according to the expected aggregate impact of productivity advances on output prices. The annual growth rate or the procedure for setting the growth rate target would have to be fixed at the constitutional level so that no range existed for central bankers' discretion with respect to interest group pressures and own interests. As a direct consequence, the degree of predictability of the value of the unit in which the domestic medium of exchange is quoted would certainly increase, though probably not as much as in the case of currency competition. But, in turn, the distortions in the market due to the nonneutrality of the money supply would at least be kept within narrow limits. At the same time the proposal would make it impossible for governments to misuse the money printing press to finance excessive public deficits, that is, to resort to inflationary public finance. No international cooperation would be required to install the arrangement.

On the cost side of this proposal, one has to recognize that the quantity of liquidity services supplied may be inefficient through disregard of any pricing rules. Further, the transaction domain for the currency in question may well be suboptimal, although one cannot know in advance, that is, without a trial, what the optimal transaction domain is. Also, cost- or X-inefficiencies (Leibenstein, 1966) may arise in particular in the absence of effective market pressures because the government would have to monitor central bank activities instead. The government would, furthermore, be the residual claimant if the revenues earned were larger than the costs, and it would have to cover current deficits in the reverse case. However, no specific investments in sunk capital are required in this setting, since the bank remains public and no rival medium of exchange exists.

Second, the institutional option advanced for comparison also acknowledges that there may be an interest in a variety of differently specified and stable units of account. Why should it not be possible, at least in the national domain, to establish property rights in the use of unit-of-account indices by granting judicial standing to contractual arrangements only if a price has been paid? A potential supplier would direct his productive effort primarily toward defining and updating the index offered, measuring and reporting its development over time, and promoting its spread. In this case the conditions for a private market in appropriate indices are established, since exclusion from the benefits would be feasible. People would be free to select the most appropriate standard in terms of varying bundles of goods and services just as in the case of currency competition. The main difference from currency competition would be that the actual payments would still be made in the principal medium of exchange, whose value would be determined by the monetary growth rule proposed above. Economic actors would consequently have the choice of divorcing the unit-of-account function from the payments function, but they could also choose to denominate calculations and contracts in terms of the unit of the principal medium of exchange. Yet the use of indices rather than units of account with preannounced values would involve additional transaction costs in so far as calculations were necessary to determine the amount of units of the medium of exchange required, for instance, to settle debts. On the other hand, the uncertainties associated with the use of units of account, whose values are the supply-and-demand determined values of circulating media of exchange, would be avoided.

One can easily see that the alternative sketched above avoids both the latent risk of an uncontested monopoly and high international setup costs associated with currency competition while having features quite similar to it. But unfortunately the advantages do not come about without costs; the list of inefficiencies is quite long. In fact, no one can say which arrangement should be aimed at except the human beings who are affected by it. All monetary institutions need to be subject to continuing critical and contestable analyses so as to proceed in the light of experience. The analyses must be conducted in an open milieu so that the diverse communities of interest affected by monetary institutions and policies can have access to conjectures about modifications in these institutions. As a result, some constituencies may be willing to implement currency competition for its advantages while accepting its risks and high decision costs. Others may choose an arrangement with lower risks or lower decision costs at the expense of some desirable features. And all may modify the rule settings chosen in the light of their particular experience. Many other options including that of a fully independent central bank (see, for example, Picht, 1988) may be discussed as reasonable alternatives to present monetary regimes.

Yet it appears that currency competition is not just one alternative among others. It is unique not because it is necessarily the best system of order, but because it provides either a valid starting point for modifications, or a reference for alternatives that ultimately address the various aspects of market failure discussed above. Consequently, existing monetary arrangements may be reviewed in light of how they address features of market failures, and at what costs—including government failure.

Notes

1. The term "BFH system" goes back to Greenfield and Yeager (1983), who credit the type of order advanced to Black (1970), Fama (1980), and Hall (1982).

2. For a discussion on the importance of rules as supplementary facilities to the market see V. Ostrom and Hennessey (1975).

3. For a recent discussion and critique of the commodity (gold) standard and the BFH system see Gustin (1984: 135–152), and Cobb (1984: 153–165) for the former, and White (1984: 699–712) for the latter.

4. In the fifteenth century, squirrel skins were used as money in Russia. As the supply of skins failed to keep pace with exanding monetary requirements, the use of whole skins was discontinued. Snouts, ears, and claws were substituted for them. These, it is claimed, gave place to pieces of skin or leather, at first of irregular shape one inch square, and later of circular form, impressed with

government stamp. It is alleged that these pieces were convertible at government depots into whole skins (Einzig, 1949: 279). About 1600, an ordinance was issued in Guatemala forbidding the export of cocoa except against payment in coin, presumably in order to avoid depleting the country's supply of currency. At that time cocoa beans were used for monetary purposes (p. 185).

5. When precious metals (i.e., gold and silver) still played the dominant role as safeguarding devices at the end of the last century, Simmel ([1900] 1978: 184) speculated on such an alternative as follows: "The value of money is based on a guarantee represented by the central political power, which eventually replaces the significance of the metal."

6. Since sunk capital serves as a collateral that grants that cheating, by unanticipatedly spending excessive quantities of the medium of exchange, is not advantageous for an owner even if the present value of the profits of the firm supplying monetary services is negative, orderly exit from the market can be expected.

7. For a related concept, see Posnett and Sandler (1985).

8. Even monetary deposits, i.e., deposits with liquidity characteristics, have been expressed in terms of ECU, although progess has initially been relatively slow because of some unattractive features of this particular unit of account (see, for example, Pfisterer and Regling, 1983: 278–280). For an up-to-date account of the progress made with respect to the spread of the ECU, see the "ECU Newsletter" of the Instituto Bancario San paola Di Torino, Sanpaola Bank.

9. For example, a plain conflict exists between avoiding shoe-leather and displacement-information costs and the minimization of "noise." The former requires price level stability, the latter a price level trend following productivity increases.

Works Cited

Black, Fischer (1970) "Banking and Interest Rates in a World without Money: The Effects of Uncontrolled Banking." *Journal of Bank Research*, vol. 1. (autumn), 9–20.

Brown, Pamela (1982) "Constitution or Competition? Alternative Views on Monetary Reform." *Literature of Liberty*, vol. 5, no. 3, 7–52.

_____ (1985) "The Nation's Money Supply: Proposals for Institutional Reform." In Catherine England, ed., *Banking and Monetary Reform: A Conservative Agenda*. Washington, D.C.: Heritage Foundation, 9–38.

Brunner, Karl, and Allan H. Meltzer (1971) "The Uses of Money: Money in the Theory of an Exchange Economy." *American Economic Review*, vol. 61, no. 4, 240–283.

Chant, John F., and Keith Acheson (1972) "The Choice of Monetary Instruments and the Theory of Bureaucracy." *Public Choice*, vol. 12 (spring), 13–33.

Cobb, Joe (1984) "Going for Solid Gold." In Pascal Salin, ed., *Currency Competition and Monetary Union*. Financial and Monetary Policy Studies, vol. 8. The Hague: Nijhoff, 153–165.

Einzig, Paul (1949) *Primitive Money, in its Ethnological, Historical and Economic Aspects*. London: Eyre & Spottiswoode.

Fama, Eugene F. (1980) "Banking in the Theory of Finance." *Journal of Monetary Economics*, vol. 6 (Jan.), 39–57.

Friedman, Milton (1962) *Capitalism and Freedom*. Chicago: University of Chicago Press.

_____ (1969) "The Optimum Quantity of Money." In Milton Friedman, ed., *The Optimum Quantity of Money and Other Essays*. Chicago: Aldine, 1–50.

_____ (1984) "Currency Competition: A Sceptical View." In Pascal Salin, ed., *Currency Competition and Monetary Union*. Financial and Monetary Policy Studies, vol. 8. The Hague: Nijhoff, 42–46.

Greenfield, Robert L., and Leland B. Yeager (1983) "A Laissez-Faire Approach to Monetary Stability." *Journal of Money, Credit and Banking*, vol. 15 (Aug.), 302–315.

Gustin, Lisa (1984) "Backgrounder on the Gold Standard." In Pascal Salin, ed., *Currency Competition and Monetary Union*. Financial and Monetary Policy Studies, vol. 8. The Hague: Nijhoff, 135–165.

Hall, Robert E. (1982) "Monetary Trends in the United States and the United Kingdom: A Review from the Perspective of New Developments in Monetary Economics." *Journal of Economic Literature*, vol. 20 (Dec.), 1552–1556.

Hayek, Friedrich A. von (1976) *Denationalisation of Money*. Hobart Paper Special, no.70, Institute of Economic Affairs. London: Hobart.

─────────────── (1984) "The Future Unit of Value." In Pascal Salin, ed., *Currency Competition and Monetary Union*. Financial and Monetary Policy Studies, vol. 8. The Hague: Nijhoff, 29–42.

Kane, Edward J. (1980) "Politics and Fed Policymaking: The More Things Change the More They Remain the Same." *Journal of Monetary Economics*, vol. 6, no. 2, 199–211.

Kindleberger, Charles P. (1972) "The Benefits of International Money." *Journal of International Economics*, vol. 2, no. 4, 425–442.

Klein, Benjamin (1974) "The Competitive Supply of Money." *Journal of Money, Credit and Banking*, vol. 6, no. 4, 423–453.

─────────── (1978) "Competing Monies, European Monetary Union and the Dollar." In Michelle Fratianni and Theo Peeters, eds., *One Money for Europe*. London: Basingstoke, 69–94.

Klein, Benjamin, and Keith B. Leffler (1981) "The Role of Market Forces in Assuring Contractual Performance." *Journal of Political Economy*, vol. 89, no. 4, 615–641.

Kolm, Serge-Christophe (1972) "External Liquidity: A Study in Monetary Welfare Economics." In Giorgio P. Szegoe and Karl Shell, eds., *Mathematical Methods in Investment and Finance*. Amsterdam: North-Holland, 190–206.

Leibenstein, Harvey (1966) "Allocative Efficiency vs. 'X-Efficiency.'" *American Economic Review*, vol. 56, no. 3, 392–415.

Menger, Carl (1984) *The Origin of Money*. CMRE Monographs, vol. 40 (April). Greenwich, Conn.: Committee for Monetary Research and Education. First published in 1892.

O'Driscoll, Gerald P., Jr. (1983) "A Free-Market Money: Comment on Yeager." *Cato Journal*, vol. 3 (spring), 327–333.

Ostrom, Vincent, and Timothy Hennessey (1975) "Conjectures on Institutional Analysis and Design: An Inquiry into Principles of Human Governance." Working paper W75-11, Workshop in Political Theory and Policy Analysis, Indiana University, Bloomington, Ind.

Ostrom, Vincent, and Elinor Ostrom (1977) "Public Goods and Public Choices." In E. S. Savas, ed., *Alternatives for Delivering Public Services: Improved Performance*. Boulder, Colo.: Westview Press, 7–49.

Paul, Ron, and Lewis E. Lehrman (1982) *The Case for Gold: A Minority Report of the U.S. Gold Commission*. Washington: Cato Institute.

Pfisterer, Hans, and Klaus Regling (1983) "Die Rolle der ECU im privaten Bereich: Geringe okonomische Anreize." In Hans Eckard Scharrer and Wolfgang Wessels, eds., *Das Europaische Wahrungssytem*. Europaische Schriften des Instituts fur Europaische Politik, vol. 60. Bonn: Europa Union Verlag, 273–283.

Picht, Hartmut (1988) "Central Bank Independence: Why Does It Make a Difference?" Paper prepared for presentation at the European Public Choice Meetings, Bergen, Norway, May 18–21.

Posnett, John, and Todd M. Sandler (1985) "Synthetic Joint Supply and the Private Provision of Public Goods." Paper prepared for the Meeting of the Public Choice Society, New Orleans, Feb., 21–23.

Samuelson, Paul A. (1954) "The Pure Theory of Public Expenditure." *Review of Economics and Statistics*, vol. 36, no. 4, 387–389.

Schneider, Harold K. (1974) *Economic Man: The Anthropology of Economics*. New York: Free Press.

Simmel, Georg (1978) *The Philosophy of Money*. Boston: Routledge and Keagan Paul. First published in 1900 as *Philosophie des Geldes*.

Tucker, George (1964) *The Theory of Money and Banks Investigated*. Reprints of Economic Classics. New York: Kelly. First published in 1839.

Vaubel, Roland (1977) "Free Currency Competition."

Weltwirtschaftliches Archiv, vol. 113, no. 3, 435–461.

_____ (1984) "The Government's Money Monopoly: Externalities or Natural Monopoly." *Kyklos*, vol. 37, no. 1, 27–58.

Wagner, Richard E. (1984) "Boom and Bust: The Political Economy of Economic Disorder." In James M. Buchanan and Robert D. Tollison, eds., *Theory of Public Choice II*. Ann Arbor: University of Michigan Press, 238–272.

White, Lawrence H. (1983) "Competitive Money, Inside and Outside." *The Cato Journal*, vol. 3 (spring), 281–299.

_____ (1984) "Competitive Payments Systems and the Unit of Account." *American Economic Review*, vol. 74, no. 4, 699–712.

Yeager, Leland B. (1968) "Essential Properties of the Medium of Exchange." *Kyklos*, vol. 21, no. 1, 45–69.

_____ (1983) "Stable Money and Free-Market Currencies." *The Cato Journal*, vol. 3 (spring), 305–326.

_____ (1984) "Deregulation and Monetary Reform." *American Economic Review*, vol. 75 (May), 103–107.

Part V

The Continuing Challenge

15
V. *Ostrom*, D. *Feeny*, H. *Picht*

Institutional Analysis and Development: Rethinking the Terms of Choice

Contingencies, Conceptions, and Social Realities

The conversations and discussions associated with the diverse papers in this volume arose from the question of what "getting the prices right" might mean. If we do not confine ourselves to monetary prices, but do allow for the implications of Philip H. Wicksteed's conception of price as the terms on which alternatives are available, we reach out to the broader realms of human choice. This poses great difficulties because all choices need to be arrayed in relation to commensurable alternatives. Conceptualizing the relevant alternatives requires sorting out different levels of analysis.

Most of our discussion in this volume has focused not upon the price of wheat, rice, maize, or other commodities but upon the choice of alternative institutional arrangements in human societies. The prices that get generated in marketplaces, with the associated experiences that people have, are products of the institutional arrangements that exist in human societies. Thus Harold Berman, in *Law and Revolution* (1983), indicates that law is an essential factor in the productive effort of any entrepreneur or economic agent.

> Law is as much a part of the mode of production of a society as farmland and machinery; farmland or machinery is nothing unless it operates, and the law is an integral part of its operation. Crops are not sown and harvested without duties and rights of work and of exchange. Machinery is not produced, moved from producer to user, and used, and the costs and benefits of its use are not valued, without some kind of legal ordering of those activities. Such legal ordering is itself a form of capital. (Berman, 1983: 557)

Traditional mainstream economists usually have glossed over the connection between law and exchange relationships by postulating the existence of law and order. But, all economic agents carry on their activities under the terms and conditions set by law or by equivalent rules in the form of enforceable customs.

A basic challenge, then, is to understand the nature and constitution of order in human societies. How do diverse forms of rule-ordered relationships affect development potentials and the terms on which goods and services ultimately become available? One difficulty arises from the circumstances that human beings, to some significant degree and cumulatively over time, shape their own social realities. In doing so they draw upon different conceptions and ways of putting together patterns of associated relationships. In turn, scholars, observers, or analysts who seek to understand the institutional arrangements that exist in human societies, also shape the conceptual tools that they use to describe and analyze the social realities that others have created. The shaping of these tools is likely to be greatly affected by the institutional endowments with which the investigator is familiar. When these same tools are applied to differing environments, the analysis may be of limited use or even misleading. We have no reason to believe that scholars or other professional analysts like lawyers, administrators, or journalists are endowed with unique capabilities that enable them to know what is true. The concepts used to analyze the way that others conceptualize and order their social realities are vulnerable to error.

We find ourselves, then, in the puzzling circumstance where scholars and related professionals are required to choose the conceptual tools that will enable them to inquire about the patterns of institutional arrangements that others have created in different human societies. The difficulties in resolving this dilemma usually leave us with perverse forms of cultural ethnocentrism. Analysts have their ethnocentric conceptions of what it means to be modern and what is entailed in development. Other peoples think of and experience themselves in relation to what they have learned within their cultural heritages. One may reach limits where it becomes difficult to go beyond the systems of concepts and rule-ordered relationships that are inherent in different cultures and ways of life, including the cultures and ways of life lived by scholars and professional analysts.

Yet, concepts—ideas—are the primary source of innovation and development in human societies. A new idea or concept, when acted upon, gives rise to new possibilities and limitations. Life would simply be a repetitious cycle of following established routines if it were not for new ideas and their place in giving rise to new potentialities for human development. It is this factor that underlies the unwillingness of most human beings to settle for cultural relativism because cultural relativism implies cultural isolation. Instead of isolating themselves, human beings reach out in order to discover what they may learn from one other. Human curiosity is not content with cultural relativism.

Because some human societies, cultures, or civilizations have achieved greater capabilities for generating new ideas, accumulating and transmitting larger bodies of knowledge and skills, and making use of knowledge and related technologies, they tend to look upon themselves as more developed, and upon others as less developed. The more developed are apt to show a significant sense of superiority, if not arrogance, in relation to those who are less developed. The ideas, conceptual tools, and ways of life of the more developed are then presumed to be superior to those of the less developed, without any serious examination of the usefulness of these ideas, conceptual tools, and ways of life for different circumstances. People who are presumed to be less developed, in turn, are apt to acquire certain ideas about the "more-developed" societies and to conclude that those ideas are the ones that yield new and improved ways of life.

Instead of looking upon economic relationships as those that apply to the production and consumption of goods and services, or to whatever is done and valued in everyday life, analysts have on occasion looked upon an economy only as the realm of trade in world markets. That image of an economy is more like Adam Smith's characterization of a "mercantile system" in book 4 of *The Wealth of Nations* than his discussion of "commerce" in society. Smith did not refer to capitalism. Privatization, in such a conceptualization, has little to do with an "informal" economy or with the use of institutional arrangements of a competitive economy to allocate resources. Official economic policy in this setting is primarily oriented toward large-scale enterprises that connect a national economy to a world economy rather than to the economic life that exists in ordinary villages and communities.

In turn, "the state" is conceived as exercising the ultimate authority to make and enforce law on the basis of a monopoly of the lawful instruments of coercion in a society. The presumption is that there must be a single center of government that has exclusive authority to decide what is lawful. When this presumption is accompanied by one that a bureaucratic system of administration is essential to a "rational legal order," the terms of choice come to be strongly dominated by national authorities. Because many businesses would prefer to operate in a protected market that excludes potential competitors, it is not surprising then to find company law, the domestic terms of trade, and access to the world economy, tightly controlled by monopolists, parastatal organizations, and their associated cartels. Under such circumstances, "privatization" cannot be expected to yield competitive market relationships in a society. Local traders are so circumscribed by legal restrictions that they can hope neither to expand the scale of their own enterprises to reach out to larger markets, nor to build the types of community infrastructures that are necessary for mutually productive ways of life.

In this context, intellectual debates about "states" and "markets," or "socialism" and "capitalism," miss their mark. Casual observation of what goes on in the lives of ordinary people in a country like Nigeria, for example, suggests that hundreds of thousands of people earn their living as traders. There must be nearly a million peasant families who not only provide for their own subsistence but trade farm products or other services as well. No Nigerian would look upon these peasant families and traders as "capitalists." Yet each is an entrepreneur engaged in a business. That business depends in vital ways upon buying and selling in what can properly be called market relationships. Most of this buying and selling occurs in the "informal" economy rather than in the "formal" economy of "parastatal" organizations and "capitalist" enterprises. Somehow the dynamics of the Nigerian informal economy is thought of as a world apart from the formal economy of large-scale enterprises controlled by parastatal corporations or "private" corporations organized under company law.

From Toyin Falola's 1984 work *The Political Economy of a Pre-Colonial African State: Ibadan, 1830–1900*, we learn that Ibadan had a dynamic trading economy of substantial sophistication before the British Empire established its hegemony over Yorubaland and other parts of Nigeria. In order to understand the economy of contemporary Nigeria, efforts like Falola's are needed in order to analyze how different sectors of the economy operate as aggregate systems, and to determine what constraints bifurcate the informal economies from the formal one. Such analyses would recognize, as Falola does, that "all institutions of society, be it political, economic or religious were blended with the economy" (Falola, 1984: 10). Falola points out that these capabilities were better reflected in the works of the "old" political economists—referring to Locke, Smith, Mill, Ricardo, and Marx—than by modern neoclassical economists. We would want to add the works of Hobbes, Montesquieu, Hume, Hamilton, Madison, and Tocqueville to any such list. The insight that all institutions of a society are likely to be blended with the economy is a recognition of the configurational nature of human societies.

Like the lawyers and economists working at the intersection of law and economics, there are other communities of scholars who view conceptual, cultural, economic, ethical, and political considerations as being closely linked in configurations of relationships that are constitutive of human societies and affect potentials for better living conditions. The work of these scholars is variously referred to as studying "public choice," the "new institutional economics," "transaction-cost economics," "institutional analysis and development," and the "new political economy." There are emerging communities of scholars in all parts of the world who share many of the perspectives and presuppositions (while disagreeing with others) used by Falola in his study of the political economy of precolonial Ibadan. This is what offers the promise of rethinking the terms of choice that are available to people in different parts of the world, and to analysts in their choice of conceptual tools that facilitate a better understanding of human potentials.

We impose conceptual distinctions upon a complex reality in order to think and communicate about complex orders. The words in a language always simplify. Yet, recourse to overly abstract simplifications such as "states" and "markets," "capitalism" and "socialism," the "modern" and the "less developed" for thinking about complex configurations of relationships becomes increasingly meaningless. Concepts and conceptual models are reified as though they were realities. Tocqueville was aware of this problem when he made the following observation:

> [T]he more I study the former state of the world, and indeed even when I see the modern world in greater detail, when I consider the prodigious diversity found there not just in laws but in the principles of laws and the different forms that the right of property has taken and, whatever anybody says, still takes on this earth, I am tempted to the belief that what are called necessary institutions are only institutions to which one is accustomed, and that in matters of social constitutions the field of possibilities is much wider than people living in each society imagine. ([1893] 1959: 80–81)

The question, then, is how can we come to terms with institutional analysis and development that is pertinent to the problems of choice confronting the peoples in different parts of the contemporary world? An attempt has been made in this volume to respond to this question. While the essays address themselves to discrete topics, each of the contributions needs to be viewed as addressing aspects that function in configurational ways with one another. The political realm is not a world apart from the economic realm, the religious realm, or the social realm. Families are key producing, trading, consuming, educational, and self-governing units in any society. They sustain an intergenerational cycle of life that is ordered in relation to conceptions and practices that have ethical and religious significance. Societies get put together as complex configurations of human relationships.

The essays in this volume were written to help clarify some of the factors that need to be taken into account in rethinking the terms and conditions that affect potentials for development in human societies. We do not claim to have found the one true way. Rather, this concluding chapter should stimulate continuing efforts to rethink the terms of choice.

In what follows we shall briefly reflect upon how the various contributions in this volume fit into a mode of institutional analysis. We shall then show how many aspects of institutional arrangements can be put together by way of explicit or implicit contractual arrangements. We shall do so only to indicate that degrees of choice are available in the way that human beings constitute ordered relationships in human societies. The command of sovereigns is not the only way to achieve ordered ways of life. Most societies, most of the time, have relied upon some combination of command structures and consensual arrangements. If we are to create alternatives to imperial orders, we must confront the problem of constituting systems of government that operate with the consent of the governed. Finally, we shall reflect upon how the mode of analysis applied in the various papers can be generalized.

In the discussions that follow it is important to recognize that normative considerations as well as positive ones enter into institutional analysis and development. Normative considerations enter in two ways. First, the positivist heuristic directs the investigator to describe the normative standards that prevail in a given human society at a given point in time. Understanding the norms is part of institutional analysis. Second, the investigator has personal and professional normative standards that should be made explicit and that may affect the analysis. Cost-benefit calculations can apply where money is used as a measure of value. Other forms of calculation inherent in normative inquiry characteristic of the rule "Do unto others as you would have others do unto you" apply to the formulation of norms, which distinguish what is prohibited from what is permitted and/or required. We presume that human beings continually strive within the latitudes of choice available to them to improve their conditions (or, equivalently, to avoid more adverse conditions). The relevant normative criterion, then, is to take advantage of opportunities to improve welfare without doing so at the cost of others.

How rule-ruler-ruled relationships can be constituted in different types of political order is viewed as problematical. Who function as rulers and who as ruled varies depending upon how political orders are constituted. It is possible in constitutional republics for citizens to set and be responsible for enforcing rules of constitutional law as these apply the persons exercising the specialized prerogatives of governmental offices. There is no universal rulership model applicable to all mankind even though rule-ordered relationships exist in all societies.

Given these circumstances, the course of inquiry applicable to institutional analysis and development needs to draw upon diverse sources of inquiry about patterns of order and development in human societies. Important contributions to institutional analysis and development are offered by studies in anthropology and in economic, legal, political, and social history (see, for instance, Schultz, 1964, 1981; Kuznets, 1966; Kravis, 1970; Rotberg, 1971; Kelley and Williamson, 1974; Pipes, 1974; North, 1981; Alexander, 1982; Berman, 1983; Hayami and Ruttan, 1985; Feeny, 1987).[1]

Choice Among Institutions

In order to clarify problems associated with different levels of analysis, we might consider a choice among wheat, rice, and maize as one that is available to most of us in some type of exchange arrangement unless we grow our own wheat, rice, or maize. We can for some purposes make comparisons that can be measured by a common yardstick, represented by a price expressed in the unit of money as a general medium of exchange. Everything that is exchanged for money as a medium to facilitate exchange transactions can be measured in the metric of that medium. In such circumstances, a degree of commensurability among dissimilar commodities can be achieved when pricing yields an equilibrating tendency between supply and demand. Goods exchangeable for money under such circumstances will be available to the potential buyer even though the price may be dear because of limited conditions of supply.

Even under these conditions, anyone making a choice among wheat, rice, or maize is confronted with many remaining incommensurabilities known only to people who have had substantial experience with the use of these grains. Markets cannot generate perfect information; but open markets, which allow for prices to be determined as a function of supply and demand, do generate an important range of information for those who are experienced traders. It is open access to the opportunities that are available in a market economy that generates a competitive market and enables most people to acquire considerable experience at trading in markets. It is the openness of access that determines the competitiveness of markets; and it is competitiveness that helps to alleviate scarcities. This is why open-access commerce is a key to what Adam Smith refers to in the title of his book, *The Wealth of Nations*. Smith's work is a serious treatise on development economics. His analysis of colonialism and mercantilism indicates some of the serious impediments to development.

When competitive conditions are not met, monetary prices alone no longer yield a commensurability that accurately reflects relationships among different goods and services. The monetary prices may be set below the equilibrium level where the quantity supplied is insufficient to meet the quantity demanded. This scarcity creates rationing, queueing, and the working out of alternative accommodations. The price at which goods are available then includes reference not only to the monetary price specified but to all of the complementary efforts—including the use of special connections, and the varieties of side payments, that must be made to secure the good or service in question, or a poor substitute, or do without. Thus, competitive market structures have an important place in achieving a high degree of commensurability in the use of money as a measure of value. In the absence of those conditions, money prices give distorted information about commensurabilities.

The welfare implications of these distortions are likely to be bound up in a structure of relationships that is both counterintuitive and counterintentional. Anyone who has lived in a "socialist" society will appreciate that the nominal money price is a weak indicator of the costs encountered by those seeking to procure goods and services. Anyone who has lived in a "capitalist" society will likewise have experienced many anomalies with regard to prices. Price theory does, however, provide rudimentary diagnostic tools by which individuals in either so-called socialist or so-called capitalist societies can begin to understand why problems of distortion in pricing arise.

The important intellectual excursion on which Louis De Alessi has taken us in chapter 11 of this book indicates how an economist addresses his problems. He builds his analysis of how markets alleviate scarcity upon explicit assumptions, and shows how patterns of exchange relationships in a postulated system of such relationships will work. One who understands the logic of this mode of analysis can modify assumptions and specify how constraints upon "market" relationships in, say, the Soviet Union will affect patterns of relationships in a "socialist" society, or how constraints on "market" relationships in the United States will affect patterns of relationships in a "capitalist" society—patterns that have many of the characteristics of a mercantile system.

Still other conditions affect the way that human beings relate to one another. This has to do with the shared community of understanding that people have about how they regard one another, what they consider to be fair, how they distinguish right from wrong, and how the aggregate orders of human societies and of nature get put together in what may be conceived as a universal order. Many of these considerations are closely associated with the presuppositions that people make as part of their religious faiths. John Taylor's "The Ethical Foundations of the Market" (chapter 12) identifies an important factor that must be taken into account in any analysis of the terms of choice in human societies. If there were no bases for trust, and no shared community of understanding about the meaning of right and wrong, then the terms of trade in exchange relationships or the patterns of reciprocity in communal and social relationships would become extraordinarily precarious. Such societies could not "develop." This is why Falola (1984) sees religious institutions as blending with economic, social, and political institutions in a society.

Ronald Oakerson's "Reciprocity: A Bottom-Up View of Political Development" (chapter 5) uses a normative approach similar to Taylor's to explore how patterns of collective order might be constituted in human society by starting with primary units of collective action beyond the domain of family groupings. His approach entails a logic that, if reiterated to apply to collectivities, might be used to constitute a democratic self-governing society in contrast to a state-governed one.

Hartmut Picht, in chapter 14, illustrates how important money is as a supporting facility for the market. He then asks whether money itself could be supplied by the open-market arrangement known as "currency competition." His analysis shows that currency competition, in order to work satisfactorily, would require a complex set of rules and levels of agreement, which would be difficult to achieve.

Vincent Ostrom, in his essay "Opportunity, Diversity, and Complexity" (chapter 13), indicates how the viability of market relationships depends upon the availability of public or quasi-public goods and services. Most operating economies will thus be mixed economies, containing both public and private enterprises. Public services need not, however, be provided by a central government. Many streets, roads, and other thoroughfares; fire protection; police services; and other such services may be communally organized in ways that are not subject to open access by competitive entrepreneurs but under terms and conditions that are collectively arranged in local communities. Reliance may still be placed upon private entrepreneurs for some aspects of those services, but under terms and conditions that are communally specified (V. Ostrom and E. Ostrom, 1977). Latitude of choice is available in putting together such services, and they need not be the exclusive monopoly of a bureaucratically controlled public service subject to the command and control of some supreme authority in the central government. Susan Wynne, "Institutional Resources for Development among the Kgalagadi of Botswana" (chapter 7), explores how extended kin relationships offer productive opportunities for taking collective action. Similarly, Amos Sawyer in his case study of the Putu Development Association in Liberia, shows both the opportunities and resources for collective action in a small community and the destructive impact of autocratic interference by a central government (chapter 8).

Yet it is important to make distinctions so that we can know where open access to exchange relationships yields an alleviation of scarcity, as against circumstances in which it means either excessive exploitation or situations where nothing gets done. Excessive exploitation yields the tragedy of the commons (Hardin, 1968). Free-riding in a public-good, open-access situation means that little or nothing gets done (Olson, 1965). Open access has variable implications in different situations. Elinor Ostrom's "Institutional Arrangements and the Commons Dilemma" (chapter 4) indicates how communities of people in diverse parts of the world have worked out resolutions to problems that arise when people share the use of common-pool resources; they do not necessarily succumb to the tragedy of the commons. The same principles apply to other communally organized public services.

When people act outside the fundamental precepts of what is proper in human relationships, retribution is one way in which others can try to "right" the "wrong." But retribution implies that an effort is made to impose a deprivation upon another as an appropriate payment for the "wrong" that had been committed. The result is a precarious situation where efforts to impose deprivations upon one another can escalate to the point of mutually destructive violence (Boulding, 1963). This is usually what is meant by warfare, and is indicative of the limits to mutually productive relationships in human societies. The possibility of a war of all against all becomes one of the sources of justification for a state to exercise a monopoly of the lawful use of force in a society. But there is reason to believe that those who exercise a monopoly over the legitimate use of force will take advantage of the opportunities that are available to them. These are the problems addressed in Vincent Ostrom's "Cryptoimperialism, Predatory States, and Self-Governance" (chapter 2). Sombat Chantornvong, in chapter 3, indicates how the basic conditions of inequality characteristic of many Asian societies yield relationships where the ruling elites exercise strong patterns of dominance, in contrast to the society described by Tocqueville in his *Democracy in America*. Amos Sawyer's "The Development of Autocracy in Liberia" (chapter 9) gives an account of how the mixed motives associated with the resettlement of former slaves and an exogenous authority relationship finally evolved into an increasingly autocratic system of government.

Human beings, thus, confront circumstances where economic, political, religious, and social institutions are closely linked and interrelated to one another. James Roumasset and Sumner J. La Croix, in "The Coevolution of Property Rights and Political Order" (chapter 10), indicate how these relationships were linked together in the coevolution of property rights and governmental structures in Hawaii prior to American annexation. They draw interesting conclusions about the way that rent-seeking may induce institutional changes that enhance efficiency.

Finally, David Feeny in "The Demand for and Supply of Institutional Arrangements" (chapter 6) indicates how the basic elements in studies of economic history and development can be used to move from a metaphor derived from studies of technological change to a framework for institutional change. Such factors as rules applicable to collective choice, other institutional arrangements, costs of institutional design, the existing stock of knowledge, expected costs of implementing new arrangements, and conventional wisdom enter into such calculations.

Institutions as Contractual Arrangements

As soon as we look at the links in human relationships and see how people indicate their intentions to one another, stipulate their shared level of understanding and agreement, and promise to act in certain ways with one another, we begin to understand how patterns of rule-ordered relationships can unfold. What Oakerson calls exchange is based upon implicit, if not explicit, contractual relationships. When one goes into a supermarket where each item has a price tag, the buyer takes what he or she wants, makes an appropriate payment to a cashier, and goes his or her own way. Words need not be spoken. Yet these actions involve an indication of intention and occur against a background of shared understanding in which each party carries out an expected performance (implicit promise) in relation to the other.

The German economist Walter Eucken (1951: 53) has emphasized that a contract is not only a way of engaging in market exchanges but can be used to create other forms of economic organization and power structure. Eucken's emphasis upon the scope of contractual relationships needs to be seen in the context of John Taylor's essay, "The Ethical Foundations of the Market," with its emphasis upon the depth of mutual understanding that is likely to be implied as people indicate their intentions and make promises to perform in stipulated ways with one another in a market setting. Contracting as a process for constituting human organization is too often ignored when the emphasis is placed upon passing a law or issuing a decree. James M. Buchanan and Gordon Tullock, in *The Calculus of Consent* (1962), have emphasized the nature of contractual relationships (unanimity) as a logical basis for constitutional government (see also Buchanan, 1975).

Recent advances have also focused upon the contractual nature of the business firm. A "firm" requires a somewhat different type of contracting, perhaps more of a covenantal character, than would be involved between buyers and sellers in a supermarket. A long-term employment contract between a proprietor and employees is constitutive of a firm or a business establishment. The continuing renegotiation of long-term employment contracts depends upon conditions of reciprocity if the contracts are to function as viable constitutions (Coase, 1937; Alchian and Demsetz, 1972; Kruesselberg, 1986: 364–381).

The usual corporation in Western systems of law has placed primary emphasis upon the contractual understanding reached by those who have put up the financial resources to make a business venture into a viable enterprise. These resources are called "capital." In the nature of the enterprise is a contractual understanding among those supplying capital—the "capitalists." Many such enterprises, however, have involved the pooling of resources by workers, peasants, or traders who have chosen to cooperate with one another to take advantage of economic opportunities that are available to them.

While Western corporation or company law may emphasize capital structures pertaining to finance, the larger nexus of contractual relationships that are constitutive of business firms must necessarily include reference to employees. Whether these contractual relationships apply only to individuals or function through intermediaries as in collective bargaining relationships, they are constitutive of the enterprise. Whether workers or capital shareholders are viewed as the basic core of the firm will make a difference to whether the business is run more like a trade union or more like a profit-earning proprietorship. If the relevant product markets are highly competitive, the difference between the two narrows significantly. If the state owns the capital structure of "worker-managed" firms, workers may then rely upon the "state" to make ends meet. Accounts rarely balance in such circumstances.

Contractual relationships can also be used to put together various types of power structure. More frequently than not, these are likely to be implicitly understood, and rarely written as formal contracts. Businessmen operating in a market may agree upon ways to deny open access to market opportunities and exclude potential competitors from entering their market. They may go even further to allocate marketing areas or market shares and to set prices to be charged. This is usually what is meant by the term "cartel." This type of institutional arrangement, contractual in nature, is designed to enhance the economic opportunity of those who are already in business to the disadvantage of future competitors, with higher prices for those who are required to buy in markets dominated by cartels. The long-term viability of such arrangements often depends upon the cartels dominating governmental decisions as well.

The nexus of contractual relationships can be broadened to form coalitions to influence or dominate the decisions taken by governmental authorities. Such methods can be used to form interest groups and political parties. When access to the political process is relatively open, competitive rivalry is likely to exist among political parties. But those who achieve dominance of the political process may find it to their advantage to restrict access. When this takes the form of a one-party system, those who control such a party find it relatively easy to maintain dominance in that society's government. We again face a monopoly of the powers of government and of the lawful use of instruments of force in a society.

Other social relationships beyond the realm of the lawful also depend critically upon implicit patterns of contractual relationships. These can take on the character of conspiracies to violate what is lawful. Military coups, revolutionary movements, and outlaw regimes are bound together by networks of contractual understandings that are usually complemented by coercive capabilities to exercise discipline and to eliminate those who betray their comrades and are identified with the "enemy." Once dominance of a government is gained by a successful coup or revolutionary struggle, those who exercise leadership prerogatives are not bound by legal constraints and are then free to impose their dominance upon others. Those who use force to prevail have breached the contractual nature of social relationships, and so often find themselves to be the victims of the new Leviathan that they have created.

The nature of contractual relationships can thus extend to the general configurations of relationships in human societies. What is important in this context is to make appropriate distinctions so that human beings understand the significance of their own actions. We implicitly enter into a great number of contracts as we buy and sell. But there is another side to these relationships. At the same time that we contract to buy or sell, we are affirming or modifying the structure of human relationships that we characterize as market, exchange, and property relationships. When we take a job, we are agreeing to a contract that is constitutive of business firms, public agencies, or other endeavors. When we communicate our intentions to one another, and signal agreements and disagreements, we are building the ties that are constitutive of human societies. When we participate in coups d'état and revolutionary movements, we presume to use instruments of coercion to war upon others and exercise dominance over others. Conditions of reciprocity are breached.

We need then to be aware of the operational, collective choice, and constitutional choice implications of what we do even in the context of everyday life. The operational level is concerned with what happens—with the relationship of actors to events. Collective action arises with reference to some community of people—family, kin, other associates and associations, and governments—that we implicitly take into account as we act. The constitutional choice level is implicated as we arrive at or modify the terms and conditions that apply to the governance of these associated relationships. It is not enough just to obey or to be exclusively preoccupied with one's narrow self-interest. Instead, what one does and how one relates to others is constitutive of human societies as ways of life.

Indicating intentions, stipulating joint understandings, and making promises always depend upon methods for enforcing promises or providing remedies for failures to perform. This is why rule making is always accompanied by problems of enforcing rules and judging the appropriate application of rules. Such arrangements can also be put together in complex systems of contractual relationships. When this is done, it is important to make distinctions that apply to rule-ordered relationships. "Rule setting" applies to legislating, "rule using" to acting, "rule enforcing" to monitoring the actions of others, and "rule adjudicating" to judging the actions of others. In simple contractual relationships, however, the respective parties may each function as legislators, actors, monitors, and judges. It is only in more complex structures that such functions become differentiated into distinguishable forms.

The level of constitutional choice, then, applies to setting and enforcing the terms for rule setting, rule using, rule enforcing, and rule adjudicating. It is entirely possible for contracting parties to declare their intentions, stipulate their shared understanding, and to make promises with respect to all these functions. Any contract of this sort has constitutional significance for those entering into such contractual relationships; indeed, it might be conceptualized as being constitutive of self-governing associations and communities. This is why we might expect to find a great deal of self-organizing and self-governing capabilities in all human societies. Systems of governance can be constituted by conceptually simple but socially complex configurations of implicit or explicit contractual relationships. There is no theoretical reason why there must be a single center that has exclusive authority to formulate and enforce rules in a society. Analysts need to understand that proclamations and decrees by governments are not the only source of law in a society.

When we have reference to millions, tens of millions, and hundreds of millions of people, such processes are likely to become highly formalized, subject to distinguishable procedures organized in distinct ways. These are ways of reducing the transaction costs for constituting and reconstituting relationships in human societies. While we sometimes refer to them as "the government," or "the state"—a sphere where we presume exclusive authority to govern— we should never forget that human beings can also realize significant potentials for self-organizing and self-governing capabilities exercised through both explicit and implicit contractual relationships. When human societies are so constituted that the institutions of government operate with the consent of the governed, the basic characteristics of those structures come close to approximating configurations of contractual relationships (Buchanan, 1975).

The institutional arrangements in all human societies must necessarily be both imperfect and incomplete. As a consequence, the most essential institutional arrangements are those that enable human beings to maintain an open public realm where people can freely communicate with one another, explore alternatives, engage in critical assessment, and consider contestable arguments in reaching an understanding about the shortcomings of existing institutions, and what might be done to alter the structure of human relationships and improve the conditions of life in the society. These conditions might apply in a family, a business firm, a trade union, various associations, a community, and in the large social aggregations that we associate with units of government. When such discussions and decisions can be publicly undertaken and acted upon, we have circumstances where societies can achieve self-governing capabilities.

The critical task in many societies, then, is how to mesh governance of relationships in the little traditions of everyday life with the governance that pertains to larger communities of relationships. It is doubtful that the most propitious way to proceed is to presume a monopoly of rulership prerogatives by those who—coincidentally—control the lawful use of instruments of coercion in a society.

Formal processes of constitutional decision making through constitutional conventions, constitutional referenda, and various forms of constitutional revision may closely approximate a process of working out constitutional contracts for each unit of government. But when constitutions are established by military decrees, revolutionary proclamations, or the enactments of governments, the basic structure of contractual arrangements is likely to be breached and replaced by unilateral assertions of authority. The predominant effect of such unilateral strategies is to yield autocratic systems of rulership.

This is why, then, we must seriously devote ourselves to understanding the various ways in which people in human societies have addressed and continue to address themselves to the nature and constitution of order in human societies. It is only as we understand the diverse possibilities that we can begin to appreciate the terms of choice that are available in different human societies. The experience of traders functioning as competitive entrepreneurs in an "informal" economy may provide basic infrastructures that offer greater opportunities and resources for alleviating scarcity than the nexus of parastatal organizations and multinational corporations. In the same way, the experience of people in villages and local communities may provide the more important infrastructures for learning how to achieve independence and self-reliance in the governance of human affairs. These potentials will not be found in government manuals and military decrees; but they nonetheless exist among people everywhere. The burden is upon analysts to identify and clarify them, as Susan Wynne and Amos Sawyer have done for the Kgalagadi and Putu.

Toward Convergence in a Theory of Institutional Choice and a Theory of Inquiry

As we have been considering the terms of choice we have also been identifying elements in a heuristic for the analysis of institutional arrangements in human societies. Whatever the focus of attention in any problematical situation, we assume that human beings confront choice and action in situations that can be represented as having to do with: (1) resource endowments; (2) the technologies that can be used to transform resources into valued goods and services, including public goods and services; (3) cultural endowments, including languages, ideas, and shared communities of understanding; (4) the preferences and aspirations of individuals; and (5) institutional arrangements that enable people to articulate preferences and order human relationships. Such efforts can be conceptualized in heuristics that are driven by different grammars of choice. Economic calculations expressed in a metric of prices, moral and juridical reasoning expressed in a logic of rules, and the use of language to draw inferential reasoning and accrue warrantable knowledge are indicative of different grammars of choice.

The more fully the structure of choice situations can be specified, the closer we can come to indicating the structure of opportunities and constraints that will motivate and confront actors in situations of this type. The elements in any such heuristic have reference to the material conditions that derive from natural circumstances. They are placed in a configuration of relationships where cultural circumstances, having to do with rule-ordered relationships and shared communities of understanding, enter into the choice situations (Kiser and E. Ostrom, 1982). We presume that there are behavioral and cognitive propensities that apply to all mankind and that underlie the cultural variations found in different societies. Further, there are prototypical situations that exist in all human societies including: (1) exchange relationships; (2) teamwork; (3) the organization of teams of teams; (4) the circumstances associated with communal or collective use of common-pool resources, facilities and properties, and public goods and services; (5) conflict and conflict resolution; and (6) rule-ruler-ruled relationships. All human action will then occur within choice-and-action situations that are variable with regard to the nature of goods, technologies, and material conditions, and also with regard to the culturally and socially defined circumstances. They will occur, however, in a context that has reference to underlying universals applicable to human nature and to prototypical circumstances that occur in all human societies.

We would further anticipate that as we use a heuristic to specify choice-and-action situations and the constraints and incentives inherent in those situations, we would begin to get sufficient closure for logical inferences to be derived about how people will act in such situations, and what consequences can be expected to follow from those action tendencies. A heuristic with an appropriate grammar of choice can thus be used to elaborate a theoretical explanation. The more fully the problematical situation can be specified, the more closely the analyst can come to specifying a theoretical *model* of such situations. Once these are understood, it is possible to take a game-theoretic or similar perspective and anticipate how actors choose strategies and act within problematical situations.

A similar use of a heuristic has occurred in the field of inquiry concerned with industrial organizations. There, the heuristic pertains to structure, conduct, and performance. The structure of an industry is presumed to exist in relation to market organization. But different forms of market structure are presumed to exist with reference to competitive arrangements, oligopolies, cartels, and monopolies. Conduct is affected by structural characteristics. Once these structured characteristics are identified, patterns of conduct require elaboration. Performance can be evaluated only in the light of both structural characteristics and patterns of conduct. Much the same heuristic, emphasizing structure, conduct, and performance, can be used to investigate political and administrative structures in the light of alternative ways of conceptualizing and designing systems of governance in human societies.

In taking such an approach we do not have to assume that the world of human experience needs to be conceptualized in such broad generalities as "states" and "societies," "markets" and "hierarchies," or "socialism" and "capitalism." We may assume instead that exchange relationships exist in all societies, that markets may take on different characteristics, and that actors in any given action situation may be confronted with both the constraints and the opportunities inherent in organizing factors that depend upon variously structured circumstances. The factors may be supplied by private or public entrepreneurs, placed in monopolistic or competitive situations. Clearly, action situations may involve multimarket as well as multibureaucratic structures (Gupta, 1985; Kaufmann, Majone, and V. Ostrom, 1986); there is no need to identify the situation with something called "the market" or "the state."

We have here the possibility that analysts can use a particular focus to "penetrate" social reality rather than to increasingly "distance" themselves from it, as Walter Eucken (1951: 105) has expressed the difference. While all choice-and-action situations will be culturally and socially defined, cross-cultural comparisons can be made by juxtaposing the culturally and socially specific situation with presumptions that might universally apply, both in human nature and in the prototypical social circumstances that can be expected to exist in all human societies. Specific analyses can thus be placed in the context of more general cross-cultural analyses.

This same mode of analysis can also be turned back upon analysts or observers and the context of the analytical situations in which they work. Analysts draw upon a shared community of understanding that pertains to the concepts used, and to how these relate to the conduct of inquiry in analytically conceptualized situations where analysts are observing other communities of people as the observed.

A key problem arises with reference to the degree to which the concepts used by the analyst can be expected to predominate in relation to what is observed. If analysts view the world as one of "markets" and "states," or "socialism" and "capitalism," will they "see" only what conforms to what they are looking for? Or do they allow themselves to see the anomalies and puzzles that cannot be adequately accounted for by reference to the concepts used to inform their analyses? We might generalize that the more the observers distance themselves from reality, the less likely they are to become aware of anomalies and puzzles.

At the same time, Eucken has warned us that other observers may become so preoccupied with "the facts" that inquiry becomes little more than heaping "facts" upon "facts." The perils of an overly generalized model, in which the analyst sees only a framework, can, like the perils of mindless empiricism, be avoided in part through an explicit specification of how the components of a heuristic fit time and place variables in particular circumstances. Theory can then be used to more closely fit empirical exigencies and derive better tests of hypotheses. Such a research strategy cannot be the sole means of intellectual inquiry, but it does have the advantage of refining theoretical inquiry to achieve a more explicit specification of problematical situations. Feeny (1987 and chapter 6 of this book) discusses the explicit testing that overturned earlier notions of surplus labor, or the presumption of inelastic supplies of agricultural goods. The need for such careful testing of theory is even more evident in the literature on institutions and development.

At this point we also need to caution that the study of human societies has to do only with quasi-causal orderings, not with determinate ones. The constraints shaped by rules and shared communities of understanding are soft constraints created by human choice rather than the hard constraints imposed by nature. Some hard constraints are operable in human experience, such as the important constraint that any one person can listen to and understand only one speaker at a time. Such a constraint creates strong oligarchical tendencies in all deliberative groups, constraints that increase as a function of group size (V. Ostrom, 1987: 92–97). Most culturally and socially defined constraints, however, occur under circumstances where actors may choose, for example, to violate a rule. Rule orderings, then, are soft constraints and can only "influence" behavior. Such influence is not, however, without significance in specifying the action tendencies inherent in choice-and-action situations.

A final puzzle remains. It is a potential lack of congruence between the conceptual apparatus used by analysts and the one used to shape the shared community of understanding that operates among people in any situation of choice. Does the observer need to take account of the way that human beings think about and experience themselves? It is hard to imagine a well-specified choice-and-action situation without indicating how actors in such situations experience themselves. On the other hand, an observer may find that the explanations offered by actors in such situations are not the best way to account for what occurs. There are both counterintuitive and counterintentional aspects that apply to patterns of human social interaction.

This problem of the congruence between the conceptions used by observers and conceptions used by people who are being observed as they think about and experience themselves may pose analytical difficulties. If people, for example, do not think of or experience themselves as either "capitalists" or "socialists," is there a danger of error being intruded into the analysis when observers think of actors in choice-and-action situations as necessarily being one or the other? Would the analysis be improved by referring to a language that is more consistent with the way that people think of and experience themselves? Instead of conceptualizing many societies as "capitalist" societies, it might be more appropriate to conceptualize them as enterprising societies. We might then analyze human social relationships according to whether they constrain or facilitate enterprising potentials. We could then admit the possibility that people might devote themselves variously to private or public entrepreneurship, or combinations of the two, in alleviating scarcity and advancing human welfare. Can "socialist" societies also be viewed from the same perspective as enterprising societies? Given the way that opportunities are facilitated and constraints interposed, what effects would be anticipated for alleviating scarcity and advancing human welfare?

In conclusion, then, we assume that problems of institutional analysis and development need to be addressed by modes of analysis that allow us to penetrate social reality rather than distance ourselves from that reality. Using a common heuristic applicable to a cross-cultural context should, however, yield a level of understanding about the action tendencies inherent in different societies and civilizations, as well as a critical self-understanding of the choice-and-action situation in which scholars and other analysts pursue their inquiries. The potential for observer error can be reduced by a critical dialogue between observers and those being observed. It is this potential that enhances opportunities for learning, innovation, and development to occur. Rethinking the terms of choice that apply both to observers and to the observed remains a continuing challenge for exploring the relationship of human institutions to potentials for development.

The need for rethinking also applies to iterative analyses in which the evolution of institutions is considered. The development process is characterized by major changes in the characteristics of societies, changes that in turn influence and are influenced by institutional change. Institutional innovations at one period become endowments in the next. Profound changes in resource endowments, technologies, cultural endowments, and preferences have important implications for the evolution of institutions, just as changes in institutions have important implications for resource use, technological innovations, the use of capital assets, cultural development, and the articulation of preferences. Thus, the use of a heuristic to inform positive analysis and to unravel the factors that are treated as elements in heuristics needs to be extended and applied to patterns of order and development in human societies. The terms of choice confronting both observers and the observed need to be thought about and rethought as the frontiers of choice are extended in human societies.

Note

1. The most important insights revealed by these studies are the following ones. First, development is characterized by pervasive structural change in the economy and society. Among the important

trends are the transitions from rural to urban and from agricultural to industrial society, and from an economy dominated by the self-employed to one in which employee status dominates. Second, historical investigations indicate that only a small portion of the growth in per capita output may be explained by the growth in per capita inputs. In spite of the importance of accumulation, it accounts for only a relatively small part of the growth in output per person. Just as we find that accumulation is not the "engine of growth," so too the historical evidence indicates, third, that although trade may greatly facilitate growth, it is not the engine either. Kravis (1970) characterizes trade instead as "the handmaiden of growth." Fourth, the fundamental engines of growth appear to be technological and institutional change, that is, the capability to derive more than ever before from the resources at hand. The generation and productive use of new technologies and new institutional arrangements are both intimately related to investments in the capabilities of human agents—the process of human capital formation. Those trying to understand and design institutions in development, then, need to recognize these important generalizations derived from previous scholarship.

Works Cited

Alchian, Armen, and Harold Demsetz (1972) "Production, Information Costs, and Economic Organization." *American Economic Review*, vol. 62 (Dec.), 777–795.

Alexander, Paul (1982) *Sri Lankan Fishermen: Rural Capitalism and Peasant Society*. Monograph on South Asia no. 7. Canberra: Australia National University.

Berman, Harold J. (1983) *Law and Revolution: The Formation of the Western Legal Tradition*. Cambridge, Mass.: Harvard University Press.

Boulding, Kenneth E. (1963) "Toward a Pure Theory of Threat Systems." *American Economic Review*, vol. 53 (May), 424–434.

Buchanan, James M. (1975) *The Limits of Liberty: Between Anarchy and Leviathan*. Chicago: University of Chicago Press.

Buchanan, James M., and Gordon Tullock (1962) *The Calculus of Consent: Logical Foundations of Constitutional Government*. Ann

Arbor: University of Michigan Press.

Coase, R. H. (1937) "The Nature of the Firm." *Economica*, vol. 4, 386–405.

Eucken, Walter (1951) *The Foundations of Economics*. Chicago: University of Chicago Press.

Falola, Toyin (1984) *The Political Economy of a Pre-Colonial African State: Ibadan, 1830–1900*. Ile-Ife, Nigeria: Ife University Press.

Feeny, David (1987) "The Exploration of Economic Change: The Contribution of Economic History to Development Economics." In Alexander J. Field, ed., *The Future of Economic History*. Boston: Nijhoff, 91–119.

Gupta, Anil K. (1985) "Socio-Ecological Paradigm for Analysing Problems of Poor in Dry Regions." *Ecodevelopment News*, nos. 32-33 (March), 68–74.

Hardin, Garrett (1968) "The Tragedy of the Commons." *Science*, vol. 162 (Dec.), 1243–1248.

Hayami, Yujiro, and Vernon W. Ruttan (1985) *Agricultural Development: An International Perspective*. Rev. ed. Baltimore: Johns Hopkins University Press.

Kaufmann, Franz-Xaver, Giandomenico Majone, and Vincent Ostrom, eds. (1986) *Guidance, Control, and Evaluation in the Public Sector*. Berlin and New York: de Gruyter.

Kelley, Allen, and Jeffrey Williamson (1974) *Lessons from Japanese Development: An Analytical Economic History*. Chicago: University of Chicago Press.

Kiser, Larry, and Elinor Ostrom (1982) "The Three Worlds of Action: A Metatheoretical Synthesis of Institutional Approaches." In Elinor Ostrom, ed., *Strategies of Political Inquiry*. Beverly Hills: Sage, 179–222.

Kravis, Irving (1970) "Trade as a Hand-Maiden of Growth: Similarities between the 19th and 20th Centuries." *Economic Journal*, vol. 80, no. 320 (Dec.), 850–872.

Kruesselberg, Hans-Guenter (1986) "Markets and Hierarchies." In F. X. Kaufmann, G. Majone, and V. Ostrom, eds. *Guidance, Control, and Evaluation in the Public Sector*. Berlin and New York: de Gruyter, 349–386.

Kuznets, Simon (1966) *Modern Economic Growth: Rate, Structure and Spread*. New Haven: Yale University Press.

North, Douglass C. (1981) *Structure and Change in Economic History*. New York: Norton.

Olson, Mancur, Jr. (1965) *The Logic of Collective Action, Public Goods and the Theory of Groups*. Cambridge, Mass.: Harvard University Press.

Ostrom, Elinor (1987) "The Implications of the Logic of Collective *Inac*tion for Administrative Theory." Working Paper W87-3, Workshop in Political Theory and Policy Analysis, Indiana University, Bloomington, Ind.

Ostrom, Vincent (1987) *The Political Theory of a Compound Republic: Designing the American Experiment.* Rev. ed. Lincoln: University of Nebraska Press.

Ostrom, Vincent, and Elinor Ostrom (1977) "Public Goods and Public Choices." In E. S. Savas, ed., *Alternatives for Delivering Public Services: Toward Improved Performance.* Boulder, Colo.: Westview Press, 7-49.

Pipes, Richard (1974) *Russia under the Old Regime.* New York: Charles Scribner.

Rotberg, Robert I. (1971) *Haiti: The Politics of Squalor.* Boston: Houghton Mifflin.

Schultz, Theodore W. (1964) *Transforming Traditional Agriculture.* New Haven: Yale University Press.

—————————— (1981) *Investing in People: The Economics of Population Quality.* Berkeley: University of California Press.

Smith, Adam (1937) *An Inquiry into the Nature and Causes of the Wealth of Nations.* Edwin Annan, ed. New York: Modern Library.

Tocqueville, Alexis de (1959) *The Recollections of Alexis de Tocqueville.* J. P. Mayer, ed. New York: Meridian Books. First published in 1893.

Wicksteed, Philip H. (1933) *The Common Sense of Political Economy.* Lionel Robins, ed. London: Routledge and Kegan Paul.

Williamson, Oliver E. (1985) *The Economic Institution of Capitalism: Firms, Markets, Relational Contracting.* New York: Free Press.

About the Authors

LOUIS DE ALESSI is professor of economics with a joint appointment in the Department of Economics and the Law and Economics Center, University of Miami, Coral Gables, Florida. His teaching and research interests are price theory and its application, with special focus on the economic consequences of using alternative institutions to control economic activity.

SOMBAT CHANTORNVONG is professor of political science at Thammasat University in Bangkok, Thailand. His research interests are concerned with democracy and development in Southeast Asia.

DAVID FEENY is professor in the Department of Economics and the Department of Clinical Epidemiology and Biostatistics at McMaster University, Hamilton, Ontario. He has published studies in economic history and development, institutional change, and health technology assessment, including *The Political Economy of Productivity* (University of British Columbia Press, 1982), as well as numerous articles in various development economics, economic history, and health science journals.

SUMNER J. LA CROIX is an associate professor in the Department of Economics and in the Social Science Research Institute at the University of Hawaii, Honolulu. He has published numerous papers concerning the economic history of Hawaii and various topics in law and economics.

NORMAN NICHOLSON is chief, Plans and Analysis Division, Office of Development Planning, Bureau for Asia and the Near East, U.S. Agency for International Development. His research interests are economic policy and institutional development.

RONALD OAKERSON is currently senior analyst and assistant director of research at the U.S. Advisory Commission on Intergovernmental Relations, Washington, D.C. He is on leave of absence as associate professor of political science at Marshall University, West Virginia. His major research interests are American local government and public policy.

ELINOR OSTROM is codirector of the Workshop in Political Theory and Policy Analysis and professor of political science at Indiana University, Bloomington. Her research interests have focused on the effects of institutional arrangements on citizens and public officials in various settings, including urban areas and diverse common-property resources.

VINCENT OSTROM is Arthur F. Bentley Professor of Government and codirector of the Workshop in Political Theory and Policy Analysis at Indiana University, Bloomington. His research interests are the nature and constitution of order in human societies, with emphasis upon the constitutional level of analysis.

HARTMUT PICHT, senior fellow at the Institute of World Economics, University of Kiel, West Germany, is currently visiting associate professor of economics at Indiana University, Bloomington. His research and teaching have focused on monetary economics, international finance, and economic development.

JAMES ROUMASSET is a professor of economics at the University of Hawaii, Manoa. He specializes in applications of neoclassical institutional analysis to peasant and industrialized economies, and collaborates on interpreting the economic history of Hawaii.

About the Authors

AMOS SAWYER, former dean of social science, University of Liberia, is currently a research scientist at the Workshop in Political Theory and Policy Analysis, Indiana University, Bloomington. His research interests include investigation of problems associated with the constitution of order and institutional development in African societies.

JOHN F. A. TAYLOR is professor emeritus of the Department of Philosophy at Michigan State University, East Lansing, Michigan. His chapter, "The Ethical Foundations of the Market," is an abridged version of the argument set forth in his Guggenheim study, which has appeared in two works, *The Masks of Society* (New York: Appleton-Century-Crofts, 1966), and *The Public Commission of the University* (New York: New York University Press, 1981).

SUSAN WYNNE is a research associate at the Workshop in Political Theory and Policy Analysis, Indiana University, Bloomington. Her research efforts have focused on the relationship between institutional design and economic development.

Index

Abdelnasser, Gamal, 46
Accountability, 6
ACS: authority of, 300; formulates constitution, 293; imperial heritage of, 301; problems of, 294, 295; repatriation sponsered by, 286
Action, choice and, situations, 459
Adelman, Irma, 249
Africa: cognitive resources of, 214; European empires in, 398; foundations of political order in, 281–85; hierarchy in, 215; indigenous setting of, 287–92; patrimonial rule in, 283; personal rule in, 283; political order in, 280; postcolonial, 27; social organization of, 288–90
African Sahel, 394
Age, in Putu, 255
Agency for International Development, 30
Aggregation rules, 123, 239
Agricultural Involution (Geertz), 14
Agriculture: research in, 191, 194; U.S. and Japanese, 193
Alanya, Turkey: Commons dilemma in, 111–12, 117–20; rules changed in, 123–26
Alexander II, Czar, 61

Ali'i nui, 322, 323, 324, 327
Allen, Robert C., 319
Allocation, efficiency of resource, 175
Ambedkar, B.R., 19
American Colonization Society. *See* ACS
American West, 394
Anderson, Terry L., 316
Application, iterative, 177
Appreciation, of unit of account, 420
Arable Land Replotment Law, 188
Aristocracy, Asian revolution prompted by, 72
Aristotle, 102
Arizona, water users in, 185
ASEAN: economic success of, 16; lack of democracy of, 17
Ashby, W.R., 63
Asia, 34, 35, 36; bureaucracy in, 73; class hierarchy in, 75; disruptions of authority in, 72; economic development in, 82–89; elections in, 75; entrepreneurial class in, 71; European empires in, 398; individualism in, 90; inequality as rule of society in, 70, 78, 89; military elites in, 76; modernization in, 90; nationalism in, sparked by Western democracy, 71;

negative human self-interest in, 81; newspapers in, 76; oligarchs of, 77; religion in, 74; revolution in, prompted by aristocracy, 72; revolutionary nationalism of, 71; and Tocqueville's analysis, 70–81. *See also* ASEAN; Southeast Asia
Association of Southeast Asian Nations. *See* ASEAN
Associations: rules of, 402; voluntary, in United Kingdom, 193; of water users in California, 184
Authoritarian regimes, 6
Authority: centralization of, 280; consolidation of, 295; disruptions of, in Asia, 72; market arrangements depend upon, arrangements, 391; operational pattern of, in Putu, 256–57; personalization of, 298–300; Poro, 290; in presidency, 297; public, 15; Putu structure of, 253–55; relationships within the family, 220–22; as rule-ruler-ruled relationship, 57; rules, 123, 124, 239; as unlimited and indivisible, 59
Autocracy: development of, in Liberia, 280–303; in Lenin, 53
Ayres, Ali, 293

Barclay, Arthur, 296
Barclay, Edwin, 297, 299
Barclay Plan, 297
Bargain, rule of voluntary, 385
Bauer, P.T., 32, 396–97, 401
Baumol, William J., 317
Bendix, Reinhard, 32
Benefits: of agricultural research, 192; reallocating, 22
Bengal, Permanent Settlement in, 187
Berkes, Fikret, 111, 118
Berman, Harold, 440
Betriebe, 390

BFH system: critique of, 409; of monetary order, 408
Bhagavad Gita, 25
Bhargava, Ravindra C., 248
Binswanger, Hans, 30
Biology, as multileveled discipline, 129
Biotechnology, 6
Bleah Kwee, 254, 255, 265
Board of Commissioners to Quiet Land Titles, 328
Bodio, 267
Boreholes, *Kgotla* near cultivation and, 231–33
Botswana, 215; Kgalagadi of, 26
Boundary, rules, 123, 239
British: imperialism, 191; surveyors, 186; tax levels of, India, 187. *See also* England; United Kingdom
Buchanan, James M., 452
Bureaucracy: in Asia, 73; military as, 74; in Thailand, 73
Burma, 74
Burrowes, Carl, 288

Cabral, Amilcar, 64; on significance of cultural heritage, 214
The Calculus of Consent (Buchanan and Tullock), 452
California: collective enterprise in, 394; incentives for suppliers of water in, 395; water resources in Southern, 108–11; water users in, 184, 394, 399
Campbell, Richmond, 103
Canadian Federal Department of Fisheries, 128
Capital: brand-name, 417; human, 345; improvements in human, 4; most valuable forms of, 213; social, 23
Capital markets, 5; develop specialized institutions, 14
Capitalism: allocation of resources under, 369; anomalies of prices under, 448; as label, 392, 393, 460

Central Plain, 186
Central Tunisia Development Project, 249
Centralization, of authority, 280
Centro Internacional de Mejoramiento de Mais y Trijo, 194
Change: becomes status quo, 177; demand for and supply of institutional, 163–71, 176–91; demographic, 177; dynamic sequences of institutional, 191–96; heuristic framework of institutional, 171; in structure of economy, 14; supply of institutional, 15, 23; technological, 162–63, 177, 189; three components of institutional, 169
Chantornvong, Sombat, 17, 20
Chao Phraya River valley, 166
Charging, technique, 425
Charles XII, 321
Charter, corporate, 181
Cheema G. Shabbir, 249
Chiefdom, Putu, 252
China, Hawaiian trade with, 326
Choice: and action situations, 459; among institutions, 446–51; constitutional, in everyday life, 455; public, 29, 30
Coase, Ronald H., 163, 317
Coercion: as central issue, 153; taming use of, 145
Coevolution, of property rights and political order, 317–21
Cognitive: heritage of Kgalagadi, 236, 237; resources, 26; Tocqueville on, heritage, 214
Collapse, of local institutions, 26
Collective action, 144, 145, 455; as misnomer, 155; primary local units of, 216–19, 270
Collective choice, conditions of, 172
Colonialism, and Western imperialism, 71
Commodity: labor as, 401; monies, 410, 411; production, 291–92; scarcity of, 356
Common, ownership, 344
Commons, John R., 171
Commons, management of, 21
Commons Dilemma, 101–8; in Alanya, Turkey, 111–12, 117–20; in Hirano, Japan, 114–17, 125–26; institutional responses to, 117–20; methodological significance and, 120–26; in Nagaike, Japan, 114–17; successful efforts to cope with, 108–17; in Toerbel, Switzerland, 112–14, 118, 125–26; in West Basin, California, 108–11, 117–20; in Yamanoka, Japan, 114–17. *See also* Game theory
Commonwealth: Adam Smith on functions of, 320; factor of, 380
Communal, over market organization, 318
Communist party, 54; as cryptoimperialism, 55
Community: demands of moral, 384; efficacy of local, 4; market as, 378
Comparative institutions, approach, 318
Competition: channeling, 353; kinds of, 369
Complexities, in modern societies, 389–93
Concepts: reified, 444; as source of innovation, 441
Conceptualization, of patterns of societies, 389–94
Conflict: and conflict resolution, 265–69; external, 266–68; internal, 265–66
Congruence, lack of, 462
Consent, terms of, 384
Constable, cannot institute society, 380
Constitution: definition of, 172; as set of rules, 149; specifies terms of government, 401; two

features of, 49. *See also* Constitutional
Constitution for the Government of the African Settlement, 293
Constitutional: changes in, order, 179; choice, 149–51; choice allows for dispersion of powers, 152; choice in everyday life, 455; choices contrast to program choices, 151; conceptualizing, order, 293–95; Convention, 294; hierarchical, order, 26; implications for currency competition, 424–27; order, 15, 23; order and collective choice, 172; order and economic development, 16; order as endogenous, 174, 175; significance of contract, 456. *See also* Constitution
Constitutive policies, 8
Consumer, interest of, 194
Consumption: cutting down on good's, 353; specialization in, 344–48
Contingent, considerations, 29
Contract, 392; constitutional significance of, 456; and property, 25; system, 5
Contractual, nexus of, relationships, 453, 454
Cook, Captain, 322
Cooperatives, development programs dominated by, 248
Copeland, Miles, 44, 399; formula of, 45–51
Corporation, reason for, 351. *See also* Firms
Corps of Engineers, 394
Corruption, of local institutions, 26
Cost: advantages, 418; decreasing, 417; displacement-information, 426; fixed, 180; of innovation, 15; of institutional design, 23; opportunity, falls, 343; postive transaction, 361, 362; of price discrimination, 363; reallocating, 22; transaction, 350, 361, 419; transaction, inhibits exchange, 346
Council of Elders: as advisory body, 256; nature of, 254; organizing population and, 264; of Penoken, 258
Coup: as illegal, 50; military, 46, 47
Covenant: of economic community, 385; unspoken, 379
Crankshaw, Edward, 61
Cryptodiplomacy, as hidden diplomacy, 44
Cryptoimperialism: American or Soviet, 59; appropriate to "Free World," 65; command-and-control structures of, 64; communist party as, 55; forms of, 44
Cuffee, Paul, 286
Cultivation, *Kgotla* near, and boreholes, 231–33
Cultivator, 178, 179
Cultural, endowments, 458
Currency competition, 33; and alternative options, 427–30; attributes of market for, 409; constitutional implications for, 424–27; as radical alternative, 407; as strategic device, 408

Dahrendorf, Ralf, 24
Davis, Lance E., 172, 191
Day, Richard H., 318
De Alessi, Louis, 31
Decentralization, 5, 24; experiments with, 249
Definitions, unit-of-account, 418
Deflation, rate, 420
Demand curves, 342; indicate maximum price, 348
Demand-and-supply approach, 162–63, 355
Democracy: Asian nationalism sparked by Western, 71; defended in its own right, 21; end of

Western imperialism and, 73; free-market economy and, 7; Greek philosophy on, 17, 19; lack of, in ASEAN, 17; Lenin rejects broad, 52; social conditions of, 91; in United States due to three major factors, 91; world not safe for, 43
Democracy in America (Tocqueville), 69, 451
Demographic, change, 177
Demsetz, Harold, 315, 318
Deposits, 421
Depreciation, of unit of account, 420
Despotism, Tocqueville on new kind of, 82, 88
Deutsch, Karl, 32
Developing countries, institutional weaknesses of, 6
Development: community, 5; community, as self-governance, 250–51; incremental, 151; political, 141–55; processes, 151–54; programs dominated by cooperatives, 248; pursuit of, opportunities, 396–404; role of participation in, 248–50; two schools of thought in, literature, 5
Dewey, John, 142
Dictatorship, and privatization, 21
Dignity: of persons, 386; as subject of rights, 386
Diplomacy, cryptodiplomacy as hidden, 44
Dissipative structures, 121
Distributive policies, 8–9
Division of labor, 379
Djilas, Milovan, 55
Donor agency, 271
Douglass, Frederick, 286
Dynamic sequences, of institutional change, 191–96

Economic: basic propositions of, theory, 341; capitalist, strategies, 282; constitutional order and, development, 16; domain derivative, 378; entrepreneurs, 29; fundamental, problem, 339; historians, 160, 161; inequality, 82; institutions, 32; law essential to, agent, 440; markets used to solve, problem, 353–60; new, history, 316; and political environment, 316; socialist, strategies, 282; success of ASEAN, 16; system that inhibits price system, 358; theory three pillars of, 159; usefulness of alternative, systems, 371. *See also* Economy
Economies-of-scale, 164, 169, 182; external and internal to producers, 416–19; internal to a supplier, 419; in research, 192
Economy: development of, in Asia, 82–89; free-market, and democracy, 7; functions money performs in, 410; increase in size and complexity of, 14; informal, 403, 443, 457; intersection of law and, 443; land-abundant, labor-scarce, 164; maintenance and growth of, 358–59; major changes in structure of, 14; as realm of trade, 442; reciprocity at core of, 142–46; study of, 160. *See also* Economic
Edict of Emancipation, 61
Efficiency, 34; of communal over market organization, 318; enhancing, 177; and environment, 316; normative criterion of, 176; organizational, 22, 28; property rights and, 316; rent-seeking and, 190; of resource allocation, 175; tradition, 316
Ehrenfeld, David W., 106

Eichelberger, James, 46
Ejido, system in Mexico, 357
Elections: in Asia, 75; in Putu, 256
Electric, U.S., power industry, 368
Emancipation Proclamation, 61
Endogenous, 177; constitutional order as, 174, 175; institutional arrangements, 173, 174; property rights as, 315
England, 320. *See also* British; United Kingdom
Entrepreneur, 22; class of, 71; economic, 29; law essential to, 440; political, 29; in the public sector, 394–96
Entry rules, 124, 125
Equality: of conditions, 70, 90; income, falls then rises, 366; wage income and, within family, 230–31
Equilibrium: of harvest-share wage with daily wages, 178; importance of, conditions, 370; monetary, 424; static analysis of, 177
Ethical, foundations of market, 377–405
Ethnic: Krahn, group, 252; rules of, inequality, 225–26
Ethnocentrism, 441
Eucken, Walter, 452, 460, 461
European Currency Unit, 415
Evolutionary, perspective, 177
Exchange: cash media of, 419–21, 421; community of, 378; as contractual relationships, 452; domestic medium of, 428; facilitating, 369; medium of, 415, 418, 420, 421; model as caricature, 144; reciprocity similar to, 143; relationships exist in all societies, 460; rule of reciprocal, 385; and specialization, 341, 349; subjects of, 381; transaction costs inhibit, 346
Exogenous, 177; demand-side, factor, 180; institutions as, 173

Factor ratios, 14
Falola, Toyin, 449; on Nigeria, 443
Family: authority relationships within, 220–22; as elemental unit of government, 221; key to society, 445; polygamous, 288; polygynous, 220, 222, 223; wages and equality within, 230–31
Feasibility of exclusion, 411–414
Federal Trade Commission, 365
Feeny, David, 19, 22, 321, 396
Feudal system, origins of, 164
Finley, Robert, 286
Finn, Huckleberry, 381, 382, 387
Firestone, 298
Firms: contractual nature of, 452; government-owned, 368; why, exist, 350; workers manage, 367. *See also* Corporation, 351
First Amendment, of U.S. Constitution, 150
Fishery, as Commons Dilemma, 111–12
Force, legitimate use of, 59
France, 320
Free inquiry, 15
Freedom, 17; combined with self-interest in Tocqueville, 95, 148; of speech, worship, and assembly, 62
Free-market economy, and democracy, 7
Friedman, Milton, 33, 408, 420, 428
Fula, of Guinea Bissau, 214
Funding, public, 191

Gain: Adam Smith on opportunities for, 340; opportunities for, 371
The Game of Nations (Copeland), 44, 45, 46, 399
Game theory: literature, 21; tools of, 122. *See also* Commons Dilemma; Prisoner's Dilemma
Gandhi, Mohandas, 25

Geertz, Clifford, 14, 24
Gellar, Sheldon, 282, 283
Gemeinschaft, 19
General Motors, 381
Germany, development fostered in, 193. *See also* West Germany
Gesellschaft, 19
Giddens, Anthony, 118
Godel, Escher, Bach (Hofstadter), 120–21
Godwin, Kenneth, 101
Goods: and services, 412; subsidies on a wide range of, 9
Gordon, H. Scott, 102
Governance: Hobbesian model of, 293; investment in, structures, 316; meshing, of relationships, 457; rules of, 172; transaction cost of, 181. *See also* Government; Self-governance
Government: central, and markets in Russia, 320; central, solution, 119; consequences of, regulation, 370; constitution specifies terms of, 401; contracting some public goods, 362; does not stimulate markets, 320; family as elemental unit of, 221; in Imperial Russia, 51; local, 147; outside state, 402; owned firms, 368; regulatory agencies, 367–68; revolutionary, 47–48; role of, in market system, 346. *See also* Governance
Grain Coast, 287
Grant, special, of limited liability, 181
Great mahele, 328
The Great Transformation (Polanyi), 14, 392
Greek philosophy, on democracy, 17, 19
Green Revolution, 34
Growth, and maintenance of economy, 358–59
Grundformen der Wirtschaftsordnung (Hensel), 389

Guinea Bissau, Fula of, 214

Hardin, Garrett, 21, 101–2, 105
Haushaltungen, 390
Hawaii, 28, 321; comparison of Thailand and, 329; new military technology in, 324; nineteenth-century, 316; population decline in, 327, 330; property rights and political order in, 322–30; religion of, 323; religion and political order in, 325; rent-seeking in, 330; sale of land in, 328; three social classes in, 322; trade between, and China, 326; trade between, and United States, 326; trade from, 326; transition to private property in, 327
Hayami, Yujiro, 168, 169, 178, 179
Hayek, Friedrich A. von, 407, 423, 426
Heide, J. Homan van der, 166
Heilbroner, Robert L., 106
Hensel, K. Paul, 389
Hicks, John, 162
Hierarchy: in Africa, 215; class, in Asia, 75; political order as, 183; principle of, 219–26; self-governance within, 269–72
Hill, P.J., 316
Hindu: non-violence in, culture, 25; society, 24
Hirano, Japan, Commons Dilemma in, 114–17, 125–26
Hirschman, Albert O., 235
Historians, economic, 160, 161
Hobbes, Thomas, 56, 58, 106, 156, 280, 293
Hofstadter, Douglas, 120–21
Homestead Act, 190
Housing developments, 361
Huntington, Samuel P., 280
Huttenback, Robert A., 191

Ibadan, 443
Ideas, dissemination of, 145

Ideology, North's framework of, 170, 173
Ilchman, Warren, 248
Imperialism: British, 191; end of, 43
Implementation, cost of, 186–87
Income: determines demand for goods, 357; distribution of, 175; equality falls then rises, 366; shift of, distribution, 181
Indigenous culture, 23
Individualism, in Asia, 90
Individuals, preferences of, 458
Indonesia, harvest-labor institutions of, 178
Industry, growth of, 79
Inequality: in Asian societies, 70; of conditions and human self-interest, 81; economic, 82; as rule of Asian society, 78, 89; rules of ethnic, 225–26
Inflation, rate, 420
Information: availability of, 4; rules, 123, 239; systems, 6
Innovation: benefits from, 182; cost of, 15; failure to provide institutional, 14; ideas as source of, 441; institutional, 12–16; for public funding, 191; in Saxony, 193; technological, 13
Inquiry: concerning industrial organizations, 459; theory of, 458
Institutional: arrangements, 173, 176, 357, 398; cost of, design, 23, 183, 184; demand for and supply of, change, 163–71, 176–91; dynamic sequences of, change, 191–96; endogenous, arrangements, 173, 174; evolution, 174; existing, arrangements, 188; failure to provide, innovation, 14; heuristic framework of, change, 171; innovation, 12–16; primary local units of, development, 152; requisites of market economy, 30; responses to Commons Dilemma, 117–20; secondary local units of, development, 152; supply of, change, 15, 23; theory of, choice, 458; three components of, change, 169
Interest rate, 359; low, 419
International Center for the Improvement of Wheat and Maize, 194
International Monetary Fund, 8
International Rice Institute, 194
International waters, 11
Interstate Commerce Act, 188
Investment, in governance structures, 316
Irrigation: investment in, 166; policy in Thailand, 165; two divergencies affected, policy, 167

Jackson, Robert H., 282, 283
Japan, 189; land-scarce, labor-abundant, 162; social norms in Thailand and, 188
Jedo, Principal, 261
Joint supply, 414–19
Jointness of use, 411–14

Kahuna, 323, 325
Kamehameha I, King, 324, 326, 331
Kamehameha II, King, 325, 326
Kamehameha III, King, 331
Kant, Immanuel, on moral law within, 386
Kapu system, 323; abolition of, 325
Kgalagadi, 215, 216; of Botswana, 26; cognitive heritage of, 236, 237; pattern of *Kgotla* organization, 227–30; politial life of, 225–26. See also *Kgotla*
Kgotla: Kgaladadi pattern of, organization, 227–30; near cultivation areas and boreholes, 231–33; nonhierarchical principles of, 226–33; as primary local unit, 216–19; rules of, formation,

Index

222–24. *See also* Kgalagadi
Khudumelapye, 229
Kikuchi, Masao, 178, 179
Kindleberger, Charles P., 413
Kinship, rules, 238
Klein, Benjamin, 407, 408
Knowledge: base, 15, 23; of institutional arrangements, 185
Konohiki, 322, 327
Krahn, ethnic group, 252
Kruesselberg, H.G., 401
Kwena, political life of, 225–26
Kweneng, 26

Labor: Adam Smith on, productivity, 318; as commodity, 401
LaCroix, Sumner J., 26, 28, 29, 190, 451
Land: communal rights to, 112–17; Hawaiian sale of, 328; private rights to, 114; production, 291–92; rights in Thailand, 329
Land Commission, 328
Land grants, in United States, 186–87
Law: essential to entrepreneur, 440; intersection of economics and, 443; of requisite variety, 63; state enforces, 442
Law and Revolution (Berman), 440
Leadership, revolutionary, 55
League of Nations, 296
Legal, established, systems, 184
Lenin, V.I., 44, 154; autocracy in, 53; formula of, 51–55; theory of revolution in, 51–55; vanguard party of, 61
Letlhakeng, 229, 231
Leviathan, 20; necessary to avoid tragedies of commons, 106
Leviathan (Hobbes), 56, 156
Liberia, 27, 28; development of autocracy in, 280–303; as high-income economy, 308; humanitarian impulse in, 300; open door policy in, 298; pacification program in, 305; president of, 257; Putu in, 269; tax in, 257
Liberian Frontier Force, 296
Lidice, 382
Lincoln, Abraham, 61
Linguistics, as multileveled discipline, 129
Liquidity: characteristic, 417; services, 424
Lloyd, William Förster, 102
Local communities, 23; lack of market institutions in, 25
Locke, John, 382, 383
Los Angeles, groundwater basins, 108, 109
Lowi, Theodore, 8, 19, 30
Luther, Martin, 381

McKean, Margaret A., 114, 117
Macroeconomic models, 161
Madison, James, 65
Maintenance, and growth of economy, 358–59
Maka'ainana, 322, 323, 324
Malaria, 34
Malaysia, 74
Mali Empire, 287
Managers, 352; monitoring, 368; workers employ, 401
Marcos, President, and "democratic revolution," 82–84
Market, 107, 460; arrangements depend upon authority arrangements, 391; attributes of, for currencies, 409; capital, 5; central government and, in Russia, 320; characteristics of, system, 341–53; closed, limits entry, 365; as commerce of insufficient saints, 379; communal over, organization, 318; as community, 378; competitive, setting, 424; conditions of peaceful, 385; ethical foundations of, 31, 377–405; facilitates specialization and exchange, 341;

failures, 5, 10, 29; government power does not stimulate, 320; highly productive, economy, 399; how, alleviates scarcity, 31; institutional requisites of, economy, 30; institutions, 29; limitations of, 360–69; "noise" introduced to, 423; open, system, 352, 356; prices, 165, 369; reciprocity between individuals in, model, 142; role of government in, system, 346; size of, increases, 180, 181; strict, 119; system and interest rate, 359; used to solve economic problem, 353–60; when, competition fails, 412
"Market Order and State Planning" (Bauer), 396–97
Marx, Karl, 53, 54, 377, 393
Mass organization, 49
Mass society, literature, 18
Mechanization, 178
Mehngee, Elder, 260
Menger, Carl, 410
Mercantilism, 393
Mexican Ministry of Agriculture, 194
Mexico, *Ejido* system in, 357
Military: as bureaucratic organization, 74; control of ecological problems, 106; coup, 46, 47; elites in Asia, 76; as intelligence system, 48; new, technology in Hawaii, 324; technology, 164
Mixed goods, 11, 12
Mockern, Saxony, 193
Model: demand-induced, 163; exchange, 144; Lugard, 256; macroeconomic, 161; market, 142; pluralist, 18; testing of, 197
Modernization: in Asia, 90; perception of, 248
Mohieddin, Zakaria, 46

Monetary: disorder, 422; equilibrium, 424; functions to monetary services, 410–14; prices, 447; primitive, systems, 410; services, 418; supply growth, 428; synthetic joint use of, services, 414–19
Monopoly: bargains at high price, 402; concern with, overstated, 364; and consumer's surplus, 366; definition of, 363; effect of, on allocation of resources, 364; natural, 11; supply advantage, 425
Monrovia, 267, 294
Moral: demands of, community, 384; law within, 386
Morris, Cynthia T., 249
Multilevel systems, 121
Munford, John P., 286

Nagaike, Japan, Commons Dilemma in, 114–17
Nation, recipe for constituting "new," 45–56
Nationalism, revolutionary, in Asia, 71
Nation-state, restores social control, 5
Natural monopoly, 11
Nazi, 382, 385
Neocolonial, 283
Neopatrimonialism, 283
Newspapers, in Asia, 76
NGO: Liberian, 251; as substitute for central government, 250
Nigeria, 443; Falola on, 443; informal economy of, 443
Nominal, money price in socialist country, 448
Nongovernmental organization. *See* NGO
North, Douglas, 163, 169, 172, 174, 189, 323
N-person relationship, 144

Oakerson, Ronald, 21, 22, 172, 216, 234, 235, 449
OAU, summit conference of, 299

Okihiro, Gary Y., 224
Oligarchs, of Asia, 77
Olson, Mancur, 145
On the Social Contract (Rousseau), 156
Operational, level, 455
Opportunities: for gain, 371; for profit, 350; pursuit of development, 396–404; trade expands production, 340
Order: nature of, in societies, 440; rational legal, 442
Organization of African Unity. *See* OAU
Organizational: nonhierarchical, principles, 226–33; principles of Kwena and *Kgotla*, 219
Ostrom, Elinor, 21, 270, 450
Ostrom, Vincent, 20, 32, 33, 147, 172, 235, 449, 451
Owners of the Land: as advisory body, 256, 257; as high council, 254, 255; meeting of, 258, 259; organizing production and, 264
Ownership, public, 12

Pair-wise relationship, 144
Panton, equivalent to, 289
Panzar, John C., 317
PAP: as administrative state, 87; and economic development in Singapore, 84–87; "liberal democracy" dispensable for, 86; monopolization of power by, 86; single-party system in, 86–87
Paradoxes of Rationality and Cooperation (Campbell), 103
Parastatal, organizations, 443
Parker, William, 163
Participation: and development, 23, 248–50; local, 5, 24
Party: communist, 54; Lenin's revolutionary, 52, 53
Parue, Dugbe Saydee, 260
Paye, Martha, 261
Payoff rules, 123, 124, 239

People's Action Party. *See* PAP
Permanent Settlement, in Bengal, 187
Peter the Great, 321
Philippines: change of government in, 400; compared to Singapore, 88; "democratic revolution" in, 82–84; harvest-labor institutions of, 178; International Rice Institute of, 194; national revolution in, 72
Picht, Hartmut, 31, 33, 449
Planning, unavoidable, 353
Pluralist model, of political development, 18
Polanyi, Karl: on "collapse" of local institutions, 26, 32; on contract and property, 25; on lack of social innovation, 14; market structures as diabolical in, 392, 397
Police, as security system, 48
Political: creating Liberian, order, 285–92; development, 141–55; and economic environment, 316; economy, 26; elites, 6; foundations of, order in Africa, 281–85; order in Africa, 280; order and property rights, 317–21, 322–30; order and religion in Hawaii, 325; relationships and reciprocity, 143
The Political Economy of a Pre-Colonial African State (Falola), 443
Polygamous, family, 288
Polygynous, family, 220, 222, 223
Poor Laws, 32
Population: decline in Hawaii, 327, 330; growth, 178; growth and technological change, 329; low, density, 164
Poro authority, 290
Position rules, 123, 124, 239
Power: maintenance of governmental, 47; monopoly on governmental, 152; unity of, 58
Predatory: elites, 26; exploitation, 393;

states, 44, 59
Price: as alternative terms, 60; anomalies of, in capitalist country, 448; changes, 423; decrease in, 347; demand curves indicate maximum, 348; discrimination, 363; distortion, 6; economic system that inhibits, system, 358; in general sense, 398; getting, right, 7, 31, 63, 387, 439; level stability, 421; monopoly bargains at high, 402; nominal, 347, 448; relative, and size of market, 165; several functions of higher, 354–55. *See also* Pricing
Pricing: pattern in cash media, 419–21, 425; rules, 428. *See also* Price
Prigogine, Ilya, 121
Primary local units, 146–49; of collective action, 216–19; conditions for productive, 234–35; of institutional development, 152; as insufficient, 153; *kgotla* among, 216–19; survival of, 270
Prisoner's Dilemma, 103–5. *See also* Commons Dilemma; Game theory
Privatization, and dictatorship, 21
Producer, interest of, 194
Production: cost of, 184; entails choice of institution, 357; functions, 350; organizing, 264; possibilities, 349; specialization in, 348–53; trade expands, opportunities, 340
Profit, opportunities for, 350
Program, formulating a, 262–65
Propaganda, 48
Property: characteristic of private, 353; by consent, 383; and contract, 25; Hawaiian transition to private, 327; paradox of, 383; private versus common, 316; production, 291–92; transformation to private, 319. *See also* Property rights
Property rights, 5, 170; alternative systems of, 359; coevolution of political order and, 317–21; complexity of, 343; constraints on, 345; different systems of, 344; as efficient, 316; as endogenous, 315; limits on private, 356; on migratory fish, 361; moving toward system of, 346; new forms of, 177; and political order in Hawaii, 322–30; and rent-seeking behavior, 320; school, 318; in Thailand, 185–86, 190, 321. *See also* Property
Propositions, economic theory based on several, 341
PRO's, financed by public treasury, 299
Public: authority, 15; choice, 29, 30; funding, 191; lands in United States, 190; ownership, 12; policy distortions introduced by, 15; pricing, goods, 10; realm. *See Res publica*; regulation, 12; sector enterprises, 10, 11
Public goods: government contracting some, 362; Samuelsonian, 362
Public Relations Officers. *See* PRO's
Putu: age in, 255; Chiefdom, 252; lessons from, 268; in Liberia, 269; operational pattern of authority in, 256–57; principles of association in, 255; rice produced by, 268; social organization, 253; society, 251; Speaker of, 258; structure of authority, 253–55; SUSUKUU withdraws from, 268; tax in, 257; Youth Association of, 258
Putu Development Association, 27, 450; assisted by NGO, 251;

history of, 257–59; as a local unit, 262; organizing, 259–62; social efficacy of, 268

Quarter, as larger social unit, 289

Rangsit, 186
Rate, inflation or deflation, 420
Reciprocity: asymmetric political relationships of, 154; at core of economic thought, 142–46; as informal, 151; learning of, 148, 149; major objection to, 153; new patterns of, 152; as *n*-person relationship, 144; as pair-wise relationship, 144; political relationships and, 143; significance of, 234; similar to exchange, 143
Reclamation Service, 394
Redistributive policies, 8
Regulation: consequences of government, 370; government, 367–68; policies, 8; public, 12
Religion: in Asia, 74; of Hawaii, 323; and political order in Hawaii, 325
Rent: controls, 356; potential, 13; seeking, 9, 19, 330; seeking and property rights, 320
Repatriation: idea of, 285–87; sponsered by ACS, 286
Representativeness, 6
Repression, 15
Requisite variety, law of, 63
Res publica, 63, 64; primary local units of, 147
Resources: allocation of, 175; availability of, 4; cognitive, 26; effect of monopoly on allocation of, 364; endowments of, 458; mobilizing, 262–65; scarce, 353; technologies to transform, 458
Revolution: Asian, prompted by aristocracy, 72; Green, 34; as illegal, 50; Lenin's theory of, 51–55; in Philippines, 72. *See also* Revolutionary
Revolutionary: government, 47–48; leadership, 55; Lenin's, party, 52, 53; nationalism in Asia, 71. *See also* Revolution
Rice: fertilizer-responsive varieties of, 178; and property rights, 185–86; riots, 267
Risk, who bears, 359–60
Rondinelli, Dennis A., 249
Rosberg, Carl G., 282, 283
Rothamsted Agricultural Experiment Station, 193
Roumasset, James, 26, 28, 29, 451
Rousseau, J.J., 156
Royal Survey Department, 186
Rulers: and instruments of evil, 58; maximization of revenues to, 170. *See also* Rules
Rules, 239; aggregation, 123, 239; of association, 150, 152, 402; authority, 123, 124, 239; boundary, 123, 239; change of, 123–26; common set of specific, 123; constitution as set of, 149; entry, 124, 125; of ethnic inequality, 225–26; four key sets of, 20; of governance, 172; information, 123, 239; of *Kgotla* formation, 222–24; kinship, 238; for making rules, 120; operational, 173; partitioning, 116; payoff, 123, 124, 239; position, 123, 124, 239; pricing, 428; ruler, ruled relationship, 57, 58, 446; scope, 123; in socialist societies, 57; variety of, 122. *See also* Rulers
Ruling class, 55–56
Russia, 321; central government and markets in, 320; Edict of Emancipation in, 61; emancipation of serfs in, 61
Ruttan, Vernon, 15, 30, 33, 168, 169, 194

Ryotwari system, 187

Samuelson, Paul A., 411
Samuelsonian, public goods, 362
Sanctions, enforcing, 264
Sandalwood: resource approached exhaustion, 331; trade, 326
"Satanic Mill," 392, 397
Sawyer, Amos, 27, 450; on social organization, 215
Sawyer, Tom, 381, 382, 387
Saxony, inovation in, 193
Scale, 12
Scarcity: conflict of interests over, 369; markets alleviate, 31
Schmookler, Jacob, 165
Schneider, Harold K., 235
Scope rules, 123, 239
Secondary local units, of institutional development, 152
Security, lack of, 164
Self-governance, 17; bedrock of, 18; community development as, 250–51; dilemma of, 269–72; fashioning own system of, 402; how population learns, 18; Tocqueville on, 20; UNRISD on community, 271. *See also* Governance
Self-interest: combined with freedom in Tocqueville, 95, 148; ideology constrains, 170; inequality of conditions and human, 81
Serfs: emancipation of, in Imperial Russia, 61; rather than slaves, 164
Service, use or enjoyment of, 414
Services: and goods, 412; liquidity, 424; monetary, 418; stabilization, 422–24; unit-of-account, 417
The Shadow of the Winter Palace (Crankshaw), 61
Shareholders, 351
Shares, transferability of, 351
Shepard, W. Bruce, 101
Shirking, 350, 352; in reciprocal relationship, 144
Shopping centers, 361
Sierra Leone, 286
Sierra Leone Frontier Force, 296
Singapore: as administrative state, 87; compared to Philippines, 88; discourages conflict, 85; economic development of, 84–88; as prosperous "capitalist" country, 85
Slaves, 17; emancipation of, in United States, 61; repatriation of, 285; serfs rather than, 164
Smith, Adam, 31, 63, 393, 442; on functions of commonwealth, 320; on labor productivity, 318; open-access commerce in, 447; on opportunities for gain, 340; on technological change and population growth, 329
Smith, Robert J., 106
Social: benefits, 164, 165, 166; exchange as misnomer, 155; experimentation, 15
Socialism: allocation of resources under, 369; European, 5; as label, 392, 393, 460; nominal money price under, 448; revolutionary rhetoric about, 400
Society: conditions of, 384; exchange relationships exist in every, 460; forming new, 292–300; free, 62; patterns of order in, 389–94; primary local units of, 146–49; Putu, 252; rules of association in, 150
South Africa, 27, 230
Southeast Asia, rubber trees in, 397. *See also* Asia
Sovereign: subjects in presence of, 59; supreme, 20
Sovereignty, theory of, 44, 56–60
Speaker of Putu, 258, 260
Specialization: in consumption, 344–48; and exchange, 341, 349; facilitating, 369; of

ownership, 360; in production, 348–53
Stabilization: services, 417, 422–24; unit-of-account, 413, 414, 415, 416, 419, 425
State, 107, 460; conceptualizing a, 391; enforces law, 442; instrumentalities as formal, 152; regulation of water in Arizona, 185
State Public Utilities Commission, 394
State and Revolution (Lenin), 51, 53
Status quo: change becomes, 177; circumstances of, 183
Stillman, Peter, 106
Stockton, Robert F., 293
Subsidies, 12; on a wide range of goods, 9
Substitution, subjective rate of, 345
Suffrage, broadening of, 180
Supply: of an input, 365; of institutional change, 15, 23; interaction of demand and, 355; of technological change, 162–63
SUSUKUU, 258–59; accusations against, 267; animating influence of, 262; role of, 263–64; withdraws from Putu, 268
Systems, multilevel, 121

Tax: levels of British India, 187; in Liberia, 257; in Putu, 257
Taylor, John, 30, 31, 449
Technological: biological, change, 189; change, 177; change and population growth, 329; demand for and supply of, change, 162–63; demand-induced model of, change, 163; innovation, 13
Thailand: British surveyors in, 186; comparison of Hawaii and, 329; democracy in, 73; as homogenous society, 75; imperialist environment of, 167; irrigation policy in, 165; land rights in, 329; loosely structured, 189; private versus government interests in, 167; property rights in, 185–86, 190, 321; social benefits for, 166; social norms in Japan and, 188
The Theory of Moral Sentiments (Smith), 63
Theory of Wages (Hicks), 162
Third World: impoverishment in, 59; market order in, 397; Tocqueville and, 69–96
Thomas, Robert Paul, 163
Timber Culture Act, 190
Tocqueville, Alexis de, 17, 20, 65, 444, 451; on aristocratic rule, 77; Asian situation and analysis of, 70–81; on association, 405; bureaucracy in, 73; on despotism, 82, 88; on entrepreneurial class, 71; equality of conditions in, 70, 74, 90; explains democracy in United States, 91; on industry, 80; on lack of political maturity, 94; on revolution, 72; on self-interest and freedom, 95, 148; self-rule in, 75; on significance of cognitive heritage, 214; on "social state," 91; and Third World, 69–96; on village or township, 146, 216
Toerbel, Switzerland, Commons Dilemma in, 112–14, 118, 125–26
Tonnies, Ferdinand, 19
Township, Tocqueville on, 146, 216
Trade: economy as realm of, 442; expands production opportunities, 340; extent of, 345; Hawaiian, 326
Traditional: communities, 23; hierarchical norms, 219; organizational arrangements, 217; organizational forms, 25
Transaction costs: of governance, 181;

imply, 350, 351; inhibit exchange, 346; limitations of, 361; and public goods, 362
True Whig Party. *See* TWP
Tswana language, 237, 240
Tubman, William, 28, 257, 298, 299
Tullock, Gordon, 452
TWP, as only party in control, 297

Unification, policy, 298
Union of Soviet Socialist Republics, 44
Unit of account, 418; depreciation or appreciation of, 420; predetermined value of, 423; production externalities of, 422–24; uncertainty in using, 426
United Kingdom: voluntary associations in, 193. *See also* British; England
United Nations Research Institute for Social Development. *See* UNRISD
United States: Emancipation Proclamation in, 61; emancipation of slaves in, 61; government, 381; Hawaiian trade with, 326; land grants in, 186–87; land-abundant, labor-scarce, 162; public lands in, 190
United States Army Corps of Engineers, 359
United States Department of Agriculture, 193
United States Department of Justice, 365
Units of account, alternative, 429
UNRISD, on community self-government, 271
Upper Valais, 112–14
Utilities, 368

Vispertal, 112–14
Voting rights, changes in, 180

Wages: and equality within family, 230–31; harvest-share wage and daily, 178; incentive for higher, 367; nationally negotiated, 358
Wants, satisfying, 342
Washington Post, 400
Water: incentives for suppliers of, in California, 395; resources in Southern California, 108–11; users in Arizona, 185; users in California, 184, 394, 399
Waters, international, 11
The Wealth of Nations (Smith), 442, 447
West Basin, California: Commons Dilemma in, 108–11, 117–20; rules changed in, 123–26
West Basin Water Association, 110
West Germany, economic process in, 390. *See also* Germany
Western imperialism: and colonialism, 71; end of, and democracy, 73
What Is To Be Done? (Lenin), 51
"Where to Begin?" (Lenin), 51, 52
Willig, Robert D., 317
Wollo, Pyne, 261
Workers: employ managers, 401; manage firms, 367
Workshop in Political Theory and Policy Analysis, 123
World Bank, 166
Wynne, Susan, 26, 450

Yamanoka, Japan, Commons Dilemma in, 114–17
Yeager, Leland B., 408, 413
Yew, Lee Kuan, 85
Youth Association of Putu, 258

Zaim, Husni el, 45
Zamindar system, 187
Zolberg, Aristide R., 281, 282
Zorzor Teacher Training Institute, 261